Comparative Federalism

Comparative Federalism uses a comparative approach to explore the contemporary nature and meanings of federalism and federation.

Providing both a detailed theoretical examination and fresh case studies, it clearly distinguishes between 'federation', a particular kind of state, and 'federalism', the thinking that drives and promotes it.

Written in a lucid and accessible style, this new text:

- analyses the conceptual bases of federalism and federation through the evolution of the intellectual debate on federalism, the American federal experience, the origins of federal states and the relationship between state-building and national integration;
- explores comparative federalism and federation, looking at five main pathways into comparative analysis via empirical studies on the USA, Canada, Australia, India, Malaysia, Belgium, Germany, Austria, Switzerland and the EU;
- explores the pathology of federations – looking at failures, successes and the impact of globalisation – and concludes with an assessment of federal theory.

This book will be of great interest to students and researchers of federalism, devolution, comparative politics and government.

Michael Burgess is Professor of Federal Studies and Director of the Centre for Federal Studies at the University of Kent.

Comparative Federalism
Theory and practice

Michael Burgess

Routledge
Taylor & Francis Group

LONDON AND NEW YORK

First published 2006
by Routledge
2 Park Square, Milton Park, Abingdon, Oxon OX14 4RN

Simultaneously published in the USA and Canada
by Routledge
270 Madison Ave, New York, NY 10016

Routledge is an imprint of the Taylor & Francis Group

© 2006 Michael Burgess

Typeset in Baskerville by Taylor & Francis Books
Printed and bound in Great Britain by
Antony Rowe Ltd, Chippenham, Wiltshire

British Library Cataloguing in Publication Data
A catalogue record for this book is available from the British Library

Library of Congress Cataloging in Publication Data
A catolugue record for this book has been requested

ISBN10 0–415–36454–X (hbk)
ISBN10 0–415–36455–8 (pbk)

ISBN13 978–0–415–36454–6 (hbk)
ISBN13 978–0–415–36455–3 (pbk)

Taylor & Francis Group is the Academic Division of T&F Informa plc.

For Marie-Louise

Contents

Acknowledgements

This book has been a very long time in the making. It origins date back thirty years to my postgraduate days at the University of Leicester in the early 1970s when I first became interested in comparative federal studies. Since then, this interest has simmered steadily until it finally came to the boil in the mid-1980s when I began to look more closely at both the western European and Canadian versions of federalism and federation, a conceptual distinction originally made explicit by Preston King in his seminal work entitled *Federalism and Federation*, first published in 1982 by Croom Helm.

My gradual acquaintance with comparative federal studies during those years at Leicester was due, respectively, to Professor Christopher Hughes and Professor Murray Forsyth, both of whom stimulated me enormously to pursue advanced research into the history, theory and practice of the federal idea in its various manifestations at different times and in different contexts. My subsequent university career advances from Plymouth to Keele to Hull and recently to Kent have each contributed something new to my own intellectual understanding and appreciation of this most fascinating of subjects. Today, however, it is to my colleagues and friends in the Comparative Federalism and Federation Research Committee of the International Political Science Association (IPSA) that I owe my greatest intellectual debt and gratitude for what is written in the pages of this book. I would like particularly to thank Franz Gress and Alain-G. Gagnon not only for their intellectual and educational insights in general but also for their invaluable friendship that I have never taken for granted. Chapter 7 derived from a joint paper that Franz Gress and myself presented at the IPSA Conference in August 2000 in Quebec City, Canada while Chapter 10 originated in another paper that I presented in Montreal, Canada at the invitation of Jules Duchastel, Universite du Quebec a Montreal (UQAM). I feel sure that the following colleagues will also not object to my mentioning their names here for they, too, have been far more influential in the evolution of my thinking on comparative federalism and federation than they will ever realise: Daniel J. Elazar, Ronald L. Watts, John Kincaid, Alan Cairns, David E. Smith, Luis Moreno, Patrick Peeters, Lloyd Brown-John, Rudolph Hrbek, Robert Agranoff, Frank Delmartino, Uwe Leonardy, and Nicholas Schmitt. I would also like to acknowledge the influential role of the Federal Trust and the significance of its lively output on federalist literature, but I especially want to mention John Pinder, its current chairman, whose work on the United Kingdom and Europe I have always read and admired for its intellectual clarity, prescience and boldness, often in the face of much hostility in this country. None of these people, it hardly needs emphasising, bear any responsibility for what is written here. Indeed, many of them would probably take issue with much of what I have written. The sole responsibility for the content of the book remains my own.

Finally I want to mention the fact that my current responsibility as the Director of the new Centre for Federal Studies (CFS) at the University of Kent at Canterbury (UoK) means that there is now, once again, a firm venue for post-graduate study and advanced research in this important subject in the United Kingdom. Thanks to UoK and the financial support of the James Madison Trust, it is possible for those interested in comparative federal studies to have an intellectual base where they can confidently pursue their research interests with the support and encouragement of staff involved with the CFS.

Introduction

The problem with studying federalism

The study of federalism construed in its broadest sense is fraught with difficulties that are reflected in both theory and practice. The term 'federal' has both an empirical and a theoretical resonance. In this book I shall argue that while such a thing as federal theory does exist, there is, as yet, no fully fledged theory of federalism. At best there is partial theory based upon rigorous conceptual analysis and the pursuit of terminological precision. At worst there is crass empiricism rooted in the failure to develop concepts and define the key terms. Without this fundamental preparation it is not possible to engage in genuine comparative analysis that has theoretical implications.

Part of the problem with studying federalism is that it is a microcosm of the problem with studying political science itself. Federalism deals simultaneously with fundamental moral questions as well as with amoral matter-of-fact issues. The former, like social diversity and individual and collective identities, are highly charged emotional questions for many people while the latter involve the routine pursuit of economic profit and security and reflect for the most part calculated and dispassionate self-interest. The moral basis to federalism derives from certain inherent virtues, such as respect, tolerance, dignity and mutual recognition, which lead to a particular form of human association, namely, the federal state or federation. The amoral foundation suggests that no such qualities inhere in federalism at all and that it is nothing more than a particular constitutional and/or political technique for achieving certain overarching goals such as territorial expansion or economic benefits and security.

Another reason why federalism has been so problematic for scholars is that it is multifaceted. By its very nature it is constitutional, political, social, economic, cultural, legal, philosophical and ideological. It spans the whole gamut of human experience. To understand federalism and federation fully and to comprehend its many faces, then, would be impossible. It has therefore a certain elusive quality about it. In political science of course it directly engages the endless public debate about power, authority and legitimacy: how human relations are best organised in order to preserve, promote and generally accommodate viable distinct identities. These considerations are not exclusive to federalism however; they are also directly related to different forms of human organisation, for example devolution, regionalism and decentralisation and, more tangentially, to issues of pluralism and consociationalism.

In this book I shall seek to overcome many of the conventional obstacles to studying federalism by adopting the conceptual distinction between federalism and federation originally introduced into the mainstream Anglo-American literature by Preston King in 1982. His *Federalism and Federation* was a new and different approach to the subject. It enabled scholars to research an old subject without becoming ensnared in the familiar but futile debate about definition.[1] All too often they simply failed to clear the first hurdle so that the endless search for the unattainable took the place of sound analysis. Clearly the definitional dogma of the past fifty years has now outlived its usefulness. King's conceptual approach avoids the monotonous treadmill of definition and redefinition by its firm focus upon conceptual analysis and refinement, which require terminological precision but not an all-embracing, omnibus definition of federalism as the *sine qua non* for further study.

In what follows, then, I shall take federalism to mean the recommendation and (sometimes) the active promotion of support for federation. A federation is a particular kind of state. It is a distinctive organisational form or institutional fact the main purpose of which is to accommodate the constituent units of a union in the decision-making procedure of the central government by means of constitutional entrenchment. But the relationship between federalism and federation is complex. Federalism informs federation and *vice versa*. And there are many federalisms that differ widely in their content. They reflect different constellations and configurations of cleavage patterns both in a territorial and non-territorial sense. Like federation, federalism is both rooted in context and its meaning determined by this. In order to understand each federalism, then, we must perforce locate the concept in its own distinct setting: historical, cultural, intellectual, philosophical, social, economic, legal and ideological. In this way we can begin to appreciate its huge multidimensional complexities. Federation, too, is similarly complex and contextual. As tangible institutional fact, it cannot be reduced to the mere end product of federalism. We do not move in a simple straight line from federalism to federation. Federation itself is governed by purpose, what King calls 'conscious self-direction'; it acts upon federalism, helping to shape and reshape both its expression and its goals.[2] The relationship between federalism and federation is therefore symbiotic; each impinges upon the other in an unending fashion.

This brief excursion into the cloudy world of federalism and federation demonstrates how futile is the attempt to capture our subject in a single neat definition. We can only examine, explore, analyse and compare in the quest for meaning. There is no treasure trove, no elusive Holy Grail waiting passively to be discovered and disinterred. One problem with studying federalism is that, as Antony Birch remarked in 1966, it is a concept that has 'no fixed meaning'. Its meaning in any particular study is 'defined by the student in a manner which is determined by the approach which he wishes to make to his material'.[3] But this does not mean that there is no conceptual foundation, no firm ground on which to gain a strong foothold. We need to use our concepts carefully but there is no doubt that they have a usefulness, a utility for comparative analysis. Federalism and federation help and encourage us to understand one of the most important and profound of human predicaments in the new millennium, namely, how people organise and reorganise themselves voluntarily to live together side by side in peaceful neighbourly association.

This introductory discussion suggests that we should not have a level of expectation that is too high or incapable of practical achievement. Federation is not a universal panacea. It is not the answer to any or every problem of human conflict. On the contrary, it is applicable only to some conflicts at certain times in particular circumstances. It is in this sense that federation is relative, contingent and circumstantial. It can often furnish the basis for a *modus operandi* without itself being the solution. This however is a different matter. What, then, lies at the root of our study? What are federalism and federation about? Let us look a little more closely at these elemental questions.

Our brief outline of what federalism and federation mean and how they are related indicates the direction in which we must proceed. S. Rufus Davis traversed this intellectual landscape in his own epic odyssey entitled *The Federal Principle: A Journey Through Time in Quest of a Meaning*, first published in 1978, and identified what he saw as the dilemma in studying federalism.[4] Consider the following extract from 'In the Beginning' in Chapter 1:

> those who travel this precarious journey into the past must not expect to find a beginning, nor one simple coherent thing, nor a single path ... it is rare to find a single 'root-meaning' waiting to be purified or compromised. And worse for the explorer, there is no register of birth for political ideas, no birth names, no book of dates. ... The origin of the federal idea is wreathed in mist, as indeed is the origin of life itself. ... there are no secure details of parentage, no reliable paternity tests.[5]

Davis reached the end of his perilous journey with a modest restatement of the Latin term *foedus*: the tie that successfully promoted and reconciled both personal and common interests. *Foedus* appeared in many different forms but its true fidelity was confined to 'the promise of communality and individuality'.[6] In other words it recognised the inherent human condition of both individual and shared needs and identities.

What lies at the root of our study, then, is a microcosm of the larger purpose of politics itself, namely, the human quest for welfare in its broadest sense. Equally broadly, the federal idea is concerned with specific forms of human association, with how we organise human relations in order to achieve welfare. Accordingly the federal principle is an organising principle and its fundamental purpose is essentially moral. Its *raison d'être* is to furnish the basis for order and stability but in a framework that formally acknowledges, protects and promotes human dignity, difference and diversity. This is its moral content and purpose. Human beings forge different forms of unity, different collectivities, which are structured and institutionalised in order to convert human goals and intentions into human achievement. The creative tension that arises out of this predicament, the dual goal of unity and diversity, gives the federal principle its special appeal.

The study of federalism and federation is problematic partly because it is primarily about the evolution of a political idea or principle that has been construed by many people in different ways at different times in different circumstances. And both confederations and federations have taken many different forms in different historical eras. Among their strengths have been their mutability and flexibility, but these have also made this form of association a very difficult subject from which to derive theoretical implications. It is, in short, a difficult topic to study because it is theoretically untidy. What conclusions we have drawn from it suggest only partial theory rather than a fully fledged theory of voluntary union among citizens and states. But at the core of the study are certain tangible, accessible qualities. Over sixty years ago, H.R.G. Greaves put it this way:

> There is a sense in which federalism, with its combination of separate unities, may be said to correspond to the nature of modern man. He is a member not of one but of many social unities. He belongs to a local area; perhaps to a church or party, to a state, to a group of like-thinking democracies, to a race, and, finally to humanity. Thus it is hardly surprising that when we come to enquire into federalism in practice we find it covers too large an area of human experience to be readily spanned in a short space. At most we can claim to suggest certain principles and conclusions from a limited comparison.[7]

It was in such Althusian terms that the notion of federalism corresponding with empirical reality was articulated in 1940. How can we find a means by which men and women can successfully determine themselves and achieve a level of self-fulfilment that corresponds with their own individual spirit and personality? What sort of state and society might facilitate this? Can federation and federal techniques be used effectively to provide a framework to enable these living, breathing tissues of society to express and determine themselves? Can they, in short, reflect an empirical social reality? And indeed which social reality do we recognise as being worthy of and amenable to the federal prescription? Complex philosophical and theoretical issues lie at the heart of such questions.

Federalism, as it is defined in this book, addresses and reflects philosophical, ideological and empirical concerns. It is multifaceted precisely because human beings are complex. It is elusive and difficult to study precisely because it arises from and reflects this complexity. And as we have already argued, federations are not simple things. They encompass and express the very variety of federalism. Like federalism, federations are both cause and effect. They reflect movement and change. Movement from one form of association to another occurs from time to time 'according as men's loyalties are more actively engaged by the bigger or the more limited purpose'. For men, as Greaves put it, may be 'members of several at the same time'.[8]

It is time to leave our Introduction and venture into the heady world of comparative federalism and federation in theory and practice. We are now armed with the knowledge that we know so little about our subject. It is useful therefore to begin this long journey with a conceptual and methodological review designed to trace the origins of the contemporary debate about federalism and federation. It is acknowledged of course that most, if not all, of the major contributors to the debate who are included here neither recognised nor utilised this conceptual distinction. But it was often implicit in their different approaches to the subject and where this is the case I have emphasised it in the review. It does no harm to their contributions to revisit them in a different age equipped with contemporary concepts. In this way the implicit can become explicit without any distortion of its intended meaning.

It would be tedious to trace in minute detail the course of the discussion of the definition of federalism that has taken place during the past two centuries and I do not intend to do that. Instead I want to locate the source of the contemporary debate by looking briefly at particular aspects of the major contributions to federalism and federation in the mainstream Anglo-American academic literature. This enables us to avoid a mere list – an identity parade – of the main contributors and to pinpoint instead particular features of their contributions which are germane to our search for the conceptual and empirical sources of the contemporary debate. It is intended that these sources can provide the important background context and meaning for the detailed investigation into the various federal models and comparative analyses to which we shall turn later in the book. With this purpose in mind, let us begin our comparative study with the conceptual and methodological review.

Part I
Concept and meaning

1 Federalism and federation

The quest for meaning

Introduction

The intellectual debate about modern federalism – its meaning and significance – can be traced back to the late eighteenth century. The peculiar circumstances that surrounded the shift from confederation to federation in the United States of America in the years between 1781 and 1789 shaped and moulded the nature of the subsequent intellectual debate in a way which had far-reaching consequences for understanding one of the most important historical innovations in modern government and politics. The American federal model established in 1789 was based upon a set of core principles that were consciously imitated by others, and in consequence it helped to spark an enduring analytical debate about what it meant to be 'federal'. In this sense the American federal precedent corresponded simultaneously to both theory and practice.

In the two separate sections of this chapter I want to examine how the meaning and significance of federalism and federation have changed over time. I want to show how these concepts have fared at the hands of prominent historians, political scientists and practitioners in the mainstream Anglo-American literature. As we shall see, the survey will locate the origins of many of the main contemporary analytical concerns about federalism and federation. These concerns were first identified and discussed by interested observers well over a century ago and our conceptual and methodological review will therefore examine the important early contributions before concentrating upon the contemporary intellectual debate. But I will notok at the lose concepts through the eyes of the various political philosophers who have also wrestled with federalism as part of their own political discourse. There are many established texts that already do this. Instead I shall refer to them only in the extent to which they have loomed large in the intellectual debate itself.

The conceptual and methodological review enables us in Chapter 2 to revisit the intellectual and empirical distinctions between confederation and federation made by Americans in the late eighteenth century. After all, the American federal experience during 1781–89 had enormous implications for government, politics, political systems and the study of political science itself during the next two centuries. And for our purposes it allows us to place the conceptual analysis of federalism and federation on a firm foundation. In Chapter 2 I will also explore some of the main philosophical conceptions of federalism post-1789 precisely because they continue in general to furnish the basis for the management of contemporary problems in politics. The question of individual and collective identities in particular represents one of the most difficult challenges for federal political systems in the twenty-first century. Let us begin, however, with Part I of the conceptual and methodological review of federalism and federation.

Conceptual and methodological review (i)

The earliest selected contribution to the intellectual debate about modern federalism was the combined effort of Alexander Hamilton, John Jay and James Madison (under the pseudonym of Publius) whose clever and pugnacious defence of the new 'compound republic' that they had helped to create turned into a veritable philosophical treatise on the blessings of federal government. And while their talent for legerdemain in explaining the shift from confederation to federation was as cynical as it was effective, their explanation of the federal form of government in *The Federalist* during 1787–88 remains impressive to this day for its logic, conviction and clarity. As Clinton Rossiter observed:

> The Federalist converted federalism from an expedient into an article of faith, from an occasional accident of history into an enduring expression of the principles of constitutionalism.[1]

We will assess the significance of Publius and *The Federalist* for the debate about federalism in the next chapter. For the moment let us resume our intellectual odyssey and move from the late eighteenth to the early nineteenth century.

In his *Democracy in America*, first published in 1835, Alexis de Tocqueville examined the complex interaction of liberty, equality and mass democracy that he had witnessed first hand in the young emergent American society of the early 1830s. His aim was to assess the implications of this democratic revolution for European states. His search for America however was not the limit of his ambitions. In practice he saw not only America but also 'the image of democracy itself, with its inclinations, its character, its prejudices and its passions' and this equipped him to write what has since become one of the classics of political science.[2] Combining the role of political scientist, sociologist and political philosopher, Tocqueville's shrewd observations of people, ideas and events not only gave him an insight into the workings of democracy but they also enabled him to identify some of the cardinal features of federalism and federation. He believed that the republican form of government depended for its vitality and permanence upon the durability of the federal system and that the federalism in the federation – America's enduring social diversity – sprang directly from the local communities, townships and provincial assemblies. 'In America', as he put it, 'the township was organised before the county, the county before the States, the State before the Union'.[3]

The implication of this for the political organisation of the United States of America was that both the spirit and reality of freedom and independence, which had characterised the townships for nearly two centuries prior to the new union, would have to be protected and preserved. In order for the local citizen to continue to practise what Tocqueville called 'the art of government in the small sphere within his reach', the 'independence of the government of each State in its sphere was recognized'.[4] The new union therefore was based upon the sovereignty of the people, but it was built from below with political authority spiralling upwards from the individual in local communities and townships via the constituent state governments to the federal government itself. Power was both shared and divided.

Tocqueville's understanding and appreciation of the federal idea cannot be entirely divorced from his general opinions and anxieties about democracy itself. But it was nonetheless federal democracy. And this meant recognition of the needs of, as well as the threat to, minorities together with an emphasis upon the limits and possibilities of government. Interestingly he also referred to specific 'Anglo-American' political values, traditions and behaviour that were tantamount to a particular federal tradition. We will return to this classification in Chapter 6. For our purposes, then, Tocqueville's contribution to the intellectual debate about federalism and federation was to acknowledge the significance of what he called the 'social condition' of the Anglo-Americans' as well as the vitality of state autonomy and the overarching role of the formal mechanisms, procedures and institutions of federal government itself. This early recognition of the social condition of Anglo-American federal democracy is useful to our analysis of the preconditions of asymmetrical federalism that appear later in Chapter 8. There is much in Tocqueville's penetrating observations about democracy in America therefore which have a retrospective value for our comparative analysis of federalism and federation.

When we turn to look at the observations of John Stuart Mill in his *Considerations on Representative Government*, first published in 1861, the focus shifts from Tocqueville's largely deductive method and his uniquely sociological-philosophical approach to understanding and explaining American federalism and federation to the British representative parliamentary tradition.[5] Indeed we encounter a very different perspective of our subject. Tocqueville was, after all, investigating American democracy, and while Mill's philosophical purpose was not that different from the French nobleman's in his desire to identify the best form of government, his empirical focus was much wider. There is however one major similarity that is of particular relevance to our brief review. Like Tocqueville, Mill, too, identified certain social preconditions necessary for federation to work successfully. These 'sympathies' were primarily those of 'race, language, religion' and, of special interest to our survey, 'political institutions', which together were most conducive to 'a feeling of identity of political interest'.[6] But Mill also mentioned another precondition that we shall discuss in more detail in Chapter 3. This is the question of the combined resources and relative size of constituent units in a federation. Mill suggested that territorial magnitude was certainly one of the considerations that should be taken into account in determining whether or not a country opted for a federal form of government. The implication of his essay was that fully fledged federation was generally the natural result of the political conditions of a large country rather than a small one.

For Mill the separate states should not be so powerful as to be able to rely solely upon themselves for military defence otherwise they would be 'apt to think that they do not gain, by union with others, the equivalent of what they sacrifice in their own liberty of action'. If these circumstances prevailed the 'internal and sectional breach' would be in danger of going so far as to dissolve the union. Moreover, the general inequality of strength between the states comprising the union should also not be too great. Mill's assertion is worth quoting at length:

> There should not be any one state so much more powerful than the rest as to be capable of vying in strength with many of them combined. If there be such a one, and only one, it will insist on being master of the joint delibera-tions: if there be two, they will be irresistible when they agree; and whenever they differ everything will be decided by a struggle for ascendancy between the rivals.[7]

While virtually only a passing reflection upon the nature of federal government, Mill's contribution to the analytical debate retains its utility to our survey for the focus that it placed upon the important preconditions of federation as well as upon the significance of representation in federal studies. These remain of crit-ical importance to contemporary accounts of federalism and federation. Shortly after Mill's brief excursion into the subject of federal representative government a major contribution to the Anglo-American intellectual debate was made when, in 1863, Edward Freeman's historical study of federation entitled the *History of Federal Government in Greece and Italy* was published.[8] As an established historian of some considerable repute and the new Regius Professor of Modern History at Oxford, Freeman had set himself the task of exhibiting the practice of federal government throughout history, stretching back to ancient Greece and the Italian city states of the Middle Ages. This book and the numerous articles that he wrote about the federal idea, Ireland and the British Empire established Freeman as an acknowledged authority on the subject of modern federalism in late Victorian England.[9] Indeed, in another classic work on federalism entitled *The Problem of Federalism: A Study in the History of Political Theory*, first published in 1931, Sobei Mogi alluded to Freeman's *History of Federal Government* as 'the first and most exhaustive survey of the federal idea and of the history of federal government'.[10] Freeman referred to himself as 'a historian of federalism' but he was a particular kind of historian.[11] Unlike Tocqueville, whose *Democracy in America* he had read and admired, Freeman was essentially an empiricist 'in the sense of being crudely hostile to all deductive or philosophical theories of poli-tics' and a fervent advocate of the 'Comparative Method' in history and politics which made him 'an inveterate classifier and lover of parallels and analogies'.[12]

Naturally these scholarly preferences determined his own particular view of federalism that continues today to furnish us with many novel insights.

Freeman's own political creed was that of the mid-nineteenth-century English 'liberal nationalist' who believed that the contemporary processes of state-building and national integration should incorporate the federal idea in order to reconcile 'as much as possible of long-established particularity with nation-state-hood'.[13] His conception of federalism, then, was that it was essentially a compromise; it was, broadly speaking, an attempt to mediate between what he called 'two extremes'. Using, as he put it, a 'cross-division to the common classification into monarchies, aristocracies and democracies', Freeman arrived at the following destination:

> A federal government is most likely to be formed when the question arises whether several small states shall remain perfectly independent, or shall be consolidated into a single great state. A federal tie harmonizes the two contending principles by reconciling a certain amount of union with a certain amount of independence. A federal government then is a mean between the system of large states and the system of small states. But both the large states, the small states and the intermediate federal system, may assume a democratic, an aristocratic, or even a monarchic form of government.[14]

According to Freeman, federation was a mechanism of compromise between two opposing political forces under any of these three classes of government. It was an intermediate state that combined the advantages of the large state – peace, order and general well-being – with those of the small state – the full development and autonomy of the individual citizen.

Freeman concluded that a federal union was 'the most finished and the most artificial production of political ingenuity':

> A Federal Union will form one state in relation to other powers, but many states as regards its internal administration. This complete division of sovereignty we look upon as essential to the absolute perfection of the Federal ideal.[15]

In summary, federation for Freeman was characterised by three essential qualities: it was artificial; it was based ultimately upon human reason; and it was entirely circumstantial. We will look again at these characteristics later in Chapter 3. Our short survey of the contribution of Edward Freeman to the analytical debate, then, suggests that his writings continue today to repay close attention. Being a huge and, for our purposes, the first major academic study of our subject, his *History of Federal Government* remains a veritable reservoir of historical analysis about the subtleties and complexities of contemporary federalism and federation. As we shall see the assumptions, values and beliefs of many of the subsequent contributors to the debate originated from this early work.

Following the English liberal tradition of political thought sustained by Mill and Freeman, it is important to include James Bryce in our conceptual and methodological review. Bryce was formerly Regius Professor of Civil Law at Oxford and an influential politician. As a Gladstonian Liberal who reached the lofty heights of cabinet government in the 1890s, he was already a well-respected scholar for his history of *The Holy Roman Empire*, first published in 1864. But his intellectual contribution to the Anglo-American literature on federalism was confirmed with the publication of his two superb volumes on *The American Commonwealth* in 1888.[16] It might appear that Bryce literally followed in the foot-steps of Tocqueville when he set out in the late 1880s to investigate the social and political life of the United States of America, but this was not so. Bryce attempted something quite different. He wanted to portray 'the whole political system of the country in its practice as well as its theory'. Unlike Tocqueville, who had produced a general treatise on democracy rooted as much in French preconceptions as in the American experience, Bryce sought to avoid the 'temp-tations of the deductive method' and instead 'to paint the institutions and people of America' as they were. He wanted 'to present simply the facts of the case', letting them 'speak for themselves'.[17]

Leaving aside Bryce's general impressions of the condition of the American Commonwealth, his views and opinions about the strengths and weaknesses of the federal political system and indeed their implications for federal systems in general still make for riveting reading. Chapters 29 and 30 of Volume I in partic-ular underline the intellectual foundation to his own consideration of federal government and conveniently furnish us with a useful analytical framework for assessing federation itself. Let us take advantage of this scholarship which is now over a century old and identify what Bryce referred to in Chapter 29 as 'the faults generally charged on federations as compared with unified governments'. These boiled down to the following seven criticisms:

1   Weakness in the conduct of foreign affairs.
2   Weakness in home government, that is to say, deficient authority over the component states and the individual citizens.
3   Liability to dissolution by the secession or rebellion of states.
4   Liability to division into groups and factions by the formation of separate combinations of the component states.
5   Absence of the power of legislating on certain subjects wherein legislation uniform over the whole union is needed.
6   Want of uniformity among the states in legislation and administration.
7   Trouble, expense and delay due to the complexity of a double system of legislation and administration.[18]

These putative weaknesses of federation go to the heart of the intellectual debate and have an enduring significance for contemporary analysis.

Bryce argued that the first four of the alleged faults were related to the nature of federal government itself which permitted 'centres of force' located in the component states that could be sustained by a constituent government, a revenue, a militia, and a local patriotism to unite them. These centres of force could form the basis of a 'resistance to the will of the majority of the whole nation' that was 'likely to be more effective than could be the resistance of individuals'.[19] But the gravity of the first two of these four weaknesses, according to Bryce, had been 'exaggerated by most writers' who had assumed on insufficient grounds that federal governments were 'necessarily weak'.[20] Bryce responded to each of these seven criticisms as they affected the USA and while he conceded some of them his general support for federation was undiminished. One defence of federal systems in particular remains of continuing relevance today, namely, that many of the problems and deficiencies associated with them were not the fault of federation itself but were endemic in the society. Consequently federation did not cause the problems but merely gave to them 'the particular form of a series of legal controversies'.[21]

When he looked at the merits of the federal system in Chapter 30 of *The American Commonwealth* Bryce insisted that he could comment only upon those advantages that the experience of the American union had illustrated. Nonetheless they retain their relevance for the purposes of our review. Broadly speaking, he identified eight distinct advantages of federation:

1   That federation furnished the means of uniting commonwealths into one nation under one national government without extinguishing their separate administrations, legislatures and local patriotisms.
2   That federation supplied the best means of developing a new and vast country because it permitted an expansion whose extent, rate and manner of progress could proceed with more of a variety of methods and adaptation of laws and administration to the circumstances of each part of the territory in an altogether more truly natural and spontaneous way than could be expected under a centralised government.
3   That federation prevented the rise of a despotic central government. Bryce observed that the following two arguments related to and recommended not so much federation as local self-government, but since this is precisely what lies at the heart of federal principles we shall, like him, include them here:
4   Self-government stimulates the interests of the people in the affairs of their own neighbourhood, sustains local political life, educates the citizen in his civic duty and teaches him that the sacrifice of his time and labour are the price that must be paid for individual liberty and collective prosperity.
5   Self-government secures the good administration of local affairs by giving the inhabitants of each locality due means of overseeing the conduct of their business.
6   That federation enabled a people to try experiments in legislation and administration which could not be safely tried in a large centralised country.
7   That federation, if it diminished the collective force of a nation, diminished also the risks to which its size and the diversities of its parts exposed it.

8   That federation, by creating many local legislatures with wide powers, relieved the national legislature of a part of that large mass of functions which might otherwise prove too heavy for it.[22]

Bryce concluded his list of merits by noting that 'all of these arguments' recommending federation had 'proved valid in American experience'. Federation was the only resource simply because 'the Americans in 1787 would probably have preferred complete state independence to the fusion of their states into a unified government'.[23]

In hindsight, it is clear that the analysis of the federal system of the USA and the insights revealed about federal systems in general in *The American Commonwealth* remain of inestimable value to us today. Bryce's mammoth work pointed up both general principles and problems of federation as well as those that pertained solely to America. In short, *The American Commonwealth* still offers more to the student of comparative federal systems than simply the American experience. It emphasises the universality of federal problems and principles. Let us look briefly at some examples of this quality in the contribution of James Bryce to our subject.

In his prefatory remarks to Chapter 30, Bryce reflected upon the motives for federation. His reflections merit lengthy inclusion here:

> There are causes and conditions which dispose independent or semi-independent communities, or peoples living under loosely compacted governments, to form a closer union in a federal form. There are other causes and conditions which dispose the subjects of one government, or sections of these subjects, to desire to make their governmental union less close by substituting a federal for a unitary system. In both sets of cases, the centripetal or centrifugal forces spring from the local position, the history, the sentiments, the economic needs of those among whom the problem arises; and that which is good for one people or political body is not necessarily good for another. Federalism is an equally legitimate resource whether it is adopted for the sake of tightening or for the sake of loosening a pre-existing bond.[24]

These reflections capture the very essence of federation. They aptly demonstrate the flexibility inherent in federal systems. Bryce considered the merits of federation in a nutshell to be 'the counterpart and consequences' of the limitation of central authority. Put simply, they were 'the qualities of federalism's defects'.[25]

Bryce also acknowledged another important feature inherent in all federal systems, namely, the question of national identity. He stated the predicament in the following way:

> The problem which all federalized nations have to solve is to secure an efficient central government and preserve national unity, while allowing free scope for the diversities, and free play to the authorities, of the members of the federation.[26]

The conundrum was whether or not it was possible to reconcile the new over-arching 'political nationality' – Freeman's 'artificial' quality – with the various local identities and diversities characteristic of the constituent units of the feder-ation. Bryce believed that the successful American national experience was due in large measure to the application of two basic devices: the granting to the federal government of direct authority over all citizens irrespective of the state governments; and the establishment of the Supreme Court to arbitrate disputes and interpret the constitution. These so-called 'mechanical contrivances' were crucial in forming what he called 'a legal habit in the mind of the nation'. However, the real value of a 'political contrivance' resided 'not in its ingenuity but in its adaptation to the temper and circumstances of the people' for whom it was designed.[27] In the USA there had been:

> On the one hand … the love of local independence and self-government; on the other, the sense of community in blood, in language, in habits and ideas, a common pride in the national history and the national flag.[28]

Political contrivances, then, merely fostered and gave legal form to 'those forces of sentiment and interest which it finds in being'. There had to be already in existence 'a mass of moral and material influences stronger than any political devices'.[29] In his supplementary note to the 1910 edition of *The American Commonwealth* Bryce expanded further on the question of American nationhood. He noted that the nation felt itself 'more than ever before to be one for all commercial and social purposes' with every part of it 'more interlaced with and dependent on all the other parts than at any previous epoch in its history'.[30] This was, he argued, principally due to internal causes such as the growth in impor-tance of federal matters, such as defence and commerce, and the increasing recognition of the need for more uniformity of regulation. These remarks about national identity in federal systems seem, at least in the American experience, somewhat anodyne but to the modern minds of the new millennium they have a much more awkward resonance when applied to less socially homogeneous soci-eties. Indeed, it is precisely the combined impact of the growth of federal government, the seemingly inexorable processes of national integration and the palpable shift in central–local relations that have been the cause of so much discontent in many socially heterogeneous federal systems. In short, the forces of centralisation have strengthened federal government and facilitated, although not legitimised, its encroachment upon the constitutional preserves of the constituent state units.

Before we leave our short summary of Bryce's contribution to our under-standing of federations and federal political systems it would be unwise to overlook the legal-historical dimension to this understanding. In the two volumes of his *Studies in History and Jurisprudence*, first published in 1901, Bryce introduced the twin notions of centrifugal and centripetal forces in constitutional law. This essay, about 65 pages in length, has been neglected in the mainstream Anglo-American literature on federations and deserves to be reinstated as an important contribution to our understanding of the forces that give rise to what we might call the 'federal predicament'.[31] In his survey of rigid and flexible constitutions, the tendencies that operate either as centripetal or centrifugal forces and the complex relationship of these factors to the formation of federations and the operation of federal political systems, he made a series of important statements and claims that remain of immense significance and not a little controversy in the contemporary debate about federalism and federation.

In particular Bryce called attention to what are often alluded to today as the preconditions of federal union. Centripetal forces were those that drew men or groups of men together into one organised community while centrifugal pressures were those that impelled men to break away and disperse. He remarked that a 'political constitution or a frame of government' – which he defined as 'the complex totality of laws embodying the principles and rules whereby the community is organized, governed and held together' – was exposed to both of these opposing forces.[32] It was context that determined whether or not the impact of a particular tendency was binding or fissiparous. Bryce identified 'obedience and individualism' as factors that could operate in both directions and added 'interest and sympathy' to the sources of these tendencies. The juxtaposition of obedience and individualism was useful because it enabled him to illustrate how both 'the readiness to submit and follow', the 'love of independence' and the 'desire to let each man's individuality have full scope' could operate in both associative and dissociative directions. Similarly with interest and sympathy. Their juxtaposition revealed how far property, industry and commerce – influences that flowed from calculation and the desire of gain – on the one hand, and the sense of community, whether of belief, taste or feeling – deriving from emotion or sentiment – on the other, could be both centripetal and centrifugal. The federal predicament was contextual and circumstantial.[33]

Bryce identified what he called 'a large and rather miscellaneous category of sources of sympathy'. These included common ancestry, the use of a common speech, the enjoyment of a common literature, religion and a group of factors that he labelled 'elements of compatibility', namely, traits of character, ideas, social customs, similarity of intellectual culture, of tastes, and even of the trivial usages of daily life.[34] His reference to 'the sentiment of nationality' was also interesting. It was based upon a complex feeling of affinities of race, of speech, of literature, of historic memories and of ideas that owed their existence to the French and American Revolutions. But the centripetal forces that impelled groups to come together to make them 'prize the unity of the state' was often accompanied by the parallel development of an opposite tendency, based on sentiment that caused men to 'intensify the life of the smaller group', making it draw apart and weaken the state. In summary, the march of civilisation tended to break down local prejudices and create 'a uniform type of habits and character over a wide area', but it also heightened 'the influence of historical memories' and rekindled resentment at 'old injuries' that disposed such groups and communities to organise themselves, assert what they deemed to be their rights and could even impel them towards separation.[35]

Bryce also identified the elements of a political strategy for framing a constitution to maintain and strengthen the unity of the state. Ideally these were trade, a common law and a common system of courts, a system of education that would spread common ideas and aspirations to the citizens and encourage a common language and common festivities, and the linking of ecclesiastical arrangements to those of secular government. Where centrifugal forces were strong, there were several constitutional contrivances that could be usefully employed to reassure citizens who were members of a significant minority community. In those cases where only a minority section of the population entertained real grievances, it was important to assuage their resentment. But at least two tendencies had to coexist for the problem to be significant: a sentiment of dislike on the part of the disaffected section towards the rest of the nation and a belief that great material advantages would be secured by separation. Leaving aside physical force, a bill of rights, intricate legal variations and the establishment of local autonomy offered the basis for achieving harmony between different communities. It was here that the federal idea was compelling. The implications of these remarks for the study of contemporary federalism and federation are self-evident and we will investigate them in more depth in Chapter 4.

Clearly the law and the constitution, history, politics and government were each indissolubly connected in Bryce's approach to studying both the preconditions of federal union and the maintenance of federal systems. But having analysed these relationships in some depth he was drawn briefly into a discussion of sovereignty and federalism – another conceptual relationship that lingered long and often agonisingly into the late twentieth century. His discussion of sovereignty was detailed but his analysis of its relationship to federalism was concise. Bryce claimed that the source of the confusion lay in the conceptual distinction between two separate but closely interrelated dimensions to sovereignty: *de jure* and *de facto*. The former was created by and concerned only law. It had nothing to do with the actual forces that existed in a state nor with the question to whom obedience was rendered in reality by the citizens in the last resort. It represented merely 'the theory of the law, which may or may not coincide with the actual facts of the case'.[36] The latter – *de facto* or practical sovereignty – on the other hand, denoted simply the strongest force in the state whether or not it enjoyed any recognised legal supremacy. And Bryce's 'Practical Sovereign' was the person or persons who could make his/their will prevail whether with the law or against the law. This was *de facto* rule.

Federations in law were states that were characterised by divided government, 'each having a sphere of its own determined by the constitution of the federation'. The legal sovereign, then, was to be found in the authority whose expressed will could bind others and whose will any other legal force could not overrule. The law, in giving this supremacy, could limit it to certain bodies and might conceivably divide the whole legislative field or executive command between two or more authorities. In a legal sense this was a 'partial sovereignty' but nonetheless a 'true sovereignty' that was capable of being divided between coordinate authorities. In modern federal states sovereign authority in its legal sense resided in the people but it was entrenched in the federal and state constitutions that could, in turn, be amended only by special legislative procedures.

Practical sovereignty was conceptually problematic. This was because obedience was achieved not so much by physical force (although this was certainly possible) but more likely by 'religious influence, or moral influence or habit'. And it was most likely to be witnessed in communities where legal sovereignty was in dispute or had simply disappeared. The relevance of this short survey for our purposes is clear. It is demonstrated in the case of the USA, where the law had no answer to the rival legal claims to federal and state autonomy – often referred to as states' rights – brought to a crisis over the question of slavery. The ensuing American Civil War was tantamount to both the redundancy of legal sovereignty and the trial of *de facto* sovereignty. War not law was the determining factor. We will return to this controversy in Chapter 2.

Before we divert our attention away from the relationship between law, sovereignty and federations, the significance of Albert Venn Dicey's *Introduction to the Study of the Law of the Constitution* for our survey of federations and federal political systems is worth more than a moment's reflection.[37] First published in 1885, this enormously influential book bequeathed a legacy that served to eulogise parliamentary sovereignty and raised the notion of the unitary state, in direct contradistinction to federation, almost to a deity. According to Dicey, the two basic preconditions for the formation of federations were: first, 'a body of countries … so closely connected by locality, by history, by race, or the like, as to be capable of bearing, in the eyes of their inhabitants, an impress of common nationality'; and, second, the existence of 'a very peculiar state of sentiment among the inhabitants of the countries which it is proposed to unite'. 'They must', he declared, 'desire union and must not desire unity'.[38] A federal state was 'a political contrivance intended to reconcile national unity and power with the maintenance of "state rights"'.[39] From this reconciliation of national unity with state independence by a division of powers under a common constitution between the nation and the individual states there flowed the following three principal characteristics: the supremacy of the constitution; the distribution among bodies with limited and coordinate authority of the different powers of government; and the authority of the courts to act as interpreters of the constitution.[40] And the constitution, which was supreme, had to be both 'written' and 'rigid' in the sense of requiring special procedures to amend it.

It is important to remember that Dicey's text was essentially a classic work on English constitutionalism based upon comparisons between it and the constitutionalism of the USA and France. And the section in his book that compared and contrasted 'Parliamentary Sovereignty and Federalism' also included short comparative studies of the American, Canadian and Swiss federations. Dicey's analysis, unlike that of Bryce, was intended to confront 'federalism' with 'unitarianism' and to demonstrate the advantages of the latter over the former. Small wonder, in this light, that Dicey's position in the British politics of the late nineteenth century was that of vehement opposition to Irish Home Rule and imperial feder-

ation. They were tantamount to national disintegration. He believed that federalism suffered from 'a certain waste of energy', preserved 'mutual jealousies' and
involved an incompatibility with 'schemes for wide social innovation'.[41]

But Dicey's legacy, which endured for almost a century, had at least one unintended consequence: it was to prove particularly unhelpful for understanding
both the concept and practice of federation. In what quickly became a classic
late Victorian exposition of the guiding principles of English constitutional law,
Dicey delivered his famous verdict on federal government in withering terms: it
meant weak government; it tended to produce conservatism; and federal political
systems meant, in practice, legalism. In short, federalism substituted litigation for
legislation.[42] Certainly Dicey's impact and influence upon the British tradition of
federalism proved especially damaging. In intellectual terms it established a
narrow legalistic conception of federation that was handed down from one
generation to the next in supine fashion. In practical terms it effectively excluded
an important option for British constitutional reform up until quite recently and
it continues to hinder clarity of thought about British national interests. It is
hardly surprising therefore that misunderstanding and confusion – not to
mention barely concealed hostility – about federalism produced the phobia that
has been a characteristic hallmark of British political culture.[43]

From the impressive scholarship of James Bryce and the unfortunate legacy of
Albert Venn Dicey we turn now to look at the contribution to federal thought of
another prominent academic contemporary, namely, Henry Sidgwick. Sidgwick
was Professor of Moral Philosophy at Cambridge between 1883 and 1900 and
his main contribution to the study of federalism and federation can be found in
two important and influential works entitled, respectively, *The Elements of Politics*,
first published in 1891, and *The Development of European Polity*, published in
1903.[44] In the latter, which was partly the result of a series of lectures delivered
at Cambridge during the closing years of the nineteenth century, Sidgwick
remarked that 'much learning and subtlety' had been applied to distinguishing
the conception of a 'federal state' (*Bundesstaat*) from that of a 'confederation of
states' (*Staatenbund*). He also claimed that perhaps 'undue importance' had been
attached to the 'aim of getting a clear and sharp distinction' between these two
concepts. 'The two notions – confederation of states, federal state – represent',
he argued, 'two stages in the development of federality'.[45]

What did Sidgwick mean by the term 'federality'? In his *Elements of Politics* he
noted that there remained 'considerable divergences of view as to the exact definition of "Federality"'. Nonetheless, it is at least clear that he meant it to
embrace a wide divergence of views about core federal principles, akin almost to
a spectrum of federality. For Sidgwick, then, a federal state had to be distinguished, on the one hand, from a unitary state with well-developed local
governments and, on the other, from a confederation or league of independent
states. But, as he remarked, 'in neither case' was the distinction 'simple and
sharp' since the balanced combination of 'unity of the whole aggregate' with
'separateness of parts', which constituted 'federality', could be 'realised in very
various modes and degrees'.[46]

Sidgwick elaborated upon his notion of federality by adding three further criteria that bore directly upon the conceptual distinction he had established between the federation, the unitary state and the confederation. These were the following factors:

1   The autonomy of the constituent units in a federation must be considerable in extent.
2   When the federality is well marked, the compositeness of the state will find expression somehow in the structure of the common government.
3   If the federal character of the polity is stable, the constitutional process of changing the constitutional division of powers between central and local governments must be determined in harmony with the principle of federalism.[47]

Let us comment briefly on each of these factors. Sidgwick had some interesting observations to make on the critical question of the relative autonomy of the constituent units in federations. Although he believed that we should not call a state 'federal' simply because the independence of the local governments in 'certain minor matters' was guaranteed by the constitution, he nonetheless insisted that 'federality' did not imply 'any definite definition of functions between the governments of the parts and the common government of the whole'.[48] His view was that the principle of federal union was much more complicated than the customary 'rough line of division' between 'internal matters' that were usually ascribed to the constituent units and 'external matters' that were the preserve of the federal government. He observed astutely that this over-simplified axiom overlooked 'matters external to the parts but not to the whole', by which he meant 'the mutual relations of the parts'. This 'intermediate region' was very important to modern states, for example, in the realms of securing free trade between 'the federated part-states'. And the reverse circumstances were also significant. There would be occasions when the so-called 'internal matters' of the constituent units would be 'of serious common interest to the whole'. Consequently the federal government ought to have the power to enforce the fulfilment of international obligations and this would sometimes involve 'interference in the internal affairs of the part-states'.[49]

With regard to the second factor concerning the incorporation of the constituent units in the structure of the federal government, Sidgwick acknowledged that this could be achieved in 'various ways and degrees'. The key issue here was one of the main concerns of both James Madison in *Federalist* 10 and John Stuart Mill, namely, vested interests and the principle of representation. Sidgwick recognised three important mechanisms to achieve this: first, equally elected state representation in some important part of the common government; second, state representatives voting not individually but collectively in a representative body of the common government, their aggregate voting power being weighted in proportion to the size of each state; and, third, the state representatives would in effect become delegates receiving instructions to conform to the wishes of the state governments. Sidgwick acknowledged however that the third mechanism would have been objectionable in a federation because it would have hampered the 'deliberative independence' of the central institution.[50]

His third factor, namely, the process of constitutional change in federations, was intriguing for its prescience. He reminded his readers that the process of constitutional change must be made more difficult than that of ordinary legislation and warned that no change should be made unless supported by the representatives not only of a decided majority of citizens but also of a decided majority of constituent states. And it seemed better to achieve the same result directly by making the legitimacy of a change in the federal constitution contingent upon the consent of a majority – whether two-thirds or three-quarters – of the legislatures of the constituent states. But Sidgwick was clearly uncomfortable with these circumstances. Indeed, the following candid statement reveals the depth of his discomfort and has obvious contemporary resonance:

> It might even be plausibly maintained that the principle of federalism, strictly taken, requires that the consent of any part-state should be given to any change in the constitutional division of powers between the whole and the parts; on the view that the powers allotted to the part-states belong to them independently, in their own right, and being not conferred by any authority external to the state, cannot legitimately be withdrawn by any such authority.[51]

After some reflection Sidgwick eventually rejected the principle of unanimity in the process of constitutional change because he believed that it would render any constitutional rule 'unalterable without revolution'. It seemed to him that this form of federality was suitable not to a federal state but rather to 'a federal union of states dissoluble at will' – a confederation.[52] But the protection of difference in federal states did draw at least some significant support from him. 'Federality', he argued, was not of course destroyed by the allotment of 'some minor special privileges' to particular constituent states. Despite the risk of instability, such 'special privileges' were hardly likely to be secure unless the federal constitution guaranteed that they could not 'be withdrawn without the consent of the privileged states'.[53]

Sidgwick, like Bryce and Freeman, regarded the conceptual distinction between federation and confederation to lie in the extent to which the central government entered normally into important direct relations with the citizens rather than acting on them only through the political institutions of the constituent state governments. This distinction he regarded as 'of the deepest character from the point of view of an individual member of the community' because it both created and sustained the 'habit of divided allegiance'.[54] And like his contemporaries, Sidgwick also believed the very nature of divided allegiance to be one of the chief disadvantages of federation. The strength and stability that federal states derived from internal cohesion tended to be 'somewhat reduced by the independent activity of local governments' especially if they could be used as 'centres of local resistance to the national will'.[55]

Sidgwick concluded his 'reflective analysis' by confirming what many subsequent commentators on federation were wont to stress, namely, that such states were merely a stage or phase in the larger, long-term processes of state-building and national integration.[56] 'It may be observed', he noted, that federation is 'likely to be in many cases a transitional stage through which a society – or an aggregate of societies – passes on its way to a completer union'. The evolution of federations into unitary states was due *inter alia* to the growth of 'mutual intercourse', the diminution of 'the narrower patriotic sentiments that were originally a bar to full political union' and the increasing inconvenience of a diversity of laws, especially in 'a continuous territory'. And partly for the same reasons, a confederation – if it held together – had 'a tendency to pass into a federal state'. Differences of race, religion and historical traditions, however, could 'indefinitely retard either process'.[57]

Sidgwick's intellectual contribution to federalism and federation, then, was conceptually rigorous and analytically perceptive. The hallmark of his approach was 'philosophical analysis', a kind of 'reflective analysis ... combined with a few empirical generalisations' that emanated from his search for 'the theory of practice'. There is evidence of a curious mixture of the deductive and the inductive in this quest, which arrived, like Freeman, at the comparative method in political science but which also emphasised, unlike him, the limits of historical explanation.[58] Our sketch of Henry Sidgwick's views on our subject brings us to the end of this section on the early contributors. Let us briefly summarise the various contributions that have helped to explain the nature and significance of our current concerns about federalism and federation.

No attempt has been made to produce an exhaustive account of every intellectual contribution to the Anglo-American academic literature from the late eighteenth to the early twentieth century. This would have been largely superfluous. Instead I have tried to point up the significant features of federalism and federation in the writings of a limited but prominent number of academic contributors – particular features that retain their relevance for contemporary discourse and analysis. Broadly speaking our short survey of selected contributions to the evolution of concept and meaning has underlined the connection between federation and the gradual emergence of mass democracy. It has highlighted, for example, the importance of the principle of representation, problems of institutional design, anxieties about the centralisation of government, the difficulties of managing different forms of conflict and the threat of secession. And it has sharpened our sensitivities to conceptual issues, especially those which distinguish federations from unitary states and from confederations. In this respect one very important consideration to emerge from the early contributions has been the emphasis upon conceptual ambiguity. By the early twentieth century we can already appreciate in the work of Sidgwick the absence of impermeable watertight compartments between the standard conceptual categories. The lines of distinction commonly drawn are not always authoritative.

On the contrary, one conceptual category can shade off into another so that, for example, a regional authority in a unitary state might enjoy a greater relative autonomy with regard to its internal affairs than a constituent state government in a federation. In other words we are reminded of Sidgwick's 'federality' which, to return to our earlier quotation, can be realised 'in very various modes and degrees'.[59]

But another purpose of this wide-ranging survey was also to locate the origins of our contemporary analytical concerns about federalism and federation. We are able now to appreciate more fully how far the sources of the continuing conceptual debate can be traced back to and identified in these notable intellectual contributions. Current concerns about federations are far from novel. It is time therefore to bring our conceptual and methodological review up to date. We will focus mainly on the post-war years because the period since 1945 is when scholarly attention paid to conceptual matters in the Anglo-American academic literature was at its most prolific, though not always its most profitable.

Conceptual and methodological review (ii)

Before we look at the contemporary period, it is important for us to acknowledge the significance of three memorable contributions – two inter-war and one during wartime – to our current understanding of federalism and federation. The first is the impressive two-volume work, which we have already mentioned, of Sobei Mogi, whose *The Problem of Federalism: A Study in the History of Political Theory* was first published in 1931.[60] According to Harold Laski, who was his tutor and who wrote the preface to the publication, this mammoth project traversed ground that it was unlikely any other scholar would travel again, at least not in quite the same way.[61] Mogi's weighty tomes combined the history and political philosophy of the federal idea in the USA, the United Kingdom and Germany with a conception of federation as 'an ideal federal form' that, in his view, had to be adopted 'more and more as real democracy progressed'.[62] His, in short, was an optimistic vision of the federal future.

The second contribution was, ironically, Laski's own and it is included here only because it is still oft-quoted, albeit *en passant*, by many students of the subject. Entitled 'The Obsolescence of Federalism', it was a short polemic, published in *The New Republic* in May 1939, which boldly announced that 'the epoch of federalism' in the USA was over. But principled denunciation was accompanied by empirical scrutiny. The arrival of powerful new economic and social forces rendered the federal idea, at least in its American form, redundant. In an age of giant capitalism, social and economic reconstruction, and minimum standards of uniform economic performance, the pressing needs of the positive state suggested to Laski that the existing federal system was a damaging hindrance to 'the implications of positivism'.[63]

During the inter-war years the concepts of federalism and federation seem not to have been particularly well developed in the Anglo-American academic literature. In an age of totalitarian experiments, the rise of socialism and the growth of the modern state and government this is hardly surprising. Mogi's massive intellectual contribution was highly informative but it did not signifi-cantly advance the cause of conceptual development. Indeed, there appears to have been no real conceptual progress beyond the established works which we have already identified above. Western liberal democratic values and assump-tions based upon a combination of American republican and British parliamentary political traditions characterised the received understanding of federalism and federation. In empirical terms the American model continued to define the conceptual and historical departure point and federation remained very much a normative model described largely in constitutional and institu-tional terms as a means of dividing sovereignty and limiting executive power in order to preserve liberty. Despite the penchant for the 'Comparative Method' in the intellectual approaches of Freeman and Sidgwick, there was certainly very little analytical basis for comparative federalism and federation during the inter-war years.

It was the threat of war and the Second World War itself that acted as the spur to a renewed interest in the federal idea. Together they had a catalytic impact upon the intellectual debate. Indeed, there was a veritable cornucopia of outpourings of federalist literature, much of it of the highest quality, in both the Anglo-American and the Continental European federal traditions between 1938 and 1945. The activities of the Federal Union in the United Kingdom and its American sympathisers together with the intellectual resistance in Europe stimu-lated much of this, with a large proportion of it understandably prescriptive, some of it widely regarded as utopian but a significant body of it having stood the test of time.[64] We will return to some of these elements in Chapter 6, but for the moment let us press on with the conceptual review. Leaving aside this important and influential body of federalist literature, which grew directly out of the deter-mination to remove the causes of war, there was one particular exception to the general paucity of academic writing on the subject. This was H.R.G. Greaves' *Federal Union in Practice,* a short comparative study, which was published in 1940.[65]

Greaves' contribution merits much closer attention than it has usually received for several reasons. First, its conceptual approach in the introductory chapter entitled 'The Nature of Federalism' was unusual for its time. Greaves' early emphasis upon the associational dimension of federalism with its strong Althusian sensitivities led him to question the role of the state, the nation and some of the conventional conceptual distinctions common at the time. He claimed, for example, that it was 'not always possible to draw clear and incon-testable distinctions' when studying federalism: 'alliance shades into league, league into confederation, confederation into federal state, federal state into unitary state'. With the prescience of a Sidgwick or a Freeman, he noted that these distinctions were 'matters of convenience' since 'many political forms merge the characteristics of one with those of another'.[66] Another reason for looking at Greaves' comparative study – with its empirical focus on the USA, Switzerland, Canada, the Union of South Africa, Australia and Germany supplemented by a brief sketch of federalism in South America and the Spanish

Republic – was its analysis of what he called 'The Causes and Conditions of Federal Union' that anticipated much of the subsequent analytical literature which we shall examine later in Chapter 3.

Together Greaves' contribution and the pedigree of the Federal Union literature combined to overcome what we might call the conceptual stagnation of the inter-war years. But it was the publication of Kenneth Wheare's classic *Federal Government* in 1946 that launched the contemporary intellectual debate. Following in the familiar English liberal intellectual tradition of Mill, Freeman, Bryce and Dicey, the thrust of Wheare's contribution was couched very much in legal and institutional terms. His 'federal principle' was defined as 'the method of dividing powers so that the general and regional governments are each within a sphere, coordinate and independent'.[67] Accordingly the criterion of the federal principle – its hallmark – was not so much that federal and constituent state governments operated directly upon the citizens but whether or not the powers of government were divided between coordinate, independent authorities. Wheare acknowledged that this definition was rigid and it is true that this rigidity extended to the point where he could confidently claim that 'any definition of federal government which failed to include the United States would be ... condemned as unreal'.[68] Indeed, his famous statement that 'the federal principle has come to mean what it does because the United States has come to be what it is' took the primacy of the American model to limits that were frankly inimical to genuine comparative analysis.[69] But even here his interpretation was far from that of a lone voice. On the contrary, it was typical of that era. Greaves, too, had earlier claimed that the USA was 'the outstanding example of a federal union'.[70]

It is imperative that we assess Wheare's major work on federal government according to the climate of the time. However we construe his weaknesses – the narrowness of his own definition of the federal principle, his excessively legalistic approach and his undue reliance upon the American experience – that together conveyed a somewhat compressed and static impression of federations and their federal governments, this should not blind us to the impressive strengths of Wheare's enduring contribution. He influenced a whole generation of thinking about the subject. And, after all, it was the first detailed and comprehensive attempt rigorously to compare the federal constitutions and governments of the USA, Canada, Australia and Switzerland in a way which continues to this day to repay close attention by students of the subject. Consequently most contemporary studies of federalism and federation still include respectful references to Wheare's classic study of federal government. This is as it should be. And it should be emphasised, too, that Wheare was looking principally at federal *governments* – why they were formed, how they were organised and how they worked – rather than at the larger picture of federalism and federation. His conspicuous neglect of federal societies, coming close to this aspect of the subject only in his brief consideration of the prerequisites of federal government, is not therefore surprising. It was a gap that would be redressed within a decade.

Wheare's classic *Federal Government*, then, remains an important milestone in the evolution of intellectual thought about federalism and federation. But it is nonetheless tempting for some critics to discredit and discard it as having outlived its usefulness. This temptation must be resisted. Time and again in our survey we will return to his comparative analysis in the continuing search for conceptual clarity and terminological precision. The value of Wheare's contribution lies chiefly in its comparative focus but there is enduring significance also in the perceptive distinction which he made between federal constitutions and federal governments, in his sophisticated analysis of the preconditions of federal union and in his belief, like Freeman before him, that federal government was essentially circumstantial.

In hindsight, Wheare's *Federal Government* was also significant for the unintended role which it played in triggering the prodigious, often contentious, but not always progressive intellectual debate about federalism and federation during the next forty years. Indeed, it became a veritable yardstick by which subsequent commentators to the debate gauged their own contributions. And it also became inevitably the victim of not a little misrepresentation and some quite severe, almost predatory, criticism. But this unfortunate predicament was also due to a unique set of circumstances that occurred during the early post-war years. The publication of *Federal Government* coincided roughly with what some might describe as a paradigm shift in the social sciences. It was published during a period of immense and turbulent intellectual change, one consequence of which was to extend the scope and enrich the content of political science so that the focus of analysis shifted away from constitutions and legal and political institutions toward more quantitative and conceptually rigorous concerns. The study of federalism and federation of course was not immune to this convulsive change.

It is true that the study of federalism and federation had in a sense always been shaped and determined by practical politics and the prevailing mode of intellectual thought and scholarship in history, philosophy, law and political science, but the dramatic impact of the Second World War, the international context of the Cold War and the emergence of the USA as both a military hegemon and the leading exponent of the so-called 'behavioural revolution' in the social sciences had a combined impact on political science the like of which was broadly comparable to the sort of profound changes wrought by epic events such as the Reformation or the Peace of Westphalia. The first indication of this notable change of focus in the study of federalism and federation to incorporate wider scholarly concerns than just the law and the constitution occurred in 1952 when William Livingston's 'A Note on the Nature of Federalism' first appeared in the *Political Science Quarterly*.[71] With the appearance of this seminal article the intellectual debate entered a new phase of development.

Livingston criticised existing approaches to the study of federalism and federation for their almost exclusive legalism. 'Legal answers', he argued, were of value 'only in the solution of legal problems'. And federation was concerned with many other problems than those of a purely legal nature. Above and beyond this legalism he claimed that there was an aspect of federation that had been largely ignored. In a famous statement the American scholar insisted that:

> The essential nature of federalism is to be sought for, not in the shadings of legal and constitutional terminology, but in the forces – economic, social, political, cultural – that have made the outward forms of federalism necessary. … The essence of federalism lies not in the institutional or constitutional structure but in the society itself. Federal government is a device by which the federal qualities of the society are articulated and protected.[72]

Put simply, Livingston stated that even the most profound analyses of constitutions, legal systems and political institutions could not inform the observer about the societies served by them. The nature of the political society could be examined only by observing how the institutions worked in the context of that society: it was their operation, not their form, that was important. Federalism was a function not of constitutions but of societies.[73]

Federalism, then, was not an absolute but a relative term. And in another oft-quoted statement he claimed that:

> There is no specific point at which a society ceases to be unified and becomes diversified. The differences are of degree rather than kind. All countries fall somewhere in a spectrum which runs from what we call a theoretically wholly integrated society at one extreme to a theoretically wholly diversified society at the other. … But there is no point at which it can be said that all societies on one side are unitary and all those on the other are federal or diversified.[74]

At this juncture in his article Livingston introduced the notion of what he called 'instrumentalities'. This term, he confessed, was a broad one and included not only constitutional forms but also the manner in which the forms were employed – the way in which the constitution and its institutions operated – together with a whole host of non-constitutional matters such as 'habits, attitudes, acceptances, concepts and even theories'. Accordingly it was not enough to check a country's constitution against an *a priori* list of the characteristics of a federal constitution in order to determine whether or not it was federal. This was an over-simplification. Indeed it was actually a very poor guide when attempting to discover whether or not the society itself was federal. Rather, an examination of the 'pattern of instrumentalities' was the best way to determine this.[75]

Livingston also noted that his 'instrumentalities' could, after a period of time, become 'rigidified and acquire a status of their own'. They could conceivably become 'ends in themselves instead of merely means toward other ends'. Intriguingly he suggested that they might even 'take on an honorific quality'; they could become 'matters of pride to the diverse elements that they served' so that ultimately 'the instrumentalities enter into and become part of the psycho-sociological complex itself'.[76] Constitutions in this respect were a classic example of how, designed principally as an instrumentality, institutions could become 'part of the complex of sociological and psychological values' that constituted the pattern of diversities. In other words the instrumentality could itself become a part of that complex of values which was the pattern of diversities.[77] The problem for students of federalism, then, was to try to distinguish clearly between society and the instrumentalities it employed. They therefore had to focus not narrowly upon the institutional patterns but upon the pattern of the diversities in the society in order to assess its federal qualities.[78]

What are we to make of Livingston's contribution? There was certainly more than a hint of Tocqueville in his emphasis upon socio-psychological values and it is easy in retrospect to understand why his critics were able to portray his work as shifting the intellectual debate too far in the direction of sociological variables. It was precisely this emphasis that enabled him to claim that federalism was a matter of degree not of kind. He was later to be accused of conceptual ambiguity in his references to federal societies, and his formulation of a 'spectrum' of federality was considered by many commentators to be terminologically imprecise. But his controversial article was helpful in the extent to which it encouraged scholars to broaden and enrich their conceptions of federalism by looking beyond mere constitutions and juridical considerations. In fact, Livingston's distinction between law, constitutions and political institutions and the societies that underpinned them was, in many ways, a precursor to the current conceptual distinction between federalism and federation that informs this book. His own conception of federalism was much more dynamic and insightful than what he obviously considered to be the static, unidimensional approach of Wheare.

But it would be a mistake to exaggerate the differences between Wheare and Livingston. After all, they both shared similar views about the role of political institutions and they both distinguished between institutional structures and the manner in which these were employed. Appearance and reality often diverge. And while Wheare drew a distinction between federal law and constitutions and federal practices, Livingston attempted to subordinate institutions to the deeper patterns of social and cultural diversity without which his instrumentalities would be, at least initially, redundant.

Before we leave Livingston's contribution, it is appropriate to mention one final important distinction that he drew in the intellectual debate, one that remains very much alive today. This was his focus upon territoriality. It is imperative that we clarify this issue because it has enormous implications for our study. Livingston acknowledged that:

> In using the term federal only in this restricted territorial sense I am taking from it some of meaning attributed to it by writers who profess to see federal elements in the various forms of pluralism, such as feudalism or corporativism. But I suggest that these writers have added a meaning that was not there before and one that introduces an element of confusion into the term.

No government has ever been called federal that has been organized on any but the territorial basis; when organized on any other it has gone by another name. ... federalism becomes nothing if it is held to embrace diversities that are not territorially grouped, ... We confuse two distinct principles when we apply the terminology of federalism to a society organized on a functional basis.[79]

This is a very interesting early emphasis upon a conceptual distinction that continues to resonate in the mainstream academic literature. Livingston accepted that it boiled down to a question of the definition of federalism and today it might seem that in this respect he construed federalism in a very narrow sense. For a commentator whose purpose was to widen and deepen our understanding of federalism this now seems somewhat ironic. But federalism, pluralism and considerations of a functional character are not as mutually exclusive as Livingston would have us believe. We will return to the question of territoriality in Chapter 5. For the moment let us continue our intellectual odyssey in search of conceptual refinement.

After Livingston's crusade against legal formalism it was not long before another major contribution to the intellectual debate added a further layer to the cumulative weight of conceptual analysis on federalism and federation. In 1955 and 1956 two articles entitled, respectively, 'The "Federal Principle" Reconsidered' Parts I and II were published in the *Australian Journal of Politics and History* by the Australian scholar S. Rufus Davis.[80] Part I was an exhaustively detailed analysis of Wheare's 'federal principle' that, for all of its impressive deconstruction, need not detain us here. Part II, however, is much more pertinent for our purposes. Davis concluded it by stating that Wheare's federal principle could convey a distinct and exclusive principle of organisation only if it was restricted to just two considerations, namely, formal juridical matters and the self-sufficiency of federal and constituent state governmental machinery. Otherwise it had no legal explanatory capacity with regard to matters of a non-legal nature. It was simply incapable of accommodating 'political and social nuances'.[81] The validity of Wheare's federal principle survived intact but in a much more impoverished form. His claim to be able to embrace the complexity of factors germane to federalism that extended beyond legal formalism was severely attenuated.

The conceptual value of Wheare's federal principle, then, was to inform the student of 'a particular kind of jural relationship in which general and regional governments may be joined, and the formal institutional arrangements in which this relationship should be expressed'.[82] Beyond this its utility was heavily circumscribed. Davis' reconsideration of Wheare's federal principle chimed closely with Livingston's earlier critique. Indeed it echoed the thrust of Livingston's foray, as the following extract from Davis' summary of the limitations of the federal principle makes abundantly clear:

> For the student of politics ... it can tell him little of the precise distribution of functions between two levels of government, the range and influence of

their functions, the precise set of fiscal relations created, the party system and the power structure within each party, the degree of cohesion and diversity in the community, their political skills and dispositions, their attitudes to the formal garment, or their wealth, traditions and usages. ... These attributes, if they are meaningful, are functions of the society, not its legal form alone.[83]

Davis' contribution to the debate about federalism in the mid-1950s, however it might seem in hindsight, was not limited solely to his unremitting dissection of Wheare's federal principle. His own analysis did bring into sharp focus other criteria of federalism and federation relevant to our quest for meaning. One significant contribution was his helpful remarks about the origins of federations. In a memorable statement repeated in his later work, he pronounced upon the circumstances that surrounded the formation and subsequent evolution of federal unions:

It is no more possible to predicate the precise motives, postulates and understandings, or predict the life which will ensue from the choice of this form of union than one can predicate the motives which lead to marriage or to predict the relationship which will ensue from the form in which the union is legally consummated.[84]

This challenging form of words about the origins and formation of federations is worth more than a moment's reflection and, as we shall see, continues to perplex and bedevil historians and political scientists seeking to explain this peculiar process of state-formation. Nonetheless, with these engaging remarks stamped indelibly on our memory, we will leave Davis' early post-war contribution and turn now to look at the work of yet another important commentator on our subject. In 1955 Antony Birch's *Federalism, Finance and Social Legislation in Canada, Australia and the United States* was published and moved the conceptual debate a stage further.[85] Birch, a Canadian, claimed that his survey of the new or proposed post-war federal constitutions in West Germany and Yugoslavia, together with those in the British Commonwealth, raised the question whether or not these countries still accorded with Wheare's classical definition. Close attention paid to the flexible nature of the numerous interactions between the federal and state authorities entrenched in the constitutions of India, Nigeria, Central Africa and the West Indies indicated that they did not. Moreover, new socio-economic developments in the established federations of Canada, Australia and the USA also suggested a similar trend away from Wheare's rigid formulation. Birch pointed in particular to two major departures:

1   Federal governments were not in practice limited to their own spheres when they passed a good deal of legislation relating to matters within the spheres of the constituent state governments as happened in both Canada and the USA regarding social welfare.

2   State governments were not in practice independent of the federal govern-
    ment when they derived a large proportion of their revenue from federal
    payments, as occurred in all three established federations.[86]

In short, practice had outstripped theory.

According to Birch, federalism was certainly not obsolescent as Laski had
famously declared. Quite the reverse. A series of new devices had made it more
adaptable and 'may even have prolonged its life'. But these early post-war developments prompted Birch to propose that 'the definition of federalism should be
reworded so as not to suggest that intergovernmental cooperation and grants'
were 'exceptions to the federal principle'.[87] He concluded his important contribution to the debate by suggesting that the new developments in the older
federations, together with the novel features of the post-war federations, illustrated how federalism had 'entered a new phase' which could conveniently be
called 'co-operative federalism':

> For whereas the guiding principle of eighteenth and nineteenth century
> federalism was the independence of federal and state authorities, the guiding
> principle of mid-twentieth century federalism is the need for co-operation
> between them. The difference is clear: the question remains whether it is
> great enough to require a rephrasing of the definition of federal government.[88]

Birch pruned Wheare's definition so that it accorded much more with contemporary post-war developments. He removed the two references identified above in
Wheare's original formulation and this left him with the following much leaner
definition: 'a federal system of government is one in which there is a division of
powers between one general and several regional authorities, each of which, in
its own sphere, is co-ordinate with the others, and each of which acts directly on
the people through its own administrative agencies'.[89] To this revised formulation could be added or subtracted a list of the chief characteristics of federal
systems of government 'in any particular period'. The essential points of distinction were therefore retained but flexibility had been introduced to take account
of new trends and developments that impinged upon federalism. Logically, then,
by the end of the century new characteristics would probably replace those that
then typified federations but 'the problem of securing political unity despite local
diversity' was likely to be more rather than less widespread and federalism
seemed to Birch to be 'adaptable enough to continue to provide the solution'.[90]
It was a note of optimism.

A decade later Birch followed up this conceptual analysis with an article entitled 'Approaches to the Study of Federalism' published in *Political Studies*.[91] In this
article he summarised the major approaches of the period and argued consistently in favour of linking conceptual analysis with contemporary political
developments. But how did Wheare and Livingston fare in this article and what
was Birch's major contribution during the mid-1960s? Echoing his earlier
remarks, Birch acknowledged that the real basis for turning away from Wheare's

approach was that it could not be usefully applied to many of the new federations that had been established since the Second World War. The reason was
simple: hardly any of them conformed to Wheare's model. The student of
comparative government was therefore confronted with a stark choice: either to
construct an elaborate model which would restrict comparative analysis to just a
few countries (as indeed Wheare had done) or to adopt a much less stringent set
of criteria that would be more all-encompassing in its scope.

Livingston's contribution came in for much more severe criticism. Birch identified three main reasons that made him doubt the utility of the largely
sociological approach. First, Livingston's spectrum of federalism was criticised
for attempting to make firm generalisations about the members of a category for
which membership was undefined. Second, his basic propositions were couched
in language that made them 'somewhat cloudy' and, finally, Livingston had
unintentionally demonstrated the failure of his approach by his inability to utilise
his own conceptual framework. Livingston's approach to the study of federalism,
on this reckoning, was much closer to that of Wheare than might have been
thought.[92] Birch concluded his article with a recommendation:

> The kind of comparative study most likely to be fruitful is that which takes
> as its starting-point the existence of somewhat similar arrangements which
> have evolved or have been devised in a limited number of countries, them-
> selves not entirely dissimilar, to meet similar needs. The object of this kind
> of study is to show how these arrangements have been modified in the
> course of time by the pressure of circumstance and by differences in the
> political traditions of the countries involved, and how far interesting points
> of similarity remain.[93]

There was much that needed further elaboration in this strategy for the comparative analysis of federal political systems and federal governments but it at least
had the merit of rooting the analysis in firm, recognised bases for comparison.
Perceived similarities in constitutional, political and legal arrangements, devised
deliberately to respond to a particular problem or set of problems, were likely to
be the product of similar political cultures and/or shared historical experiences.
Beginning with similarities in order to underline differences was the approach
that Birch preferred, primarily because it was feasible.

Birch's oft-quoted article was a timely reappraisal of the intellectual debate
about federalism that took place during the mid-1960s but it appeared after a
number of significant modifications to the approaches of Wheare and
Livingston had already been made. The first of these revisions applied to
Wheare's rigid notions of 'coordinacy' and 'independence' in his definition of
federal government. In *The Structure of American Federalism*, which was published in
1961, Maurice Vile insisted on the substitution of the concept 'interdependence'
for that of 'independence'.[94] And the gradual shift away from Wheare's restrictive model was accelerated with the portrayal of federalism as something
completely different from a static pattern of government.

Carl Friedrich, who had already published Johannes Althusius' 1603 Latin version of *Politica methodice digesta* in 1932, circulated a research paper entitled 'New Tendencies in Federal Theory and Practice' at the Sixth World Congress of the International Political Science Association (IPSA) in Geneva, Switzerland in September 1964.[95] As a highly respected scholar of federalism who understood both the philosophical and historical complexities of the Continental European federal heritage, Friedrich's paper naturally attracted considerable attention. In it he established what was quickly dubbed 'federalism as process'. Friedrich defined federalism as 'a union of groups, united by one or more common objectives, but retaining their distinctive group character for other purposes'.[96] But this definition could be stretched beyond the federal state; it could also be applied to an alliance, that is, a functional association of states; or a union of groups within a state. Friedrich was keen to emphasise the 'process of federalising' rather than the terminal end-point of that process. He had already outlined the main contours of this new approach in an important albeit neglected essay entitled 'Federal Constitutional Theory and Emergent Proposals' in 1962 and had clarified the crucial relationship between federalism and constitutionalism.[97] Friedrich believed that federalism was actually a species of the larger genus of constitutionalism and that a federal constitution was 'a subdivision of the general kind of process involved in modern constitutionalism':

> Federalism can be, and often has been, a highly dynamic process by which emergent composite communities have succeeded in organizing themselves by effectively institutionalising 'unity in diversity'. ... A conception of federalism in dynamic terms ... fits the notion of federalism as process into the notion of constitutionalism as process, and understands the relation between the inclusive community and the component communities as a system of regularized restraint upon the exercise of governmental power so as to make power and responsibility correlative with the structure of a composite and dynamic community, its interests and needs.[98]

This emphasis upon constitutionalism in the interpretation of federalism sprang primarily from nineteenth-century liberal concerns for protecting freedom and autonomy by placing constitutional limitations upon executive power. It recalled the spirit of Mill, Freeman and Bryce. But Friedrich's focus upon constitutionalism in political science extended far beyond the narrow confines of constitutional law. He construed federalism as part of the irresistible march of modern constitutionalism and democracy that sought to combine a maximum of freedom with the necessary authority. Unlike his illustrious nineteenth-century predecessors, he was at pains to point out that it was imperative 'not to confuse the process itself with particular divisions of power and authority' which might have been characteristic of it 'under particular circumstances of time and place'.[99] Constitutionalism, like federalism, was not 'a fixed and unalterable plan'. Neither should it be construed as 'a static pattern, as a fixed and precise term of division of powers between central and component authorities'.[100]

The novelty of this approach to the study of federalism and federation was appealing in the intellectual climate of the mid-1960s. It stretched the concepts further than they had been extended before, enabling scholars, and especially systems theorists, to move much more easily between the national and the international worlds of political science. The boundaries of the state could be breached with a certain aplomb. Federalism was construed in terms of trends and patterns of integration and differentiation in a wide variety of political systems and organisations in which decision-making was divided between a central authority and a number of regional units. The basis for a dynamic approach to comparative federalism and federation was established and the attention of scholars could be directed towards identifying the factors that promoted integration and those that impeded it. The American political scientist Karl Deutsch had already laid bare the foundations for just this kind of analysis as early as 1957 when his *Political Community and the North Atlantic Area* focused upon the conditions for federal integration, described as an 'amalgamated security community'.[101] The study of federalism, we are reminded, reflected changes taking place in the larger intellectual discipline of political science itself.

Friedrich's 'federalism as process' of course was not without its critics, and Birch acknowledged that there was 'a certain price to pay' for defining federalism in such general terms. In his eagerness to present federalism as dynamic rather than static he had made it difficult to know whether or not certain political systems could be regarded as federal 'at any particular time'.[102] His approach portrayed the relationship between process and structure in ambiguous terms and it did not explain precisely how we could know for sure that a so-called 'federalising process' had even begun. There were, then, many penetrating and insightful observations in Friedrich's contribution but it is fair to say that many, if not most, of his contemporaries in the intellectual debate found the basic premises of his work to be either flawed or simply too obscure to be adopted as the new definitional mantra.

At the same IPSA Conference in 1964 Christopher Hughes presented his paper entitled 'The Theory of Confederacies', which harked back to his inaugural professorial lecture 'Confederacies' that had been delivered in November 1962 at the University of Leicester.[103] Hughes' idiosyncratic contribution was to conflate the terms 'confederation' and 'federation' as a form of unitary government 'of the fully constitutional type' and as contradistinguished from confederacy which was a species of 'late absolutism or early constitutionalism'.[104] In this manner, Hughes was able to look at the familiar in an unfamiliar way. Confederacy was an earlier, tougher kind of state than the federal–confederal category. And confederacy was a 'thing' – an historical reality – while federalism–confederalism was a mere classification of unitary, fully constitutional government with some institutions borrowed from confederacy. This peculiar interpretation has been largely neglected in the mainstream literature probably because it completely rearranged the conceptual furniture in the debate and sought to reinstate an historical phenomenon that, according to Hughes, had been unjustifiably discredited. These mental acrobatics however were reminiscent of the controversies that surrounded Hamilton, Jay and Madison in their late-eighteenth-century defence of the new improvised American constitutional project outlined in *The Federalist Papers*.

In the same year that Friedrich had introduced the notion of federalism as process, William Riker's *Federalism: Origin, Operation, Significance* proclaimed that the twentieth century was an 'Age of Federalism' which was 'a constitutional bargain'.[105] Riker's formal definition of federalism was prosaic. He claimed that it was 'a bargain between prospective national leaders and officials of constituent governments for the purpose of aggregating territory, the better to lay taxes and raise armies'.[106] This bargain, when taking the form of a constitution, was federal if it included the following criteria:

1   Two levels of government ruling over the same land and people.
2   Each level must have at least one area of action in which it is autonomous.
3   There is some guarantee of the autonomy of each government in its own sphere.[107]

Riker believed that since his 'class of federal bargains' was 'large enough to admit of some generalizations', it was possible for the political scientist to rise above mere historical commentary even though 'each instance of a federal bargain' was embedded in 'a unique historical context'.[108] Although his formal definition of federalism incorporated parts of Wheare's classification of federal government, it is clear that he was not impressed by Wheare's analysis. Indeed, Riker described Wheare's classic *Federal Government* as 'highly legalistic in tone', a book which displayed 'very little understanding of political realities'. In hindsight, his reference to Wheare's 'provincialism' and his 'fairly consistent misinterpretation of federalism' was an early indication that conceptual evolution had become conceptual battleground.[109] And the battle had been joined. In his detailed examination of the conditions necessary for the striking of a specifically *federal* bargain and its subsequent maintenance, Riker had effectively reinstated politics and the role of political elites in the formation of federations. Economic, social and cultural–ideological factors might have been widely regarded at this time as fundamental prerequisites to federal integration but none of them could have any real significance without first taking into account the political environment which was pivotal to federal state-building.

There is much in Riker's 1964 contribution that continues to be of interest to students of federalism and federation today. Both his trenchant approach to the subject and the quality of his analysis remain instructive. In retrospect, he can be considered to have swung the pendulum of interpretation back from constitutional law, sociology and contemporary systems theory to political science – or to 'the political' – as detailed non-normative empirical analysis. Today the main sources of continuing controversy in Riker's early work probably boil down to the following four propositions:

1   That the politicians who offer the bargain desire to expand their territorial control usually either to meet or prepare for an external military or diplomatic threat.
2   That the politicians who accept the bargain, giving up some independence for the sake of union, are willing to do so because of some external military–diplomatic threat or opportunity.
3   That federalism must not be construed as political ideology.
4   That it is the structure of the party system that determines the maintenance of the bargain.[110]

The first two propositions have to do with the origins and formation of federations while the third is concerned to refute the causal linkage between federalism and freedom and the last has as its focus the structure of the party system as an intervening variable in maintaining federal political systems.

Riker certainly conveyed the impression that federalism had no unique virtues, moral or otherwise, apart from 'providing interstices in the social order' in which personal liberties could thrive. In answer to the candid question whether or not federalism was worth keeping, he remarked that one had to 'look to what they do and determine what minorities they favor'.[111] There seems little doubt that he regarded federal systems as of no particular significance other than reflecting organised entrenched interests. This impression was reinforced in 1969 when his somewhat curmudgeonly review article entitled 'Six Books in Search of a Subject or Does Federalism Exist and Does it Matter?' was published in *Comparative Politics*.[112] In his brief examination of pairs of countries that he described as having 'about the same political culture' – one federal and one unitary – Riker concluded that at least in the maintenance of local autonomy what counted was 'not the rather trivial constitutional structure, but rather the political and economic culture'. Indeed, federalism was 'no more than a constitutional legal fiction' that could be given 'whatever content' seemed 'appropriate at the moment'.[113] Riker even reproached himself for the 'misdirection of so much scholarly effort' in the study of a subject that had turned out to be a mere fiction. The only important function that federalism fulfilled lay in persuading regional politicians to accept the formation of a central government.[114] His so-called 'Age of Federalism', so loudly trumpeted in 1964, had turned into an intellectual fallacy just five years later:

> Federalism *qua* federalism is significant at the beginning of a central government as a way to bring in regional governments with the promise of autonomy. Once the central government is actually in operation, however, what maintains or destroys local autonomy is not the more or less superficial feature of federalism but the more profound characteristics of the political culture.[115]

Riker however seems not to have learned his own lesson. Despite his apparent contempt for federalism in 1969, he evidently found the subject to be sufficiently worthy of further reconnaissance when in 1975 he surveyed it again in some considerable detail in the much-thumbed *The Handbook of Political Science*.[116] Over 79 pages he carried out an in-depth exploration of the subtleties and complexities of federalism that even today is an invaluable resource for students of the subject. We will not investigate the further evolution of his views and ideas here because we will refer to them later in various parts of this book. For the moment let us switch our attention to six other notable contributors to the intellectual debate of the 1960s. These are, respectively, Morton Grodzins, Daniel Elazar, Ronald L. Watts, Thomas Franck, Michael Stein and Geoffrey Sawer. We will look very briefly at each of them in turn.

Both Grodzins and Elazar hold positions that reside in the category of 'Federalism as Sharing', leading S. Rufus Davis to denote them 'The Twentieth Century "Doctors"' of federalism.[117] Their joint position is cemented by a forthright rejection of 'dual federalism' – the idea of watertight jurisdictional compartments between the federal government and the constituent state governments – and its replacement by 'cooperative federalism' in the American polity. Grodzins' famous metaphor of the 'marble cake' of functional interpenetration, policy entanglement and essentially intergovernmental relations to characterise American federalism was outlined in his *The American System: A New View of Government in the United States,* edited by Elazar and published in 1966.[118] Probably the two most well-known early contributions of Elazar are *The American Partnership*, published in 1962, and *American Federalism: A View from the States*, which appeared in 1966.[119] But Elazar's overall contribution to the study of federalism cannot be confined to the American model, considerable though that is. His general contribution extends far beyond this into political theory and philosophy and international and comparative politics. Indeed, as the first editor of *Publius: The Journal of Federalism* in 1973, his role in promoting research and a wider public interest in the subject has been simply invaluable.[120]

Elazar, like Friedrich, was one of the few American scholars of federalism who both understood and appreciated fully the significance of the Continental European federal tradition as well as its Anglo-American counterpart. It is also fair to add that his own mental predisposition to 'think federally' – which is rooted in the intellectual heritage of the distant Judaeo-Christian past and traced back to the tribal times of the Israelites – has made him something of a guru of federalism in the eyes of his academic contemporaries and several advisory bodies in both the USA and Israel. In his ideological predilection for federal ideas and federal solutions to contemporary problems, Elazar clearly practised what he taught and preached.

Turning to a leading Canadian contributor to the intellectual debate, namely, Ronald L. Watts, we must concentrate our attentions upon his classic *New Federations: Experiments in the Commonwealth* published in 1966.[121] As a student of Kenneth Wheare, it might be expected that his contribution would seek to revise, extend and embellish some of his tutor's original work in *Federal Government*. And this he did with considerable scholarly prowess in an important comparative work on the new post-war federations in the British Commonwealth. He focused principally upon six major federal experiments – India, Pakistan, Malaya (later Malaysia), Nigeria, Rhodesia and Nyasaland, and the West Indies – in the years between 1945 and 1963, but the comparative empirical purpose also yielded up interesting conceptual modifications. These can be summarised for our purposes in the following five observations:

1   That there are enormous variations of the federal principle rather than one simple pattern. These include institutions, the distribution of authority, the scope of the functions assigned to each tier of government, degrees of mutual independence and interdependence, the institutional arrangements for the protection, amendment and administration of the distribution of functions and for the organisation of central legislation and administration, as well as the organisation of government within the component territorial units. These lead to new forms or adaptations of federal government.
2   That the problem of classification becomes more difficult as we turn away from constitutional law and towards definitions which include political and administrative practice and social attitudes. In some cases where there is a blend of unitary and confederal institutions no particular principle may predominate.
3   That federal experiments were in practice the only possible constitutional compromise in the particular circumstances.
4   That 'dual federalism' had given way to 'interdependent federalism' confirming a single integrated political system in which central and constituent state governments were interlocked and in practice related to each other without either being subordinate to the other.
5   That it is in the interplay and interaction of federal societies, federal political systems, federal constitutions and the practices and activities of federal governments that research on federalism should focus.[122]

Watts clearly harnessed several elements of both Wheare and Livingston to his conceptual cause without being confined by either of them. And in his construction of federalism as essentially circumstantial – a compromise between the conflicting demands for unity and diversity in a society – he followed in the footsteps of Edward Freeman. Watts also embellished Wheare's seven key factors leading to a desire for federal union, adding four further 'motives for union' that his own empirical study had suggested to him.[123] We will return to this aspect of the debate in Chapter 3.

Thomas Franck's inclusion in the pantheon of contributors to the intellectual debate in the 1960s is justified by reference to his much-quoted 1968 work entitled *Why Federations Fail*.[124] This contribution from another American scholar was, as the title implies, a pathology of four federations, namely, the West Indies, Malaysia, and Central and East Africa. As a post-mortem on the demise of these federations, the comparative research was based upon the self-confessed normative premise of 'gaining knowledge necessary to prevent other failures'.[125] And at the root of Franck's diagnostic analysis about the diseases to which federations were prone to succumb was the question surrounding the exportability of an idea that had worked so successfully in the USA. His concern to learn lessons from comparative analysis while eschewing 'facile generalizations' about the failure of federations prompted him to adopt a cautious approach when confronted by terminological and definitional problems:

> What this definitional problem suggests is not that a single, highly structured definition of federalism is needed. Rather it is that there be greater under-standing of the nearly infinite number of variations that can be played on the federal theme and that the difficulties of engineering a union of nations only begins when the leaders agree to federate and their subalterns sit down to work out what is too often called 'the details'. It also suggests that the content of a federal arrangement need not be governed by a historically fixed pattern, that the concept of federalism is malleable enough to bend with the realities.[126]

Franck was convinced that his empirical approach was more useful for an accu-rate understanding of federalism than previous contributions which relied solely upon stipulative definition. And his assertion that there are in practice infinite varieties of the federal theme rather than a single, narrow definition followed Watts in confirming the movement away from Wheare's increasingly outmoded position.

There was of course more to Franck's pathology than a comparative analysis of federal failures. Indeed, Franck regarded the outcome of his study – the nega-tive factors assembled to help explain the breakdown of federations – as furnishing scholars with clues to the necessary preconditions of success. But caution had to be applied in this purpose. The conclusions that could legiti-mately be drawn from his empirical study had only limited value. In short, their implications for either success or failure in general terms had to be judged very carefully. He made no great claims that scholars could deduce universal princi-ples about federal experiences from them. There were other interesting points that he raised about both successes and failures in federal experiments but we will postpone discussion of them until Chapter 11. Meanwhile let us turn to the fifth of our contributors, the Canadian scholar Michael Stein.

Stein's review article entitled 'Federal Political Systems and Federal Societies' appeared in *World Politics* also in 1968.[127] Referring in particular to Livingston and Watts, Stein complained about the imprecision of the concept of federal society. Was it possible to distinguish between a society that was federal and one that was not? And indeed what utility was there in identifying a federal society? For Stein it could be usefully applied only if it was confined to a society that was 'both polyethnic and multilingual in makeup'.[128] Following Livingston he argued that the major cleavages defining societies of this type were a product of ethnic and linguistic differences that were territorially concentrated. Other forces such as religion, geography and economics merely reinforced these primary deter-mining factors. In adding a flavour of Riker to his interpretation, Stein claimed that if ethnic and linguistic differences were present then political leaders representing these distinctive communities would 'bargain' for sufficient autonomy for themselves and their followers. Once the bargain was struck, however, societal forces would act on and be shaped by the political structure of federation. This enabled him to harness the work of Aaron Wildavsky to his cause. Wildavsky distinguished between 'social federalism' and 'structural federalism' and this distinction lay at the heart of his explanation for the retention of federal political forms where the social makeup of territorially based communities would seem initially to render them redundant.[129] Stein's definition of a federal political system, rooted in Eastonian premises, was clearly synthetic. He sought fruitfully to combine the work of Livingston, Watts, Riker and Wildavsky:

> A federal political system, then, in my view is that form of political system (of a nation-state) in which the institutions, values, attitudes and patterns of political action operate to give autonomous expression both to the national political system and political culture and to regional political subsystems and subcultures (defined primarily by ethnic-linguistic factors). The autonomy of each of these systems and subsystems is counterbalanced by a mutual interdependence. This balance maintains the overall union.[130]

In this way the concept of federal political systems could incorporate both 'pure power political relationships' and 'more inclusive socio-political patterns of action'. Accordingly the patterns of political relationships in Stein's so-called 'polyethnic federal systems' that were comparable were those which operated within the limits set by the federal bargain, but they also emanated from comparable territorially based cleavages in these societies. Thus was the link established between specifically 'federal' or polyethnic factors in a society and the 'federal' patterns of power-political relationships that existed in every federal political system.[131] Stein's synthetic approach was thus built upon the preliminary distinction between the essentially Rikerian political bargains, compromises and balances of power relationships, on the one hand, and the identities, values and interests characteristic of the territorially based cleavages that were channelled through both formal and informal structures, on the other.

In his review article Stein raised many important issues about federal systems and federal societies that remain today to be properly clarified. There were more questions than answers. For our purposes, however, we can summarise Stein's contribution as the following three conceptual and analytical claims:

1   The relationship between the concepts of federal political system and federal society and between federal and non-federal societies is unclear and requires further detailed examination.

2   Where comparatively homogenous societies sustain federal structures it is possible to have federal political systems without federal societies.

3   Ethnic-linguistic differences between separate distinct communities tend to polarise around the federal structure because political power, both potential

and actual, exists for these communities within the spheres of jurisdiction and functions assigned to them by the federal legal-political structure so the possibility emerges that federal political systems can both create, perpetuate and even exacerbate conflicts.

The chief merit of Stein's contribution was to attempt a new synthesis of existing approaches to the study of federalism. He believed that some kind of consensus among scholars about the meaning of 'federal society' had been reached but he sought a fusion principally of Livingston and Riker in order to bridge the gap between the political and sociological positions. It is also fair to say, with the advantage of hindsight, that Stein's conceptual tussle with the interaction of sociological variables – construed as cultural–ideological or 'polyethnic' elements – and political structures and relationships was not very far away from the contemporary usage of federalism and federation. In short, it is possible to recognise in the early studies of Livingston, Stein and Wildavsky the first, albeit implicit, indications of a conceptual distinction between federalism and federation.

Let us turn now to the Australian scholar, Geoffrey Sawer, whose *Modern Federalism* was first published in 1969. His most significant conceptual contribution was a comparative work that classified federalism into the following three 'stages of federalism': coordinate; cooperative and organic.[132] These were rough descriptions of the ways in which 'a system with basic federal principles may operate, or of its dominant style at a particular time'.[133] Sawer preferred this approach to the study of federalism because he considered that attempts to define either the word or the thing were 'likely to be futile'.[134] Nonetheless, he was compelled perforce to utilise a minimalist interpretation that he described as 'geographical devolution with guarantees for the autonomy of the units', something that even at the time took caution beyond reasonable limits.[135] His most memorable phrase was that a federal constitutional system was 'a prudential system best suited to the relatively stable, satisfied societies of squares' and it deserves to be quoted in full:

> It is not a swinging system. People are not likely to go to the stake, or the barricades, to defend federalism as such. They may undertake heroic actions for the sake of some value which federalism happens at the minute to favour, and may even then inscribe federalism on their banner – 'Liberty and Federalism' – 'Equality and Federalism' – but never just 'Federalism'.[136]

This statement was not as flippant as it might at first have seemed. It resonated closely with much of what had preoccupied Thomas Franck, namely, the question of federalism as a thing of value in itself. What did federalism signify? What was its intrinsic value? Indeed, was there any particular 'essence' to federalism? Did it have any quintessential moral value or was it merely a political contrivance in Riker's sense that had no special significance other than the reflection of contingent, circumstantial vested interests?

These elemental questions, implicit in much of the Anglo-American literature during the 1960s, brought the conceptual development of federalism to something of a watershed by 1970. The intellectual debate appeared simply to have petered out. In his *Comparative Federalism: The Territorial Dimension of Politics*, which was published in 1970, Ivo Duchacek confirmed this unhappy destination:

> There is no accepted theory of federalism. Nor is there an agreement as to what federalism is exactly. The term itself is unclear and controversial. ... Federalism has now become one of those good echo words that evoke a positive response but that may mean all things to all men, like democracy, socialism, progress, constitution, justice, or peace. We see the term applied to almost any successful combination of unity with diversity.[137]

S. Rufus Davis concurred. In 1972 he wrote that 'there has rarely been a time in the history of the subject when it has been in a more depressing and uncertain condition than it is now'.[138] The air of stagnation and disillusion appeared to be rooted in the paradox of plenty:

> The more we have come to know about it, the less satisfying and the less reputable has become almost the whole of our legacy of federal theory. Virtually all of the perspectives of politics have contributed to the decline of the federal Humpty-Dumpty. ... Almost all the older propositions attributing universal qualities to federalism are either emasculated, surviving in a new language, or defended by new rationalizations. ... Put directly, it may be doubted whether it is possible to make any further progress with the term 'federal', or any of its variants.[139]

In an essay entitled 'Against Federalism', which appeared a year later in 1973, Preston King warned against the attribution of so-called 'universal qualities' to federalism.[140] On the contrary, he argued that it was not universally valid. If it was defended as a doctrine that trumpeted universal, *a priori* truths, it would fail simply because it was in reality only circumstantial: in some cases it would prove to be relevant and applicable while in others it would be palpably inappropriate and inapplicable.[141] And in the same year Maurice Vile summarised the complaints in simple language:

> This particular game is played out ... the slippery slope upon which W.S. Livingston embarked in the nineteen fifties has reached its *reductio ad absurdum*. The time has now come to reassess federal systems in terms of a definition which actually does help us distinguish between differing kinds of political system.[142]

The gloom was further compounded in 1977 when Vile returned more purposively to engage the intellectual debate about federalism. In an essay entitled 'Federal Theory and the "New Federalism"', Vile reflected upon the 'great outpourings of literature on the subject' since 1945 with the following sober conclusion:

> The theory of federalism can hardly be said to provide a satisfactory basis for the understanding of a system of government so widespread in its application or intended application. Indeed, a 'theory' of federalism hardly exists today, largely it is suggested, because much of the theoretical effort of the last thirty years has been devoted to the discussion of the definition of federalism in such a way as to leave little or no basis upon which to build any sustained theoretical structure.[143]

Vile believed that the struggle to arrive at a neat definition of federalism was futile because such attempts oversimplified the problem by treating the whole political system as if it were a single variable. Rather, what was required was a model of the federal state that could cope with complexity, with the need to take into account the continuously changing nature of the reality of political systems, and that avoided either the rigidity of earlier definitions or the vacuity of the later ones.[144] Vile simply shifted the debate from definition to developmental model. He resurrected Livingston's earlier emphasis upon federalism as being essentially 'a particular aspect of the general problem of decentralisation' and was convinced that it had to be seen 'in that context'.[145] Federalism was distinctive as 'a cluster of different techniques' used to 'try to establish and maintain a particular kind of balance or equilibrium between two levels of government, albeit a moving, changing equilibrium'.[146] The basis for this differentiation derived from his view that relationships between two levels of government – whether federal or not – depended upon two separate but intimately related factors:

1   The degree of independence from the other that each level of government enjoys.
2   The extent to which two levels of government are interdependent such that neither level can subordinate the other to it, nor act wholly independent of the other across the whole range of government functions.[147]

In consequence the study of federalism became 'all those techniques, constitutional/legal, political, administrative and financial which serve to maintain or to erode, the balance between mutual independence and interdependence between levels of government', and it emphasised the need to 'explore the interrelationships between the different structures of the political system in this process.[148]

This was probably the most sophisticated approach to the study of federal political systems in the Anglo-American literature at that time. It was not however without certain flaws. Two criticisms were immediately evident. The first, which also typified the work of Watts, was Vile's description of 'a particular kind of balance or equilibrium'. The notion of 'balance' had been common among writers on federalism but it was really a nineteenth-century liberal legacy the practical utility of which was highly questionable. Indeed, Vile's own statements concerning relationships between two levels of government did not 'exclude' the possibility of serious conflict over jurisdiction where the federal government could conceivably overrule local governments thus highlighting the reality of federal supremacy in certain circumstances. And Preston King had already argued quite cogently that federal supremacy did not leave much room for an effective theory of balance.[149]

The second criticism was Vile's reference to 'the general problem of decentralisation' for modern federalism. Clearly the delineation of a decentralised political system presupposed the existence of a centre that did not control all the lines of political communication and decision-making. Nevertheless the term 'decentralisation' had to be employed with great caution when applied to federal states because of their contractual origins. The federal–local relationship was better expressed as contractual limited centralisation, a description that more accurately reflected centripetal forces at work in all modern states combined with a constitutional obligation not to smother local autonomy.

One strength of Vile's developmental model was that it acknowledged the complexity of federalism and its multidimensional character: constitutional, legal, political, economic, social, ideological, territorial, and cultural. Part of the failure to arrive at satisfactory conclusions about federalism was due to the fact that different scholars had been investigating different parts and dimensions of the same concept. Different schools of thought had exalted different components, claiming either that their part captured the elusive 'essence' of federalism or that others were of only marginal significance. We are reminded of Birch's remark that federalism had no fixed meaning; its meaning in any particular study was defined by the student in a manner that was determined by the approach which the student wished to make to the subject.[150]

A second virtue of Vile's model was precisely its developmental capacity to furnish a comparative treatment of federations at particular stages or phases in their evolution. Vile did not believe that scholars should simply assume that every federal state would follow an identical path of development. Using this model he claimed that several countries could be analysed in the same way in order to examine 'the particular mix of variables in the system' and the way in which that mix changed and evolved under the pressure of changing circumstances.[151] But did Vile manage to escape from the definitional problem? And was he correct to suggest that there were no realistic boundaries that distinguished federations from non-federal states? His own model, after all, was based upon a set of assumptions about what 'federal' meant, what kind of political institutions were associated with federations and even the prior existence of a 'federal spirit'. His 'clusters of techniques' seem simply to have been the means by which federal states became either more centralised or more decentralised and could equally have been a description of consociationalism as much as federalism.

Our brief survey of Vile's developmental model brings us almost to the end of this section on the conceptual and methodological review. It is clear that by the end of the 1970s a scholarly consensus of sorts about federalism had emerged. Agreement had been reached about the futility of pursuing an elusive, all-embracing definition intended to encapsulate all of the complexities and subtleties that inhered in federalism. The debate, in short, was going nowhere. There appeared to be a moratorium on the mental process of definition. The logical implication therefore was that a different approach was needed to break loose from this definitional straitjacket.

The intellectual impasse was broken in 1982 when Preston King's *Federalism and Federation* was first published and made explicit what had always been implicit in the mainstream literature.[152] Thereafter the conceptual distinction between federalism and federation has acquired sufficient international scholarly recognition to warrant its inclusion since 1985 in the title of the Comparative Federalism and Federation Research Committee of IPSA. It is important to note, however, that not every scholar of federalism has adopted this approach. The conceptual distinction has not been agreeable to everybody and even when it has been tolerated its logical analytical implications have not always been well received. Murray Forsyth described a rigid adherence to the distinction as simply 'pretentious' – an unhelpful 'red herring' – while another recent writer, Jenny Robinson, rejected the assertion that 'one can separate a process of federalism from the institutional arrangements of federation' when looking at the case of South Africa.[153]

Far from being damaging criticisms, such reservations are to be welcomed because they indicate a healthy intellectual climate. They confirm the vitality of the conceptual debate. After all, it was Kenneth Wheare who remarked about his own contribution in 1946 that 'It is proper to add that this definition of the federal principle is not accepted as valid by all students of the subject'.[154] Nonetheless, the conceptual distinction between federalism and federation upon which this book is firmly based has certain obvious advantages over earlier approaches which took as their departure point a specific, often narrow and restrictive, definition suggesting only essential elements guaranteed to be the subject of endless revision. In contrast, Preston King's conceptual distinction is able simply to bypass this particular problem. And in so doing it has the conceptual capacity to open up the subject by riveting our attention upon the essentially dynamic, changing relationship between federalism as a multidimensional driving force and federation as its institutional, structural and systemic counterpart. They are, in a nutshell, two sides of the same coin, as King noted in his memorable observation that 'there may be federalism without federation', but there can be 'no federation without some matching variety of federalism'.[155]

It is worth noting that a modest revision to this conceptual distinction was made by Watts in 1994 and reiterated in 1998 so that the term 'federalism' is identified as a normative concept and 'federation' is categorised as species of the larger genus 'federal political systems'.[156] This rearrangement of the conceptual furniture appears to have been influenced by Elazar's interpretation of federalism in his *Exploring Federalism*, first published in 1987.[157] Elazar's focus upon 'varieties of federal arrangements' prompted Watts to use the term 'federal political systems' as a 'genus of political organization which provides for the combination of shared rule and self-rule'. This allowed him to construe federal political systems as a broad umbrella concept encompassing 'a variety of species' such as those that Elazar had previously identified: federation, confederation, federacy, associated statehood, unions, leagues, constitutional regionalisation, and constitutional home rule.[158] Clearly this classification has the advantage of flexibility and is much more all-embracing than the narrow bifocal distinction between federalism and federation, but while it correctly endorses federalism as a normative idea it nonetheless has the effect of subordinating federation to a mere species of a genus that itself remains somewhat ambiguous. Moreover, federation (as a federal *state*) is something that, by virtue of its very statehood, sits uncomfortably in the mixed company of Elazar's 'varieties of federal arrangements'. Here we are reminded of Forsyth's solemn warning that 'with sufficient effort it can be detected almost everywhere'.[159]

We have now reached the end of our selected conceptual and methodological review of the mainstream Anglo-American literature which has taken us from the confederal–federal controversy inherent in *The Federalist Papers* of the 1780s to the federalism–federation debate over two centuries later. But before we conclude this chapter on the quest for meaning it is imperative that we mention the existence of a rival intellectual federal tradition to that of the Anglo-American type the cultural roots of which lie in Continental Europe. A brief preliminary survey of this rich intellectual tradition of federalism is necessary both to widen the conceptual review and to serve as the basis for the much more detailed comparative analysis in Chapter 6.

Appropriately it has been recent research on the Anglo-American tradition of federalism that has indirectly revealed the existence of a strand of federal thought unknown to most scholars of federalism until now. It is a source of European federalism quite different from the familiar modern, secular, liberal Enlightenment thinking derived from Hobbes, Locke and Montesquieu, and it is located in what is called 'covenant' theory. As we will discover in Chapter 6, this investigation brings the existence of two quite distinct political traditions of federalism into sharp focus. And by bringing them closer together it furnishes the basis for some significant comparative reflections that serve to deepen and enrich our historical and philosophical understanding of a 'federal' Europe.

The publication in 1991 of the revisionist monograph entitled *Fountainhead of Federalism: Heinrich Bullinger and the Covenantal Tradition* written by two American academic specialists in theology, Charles McCoy and J. Wayne Baker, identified a hitherto-unknown dimension of Anglo-American federalism best described as the Biblical–Reformed–Puritan ethical religious strand of federal thought the intellectual origins of which stretched back to the sixteenth century.[160] This recent research effectively established strong connecting links between the philosophical ideas of Heinrich Bullinger, a Swiss theologian-philosopher, and the evolution during the seventeenth and eighteenth centuries of covenantal federalism in the American colonies of the New World.

In modern times, covenantal theory is most closely associated with the American contributions to federalist scholarship of Vincent Ostrom, Daniel Elazar and John Kincaid. It is, above all, a biblical perspective of federalism according to which the concept of covenantal federalism embodies a set of normative principles that bind partners together in a moral contract or agreement of trust. The act of coming together remains a 'political bargain' in Riker's sense but it is much more than just this. It is also based upon mutual recognition, tolerance, respect, obligation and responsibility. Indeed, Elazar referred to the genesis of such an arrangement in the original relationship between God and man and which descends from the Bible. Elazar's own research arrived at the conclusion that a major source of the covenantal idea was both *The Federalist Papers* of Hamilton, Jay and Madison and the 1789 American Constitution itself.[161] Further research by Donald Lutz has underlined the crucial link between the political ideas of Bullinger and Johannes Althusius, the German Calvinist intellectual, and their gradual infiltration into the seventeenth-century constitutions of the American colonies.[162]

One upshot of this recent research is to broaden our conventional perspective of the Anglo-American tradition of federalism to include certain significant elements of the Continental European federal tradition. There has been, in other words, a cross-fertilisation of Anglo-American and Continental European federal political ideas. Continental European federalism can no longer be limited to Roman Catholic social theory embedded in the papal encyclicals and to the established political thought of the likes of Kant, Rousseau, Montesquieu, Pufendorf, Proudhon and Kropotkin. It must be revised to incorporate these recent research developments that suggest a much more complex and variegated political tradition than was hitherto believed.

Having briefly introduced the Continental European tradition of federalism and its relatively unknown links with the Anglo-American federal tradition, it is time to bring this chapter to a close. We are reminded of our main purpose which was to locate the major sources of the contemporary arguments and disputes about federalism and federation. And we have shown that much if not most of the basic assumptions and premises that inform the contemporary discourse about federal states – their strengths, weaknesses and fundamental characteristics – can be located in a literature which stretches back at least two centuries and often further. It is now time to return to the American federal experience and revisit the labyrinthine intellectual debate about history, philosophy and politics that surrounded *The Federalist Papers* of the late eighteenth century. This is necessary in order for us to complete the conceptual background to our subject. After all, the theoretical implications of this debate still reverberate around the contemporary discourse about federalism, federation and confederation. We will begin by looking at the broad contours of the American federal experience and then explore the implications of this experience for contemporary debate.

2 The American federal experience

Introduction

In this chapter we will revisit the intellectual and empirical distinctions between federation and confederation made by Americans in the late eighteenth century. This will help us to understand why the contemporary conceptual debate about federalism, federation and confederation has proved to be so problematic for political scientists. It is one important and extremely troublesome legacy of the American federal experience. In order to understand precisely how and why we have arrived at this awkward destination it is necessary therefore for us to unravel what remains a remarkable episode in the history of both an idea and a practical reality. In short, we must perforce return to the past.

My purpose in this chapter, then, is to address the following three concerns: first, to analyse and explore the origins of American federalism; second, to investigate the late-eighteenth-century intellectual debate about federation and confederation in the USA; and, third, to examine some of the main philosophical conceptions of American federalism that focus upon the interplay between the individual and the community as identities that are distinct but also intimately related. These three separate strands of the American federal experience are connected in a way that enables us to place our conceptual analysis on a firm foundation. In a nutshell, they contextualise the intellectual debate.

The first section locates the origins of American federalism in a complex historical setting by looking at the interaction of three influences peculiar to the USA that together shaped the first modern federation in 1789. The second section brings us face to face with what I shall call the 'confederal–federal' debate. This was essentially an intellectual debate about the precise nature, type and significance of the novel union that the founding fathers had forged, but the structure of the debate also furnishes us with an intriguing insight into the political uses and abuses of history. Indeed, the controversy about historical continuities and discontinuities in the making of the union at the end of the eighteenth century continues to resonate at the beginning of the new millennium.

The third section, which looks at some of the main philosophical conceptions implicit in pre-1789 confederalism and post-1789 federalism, catapults us into the deeply contentious world of competing and overlapping identities that has continued to reverberate in modern federal theory. Questions concerning individual and collective identities, minority rights and the principle of representation remain hotly contested in federal polities and ensure that the debate about the nature and purpose of such unions retains its contemporary relevance. With these thoughts in mind, let us turn to look at the first section, which is devoted to the origins of American federalism.

The antecedents of American federalism

The origins of the federal idea in the USA are both complex and deep-rooted. They stretch back to the seventeenth and eighteenth centuries, long before the familiar defining landmarks of 1776, 1781, 1787 and 1789, and they criss-cross three distinct dimensions to our subject, namely, Continental European philosophical thought, British imperial politics and American colonial practice. In Chapter 1 we mentioned in brief the significance of both Heinrich Bullinger and Johannes Althusius and we will return to them in Chapter 6. For the moment however let us concentrate our attentions upon the relevance of both the British imperial and the American colonial experiences.

The idea of a British federal discourse during this historical era seems initially paradoxical given the nature of the Anglo-American relationship. The constitutional and political relationship between the mother country and her American colonies was unequivocally one of the superordinate and the subordinate. But the British were not averse to constitutional and political experimentation and adjustment when it was deemed necessary to maintain the order, stability and integrity of the state. Nor were they averse to various forms of constitutional innovation in order to maintain the integrity of the empire. The legislative union between England and Scotland in 1707 is one obvious example of the former but British imperial relations in the seventeenth and eighteenth centuries were also a fertile area for a variety of novel and different political relationships. The irony is that these evolving forms of colonial autonomy ultimately failed to prevent the rupture of 1776 and the subsequent loss of the American colonies, an imperial breach that most British statesmen never ceased to regret and deplore.

The federal idea surfaced intermittently in a series of 'empire federalist ideas' of which the most persistent was colonial representation in the British Parliament.[1] First urged for Barbados in 1652, colonial representation was one way of incorporating the constituent parts of the empire into the central institutional framework. Adam Smith had recommended it in his enormously influential *The Wealth of Nations*, first published in 1776, and in 1778 the British peace mission to the rebellious American colonies, led by Lord Carlisle, was authorised to offer representation in Parliament to them along with the acknowledgement of the practical supremacy of Congress in American affairs. Moreover, as the empire evolved during the eighteenth and nineteenth centuries, the development of local colonial autonomy was sometimes construed as akin to some form of shadowy but workable federal relationship. Much of this was assumed and unspoken: 'a division between central and local powers, even when the latter are delegated and theoretically revocable, will work in a federal sense and come to be thought of in that way'.[2] The British imperial–colonial relationship, then, was a fertile policy arena for many different and often quasi-federal political ideas. And it should be noted that they were practical suggestions to perceived problems of that evolving relationship, especially once the American colonies had left the empire.

Turning now to the indigenous political ideas and the practical local governmental experience of the American colonies, it is clear that this, too, is an important dimension to the origins of the federal idea in the USA. Donald Lutz has already remarked that political relationships in colonial America potentially existed at three distinct levels: the intracolonial, the intercolonial and, finally, the colony–mother country. And as he observed, 'it is interesting that in the first and third instances, the solution tended to be federalism'. However it was 'a federalism that was unconscious, was not derived from theory and had no name to describe it'.[3] The colonies, he reminded us, were each a collection of towns or counties rather than a single, undifferentiated entity. Plymouth Colony, for example, was eventually composed of seven towns, each with its own town meeting. But since the charters establishing the colonies and signed under the royal seal, the highest civil authority, recognised only a single entity – a colony – the various constituent parts of the colonies responded by writing federal documents, such as the Fundamental Orders of Connecticut (1639) and the Acts and Orders of Rhode Island (1647). These created 'a common colony-wide government with limited powers while preserving town governments to operate in their own sphere of competence'. Echoing Tocqueville's famous observations, Lutz also noted that 'both town and colony governments were often derived in form and substance from covenants' and that even when they did not derive from covenants 'colonial governments functioned effectively as federal polities, having been built up from below'.[4]

The early seventeenth-century American colonies were permitted to form and operate their own governments provided that the laws passed by them in their local legislatures did not conflict with the laws made by the English Parliament. And England had good reasons to grant charters to the colonies. Given the difficulties of travelling between the colonies and England – a minimum two-month round trip – the mother country could not realistically administer them. Added to her preoccupation with the Civil War and the real threat of French expansionism in the New World, the imperial power found it convenient to encourage local self-government and administration based largely upon the 'obvious needs of practicality': the relationship between colony and mother country was 'federal in operation, although not federal by design'.[5]

In their understandable obsession with the Philadelphia Convention (1787) and the subsequent ratification of the second American Constitution (1789), political scientists have often overlooked this aspect of American constitutional development and have accordingly underestimated the practical realities of the colonial experience in contributing an indigenous aspect to American federalism. It is vital to appreciate that by the time of the American Declaration of Independence (1776) the colonies had been in existence as functioning polities, with varying levels of autonomy, for over a century and a half. Indeed, as Lutz has emphasised, the evolution of state constitutions were the culmination of a very long development: 'Americans wrote and evolved protoconstitutions containing all the elements later to be found in state and national constitutions'.[6] In this sense therefore the rudiments of Anglo-American federal political thought must be traced back to those documents that established local self-government on American shores during the early seventeenth century.

What, then, of inter-colonial federalism? Lutz noted that there was a distinct lack of interest among the early English colonists under either region-wide confederations or a continent-wide government. His explanation for this indifference lay in early Whig political thought: 'the American Whig devotion to local control made the Whigs highly resistant to confederations larger than a single state'. Preference for local control over political unions 'at a distance' also fuelled a suspicion that 'any continental government would be source of danger' even if it used 'standard Whig institutions'.[7] But this is not to say that such schemes and plans did not exist. On the contrary, there were a considerable number of such plans. Among the most prominent of these were the following: the New England Confederation (1643) created by the colonists; the Commission of the Council for Foreign Plantations (1660) devised in England; William Penn's Plan of Union (1696); the Report of the Board of Trade on the union of New York with other colonies (1696); the plan of the Lords of Trade (1721); and the Albany Plan of Union (1754) written by Benjamin Franklin.[8] According to Lutz the last of these – the Albany Plan – was 'one of the first serious designs for an intercolonial government' and it came 'much closer to a federal system' than did the later Articles of Confederation (1781).[9]

What is abundantly clear from this brief survey of British and American federal ideas and experiences is that the origins of American constitutional history and the federal idea stretch back almost two centuries to the first settled colonies in the early seventeenth century. Lutz's research demonstrates that the only way to arrive at a proper appreciation of the American federal political tradition is to investigate what occurred much earlier than the late eighteenth century. This viewpoint has now become the new orthodoxy, as Charles McCoy and J. Wayne Baker confirm:

> Though ignored by most historians of the Constitution, there is a tradition of federalism that pervaded the entire colonial era, developed in distinctive ways apart from European thinkers, and formed the background of experience upon which the leaders of the Revolution and new nation relied as they shaped the institutions of what became the United States of America.[10]

Clearly the key to understanding this aspect of the American tradition of federalism is 'political experience'; it was the actual practice of local, colonial self-government over many years that helped to mould a distinct federal political culture. This relatively recent research shows that if we are prepared very carefully to study and analyse the constitutional history of the early colonial and subsequent state documents, it is possible to see a continuous, unbroken tradition of federal political thought and practice that is indigenous to America and the Americans. The major events and circumstances of the later eighteenth century must not be allowed to obscure that much deeper-rooted continuity which was so vital to the gradual emergence of American federalism. While those who shaped the social institutions of colonial America, prosecuted the Revolution and produced the US Constitution might have had 'some indirect or direct influence on them from European thinkers', these American leaders were 'primarily persons who relied on their immediate context, the tradition in which they were trained and the experience accumulated on American soil'.[11] Small wonder that two of the founding fathers of the new extended republic, James Madison and Alexander Hamilton, could describe its advantages in the language of David Hume with great equanimity in *The Federalist Papers*.[12]

This brief survey of the antecedents of American federalism suggests a very long and extremely complicated progeniture. It certainly encourages us to reappraise the significance of the period 1781–89. The first experiment with the federal idea in the Articles of Confederation was not the result of an abstract paper plan devoid of historical experience to recommend it. On the contrary, it was rooted in the evolution of what Lutz has called colonial 'protoconstitutions', which were 'essentially an interplay between the problems arising from the environment in which Americans found themselves and European ideas that were selectively appropriated to help solve these problems'. But 'no one idea or tradition monopolized American thinking'.[13] This conclusion is corroborated by McCoy and Baker, who have also acknowledged that 'the major sources of federalism in America were the federal theology, the federal political philosophy and the federal practice in societal institutions brought by groups coming from Europe to establish colonies and developed in distinctive ways in the 180 years from Jamestown to Philadelphia'.[14] Having finally arrived at Philadelphia in 1787, let us shift our focus to the second section of the chapter that looks in considerable detail at the epic constitutional debate that engendered what some opponents of the new federal government regarded as the greatest intellectual deception of the age.

Federation and confederation: Publius revisited

In his *Democracy in America* Alexis de Tocqueville observed that 'the human mind invents things more easily than words; that is why many improper terms and inadequate expressions gain currency'.[15] His reference to the use of 'words' to describe 'things' and to the general difficulties of terminological precision and conceptual definition lay at he heart of the great constitutional debate of 1787. Indeed, no better example of this awkward predicament existed than that of *The Federalist* which, under the heading of *Publius*, sought to persuade New Yorkers to vote in favour of the new constitution drawn up in the summer of 1787 at the

Philadelphia Convention in Pennsylvania. And it should be noted at the outset of our short reappraisal of 1787 that the new constitution promoted by Alexander Hamilton, James Madison and John Jay was itself the result of a series of extremely difficult compromises at the Constitutional Convention between vested interests 'compelled to sacrifice theoretical propriety to the force of extraneous considerations'.[16] Madison acknowledged the significance of terminology and the difficulty of terminological precision in the following way:

> The use of words to express ideas. Perspicuity therefore requires not only that the ideas should be distinctly formed, but that they should be expressed by words distinctly and exclusively appropriate to them. But no language is so copious as to supply words and phrases for every complex idea, or so correct as not to include many equivocally denoting different ideas. Hence it must happen that however accurately objects may be discriminated in themselves, and however accurately the discrimination may be considered, the definition of them may be rendered inaccurate by the inaccuracy of the terms in which it is delivered.[17]

The Philadelphia Convention was called into existence by the Continental Congress – a meeting of the constituent states of the American Confederation – 'for the sole and express purpose of revising the Articles of Confederation'.[18] But as is now well known, the 55 delegates from 12 states who met in secret deliberation to revise the Articles exceeded their formal brief and constructed a new and very different constitution. The proposed constitution that *The Federalist* strove so fiercely to defend was, as Madison famously put it, 'in strictness, neither a national nor a federal Constitution, but a composition of both'.[19] Since it contained a mixture of republican, federal and national elements, there was no single word to describe it.

In hindsight, it is clear that the great American debate of 1787–89, especially as we follow it in the gripping pages of *The Federalist*, was more than just a loud war of words. Words convey meaning but they can also be used deliberately to mislead and deceive political opponents. One of the great ironies of the late-eighteenth-century American debate surrounding the ratification of the new constitution was the way in which its formidable proponents virtually commandeered the term 'federal'. It was certainly no accident that they chose *The Federalist* as the title of the essays published in 1788 and the vehicle for their public-relations exercise. We are reminded that the founding fathers of the American Constitution had a very different understanding than we do today of what 'federalism' meant. The conventional late-eighteenth-century American understanding of the term was what existed according to the Articles of Confederation during 1781–89 rather than what succeeded them. The prevailing conceptual distinction was between confederal (or federal) government and unitary (or national) government. There was no separate and distinct category for what later came to be known as 'federal' government. In an elegantly written essay, Martin Diamond put it this way:

> We now give the single word federal to the system the framers regarded as
> possessing both federal and national features. This means that we now deem
> as a unique principle what *The Federalist* regarded as a mere compound. ...
> The men we have come to call the 'anti-federalists' regarded themselves as
> the true federalists. ... the opponents of the Constitution fought as the true
> defenders of the federal principle. Everything that *The Federalist* says about
> the federal aspects of the Constitution must be understood ... in the light of
> its great necessity: the demonstration that the Constitution should not be
> rejected on the grounds of inadequate regard for the federal principle.[20]

It is important to remember that one purpose of *The Federalist* was to attack
the traditional understanding of federalism. It sought deliberately and some
might say desperately to muddy the waters so that much less was required for a
new political system to be deemed fully federal. Hamilton in particular was
determined to create a federal test that the proposed new constitution could
easily pass.

If we summarise this part of section two, it is clear in retrospect that after the
ratification of the Constitution in 1789 there had been a significant substantive
change in the nature of the American union. This represented an empirical shift
away from confederation to a much more consolidated form of union – what
was often referred to as a 'compound republic' – in which the national characteristics were expected ultimately to predominate. And it was precisely this
movement away from the Articles of Confederation that later gave rise to a new
conceptual distinction in political science between confederation and federation.
It was however a gradual rather than an abrupt change.[21] As Diamond astutely
observed:

> *The Federalist* had no novel understanding of what is federal, it only departed
> from others in regarding the simply federal as radically inadequate for the
> purposes of the Union it had in mind. It did have a novel understanding of a
> new thing, not simply a federal thing but a compound which it was happy to
> have men call by the old name federal. ... the Convention ... avoided past
> confederal errors by creating a Union which was radically less federal. ...
> What was wrong with the Articles and other confederacies were the essential
> federal principles themselves. The great teaching of *The Federalist* is not how
> to be federal in a better way, but how to be better by being less federal.[22]

This conclusion remains contentious. In a nutshell it claims that in reality the
new American Constitution actually departed from the established and accepted
understanding of federalism. Hamilton confessed that there was 'an absolute
necessity for an entire change in the first principles of the system'; it was so 'radically vicious and unsound' that it required not mere amendment but 'an entire
change in its leading features and characters'.[23] Consequently the new constitution altered the conventional federal form by 'subtracting from it certain
decisively federal features and adding to it certain decisively national features'. In

other words the significant contribution of *The Federalist* was 'the presentation and justification of a new form of government, neither federal nor national, but an admixture of both characters'.[24] And this interpretation has the authority of none other than Tocqueville to recommend it:

> Here the central power acts without intermediary on the governed, administering and judging them itself, as do national governments, but it only acts thus within a restricted circle. Clearly here we have not a federal government but an incomplete national government. Hence a form of government has been found which is neither precisely national nor federal; but things have halted there, and the new word to express this new thing does not yet exist.[25]

Tocqueville's remarks – written in 1835 – bring us back once again to the thorny question of classification in political science. Do we invent a new word – a neologism – to describe a new thing or do we simply regard it as an unknown quantity that is neither fish nor fowl? Should we leave the novel thing in the unsatisfactory category of an intellectual puzzle or should we attempt to shoehorn it into an established classification? As usual there is no handy Procrustean bed. The quandary of those engaged in this terminological warfare two centuries ago acts as a constant reminder to us today of the eternal problem of how to use words to express basic ideas and concepts with both clarity and precision.

One important legacy of this remarkable American journey – the processes of state-building and national integration – was the conceptual displacement of the confederal category. But this was not all. There was also a concomitant legacy of considerable intellectual significance. This was that the new conceptual distinction between confederation and federation had an entirely unexpected consequence. Few could have foreseen the enduring stigma that would eventually be attached to the label 'confederation'.

Let us probe this legacy a little further. Put simply, the practical weaknesses of the Articles of Confederation were both undeniable and evident for all to see. Delegates to the Federal Convention, while certainly not unanimous about them, were broadly agreed about their overriding deficiencies. When Edmund Randolph, one of the delegates from Virginia, opened the main business of the Convention on 29 May 1787 he identified the following five main defects of the Confederation:

1   That it produced no security against foreign invasion because Congress was not permitted to prevent war nor to support it by its own authority. It also had no power to enforce the constituent states to honour international agreements signed in its name, nor did it possess any permanent administration to sustain effectively its decisions.
2   That it possessed no constitutional power to check quarrels between the states and the union, nor a rebellion in any of them, and it did not have the means to interpose according to the particular exigency.

3   That there were many advantages that the USA might acquire in a federal union but which were not then available under the existing confederation, such as customs duties, protection from the commercial regulations of other states and the promotion of commerce in general.
4   That the existing union could not protect itself against encroachments from the constituent states.
5   That the Articles were not superior to the constituent state constitutions.

Randolph acknowledged that the authors of the Articles 'had done all that patriots could do, in the then infancy of the science, of constitutions, and of confederacies', but its inherent weaknesses strongly suggested that the Confederation ought to be 'so corrected and enlarged as to accomplish the objects proposed by their institution; namely common defence, security of liberty and general welfare'.[26] The Articles therefore stood condemned by their failure to fulfil their own stated objectives.

However, in launching a fierce attack upon the Articles in *Publius*, which he was compelled to do, Hamilton's critique had a far-reaching, if unintended, intellectual impact. It helped subsequently to tarnish the reputation of confederations in general and it encouraged some historians and political scientists to dismiss them as hopelessly inadequate forms of union. Not for the first time was history written by those who had triumphed. Let us look briefly at this unfortunate legacy before returning to our discussion of *Publius* and its general implications for the study of modern federalism and federation.

Since 1789 the term 'confederation' has often been used in a pejorative sense. Political scientists and historians have frequently dismissed confederal government as both weak and transient. Indeed there has been a general tendency to regard it as a mere transition on the road towards federation – that more perfect union. The American federal experience is held as the defining model. Accordingly, confederations will either drift apart or they will form a new state. In his study of the theory and practice of confederation, Murray Forsyth has acknowledged that the German *Bund* of 1815–66, the Swiss Confederation established in 1815 and 'perhaps above all' the American Confederation of 1781–89 have 'all suffered harsh treatment' at the hands of academics and publicists.[27] He was certainly correct to emphasise the American example. In his classic study of the Continental Congress, Edmund Cody Burnett confirmed that 'it has been much the practice to heap criticisms' upon the Articles and 'even to treat it with a measure of scorn'.[28] Unlike Burnett, however, Forsyth concluded that there was 'an understandable basis for the scorn which is conventionally heaped on confederations'. This was because once a community had achieved the lofty goal of statehood it tended to 'look back with almost amused disdain on the efforts at unity that fell short of statehood'.[29]

For Hamilton of course the first federal constitution – the Articles of Confederation – was simply inadequate for its purposes. His assertion that the government of the USA was palpably 'destitute of energy' enabled him to identify, as he saw it, the real lacuna in confederation:

The great and radical vice in the construction of the existing Confederation is in principle of *legislation* for *States* or *Governments*, in their *Corporate* or *Collective Capacities*, and as contradistinguished from the *Individuals* of whom they consist. ... But if ... we still will adhere to the design of a national government, ... we must extend the authority of the Union to the persons of the citizens – the only proper objects of governments.[30]

In this famous passage from *Federalist* 15, Hamilton struck a savage blow at the Confederation by revealing what he took to be the underlying impotence of the union. He believed that such polities had been 'the cause of incurable disorder and imbecility'.[31] Consequently what was needed to remedy this condition of affairs was 'energetic government' by which he meant the 'augmentation of federal authority' at the expense of the constituent state governments. And in order further to condemn existing federal principles as irretrievably deficient both Hamilton and Madison used *Federalist* 16–22 to conduct a short but relatively extensive historical survey of all earlier confederations (called 'confederacies').

The result of their brief historical examination of previous confederacies – which included the ancient Greek and the German, Swiss and Dutch cases – was far from surprising. They had a vested interest in deliberately maligning confederal experiments and produced a damning indictment of existing federal principles and assumptions. Their conclusion was unequivocal: confederacies in general either survived to live contemptibly or perished miserably precisely because of their fidelity to federal principles that were deemed erroneous:

The important truth ... is that a sovereignty over sovereigns, a government over governments, a legislation for communities, as contradistinguished from individuals, as it is a solecism in theory, so in practice it is subversive of the order and ends of civil polity.[32]

Small wonder, in this light, that modern confederation – as a union of states – became the victim of rough justice. The prosecution was vindictive. In turn, confederal government has acquired the reputation of being weak, anarchic and highly unstable – a danger to internal order and external security. And these images seem to have been passed down from one generation to the next so that the stigma of confederation has become part of an almost unquestioning conventional wisdom. But if there seems to have been a well-organised body of opinion in the Federal Convention, so ably buttressed and sustained by *Publius*, which was broadly supportive of these trenchant criticisms of the Articles, were their arguments as popular or as convincing as their ultimate victory would have us believe? In practice there was strong evidence to the contrary which suggested that elite opinion in reality was deeply divided about both the arguments against the Articles and the conclusions that seem to have flowed from them.

Victory, it has been said, has a thousand fathers while defeat is an orphan. History has not been kind to the so-called 'anti-federalists' who up until 1787–88 were the real federalists but who, having been so abruptly and unceremoniously outmanoeuvred and dislodged thereafter, were portrayed as federalism's sworn enemies. Because they failed effectively to combat both the rhetorical flourishes and the public-relations campaign waged by *Publius*, the anti-federalists were consigned to the margins of American constitutional and political history, their initial defeat subsequently reinforced by the lost cause of states' rights in the American Civil War (1861–65). But their initial failure to resist the devastating combination of intellectual acumen and political shrewdness displayed by *Publius* meant that they were simply unable either to halt or ultimately to reverse the momentum for constitutional reform generated at the Federal Convention. It is however important that we do not completely dismiss the arguments of the anti-federalists and brush them aside as if they were merely the debris of history for though they were the historical casualties of Philadelphia they were also the unsung defenders of a federalism whose principles and assumptions have never been entirely discarded.

The anti-federalists' scepticism about the founding fathers' invention – the compound republic – was grounded in their deep concern for the preservation of liberty. If we examine the many detailed objections to Hamilton, Jay and Madison's propaganda exercise in favour of the new Constitution, we find that this, above all else, was the overriding concern that served to unite what was in reality a disparate band of critics. And it is important to note that criticism of the Articles was not tantamount to agreement about how they should be reformed or whether they should be replaced. Anti-federalists such as George Mason, Patrick Henry and Richard Henry Lee of Virginia together with George Clinton and Robert Yates of New York were all highly respected professional gentlemen who furnished formidable opposition to the ratification of the Constitution. It was not a foregone conclusion. They represented the anti-federalist mind – a complicated mind that, although sceptical, was always more than just a negative predisposition. What united them – apart from the over-arching fear of the loss of liberty – was a firm belief in republican government, the need for a bill of rights, opposition to unlimited taxing power, fear and disapproval of mob violence, disorder and anarchy, anxieties about standing armies in peacetime and a consistent scepticism about consolidated government. Their experience of, and opposition to, monarchy, aristocracy and imperial tyranny at the hands of the British did not predispose them to welcome the idea of a new – and inevitably remote – consolidated American federal government with its equally inevitable problems of citizen and state representation, financial mismanagement and corruption. In short, they had not fought a war and ejected the British from North America in order to replace them with a new despotism.

If we look briefly at a sample of anti-federalist literature, we can appreciate how far the main targets of their searching critiques converged upon two particular questions, namely, the dangers of the proposed consolidated or national government to liberty and republican principles and what was construed as the largely fallacious diagnosis of the ills of confederation. Typical of the clarity and force of the anti-federal mind was the devastating critique of 'Brutus', who exposed the new constitution for what he believed it really was:

> It appears from these articles that there is no need of any intervention of the State governments, between the Congress and the people, to execute any one power vested in the general government, and that of the Constitution and laws of every State are nullified and declared void, so far as they are or shall be inconsistent with this Constitution, or the laws made in pursuance of it, or with the treaties made under the authority of the United States. The government, then, so far as it extends, is a complete one, and not a confederation. It is as much one complete government as that of New York or Massachusetts; has as absolute and perfect powers to make and execute all laws, to appoint officers, institute courts, declare offences, and annex penalties, with respect to every object to which it extends, as any other in the world. So far, therefore, as its powers reach, all ideas of confederation are given up and lost. ... In the business ... of laying and collecting taxes, the idea of confederation is totally lost, and that of one entire republic is embraced. ... what is meant is, that the legislature of United States are vested with the great and uncontrollable powers of laying and collecting taxes, duties, imposts and excises; of regulating trade, raising and supporting armies, organizing, arming, and disciplining the militia, instituting courts, and other general powers; and are ... invested with the power of making all laws, proper and necessary, for carrying all these into execution; and they may so exercise this power as entirely to annihilate all the State governments, and reduce this country to one single government.[33]

'A Farmer' whose anti-federalist mentality also inclined him to plain speaking confirmed this excoriation by 'Brutus' of what seemed to lie concealed beneath the surface of the federalists' constitutional remedy:

> All the prerogatives, all the essential characteristics of sovereignty, both of the internal and external kind, are vested in the general government, and consequently the several States would not be possessed of any essential power or effective guard of sovereignty. ... it is evident that the consolidation of the States into one national government (in contradistinction from a confederacy) would be the necessary consequence of the establishment of the new constitution, and the intention of its framers – and that consequently the State sovereignties would be eventually annihilated, though the forms may long remain as expensive and burdensome remembrances.[34]

Patrick Henry focused his anti-federalist mind upon the very legitimacy of the whole historic event when he urged those in the Virginia Ratifying Convention to ask themselves precisely how and according to whose authority they had allowed themselves to arrive at such a fateful destination. Referring to the Philadelphia Convention, he declared:

I am sure they were fully impressed with the necessity of forming a great consolidated government, instead of a confederation. That this is a consolidated government is demonstrably clear; and the danger of such a government is, to my mind, very striking. I have the highest veneration for those gentlemen; but, sir, give me leave to demand: what right had they to say 'We, the people?' My political curiosity, exclusive of my anxious solicitude for the public welfare, leads me to ask: Who authorized them to speak the language of 'We, the people', instead of 'We, the states?' States are the characteristics and the soul of a confederation. If the states be not the agents of this compact, it must be one great, consolidated, national government, of the people of all the states. ... That they exceeded their power is perfectly clear. The federal Convention ought to have amended the old system; for this purpose they were solely delegated; the object of their mission extended to no other consideration.[35]

Turning to the federalists' diagnosis of the failures of the Articles of Confederation, which had been so badly mauled by *Publius*, this also cut no ice with the anti-federalist mind. Entitled 'the Centinel of the people's liberties' (abbreviated to 'Centinel'), the anti-federalist mind focused sharply upon the allegations made against the articles only to expose what it took to be a largely unfounded indictment:

We should ... be careful ... not to impute the temporary and extraordinary difficulties that have hitherto impeded the execution of the confederation to defects in the system itself. For years past, the harpies of power have been industriously inculcating the idea that all our difficulties proceed from the impotency of Congress, and have at length succeeded to give to this sentiment almost universal currency and belief. The devastations, losses and burdens occasioned by the late war; the excessive importations of foreign merchandise and luxuries which have drained the country of its specie and involved it in debt are all overlooked, and the inadequacy of the powers of the present confederation is erroneously supposed to be the only cause of our difficulties. ... What gross deception and fatal delusion![36]

These representative examples of the anti-federalist position in relation both to the alleged practical defects and deficiencies of the Articles and the perceived threat to liberty posed by what was a real substantive change in the nature of American federal government confirm that the intellectual debate was more than merely the cant of the day. Real practical issues of government were at stake. *The Federalist* was brilliantly argued and ingeniously persuasive but it was not without its own weaknesses and inconsistencies. The ability of the anti-federalists to expose these but their failure adequately to convince the ratifying conventions to reject the federalists' remedy was their tragedy. In consequence far too much reliance has been 'placed upon this single volume as the embodiment of federalist philosophy'. Had there been a much more searching analysis of the writings of other federalist publicists it is likely that further inconsistencies would have emerged and the anti-federalist position would probably have been revealed to be just as 'imaginative, perceptive and farsighted as that of the victors in the debate over the Constitution'.[37]

But was the anti-federalist case itself defensible? Were the anti-federalists correct in their claim that the conceptual shift from confederation to federation embodied such a significant practical change in the nature of American government that something entirely new and different had been constituted? Had the Federal Convention, in short, crossed the Rubicon? Here we are compelled to return to the language and terminology of *The Federalist*. In *Federalist* 9 Hamilton sought carefully to undermine this entrenched anti-federalist position by striking at the fundamental assumptions on which it was based. We are reminded of the anti-federalist position that was lucidly outlined by 'A Farmer':

> There are but two modes by which men are connected in society, the one which operates on *individuals*, this always has been, and ought still to be called, 'national government'; the other which binds *States* and *governments* together, this last has heretofore been denominated a 'league' or 'confederacy'. The term 'federalists' is therefore improperly applied to themselves, by the friends and supporters of the proposed constitution. This abuse of language does not help the cause. ... They are 'national men', and their opponents or at least a great majority of them, are 'federal' in the only true and strict sense of the word.[38]

The 'only true and strict sense of the word' implied that the laws of a national government operated directly upon the persons and property of individuals rather than solely on the constituent states as they would in a confederation. Indeed, in the secrecy of the Federal Convention, Madison himself had confessed as much when he remarked that 'whatever reason might have existed for the equality of suffrage when the Union was a federal one among sovereign States, it must cease when a national Governt. should be put into the place ... the acts of the Gen'l Govt. would take effect without the intervention of the State legislatures'.[39]

Hamilton, who dodged nimbly between the polar extremities of tyranny and anarchy, persistently pursued this linguistic and conceptual legerdemain. We shall quote him at length:

> A distinction, more subtle than accurate, has been raised between a 'confederacy' and a 'consolidation' of the States. The essential characteristic of the first is said to be the restriction of its authority to the members in their collective capacities, without reaching to the individuals of whom they are composed. It is contended that the national council ought to have no concern with any object of internal administration. An exact equality of suffrage between the members has also been insisted upon as a leading feature of a confederate government. These positions are, in the main,

arbitrary; they are supported neither by principle nor precedent. It has indeed happened that governments of this kind have generally operated in the manner which the distinction, taken notice of, supposes to be inherent in their nature; but there have been in most of them extensive exceptions to the practice, which serve to prove, as far as example will go, that there is no absolute rule on the subject. ... The extent, modifications, and objects of the federal authority are mere matters of discretion. So long as the separate organizations of the members be not abolished; so long as it exists, by a constitutional necessity, for local purposes; though it should be in perfect subordination to the general authority of the union, it would still be, in fact and in theory, an association of states, or confederacy.[40]

Hamilton's argument was essentially two-pronged: first, there was no hard and fast rule about what precisely constituted a confederation; and, second, the shared and divided nature of power in the proposed constitution effectively confirmed the autonomy and integrity of the constituent states in the revised federal union. The direct representation of the states in the Senate, their incorporation as constituent parts of the national sovereignty and the various 'portions of sovereign power' exclusive to them rendered the arrangement fully congruent with 'the idea of a federal government'. Hamilton, it should be remembered, regarded these criticisms of the anti-federalists as 'the novel refinements of an erroneous theory'.[41]

From the distance of two centuries, how can we resolve this elemental dispute between the federalists and the anti-federalists? Was it merely, as Hamilton suggested, more subtle than accurate? Were the disputed distinctions made by the anti-federalists really only arbitrary, supported neither by principle nor precedent, nor subject to extensive exceptions? The attempt to answer these questions has been unavoidably complicated by the compelling nature of the federalists' victory over the anti-federalists. We must recall that *Publius* could not afford to allow the anti-federalists to reject the proposed constitution on the explicit grounds of its fundamental disregard for the (con)federal principle. The claim of continuity with the past was crucial to the federalists' success. But their triumphal usurpation of the term 'federal' also had the inescapable consequence that it would henceforth come to be associated solely with the new constitutional settlement ratified in 1789 rather than with what existed before then.

One irony of these circumstances was that the federalists' insistence upon a continuity between pre- and post-1789, which was largely expedient for the purpose of victory, resulted in a conceptual rupture with the past. In this curious way the term 'federal' came irrevocably to monopolise the subsequent discourse on the nature of American government after 1789 while the term 'confederal' was confined strictly to the Articles. It would seem, then, that at least part of the answer to the question concerning the anti-federalists' disputed distinctions with Hamilton was that both positions were defensible. Recent research on confederations has emphasised that although the Articles did operate mainly upon the constituent states of the union, they did not do so exclusively. In certain notable respects they also operated directly upon individuals.[42] Hamilton was right; the historical experience of confederation, apart from some obvious core principles, has never suggested a clear-cut, unambiguous conceptual definition. There was some considerable scope for practical variations on the confederal theme but the position of the anti-federalists was also perfectly justifiable. The targets of their complaints against the proposed constitution depended upon which aspects of the novel arrangements they believed to be the most dangerous to liberty and therefore the least defensible. For them the onus on making a convincing case for moving from the *status quo* to revising the Articles lay squarely with the federalists. The argument comes full circle when we return to the familiar anti-federalist rebuke that the Federal Convention exceeded its brief and replaced rather than reformed the old confederal system.

Another approach that attempted to reconcile the positions between the federalists and the anti-federalists in this dispute is Martin Diamond's classic essay entitled 'What the Framers Meant by Federalism'.[43] In this investigation Diamond unravelled what was an intricate argument to explain precisely how the anti-federalists succumbed to the skilful political strategy of Madison and the federalists at the Federal Convention. The gist of his conclusion is relevant here. In brief it hinges upon the federalists' insistence that the ends of union could never be effectively achieved by the federal principle alone. Much more was required from the Articles if what both the federalists and the anti-federalists wanted was to be secured. Consequently the task of the federalists was to manoeuvre the anti-federalists into a position where they were forced to acknowledge the inadequacy rather than the irrelevance of the federal principle itself. Once this was achieved their position became untenable. In the end the Articles of Confederation – as the first federal constitution of the USA – was simply marooned. It became indefensible. All that the anti-federalists could do was to fight a rearguard action and try to incorporate as many federal features into the final outcome as best they could.

This is how Diamond accounted for the emergence of the novel 'federation' that was ratified in 1789. The term 'federalism' was 'truly the middle term' between confederal and national government because it modified and then combined 'the best characteristics of the other two forms'. This combination was thought to create 'a new and better thing to which is given the name feder-alism'.[44] One irony evident in this explanation, then, is that in attributing the term 'federal' to the system the framers regarded as possessing both federal and national features, 'we now regard as a unique principle what they regarded as a mere compound'. Clearly to use the term 'federal' to describe both the 'federal' and 'national' features of their plan was 'to lump under one obscuring term things they regarded as radically different'.[45] But this was because the federalists were forced to make concessions to the anti-federalists in order to achieve a workable compromise. The final outcome was what Diamond called 'the famous compromise', namely, the 'composition' of both federal and national elements. And it is important to remember that the ideas that supported the original feder-alist position 'have long retained their vitality in American politics':

the federal elements which have found their way into the Constitution have always supplied historical and legal support to recurring expressions of the traditional federalist view. It is necessary to acknowledge the survival of this view and the grounds for its survival. But it is impossible to understand the work of the Convention without seeing that the view survived only after having first been shaken to its very root, and hence that it survived only in a permanently weakened condition.[46]

In this regard we can understand why Lutz could suggest that modern federalism and the American Constitution did not so much replace the Articles 'as evolve it'. The former were built upon the latter 'as a revision in an earlier experiment that had been found to be flawed'. In other words the American federation was 'not simply founded in 1787, but refounded upon a base that had been laid earlier in the Articles of Confederation'.[47]

This conclusion is perfectly defensible as far as it goes. But in refusing to pursue the full implications of the substantive change in nature and character of the new political union established during 1787–89, it does not convey the real significance of the American federal experience. This is that the federalists did not merely design a revised but still basically confederal union; they actually created the basis for a new state, namely, a federation. They had moved away from the idea of a union of states, based on (con)federal principles, and towards the concept of a single national state. It was a qualitative change in the nature of the thing itself.

If we summarise this section, which has revisited *Publius* in order principally to buttress the conceptual foundation to the book, we can easily appreciate the enormous complexities and paradoxes that inhere in our subject. The devious duplicity and the labyrinthine twists and turns in the intellectual debate ensure that students of federalism and federation must constantly return to *The Federalist Papers* to reappraise and reassess their continuing significance for an understanding of contemporary federal political systems. As Diamond emphasised, the American federal experience has effectively converted a mere compound into a unique principle that has endured.

It is time to move to the third section of the chapter and examine some of the main philosophical conceptions of federalism post-1789. In order to do this, however, we will look first at some of the main philosophical issues that informed the intellectual debate about federalism in 1787. Let us begin with a brief survey of these questions.

Federalism and federation: philosophical conceptions of individual and community

What were the main philosophical issues and assumptions that characterised the age of *Publius* and the Federal Convention? What were Hamilton, Jay and Madison and the men who assembled at Philadelphia in the summer of 1787 seeking to achieve in terms of philosophical goals and how did they integrate these into the basis of their new federation? The political ideas and philosophical conceptions that infused the constitutional debate about the shift from confederation to federation read today like a political-science lexicon of basic terminological definitions. The political propaganda of *Publius* also operated as a political-science manual that conveyed to interested publics the basic elements of modern government. In retrospect the whole episode was essentially about the origins of American constitutionalism but in returning to first principles the collected letters of *Publius* acquired a tangible, if entirely unforeseen, universality of meaning and significance that extends well beyond the American federal experience.

If we focus narrowly upon the conceptual elements of political discourse, we confront *inter alia* the following: representation, consent, authority, legitimacy, obligation, responsibility, accountability, virtue, morality, humility, sovereignty, law, power and the common good or general welfare. These in turn have spawned the rule of law, balance of power, separation of powers, public versus private interest, tradition and hierarchy. If we concentrate on political ideas and movements, we find the following: liberty, equality, justice, natural rights, constitutionalism, democracy, republicanism, whiggism, toryism, conservatism, liberalism, secularism, voluntarism and utility. And if finally we search for the philosophical foundations of American federalism we will locate them not only in the Commonwealth legacy of the failed English republican revolution of the seventeenth century – and especially in the writings of James Harrington – but also derivatively in the works *inter alia* of Niccolò Machiavelli, John Locke, Algernon Sydney, John Milton, David Hume, Jean-Jacques Rousseau and Charles Montesquieu.[48] As Lutz has asserted, the pattern of influences was multiple, varying from one philosophical text to another: 'the debate surrounding the adoption of the U.S. Constitution reflected different patterns of influence than did the debates surrounding the writing and adoption of the state constitutions or the Revolutionary writing surrounding the Declaration of Independence'.[49] Nor should we forget the crucial impact of legal thinking in the late eighteenth century. In the realm of legal thought the influence of the English constitutional lawyer William Blackstone loomed so large that between 1780 and 1800 he was the most cited individual author in American political literature.[50] After all, 35 of the 55 framers were lawyers by training and the whole revolutionary enterprise was about both legal and constitutional rights.[51] It is hardly surprising, then, that the indigenous, almost homespun, American philosophy of federalism that crystallised at the end of the eighteenth century had a long convoluted progeniture.

Bernard Bailyn has pointed out that in the years between the discussions about the colonies' relations to Great Britain and the construction of the first state constitutions there was 'a continuous, unbroken line of intellectual development and political experience' that bridged two intellectual worlds:

> The mid-eighteenth century world, still vitally concerned with a set of ideas derived ultimately from classical antiquity – from Aristotelian, Polybian,

Machiavellian, and seventeenth century English sources, and the quite different world of Madison and Tocqueville. Between the two was not so much a transition of ideas as a transformation of problems.[52]

As we have seen, these problems had their origins in a chain of unique circumstances wherein the value of political ideas applied to problematic developments yielded a practical experience that was heeded above everything else. The revolutionaries developed a new set of assumptions about constitutions after 1775 and it is to the circumstances that surrounded the making of the state constitutions like those of Virginia, Pennsylvania and Massachusetts that we must turn if we want more fully to understand what one writer has described as 'unquestionably the most brilliant and creative era in the entire history of American political thought'.[53] This local political experience shaped the destiny, in very much an immediate and practical sense, of constitutionalism in the USA.

What, then, was the mainstream thinking behind the construction of these state constitutions that later informed the Philadelphia Convention? Why, for example, did many of them include such features as judicial review and a bill of rights that were absent from the new federal constitution ratified in 1789? To answer these questions and those above we must turn now to consider the philosophical ideas and assumptions that drove both the federalists and the anti-federalists to combine liberty with authority in order to safeguard property, promote commerce, trade and general welfare, and to restore political stability.

The twin pillars of republicanism and democracy underpinned the gradual shift from confederation to federation. Their meaning, however, was somewhat ambiguous. We know that by the end of the War of Independence most Americans had come to believe that their government had to be republican, but what did this mean to them? In *Federalist* 39 Madison acknowledged that the inherent ambiguities of the republican form 'were an answer to this question to be sought ... in the application of the term by political writers to the constitutions of different states, no satisfactory one would ever be found'. The term 'republican' had clearly been used with 'extreme inaccuracy'. But Madison defined it unequivocally as 'a government which derives all its powers directly or indirectly from the great body of the people'.[54] It certainly meant support for popular government and consistent opposition to both monarchy and aristocracy, although not to what was widely perceived as the balanced constitution of England. At the very least, republicanism meant popular sovereignty – political authority enshrined in 'the People' – and self-government based upon consent. But Iain Hampsher-Monk has emphasised just how complicated and controversial the meaning of republican thought remains, particularly among Americans, to this day. It contained several different strands of meaning, having different emphases, which could lead in many different directions.[55] There were in reality several shades of republican ideology.

Democracy, however, was less problematic. It was often associated in the colonists' minds with republican principles and sometimes used synonymously by them. But they did not mean the same thing. Democracy was what Samuel Finer has called a 'homonym' – one word with many meanings – and the colonists' understanding of it was naturally very different from the way that we construe it today.[56] As Bailyn remarked, the term 'republic' conjured up for many the positive features of the seventeenth-century English Commonwealth that marked 'the triumph of virtue and reason' while 'democracy' was a word that denoted 'the lowest order of society as well as the form of government in which the commons ruled' and was generally associated with 'the threat of civil disorder and the early assumption of power by a dictator'.[57] Fears of so-called 'democratic despotism', of the dangers of democracy succumbing to demagogues, were rife in the early revolutionary years and it was no accident that Madison had distinguished between republicanism and democracy principally by restricting the latter to direct or 'pure democracy'. To most colonial minds at the end of the eighteenth century, democracy meant some kind of broad propertied oligarchy in which 'the lower orders' knew their station in life.

Republicanism and democracy were indissolubly connected to an emerging constitutionalism in America in the last quarter of the eighteenth century. This meant that the fundamental law of the constitution, based upon popular sovereignty, was established by the people as the constituent authority in the state and in whose name they governed themselves. Consequently constitutional law was a special law made by the sovereign people that authorised government via legitimacy and defined individual rights while conferring some powers on state governments, some on the federal government and, should they prefer it, the residuum reserved to themselves, as they did in the Tenth Amendment to the Constitution of 1789. One legacy of this emergent constitutionalism, then, was the division of power between the central (national) authority and the constituent state authorities in all federations. Small wonder that federal states have since come to signify 'constitutional federalism' in the sense of what constitutionalism means in particular and governance in general. Constitutionalism has in other words become a question of philosophy that incorporates certain ideas and assumptions about the limited nature of government and its underlying purpose.[58]

Together these three political ideas and movements of the American federal experience – republicanism, democracy and constitutionalism – embraced the elemental notions of liberty, equality, justice, representation, consent, authority, legitimacy and accountability. But they also compelled *Publius* to consider very carefully the relationship between individual and collective rights, interests, responsibilities and identities. Madison in particular was instrumental in wrestling with what he construed as the problem of 'faction' and its relationship to the broader question of majoritarianism versus minoritarianism. Attention to this particular problem was inescapable if *Publius* wished to present a convincing case for both the protection and maintenance of liberty and the need to link them to the extended republic. *Federalist* 10, then, remains pivotal to any discussion of the philosophical conceptions of individual and community that are so bound up in our comparative study of federalism and federation. We will therefore conclude this section with a short survey of what has become one of the most difficult and troublesome conflicts to attempt to manage and resolve in contemporary federations.

Hampsher-Monk has described *Federalist* 10 as 'one of the nerve centres' of the defence of the constitution by *Publius* for the way that it resynthesised 'the worrying issues about size, faction and democracy into a mutually supportive whole'.[59] It is, in other words, difficult to overestimate its significance to any serious study of federalism and federation because it goes to the very heart of what federal democracy was, is and ought to be about. Consequently its implications for contemporary federations are self-evident, although this is sometimes either forgotten or ignored by contemporary writers. Let us begin with Madison's definition of what constituted a faction:

> By a faction I understand a number of citizens, whether amounting to a majority or a minority of the whole, who are united and actuated by some common impulse or passion, or of interest, adverse to the rights of other citizens, or to the permanent and aggregate interests of the community.[60]

Madison believed that, 'the great object' of the constitutional negotiations was 'to secure the public good and private rights' against the danger of faction and to reconcile them simultaneously with both 'the spirit and the form of popular government'.[61] Accordingly republican principles contained a republican remedy but this hinged decisively on 'the greater number of citizens and greater sphere of country' over which a republic 'may be extended'.[62] Madison's ingenuity, as is well known, turned on its head Montesquieu's insistence that successful republicanism could be achieved only in small states. His famous triad of principles – representation, the greater numbers of citizens and the greater extent of territory – together yielded the extended republic. But what are we to make of his references to 'the rights of other citizens' and 'the permanent and aggregate interests of the community' in his definition of faction?

For our purposes *Federalist* 10 has another significance that relates to contemporary federalism and federation. This is that it exposes and underlines the fundamental tension between the citizen in his individual and collective capacities. The tension is bound up with the question of representation: who or what is represented in a federation? Madison's distinction between a republic and a democracy highlights the quality of dual loyalties and interests and split-level identities in the federal state. The citizen is represented as an individual member of the union and simultaneously as an individual member of a constituent unit of that union. He therefore has rights in both of these constitutional arenas. But he is also a member of two distinct communities and has a communitarian dimension to his identity. The tension in relations between these two dimensions of the citizen constitutes the federalism that is peculiar to federation. We can therefore interpret Madison's construction of a faction as 'adverse to the rights of other citizens, or to the permanent and aggregate interests of the community' to refer precisely to the sort of dual loyalties and interests and split-level identities described above. It serves to underline the philosophical, constitutional and political conceptions of individual and community. In its most elemental Aristotelian sense, it suggests that federation formally recognises the individual citizen as part of the larger society. He is, in short, part of a polity with common interests over and above his own narrow concerns.

Our brief textual exegesis of *Federalist* 10 indicates that republican representation (or the 'representativeness' of representation) based upon 'a happy combination' of the large and the small polity in the new federation was Madison's 'republican remedy for the diseases most incident to republican government'.[63] The extended compound republic would control the effects of faction by a series of checks and balances. In *Federalist* 51 Madison acknowledged that in seeking to protect 'one part of the society against the injustice of the other part' – where for example a minority of states or people was oppressed – 'ambition must be made to counteract ambition'. The answer lay in comprehending in the society:

> so many separate descriptions of citizens as will render an unjust combination of a majority of the whole very improbable, if not impracticable. ... Whilst all authority in it will be derived from and dependent on the society, the society itself will be broken into so many parts, interests and classes of citizens, that the rights of individuals, or of the minority, will be in little danger from interested combinations of the majority.[64]

The point was that there would be different majorities and minorities for different policies in separate policy arenas. And these majorities and minorities would be in a constant state of flux. *Publius* therefore recognised the difficulties inherent in seeking to reconcile the distinct interests of the larger union with the separate but related interests of its constituent parts. These boiled down to the self-interest and self-determination of the citizen in his individual and his collective or communitarian capacities.

The conceptions of individual and community in this late-eighteenth-century pursuit of good government understandably reflected a much sharper concern for state interests and identities than is perhaps evident in the USA today. Madison's much-vaunted 'diversity in the faculties of men' was something that had not yet been subjected to the penetrating and corrosive processes of state-building and national integration that were then only in their infancy. Nonetheless it is important for us to recognise the significance of these basic conceptions of individual and community – many aspects of which have endured – for the comparative study of federalism and federation. The juxtaposition of individual and community, of individual and collective interests, identities and rights, is immanent in all federations. It is, indeed, the *raison d'être* of federation *qua* federation.

Conclusion: appearance and reality

The American federal experience can be conveniently summarised in the following nine milestones: the antecedents of federalism, the Declaration of

Independence, the Articles of Confederation, the creation of the state constitutions, the Continental Congress, the proceedings of the Federal Convention, the Federal Constitution, *The Federalist Papers* and the anti-federalist essays. Together they express a remarkable combination of philosophical influence, practical experience and political theory and discourse that stands as a monument to the search for good government. Any comparative study of federalism and federation is compelled repeatedly to return to the American federal experience not because it is the prototype making all subsequent federations mere carbon copies but because many aspects of that experience retain a significance for contemporary federal experiments.

In hindsight we can appreciate just how contingent and circumstantial the experience was. Samuel Beer has recently challenged the orthodox assertion, personified in the conclusion of Martin Diamond, that the American Constitution was the outcome of a series of compromises so great that it lacked a coherent overall rationale. His interpretation of the emergence of what he has called 'national federalism' hinges conversely upon an intricate analysis that traces the USA as a single sovereign people back neither to the Articles of Confederation nor even to colonial independence but specifically to the Continental Congress. According to his skilfully argued thesis, it was the Continental Congress that acted as the constituent power of the people in authorising the transition from colonial independence to statehood.[65] Beer, however, does not deny that the American federal experience was extremely complex, with many unexpected twists and turns, and that the unprecedented compound republic led eventually to what in late- eighteenth-century parlance was widely regarded as a consolidated union. That this was the result of a series of difficult and hard-fought compromises forged during and shortly after the Federal Convention is incontestable. Why else did the Convention concede the well-known anti-federalist proposal – a bill of rights – despite opposition from both Madison and Hamilton, which was later entrenched in the first ten amendments to the Constitution? This concession was about the protection of liberty from the centralisation of power rather than a feud over federalism, just as the concern expressed about the proposed judicial system in *Federalist* 78 crystallised fears of judicial review and a flexible interpretation of the Constitution that would favour the expansion of central (federal) government. Clearly, the federalists did not have it all their own way; they were forced to include more federal features in the new constitution than they would otherwise have preferred because the anti-federalists foresaw with remarkable accuracy many of the consequences of national federalism. But however ingenious the founding fathers were in blending federal and national characteristics the Articles of Confederation, which was the authentic federal union by established historical standards, did not fail because of its purported weakness as such but rather, as Diamond observed, because Americans sought so much from it:

> The Confederacy under the Articles was not a weak league. On the contrary, it was a very good league as leagues go. Measured against other

confederacies and by standards appropriate to confederacies, the Confederacy comes off very well. But that was not how the delegates were measuring it. They were measuring it by standards appropriate to nations because they wanted from the central body what only a national government could supply.[66]

This important observation alone explains why historians and political scientists persistently query the process by which the Confederation was almost completely emptied of substance by the federalists. And it will surely continue to stretch credulity when we are reminded that the federalists 'could use one name while pursuing a goal that was the opposite in fact'.[67]

This controversy, which we can depict as national federalism versus compact federalism, turns inevitably on how the origins and actions of the Continental Congress are interpreted. The evidence remains disputed. Informed opinion is divided. But it is at least clear from *The Federalist* that in relations between the two distinct principles of federalism and nationalism the latter was expected ultimately to triumph. *The Federalist* sought to reconcile federalism with the strengthening of central government in a way that did not allow its opponents to construe the constitutional outcome as a consolidated union. In his reference to the new union as an 'incomplete nation' Tocqueville had put his finger firmly on the issue that underlined the nature of the conundrum, namely, how far the interaction of these two principles in the compound republic could work in practice. They seemed irreconcilable precisely because they were incompatible. The inference was either that one principle would prevail over the other or that the compound republic would simply have to exist in perpetual discord.

If federalism had a yardstick of measurement – a gold standard – in the late eighteenth century it is usually assumed to have been the Articles. In assessing the American federal experience however it is very difficult to avoid being pulled reluctantly into the fierce debate about what the intentions of the founding fathers were. There are many different schools of thought and we must not be deflected from our main purpose in this conclusion. What, then, does a study of this experience tell us about contemporary federalism and federation? The American federal experience seems to be engulfed in so many different controversies as to make almost any conclusion a risky business. It is hardly surprising therefore if today federalism, federation and confederation remain highly contested and contestable concepts.

Nonetheless, even in this inhospitable intellectual climate it is possible with the considerable advantage of hindsight to make some measured judgements that have a contemporary significance. We can understand perfectly well for example how the modern federal state originated. It came into existence in the most bizarre of circumstances. Federal ideas, concepts and principles have existed from time immemorial and owe nothing to the American model for their provenance, but it is the American federal experience that transformed our understanding of these established ideas, concepts and principles. Together the Federal Convention, *The Federalist* and the anti-federalist essays had the effect of strengthening the unitary and national elements in the new federal union so that it moved much closer to what was widely understood to be a consolidated (national) union with a national government. This is why Christopher Hughes defined modern federal government as 'a classification of unitary governments of the fully constitutional type'.[68] In late-eighteenth-century political thinking, we are reminded, there were only two types of government that were considered to be mutually exclusive: confederal (or federal) and unitary (or national). It was the founding fathers who created a new form of government – the compound republic – to which they gave the old name 'federal'.

The American federal experience, both in appearance and reality, was an adventure that explains why the concepts of federalism and federation have had such a chequered history. They have not been able to escape from their past. Consequently their conceptual evolution has been constantly embattled due to the interaction of two main factors, namely, the extraordinary circumstances of their transformation in meaning, definition and significance after 1787 and the context in which they took shape at the dawn of the age of mass politics. Small wonder therefore that political scientists have failed to agree upon a precise definition of these terms let alone construct much of a theoretical framework of analysis. If the appearance of modern federalism and federation has been so contingent and circumstantial it should not surprise us if the problems of conceptual analysis, definition and methodology have proved in turn to be so intractable. Given this colourful past it would seem that only a theory of circumstantial causation could successfully overcome these difficulties.

The reality of federalism and federation of course has always been more than just an American template. Federalism and federation have retained their characteristic relationship to the processes of state-building and national integration but it is a relationship in which enormous variations have emerged and developed. Beer's 'national federalism' has not been replicated in every modern federation. Nor should we expect it to be. Canada in this respect is not like Germany, and neither of them is like the USA. Nonetheless we are constantly driven back to the American federal experience because the unremitting pursuit of good government necessarily involves a return to first principles. And we find these, still fresh and unvarnished, in *The Federalist*. The writings of Madison and Hamilton, in particular, have a universality of meaning and significance that transcends generations of change. Consequently their fears and anxieties about the nature of government are still with us today. *The Federalist* grappled with many, if not most, of the difficult constitutional and political problems that continue to challenge contemporary political systems. In short, the American federal experience has a compelling relevance that extends far beyond the USA both in time and place.

It is clear, then, that many of the contemporary arguments and debates about federalism and federation have already been well rehearsed in *The Federalist*. This explains why so many scholars from Edward Freeman to Maurice Vile have often relied heavily upon the American federal model for their definitions of the federal state. Our conceptual and methodological review in Chapter 1 confirms this. It is perfectly understandable. In our comprehension of federalism and federation, then, we must not be confined by this model, but nor should we ignore it. Contemporary references to it are not necessarily vitiated by the peculiarities of the American federal experience. It need not contaminate other federal experiences unduly. In this book we shall recognise the unique historical, structural, institutional and cultural qualities inherent in every federalism and federation. The American federal experience has been discussed in some considerable detail in this chapter simply to furnish the book with an indispensable historical and philosophical context. It locates the origins of contemporary political discourse, complements the conceptual and methodological review in Chapter 1, and conveniently prepares the ground for an extensive and long overdue survey of the origins and formation of federal states in Chapter 3. In moving forward to the next chapter therefore we are not leaving the American federal experience behind us. On the contrary, its influence is inescapable and incontrovertible and we shall return to it repeatedly in our quest to explain and understand how and why federations are formed.

3 Federalism and federation
The origins and formation of federal states

Introduction

In this survey of the origins and formation of federations, it is important for us to make a clear preliminary distinction between 'origins' and 'formation'. Most of the primary contributions to the mainstream literature have concentrated their attentions on the origins of federal states while much less attention has been paid to their formation. Indeed, it is customary for scholars to identify two predominant motives in their quest to locate the origins of federations, namely, defence and security goals, on the one hand, and economic and commercial objectives, on the other. The former concerns have led to the creation of a defence union for military purposes (a *Kriegsverein*) while the latter preoccupation has led to the emergence of a customs union for economic benefits derived from the increased flow of trade and commerce (a *Zollverein*). It is, however, notable that the single most important area that has been identified as the critical factor in the origins of both confederations and federations has been defence and security. In his masterly historical survey of confederations that briefly sketched out the theory and practice of federal unions in Switzerland (1291–1798; 1815–48), the United Provinces of the Netherlands (1579–1795), Germany (1815–66) and the USA (1781–89), Murray Forsyth has confirmed that the 'classic confederation is basically a unity capable of waging war'.[1]

It should not surprise us that this singular focus upon defence and security with respect to the origins of federal unions or confederations should extend beyond unions of states to federations, especially if we begin our survey with *The Federalist Papers*. Even the briefest of glances at the first nine papers confirms that military and foreign affairs, together with questions of internal security, were the principal objects of concern.[2] William Riker, one of the most influential contributors to the intellectual debate about federalism, was not slow to reaffirm 'the primacy of the military motive' in the adoption of what he called the 'centralized federalism' of the new compound republic.[3] But in his eagerness to underline the overriding significance of the military-diplomatic advantages of federation, Riker did concede that 'economic concerns were felt' and these, too, were acknowledged in *The Federalist Papers*.[4] The reality of the circumstances that explained the origins of federal states, then, had to include economic, commercial and welfare conditions. Forsyth also emphasised that confederations were rarely concerned with defence and security alone; there was an intimate and reciprocal relationship between the goal of security and the goal of welfare and it was impossible to 'escape the logic of this interdependency'.[5] With this complex interdependency in mind, let us turn now to focus sharply upon why and how federations come into existence.

In this chapter I want to re-examine the origins and formation of federations with a view to revising and updating some of the old arguments in the mainstream literature. This task is in some ways quite straightforward while in other respects it presents us with fresh problems and difficulties previously absent or studiously avoided. In order to return to the world of generalisations about the origins of federations, it is necessary first to rehearse some of the earlier arguments about why people choose to unite in the federal form as opposed to any other form of union. To convey the complexity of the subject we will look at the following three sections: first, the old debate on the origins of federations; second, a close look at some familiar and some less familiar case studies about the motives for union that raise important questions about historical interpretation for the purpose of comparative politics; and, third, a conclusion that reassesses and reappraises the influential contribution of William Riker to this intellectual debate together with a new theoretical proposal that revolves around the idea of circumstantial causation. Let us begin by returning to the old debate on the origins of federations.

The intellectual debate about the origins of federations

The debate about the origins of federations, which is most closely associated with Riker, was bound up, as we saw in Chapter 1, with the reassertion of the exclusively political approach to the striking of a federal bargain that created a federal constitution. Consequently Riker sought to identify a series of generalisations about the conditions under which federations are created. While historians stressed the 'unique historical context' of each federal bargain, which Riker was happy to acknowledge, the political scientist in him wanted to identify a set of factors common to the origins of every federal state.[6] This would reveal a consistent pattern of behaviour that was empirically verifiable and had significant theoretical implications. His analysis of the 'bargain invented at Philadelphia' led him to propose a two fold hypothesis that he sought to test by examining the origins of 18 existing federations together with nine previous federations that had failed.[7] The conditions that formed the basis of his hypothesis were:

1   A desire on the part of the politicians who offer the bargain to expand their territorial control by peaceful means, usually either to meet an external military or diplomatic threat or to prepare for military or diplomatic aggression or aggrandizement.

2   A willingness on the part of politicians who accept the bargain to give up some independence for the sake of union either because of some external

military-diplomatic threat or opportunity. Either they desire protection from an external threat or they desire to participate in the potential aggression of the federation.

For the sake of brevity, Riker referred to these two predispositions as (1) the expansion condition and (2) the military condition.[8] Moreover, the evidence from his comparative exploration of the other federations led him to state categorically that these two conditions were necessary to the 'occurrence of federations'.[9]

The debate on the origins of federations was swiftly engaged. Shortly after the publication of Riker's two conditions, Antony Birch reviewed Riker's propositions with reference to developments in Nigeria, East Africa and Malaysia and concluded by revising and expanding these conditions to include (1) the desire to deter internal threats and (2) the willingness to have them deterred.[10] Riker readily conceded these revisions a decade later in his mammoth review of federalism published in *The Handbook of Political Science*.[11] In his focus upon 'the immediate political act of federation', he was always concerned to locate 'the conditions … most descriptive of reality' and this undertaking drove him to conduct a survey of the major contributors to the debate about the origins of federations.[12] Of necessity this brought him face to face with the theoretical claims of Karl Deutsch, Kenneth Wheare and Ronald Watts, whose respective analyses of the conditions of federalism he examined thoroughly.[13] His conclusions are worth reviewing and reassessing for our purposes because they are now thirty years old and it is pertinent for us to consider how they have stood the test of time.

In retrospect, Riker's approach to the study of the origins of federations reflected the intellectual turbulence in political science that was characteristic of the 1960s and 1970s. His primary task was to reassert the *political*; he was convinced that federalism was neither an economic nor a sociological phenomenon but essentially a political affair. Above all, he wanted to theorise about the origins and formation of federations so that political scientists would have what Maurice Vile wanted, namely, a 'sustained theoretical structure'.[14] Where, then, did Riker's detailed analysis of the origins of federations leave us? What did his theoretical concerns bequeath us today?

The Rikerian legacy is one that has endured probably because his basic premises were quite simple. He grounded his approach in the assumption that men in politics behave rationally in making bargains that involved mutual benefits. This pursuit of self-interest could be applied to constitution-making, which, after all, was participation in a rational political bargain. The conditions that he identified as being necessary to the successful conclusion of constitution-making were pertinent to one particular kind of constitution, namely, the formation of federal constitutions that created federal states. Consequently, for federations to appear it was necessary that there should be some significant threat and that this would be sufficient to compel the participating actors to strike a bargain or compact that would be mutually beneficial. Without these two necessary political conditions of 'a desire to expand and a willingness of provincial politicians to accede despite provincial loyalties', federations could not come into existence. This set of assumptions and propositions, based upon the theory of rational political behaviour, enabled him to claim at the very least 'a partially verified' political theory of their origins.[15]

The reaction to Riker's scientific approach to his subject and the bold theoretical claims that he made was clinical and uncompromising. S. Rufus Davis left no shred of doubt as to what he thought of Riker's 'quasi-scientific style' that sought to rise above the unique historical and cultural setting of each federal experience. In a scorching attack upon his 'lab-science mode' of analysis, Davis refuted Riker's claims about his two political conditions: they might be highly plausible but they were not proof because they applied in all unions so that his arguments resulted in 'a mere truism'.[16] To take just one of these two conditions – the military condition – security motives were present in the calculations of all communities that sought greater strength through association. The possible variations in the ways in which security or threat might present themselves were endless, and where it was one of a compound of factors it might be dominant, conspicuous and constant, or it might be secondary, negligible, remote, vague and inconstant. Or, finally, what was perceived or what was believed to be a security or a threat situation, and the levels of apprehension or the intensity of the belief, might vary profoundly in the calculations of each party contemplating some form of security association. Davis concluded that it was to be expected that every writer would note the presence of the military-security factor in the list of motives for federal union but that only Riker had attributed such overriding significance to it. In reality the proposition that these two factors were present at the birth of each federation was to 'state a commonplace that is hardly worth noting'.[17]

The second searing indictment of Riker's theoretical claims came from Preston King, who described his internal-external threat condition as 'intuitively attractive' but analytically 'imprecise' and ultimately 'trivial'.[18] Rather like Davis, he claimed that since the existence of military-security threats was present in all unions, then so must it prove in any specific case of successful federal union. Indeed, even if it was possible to make the threat criterion more precise, it remained that the number of cases that we could test would be so small that our results could not possibly justify 'that degree of certainty' that Riker was disposed to accord them.[19] The *coup de grâce* to Riker's assertive claims was administered with calm assurance:

> In short, it is always possible to play up the case for a threat where a federal entity comes into being, as also to play it down where federation fails. For if a federation is formed from fear of other powers, and formed equally from mutual fear of those states which federate, then virtually any type of fear must provide grounds for federal union. … To stipulate a condition which is not only necessary for a given development, but also for distinctly opposed or contrary developments, is not very enlightening.[20]

The gist of King's critique of Riker was that the central case made 'for a strict correlation between the emergence of federations and the presence of a threat to local units is simply unclear (even self-contradictory) in what it maintains'. Consequently the very basis of Riker's theoretical claims was emptied of substance: the arbitrariness, imprecision and circularity of the argumentation vitiated them at their source.[21] These two principal critiques of Riker's political theory effectively revealed it as having little or no explanatory value and certainly undermined his claim that the existence of military threats served above all to mark the origin of a federal government as distinct from other forms of union.

We can see from this brief sketch of the old debate on the origins of federations, which began with Riker's original theoretical efforts forty years ago, that the principal purpose was to explain *why* federations are formed rather than *how* they are formed. Yet it is equally important for us to understand the formation of federations just as much as it is to know why they are formed. Indeed, we need to appreciate more fully than we do just what exactly the nature of the relationship is between these two separate but related questions. Riker certainly broached the subject when he couched his initial arguments in terms of those participants who 'offer' the bargain and those who 'accept' it, but his flawed reasoning meant that much of what he claimed was superficial and oversimplified. The key that can unlock this particular door lies in the very concept of 'bargain' itself. Let us look a little closer at the use of this term.

We will recall that for Riker federation was essentially 'a constitutional bargain among politicians'.[22] However, his elaboration of the concept of bargain meant in practice that it was an agreement 'between prospective national leaders and officials of constituent governments for the purpose of aggregating territory, the better to lay taxes and raise armies'.[23] This meant that the former group of actors desired to expand its territorial control and saw in federation 'the only feasible means to accomplish a desired expansion without the use of force', while the latter party to the bargain were the officials of the constituent governments who accepted the limitations on their independence either because of a desire for protection from a military threat or as a result of their desire to participate in the potential aggression of the federation.[24] There are a number of problems with the assumptions built into this construction of the nature of the bargain – of *how* such federations are formed. I have identified them in the following way:

1   There is an implicit assumption that it is possible to distinguish between those who offer the bargain and those who accept it when in practice this is often extremely difficult, if not impossible.
2   It is taken for granted that it is always the 'prospective national leaders' who offer the bargain and 'the officials of the constituent governments' who accept it when this is not necessarily the case for every federal formation.
3   There is an implicit assumption of a clear delineation on role(s) between the national (central) elites and the subnational (regional) actors when in reality

the 'prospective national leaders' are frequently officials of the constituent governments and *vice versa*.

4   There are very often other links, such as membership of the same political party or of the same religious or ethnic group, that overlap and complicate the picture, serving to undermine the neat demarcation between so-called central and regional actors.

5   The existence of role accumulation makes it impossible in practice to assess in which capacity the delegate to a constitutional bargain is acting.

6   It is based upon an implicit assumption that we know the political convictions that motivate the parties and participating actors.[25]

These caveats to the utility of Riker's bargain constitute very real obstacles to both historical interpretation and political analysis, and they are factors that we shall have to take into account in the next section when we explore the motives for union. There seems little doubt that any serious analytical discussion of the origins and formation of federations must avoid what Davis observed when he interrogated Riker's historical version(s) of defining federal moments: 'it is difficult to resist the impression that Riker translates history with the reductionist zeal of a salvationist, an apocalyptic or materialist historian. Indeed, modified or totally contrary accounts may be and have been given of every instance he discusses'.[26] The dangers and pitfalls of the uses and abuses of history could hardly be put more plainly.

The motives for federal union

In the light of the controversies that continue to surround the intellectual debate about the origins and formation of federations, it is imperative that we tread very carefully when we seek to re-examine and reappraise why and how such states come into existence. The following section will be devoted to a brief discussion of historical events and developments in Switzerland, Canada, Australia, India, Malaysia, Austria and Germany in the hope that these case studies will shed some fresh light on the factors involved in the establishment of federations. As we shall see, the motives for union are not difficult to identify in a general sense but it remains very much a matter of conjecture as to how far we can prioritise them. In some cases the political factors might outweigh the socio-economic factors, while in other respects the reverse might be the case. Certainly it is not possible to reduce the variety of factors impinging on the federal bargain, as Riker contended, to two simple criteria of necessity. The complexity of each historical experience makes this much more difficult than Riker's bold analyses would have us believe. Moreover, it is important to recognise analytically that there is a two-step process involved in the creation of a federation: first, the desire for union and, second, the decision to have a federal union. We will look at each case study in the order in which it achieved the status of federation.

Switzerland

Switzerland became a federation in 1848 but its federal origins stretch back to 1291 when the three tiny rural Alpine communities of Uri, Schwyz and Unterwalden entered into a league of mutual defence – designated an *Eidgenossenschaft* (Oath-Fellowship) – to protect themselves against the encroachments of the house of Habsburg. Subsequently the old Swiss Confederation grew up gradually in the late medieval period as a process of aggregation, adding new communities to the original nucleus so that by 1353, when Bern joined, the League totalled eight cantons and by 1513 the accession of Appenzell raised it to thirteen. The number of constituent units remained at this figure until the changes induced by the French Revolution swept them away in 1798. Change followed change and after Napoleon's experiment with the Mediation Constitution in 1803 – a confederation with a strong centre that lasted until 1813 – it was only in 1815 that the multilingual structure that we recognise in Switzerland today first began to take shape. What had been essentially a Germanic unity was finally broken as a number of French-speaking territorial communities, together with Ticino, the only Italian-speaking area, were admitted to full canton status and re-established Switzerland as a loose confederation of 25 cantons based upon a treaty that guaranteed collective security by mutual assistance. Up until the *Sonderbund* Civil War when the seven seceding conservative Catholic cantons were soundly defeated by the liberal Protestant cantons in 1847, Switzerland had been a league of states. With the introduction of a new constitution in 1848, ratified by a popular vote of both the citizens and the cantons, it became a federation. Revised in 1874 and more recently in 1999, it is the federal constitution of 1848 that contained most of the organisational framework that characterises the Swiss polity today.[27]

The most pronounced features of this long federal progeniture in Switzerland are its slow, almost organic, accumulation of customs, conventions and political usages built up from below that have informed its political institutions. At the very core of its existence has been the ever-present pulse of the cantons and communes, both rural and urban, that have preserved the vitality of liberty, self-determination and citizen participation in local affairs. An accurate summary of the Swiss federal evolution therefore would have to include a combination of strong American influences, a unique admixture of political institutions and an indigenous political culture rooted in the spirit of *Bundestreue* – of reciprocity, mutual trust and understanding, tolerance, dignity, partnership and respect for and recognition of minorities – that values consensus, conciliation, compromise and consent above crude majoritarian calculation.[28] In short, the notion of *Eidgenossenschaft* refers to a covenant, a moral basis, to preserve and promote the politics of difference and diversity.

In hindsight it is clear that the conceptual shift from confederation to federation in 1848 was occasioned by what was in effect a Swiss civil war and to this extent Riker's military-diplomatic condition is fulfilled. But the creation of a federation in Switzerland cannot be interpreted in so peremptory a fashion without taking into account a host of other factors. In the context of military affairs the old confederation had suffered no less than four internal religious wars between the sixteenth and eighteenth centuries and had recovered to re-establish confederal union. There were reasons other than just military conflict that account for the creation of the Swiss federation in 1848. Wolf Linder has identified the following factors: economic reasons, external pressures, democracy and social values and the combination of democracy with the federal idea.[29]

By the mid-nineteenth century, industrialisation had reached many cantons creating new urban elites with vested interests in removing the boundaries of cantonal markets that were obstacles to economic activities. The federal constitution extended the powers of the centre from security and laid the foundations for a common economic market so that Switzerland became an economic unity.[30] An additional reason for a conceptually decisive shift to federation was the external environment that finally persuaded the cantons to reduce their future vulnerability to foreign pressures by buttressing their collective security. It was no accident that the 1848 constitution referred to federal responsibilities to guarantee the independence of the Swiss nation in 'unity, force and honour' as well as to uphold internal security and order.[31] A third reason for creating the federation must be sought in the long-term process of democratisation that had been fomenting in many of the cantons since the French Revolution of 1789. The spread of democratic ideas interacted with the venerable Swiss cultural heritage that had already familiarised Swiss people with individual self-responsibility and different forms of communalism or collective decision-making. This focus upon an indigenous Swiss political culture of local political practices and customs was elegantly described by James Bryce in his *Modern Democracies*, first published in 1921:

> The internal political institutions of the allied communities varied greatly. The rural cantons were pure democracies, governing themselves by meetings of the people. Of the cities, some, like Bern, were close oligarchies of nobles; in others oligarchy was more or less tempered by a popular element. ... Swiss political institutions have been built up on the foundations of small communities, rural and urban, accustomed to control their own affairs. ... the commune was from the earliest times a potent factor in accustoming the whole people to take interest in and know how to handle local affairs, every man on a level with his fellows. It is still the political unit of the nation and the focus of its local public life. ... Local self-government has been in Switzerland a factor of prime importance, not only as the basis of the administrative fabric, but also because the training which the people have received from practice in it has been a chief cause of their success in working republican institutions. Nowhere in Europe has it been so fully left to the hands of the people. The Swiss themselves lay stress upon it, as a means of educating the citizens in public work, as instilling the sense of civic duty, and as enabling governmental action to be used for the benefit of the community without either sacrificing local initiative or making the action of the central authority too strong and too pervasive.[32]

This indigenous political culture suggests that democratisation came from both 'above' and 'below'. Certainly the decision to place the extension of political rights in the new constitution under the guarantee of the federal government was really building upon a solid foundation of local experience of communal affairs. And the link with the federal idea was in a sense obvious; its implications for the democratisation of a multilingual collection of communities meant that power-sharing between central government and the cantons could furnish 'different answers to the same questions', answers that 'corresponded to the preferences of different ethnic or religious groups'. Federation permitted different cultural communities to coexist and it served to protect minorities.[33]

In summary, then, the origins and formation of the Swiss federation in 1848 are much more complex than Riker's simple military and expansion conditions indicate. The presence of an internal security threat might have been a necessary factor to help explain why the Swiss desired to restore their union, but its very presence was not a sufficient reason to explain why the Swiss demonstrated a desire for federation.

Canada

Canada became a federation in 1867 and had the distinction of being the first country to combine the parliamentary tradition of responsible government, based upon the Westminster model, with federal principles. The significance of this for political scientists rests primarily upon the novel idea of seeking to reconcile two fundamentally opposing political concepts of governmental organisation. The British parliamentary tradition is rooted in certain preconceptions about order and stability that find their expression in a fusion of executive and legislative powers so that strong executive authority results from an ability to maintain a majority among the elected representatives in parliament. Federal principles, in contrast, have as their principal goal the territorial dispersion of power that is concerned with dividing and sharing powers and competences between different parts of the polity. The former is most commonly understood to produce unitary, centralised government resulting from simple majoritarian procedures while the latter is predicated upon a federal, decentralised government that can accommodate minorities within changing multiple or compound majorities.

Most of the standard commentaries about the origins of the Canadian federation focus upon four main factors: political stalemate in the province of Canada, the threat from the United States, economic imperatives and the noble vision of the 'national dream'.[34] But the reality, as usual, is more complex. The formation of the federation seems to be relatively uncontroversial. A textual exegesis of the confederation debates emanating from the two colonial conferences at Charlottetown and Quebec in 1864 that culminated in December 1866 in a third conference in London in which the British government participated certainly corroborates the evidence for this conventional interpretation. However, there remains much that is obscure about the origins of the federal idea. Ged Martin acknowledged that the confederation proposal was first broached in 1858 by Alexander Galt in the Cartier–Macdonald administration as a federation of two or three units, or a federation of Canada with the north-west, or as a union of all the provinces, but he also recommended that historians should have 'a wider appreciation of the position of the British North American provinces within a context framed by the United States and shaped by Britain' so that federation should be seen 'not as a solution dictated by the specific circumstances of the mid-1860s, but rather as a long-maturing idea which came to blanket the political discourse of that era because it could be argued … that its time had come'.[35]

The timing of the event seems to evince scholarly consensus among historians and political scientists. There is agreement that the British North America (BNA) Act of 1867 (now called the Constitution Act (1867)) did not emerge suddenly or as a dramatic document. Its roots can be traced back to earlier constitutional documents including the Quebec Act (1774) and the Act of Union (1840) so that it was not the result of any single convulsive event or set of events in the 1860s but was construed rather 'as a vehicle by which more specific aims might be realised'.[36] In particular the creation of a federal Canada owed more to 'a vigorous and confident Upper Canada, which saw it as the best way of escaping from the political log-jam of the existing province, and as an acceptable framework for the prosecution of other projects'. The British role was therefore not one of pressure and command, but 'rather context and support'.[37] In a nutshell, it was the combination of indigenous political forces and interests in the province of Canada, together with the support of the British government, that brought what had been in the air for decades to a successful conclusion. And it should be remembered that stiff opposition to the creation of a federation was immanent in the Maritime provinces of Nova Scotia and New Brunswick while British Columbia and Prince Edward Island did not enter the union until 1871 and 1873 respectively, with Newfoundland waiting for eighty years before it too joined Canada.[38]

The evident complexities and subtleties of the origins and formation of federation in Canada in even so short a survey as this underlines the superficiality of Riker's claims in both 1964 and 1975 that 'for a brief period in the 1860s the United States seemed an immediate threat to Canada, and that was when the Canadian federation was formed'.[39] Detailed historical analysis demonstrates that his conclusions simply do not stand up to close examination. Federation in Canada 'had almost nothing to offer by way of improvement in local defence, and was equally irrelevant to – if not diversionary from – westward expansion'.[40] Consequently we can conclude by refuting Riker's claims that Canada 'exhibits both conditions very clearly'.[41]

Australia

The reasons why Australia became a federation in January 1901 must be set against the background of British imperial relations in the nineteenth century,

colonial constitutional and political evolution, important socio-economic interests and developments and, not least, geographical size. Added to the interaction
of these broad factors, we must include the particular role of political elite leadership, the press, political parties, trade unions, farmers and industrialists.

One of the most significant reasons that made some sort of union in Australia
both feasible and desirable is quite commonplace in their political literature,
namely, the relationship between the size and composition of the population and
the size of the political units. Bryce commented upon this in his *Modern
Democracies* when he observed:

> during its earlier years, when the character of each colony was being
> formed, each lived an isolated life, busied with its own local concerns,
> knowing little about the others, and knowing still less, until telegraphs were
> laid along the ocean bed, of the great world of Europe and America. Not
> only each colony, but the Australian people as a whole, grew up in
> isolation.[42]

This theme of isolation, which is also present in the Canadian psyche, haunts the
literature and became part and parcel of first the colonial political cultures and
later the national, political culture of Australia. The hallmark of Australia's
social, economic, political, constitutional and cultural development finds a
powerful resonance in Geoffrey Blainey's magnificently titled *The Tyranny of
Distance*, and it was acknowledged by J.D.B. Miller, one of Australia's leading
political scientists, to be the dominant characteristic of the federation at its very
inception:

> In 1901 there were six states, each with its own bicameral legislature accus-
> tomed to loud and not very dignified debates on economic development and
> sectional advantage ... There was little sense of common Australian
> achievement, each colony having developed in isolation and possessing
> something of a local patriotism.[43]

The political implications of this sense of isolation, borne of a sparse but homogenous population of British settlers in a distant continent, must be connected to the
slow, piecemeal constitutional and political development of colonial self-government in the mid-nineteenth century. They should also be connected to the
emergence of increasing public expectations of colonial government, especially in
the area of economic development. Jean Holmes and Campbell Sharman have
referred to this as one of the 'historical residues' of Australian federalism:

> Their autonomy was a formal recognition of the importance of the pattern
> of diversity that had developed as a result of the thrust of pastoralists, free
> settlers and emancipists into the interior from the base of the separate parent
> coastal settlements. At the same time, the harshness of the inland environ-
> ment and the uncertainty attached to economic development dependent on

overseas markets led the newly enfranchised citizens to demand that their representative parliaments provide the irrigation schemes, transport systems and port facilities necessary to counter the rigours of Australian rural life. Within the diversity of autonomous colonial governments, a pattern of centralised administration was established to give effect to these electoral demands in the first fifty years of self-government in Australia's separate colonies. It set a pattern to the political arrangements which still prevails.[44]

Holmes and Sharman demonstrate that Australia's geography and economic development, together with its separate, autonomous and self-contained political structures and administrations, effectively paved the way for 'a federal rather than a unitary national political system in the twentieth century'.[45] Similarly Geoffrey Sawer claimed that it was the experience of responsible parliamentary self-government, for periods up to half a century, which instilled in some of the colonies a resolute sense of political integrity resistant to wider political union. Responsible self-government that was introduced in New South Wales, Victoria, South Australia and Tasmania in 1855–56 and which extended to Queensland in 1859–60 and Western Australia in 1890 served both to underline and ultimately to reinforce the sense of state differences that defined Australian diversity. Sawer could therefore claim that in spite of 'close cultural similarity and common interests their people had no desire for complete union'; only 'a federal association was clearly indicated'.[46]

This short summary of the origins of federation in Australia suggests that in his eagerness to confirm his theoretical claims, Riker oversimplified the military condition deemed vital to his analysis. Indeed, if we return to Riker's original 1964 survey of the origins of federations we can easily detect the hesitation that he displayed when looking at the case of Australia: 'although the recognised military need is not so obvious in the case of Australia as in most others, military concerns were the ostensible reason for the federation movement and were probably crucial to its consummation'.[47] His 1975 survey immortalised the hesitation when he remarked that 'there was an external military threat, but it was probably weaker in the Australian case than in others we have so far examined'.[48] Statements such as these were hardly strong grounds for the claims that he had made earlier for a political theory of the origins of federations.

Riker's reading of history was certainly correct to state that the federal idea among the Australasian colonies had existed from about the 1850s, but his interpretation of the 1890 Federal Conference, the first Federal Convention in 1891, the second Federal Convention in 1897 and the subsequent colonial referendums in 1899 that led to the 'Commonwealth of Australia' in 1900 exaggerated the significance of the external military threat. There was some public anxiety about the presence of the Germans in New Guinea, the French in the New Hebrides and the Japanese in Korea in the decade between the mid-1880s and mid-1890s, but the evidence is not strong enough to support Riker's claim that these events were the catalyst that accelerated the movement toward federation. Miller considered 'the sensitivity of many Australians about defence' to be merely 'one contributing influence'; Sawer put it more succinctly: 'though some worries about effective defence contributed to the federating frame of mind; expected economic advantages were more important'.[49] More recently Brian Galligan engaged the debate with an unequivocal swipe at Riker's persistent assertion about the military condition.[50] He believed that Riker seemed to be 'plumping for a simple and challenging hypothesis'; the military threat of Japan and Germany was 'only a partial cause of federation and less significant than economic and nationalistic reasons'.[51]

This short survey of the origins and formation of federation in Australia indicates that while the federal idea was not a popular concept that ever captured the imagination of the mass publics, it was always likely to be the most acceptable option to colonial independence on the one hand and a unitary solution on the other. There was sufficient substantive diversity in the history, political autonomy, economic development, geographical expanse and the tyranny of distance to warrant just such a constitutional response. But as we shall see at the end of the section, this response was no mere replica of the American, Swiss or Canadian federal models; it contained 'indigenous qualities' that are often 'overlooked'.[52]

India

The origins and formation of India as a federation in 1950 are predicated upon several ambiguities. First, the term 'federal' was conspicuous for its studied ambiguity in the constitutional debates of the elected Constituent Assembly that adopted the new constitution. The division of opinion among political elites about the implications of this word reflected a wide spectrum of ideas that ranged from positive views about unity, domestic stability, decentralised government, the protection of minorities and British political influence, on the one hand, to fears and anxieties about civil war, separatist movements, political disorder, and open rioting, anarchy and general chaos, on the other. Second, the chronology of events that wrought the partition of India in August 1947, establishing the two independent Dominions of India and Pakistan, altered both the perceptions of and the pressures for federation. Third, the overwhelming dominance of the Congress Party representing the Hindu population of India predisposed political elites to emphasise a strong federal centre at the expense of the constituent state units. Consequently the Indian Constitution was, in the words of one of the standard commentaries, a document that expressed 'general principles and humanitarian sentiments' that mingled with 'those embodying level-headed practicality and administrative detail'. It was, in short, a product of the idealism and social content of the independence movement combined with 'the Assembly members' experience in government and of the exigencies of the times'.[53]

Most conventional interpretations of the origins of federation in India take their departure point as either 1858 when the Government of India Act made the Governor-General responsible to the Secretary of State for India acting on behalf of the British Crown, or 1861 when the Indian Councils Act was introduced that granted powers to pass legislation on local subjects to Madras and Bombay and subsequently to new provinces that were created. The underlying point is that 'if one word could sum up the post-1858 administration of British India it was "decentralization"'.[54] The milestones along the road to federation included: the India Councils Act (1892), the Government of India Act (1909), the Government of India Act (1919), the Simon Report (1930) and the Government of India Act (1935). One outstanding similarity between India and the federations of Canada and Australia is that it, too, was created by a process of what Bidyut Chakrabarty has called the 'unpackaging of empires', the devolution of imperial power.[55] This process ensured that after the British had left the unitary character of the imperial administrative legacy would simply be taken over by the Indian National Congress so that the federal idea began its life in an independent India with the notion of a strong central authority.

If we identify the main driving forces that led to the creation of the federation in 1950, the following motives loom large in the mainstream literature:

1   The interaction of the British colonial pattern of centralisation and the thinking of the Indian political leadership.
2   The British desire to bring together within a single constitutional system the parts of India under indirect rule – the princely states – and those under direct rule – the British provinces with representative institutions.
3   The British concern about communal rights and communal status between Hindus and Muslims meant that issues of states' rights were generally subordinated to the larger, more dangerous, challenge of seeking to accommodate Muslim anxieties within a united India.
4   The experience of partition in 1947 demonstrated the inherent dangers of separatism to those constructing the constitution and predisposed them to favour centralisation.
5   The goals of economic development and modernisation seemed to require a strong central authority capable of directing the economy.
6   The existence of a highly centralised, hegemonic mass party and the absence of a strong state and regional parties supported a centralised federal formula.[56]

The overriding conclusion to these turbulent events is that 'although no one seemed to seriously question the notion that India should be a federal republic, a variety of factors combined to ensure that the form of federalism would be highly centralised'.[57] Clearly the significance of British imperial influence cannot be underestimated even if all of the elements present in the Government of India Act (1935) were not fully implemented immediately after its introduction because of opposition by the princely states and by the leaders of different political parties. But it is also true that the federal constitution that emerged from the Constituent Assembly was not merely a British template. This would be to ignore the importance of indigenous Indian elites who 'produced new modifications of established ideas about the construction of federal governments and their relations with the governments of their constituent units'. Indeed, the Assembly 'produced a new kind of federalism to meet India's peculiar needs'.[58]

Given the complexity of the circumstances that surrounded the federal bargain during the period 1946–49, it was perfectly possible for Riker to claim, as he did, that his federal pre-requisites – the expansion condition and the military condition – were both evident in the creation of the Indian federation. There is no doubt that in the maelstrom of events and the turbulence of the circumstances characteristic of these years the sense of an internal/external threat existed for both Muslims and Hindus before and after partition, but why this factor should necessarily yield a *federal* state remains unclear. Moreover, the notion that the incorporation of the princely states fulfils Riker's expansion condition is also questionable. His claim that they were forced into the new union, which expanded by conquest rather than federalism, sits uneasily with his overall thesis about willing partners making federal bargains.[59]

Malaysia

The modern federation of Malaysia, formerly Malaya, has origins that can be traced back at least to 1895 when the Federated Malay States (FMS) – Selangor, Perak, Pahang and Negeri Sembilan – was formed by the British colonial administration. This was not a federation in the accepted sense of the term, but the real significance of the Treaty of Federation for our purposes 'lies in the idea of federation implicit in it: an idea which paved the way for the ultimate establishment of true Federal Government in Malaya'.[60] This left five other Malay states – Johore, Kedah, Perlis, Kelantan and Terengganu – under British protection outside the FMS as the Unfederated Malay States (UMS) until the Japanese occupation of Malaya during 1942–45.

The British imposition of the Malayan Union in 1946 comprised the former FMS, UMS and Straits Settlements states of Penang and Malacca and was the first time that all eleven Malay states had been brought together under one administration, but it lacked popular legitimacy and was fiercely opposed by the United Malays National Organisation (UMNO). The strength of the opposition eventually led to its abolition in 1948 and it was replaced in the same year by a new federal constitution.[61] The Federation of Malaya Agreement created the Federation of Malaya with the same states and settlements but this time it formally recognised the identity of the Malay states, strengthened the special status of the Malays *vis-à-vis* the Chinese, Indian and other non-Malays and introduced a highly restrictive citizenship law that actively discriminated against non-Malays. In practical terms, the new federation had strong unitary features with a highly centralised federal government that was designed to foster a sense of national unity. The constitution did not guarantee the autonomy of the constituent states nor did it address the issue of states' rights; its principal purpose was to accommodate communal pressures that reflected the heterogeneity of the population and centred upon issues of citizenship, language, religion, Malay privileges, education and the position of the local Malay rulers.

The entrenched position of the Sultans, rather like the local princes in India, had attracted strong individual allegiance in some states as a result of the long British colonial administration and this ruled out a unitary state. Consequently federation allowed the British to maintain and formally recognise the individuality of the constituent states (and their rulers) which retained those powers traditionally associated with the rulers, such as Malay customs, religion and local land issues, while it simultaneously accommodated the socio-political concerns of the Malays for special treatment in respect of ethnic diversity.[62]

With the creation of the new federation in 1948, one feature characteristic of Malaya is particularly interesting, namely, the notion of non-territorial federation. Styled a 'racial federation' by some commentators, the chief identifying diversities of Malaya were not territorially grouped, thus the Chinese and Malay elements of the population in particular were present in almost equal proportions in some states with the Indian community standing, in a sense, as a balancing force. None of the three largest communities therefore could make territorial claims for autonomous homelands. According to Dikshit, a federal form of government was adopted 'not because of but in spite of "racial" diversity, though the pattern of the real predominance of the two leading communities had created a politico-geographic situation that favoured a federal rather than a unitary organization of the state'. The communal distribution of the population meant that a federal rather than a unitary state structure would allow the Malay population in the eastern Malay states to resist the economic threat of Chinese competition that had come to dominate the western states. In a nutshell, the interaction of communal, territorial and economic diversities produced a unique set of circumstances that allowed federation to rescue the Malays from the threat of Chinese economic dominance.[63]

Watts described the Federation of Malaya as 'a hybrid somewhere between unitary and federal government' and he noted three key factors that served to reinforce the progressive increase of central authority during its nine-year existence: first, the communist threat promoted centralised administration; second, the experience of elected representation and self-government converted the central institutions into an instrument of Malay nationalism; and, finally, the political and governmental hegemony of UMNO under the leadership of Tunku Abdul Rahman ensured central influence in state politics.[64] When independence for Malaya arrived in 1957 the opportunity had also arrived to overhaul the federal system and this was carried out in a way that effectively increased the legislative authority of the constituent states while simultaneously reducing substantially their executive responsibilities. The Independent Constitutional Commission (known as the Reid Commission after its chairman, Lord Reid), on which no Malays were represented, was charged to establish a strong central government giving the constituent units a measure of autonomy, to safeguard the position of the Malay rulers, to create a constitutional head of state chosen from among the Malay rulers, to confirm a common nationality for the whole of the federation, and to safeguard the special position of the Malays and the legitimate interests of other communities. The Reid Commission Report that contained the draft federal constitution for an independent Malaya built upon the Federation of Malaya Agreement of 1948 and was clearly influenced by a combination of the Indian, British and American Constitutions.[65]

In the post-war march towards federation, Singapore had been deliberately omitted from successive schemes of all-Malayan union largely because the inclusion of its predominantly Chinese population would have relegated the Malays to a minority and both its economic interests and political leadership were sources of concern to the Malays. However, the intensified threat of a communist takeover there convinced the Malayan leadership to respond to the overtures of the Singapore premier, Lee Kuan Yew, to join the federation. At the same time negotiations began for the inclusion of the British Borneo territories in a new federal Malaysia in order principally to provide a counterweight against the increased Chinese strength consequent upon the inclusion of Singapore. When the negotiations came to fruition, after elections in the two larger Borneo territories of Sarawak and Sabah (North Borneo), Singapore, Sabah and Sarawak (the Sultan of Brunei decided against accession) joined to the states of Malaya to form the wider Federation of Malaysia in September 1963. Watts claimed that although the 1957 federal constitution was retained in form, the changes made to it by the Malaysia Act (1963) were in practice 'so substantial as to create a new federal structure', but the integrity of the new federation did not survive more than two years as the Singapore Chinese and the mainland Malays quickly became embroiled in a power struggle that led ultimately to the expulsion of Singapore from the federation in 1965.[66]

In summary, the origins and significance of the federal idea for, first, Malaya and, second, Malaysia stretch back at least to 1895 while the vision of a federal union that would include Singapore and the three Borneo territories had also been foreshadowed by early post-war events and circumstances both in British colonial relations and locally in south-east Asia. Riker claimed that his military condition had been present 'owing to the existence of communist guerrillas, supported from China', whereas the expansion condition 'was present owing to the necessity of reconciling the previously federated states'. Moreover, the existence of Indonesian hostility and reluctance on the part of Singapore and the Borneo states to accept Malayan domination was tantamount to a set of circumstances that fulfilled 'both conditions of the hypothesis'. Indeed, apart from 'habit and provincial loyalties', Riker argued that it was 'fear of Chinese domination' and the 'even greater fear of Indonesia' that demonstrated the applicability of his bargaining conditions.[67]

In hindsight there is no doubt that both the perception and the reality of an internal and an external threat characterised the formation of the federations in 1948, 1957 and 1963. This is not in dispute. What remains contestable, however, is the sort of reductionism that led Riker to oversimplify what was a much more complex set of circumstances than his hypothesis would admit. For example, his trite observations overlooked the crucial context of Singapore's underlying motive for federation. Lee Kuan Yew's reasons for entering the new federation of Malaysia in 1963 were strategic. With a population that was 80 per cent Chinese,

Singapore's membership of Malaysia could certainly not harm its singular interests while it served ultimately as a stepping stone to complete independence in
1965 – an independence, it should be noted, that occurred from Malaysia rather
than the much more hazardous route from former British colonial status. In retrospect, Lee Luan Yew had good strategic reasons for both of these constitutional
decisions in 1963 and 1965. Furthermore, Riker's suggestion that the expulsion of
Singapore in 1965 can be explained by recognising that Indonesia was 'not as
dangerous as it seemed' is entirely unconvincing.[68] Dikshit confirmed that 'any
military threats' to Singapore's existence were 'secondary to the economic considerations which reigned supreme in the minds of its leaders'.[69]

Equally, the role of Brunei was glossed over by Riker in his sketch outline.
Brunei was selectively omitted presumably because it did not join Malaysia
while both Sabah and Sarawak did, but just as the economic significance of
Brunei's rich oil revenues could be used as a reason for its decision to stay
outside the union, so the importance of economic factors should not be ignored
when explaining why Sabah and Sarawak took the opposite view. Dikshit
claimed that while security concerns were the main motive in the Malayan
move towards Malaysia, 'in the case of the Borneo territories economic motives
were equally, if not more, significant'. Indeed, 'the economic considerations
were ... the primary factor behind the overwhelming support for the Federation
proposal in the September 1961 referendum in Sabah and Sarawak.[70]

In conclusion, then, we can confirm that in the case of Malaysia 'diplomatic
and strategic considerations were openly paramount' in the motives for enlarging
and adapting a federal union that already existed.[71] Riker conceded the criticisms of Birch and revised his military condition to include both internal and
external threats that were explicit in the Malaysian case study, but in the light of
Lee Kuan Yew's political strategy in Singapore his much-vaunted expansion
condition also required some attention.[72]

Austria

Federal forms of social and political organisation in Austria can be traced back
to the Holy Roman Empire, the Habsburg Empire and later Austria-Hungary
(the Dual Monarchy) in the wake of the *Ausgleich* formed in 1867. The policy of
'divide and rule' orchestrated by the Austrians and the Magyars allowed them to
share imperial power until the end of the First World War that occasioned the
collapse of the empire. In 1918, as the non-German nationalities broke away to
form independent states, Austria was effectively marooned as a rump state.
Initially a unitary state under the name *Deutschosterreich* was set up in the German
parts of the old empire but the central government in Vienna was unable to
establish unchallenged authority over the regional governments of the crown
lands of the former Austrian monarchy in Vorarlberg, Salzburg, Upper Austria,
Lower Austria, Styria, Tyrol, Carinthia and Burgenland. The disappearance of
the central imperial authority had left a post-war political vacuum and most of
these crown lands had resorted to the provincial charters introduced by the

Landesordnungen of 1861. Between 1918 and 1920, when the federal constitution of the First Republic was introduced, a tangled skein of events and circumstances led to these former imperial lands effectively reinventing themselves as new *lander* in the Austrian federation.

The complexity of events and circumstances in the early post-war years derived from the strains and tensions surrounding regional diversities based upon socio-economic and cultural differences that had enormous political and constitutional significance. Divisions between industry and agriculture, between city (Vienna) and rural societies and between Catholic conservatism and the socialist-dominated capital (Vienna) produced a constellation of cleavage patterns that made it 'obvious that, if Austria was to exist at all as an independent State, the form of her constitution must be pronouncedly federal'.[73] In such circumstances it was hardly surprising that post-war Austria became a veritable battleground between socialist and Christian-social camps (*Lager*) struggling to secure control of the new state. The formation of a federation in Austria, then, was forged from extremely unpromising circumstances that wrought an antagonistic compromise. The two main *Lager* parties were 'the architects of the constitution of the First Republic', but at its very inception the federation lacked democratic legitimacy, a situation exacerbated by the lack of an Austrian national identity and large question marks placed over its economic viability.[74] Consequently the creation of what on the surface was a nationally homogenous federal state only imperfectly concealed deep fissures about how the political system should be structured. In practice the federal political system was first reformed to strengthen executive power in 1929 and then dismantled in 1934 after a short civil war that brought Dolfuss to power at the head of an authoritarian clerical regime. He set up a corporatist state structure known as the *Standestaat* and this was itself replaced in 1938 by the *Anschluss* with Nazi Germany that reduced Austria to a constituent unit of the Third Reich as the province of *Ostmark*.

At the end of the Second World War in 1945 the chief characteristic of Austria's reconstruction was constitutional and political continuity. Indeed, the establishment of the Second Republic was largely undertaken by the same political parties that had created its unfortunate predecessor. The Allied powers allowed the 1920 constitution to be reinstated along with the extensive amendments that had been introduced in 1929 and the Austrian *lander* were recreated along their 1938 borders. Once its occupation status ceased in 1955 and the Soviet Union and Allied forces withdrew, Austria regained its full state sovereignty. The Second Republic benefited from a series of significant changes to the Austrian political environment that gave it a much better chance of survival than its abortive forerunner. First, it had emerged from a decade of occupation by foreign powers, an experience that in itself served to unite Austrians while it also confirmed the federation's territorial boundaries and its distinct sense of separateness from post-war West Germany. Second, there was a significant change in the parties' ideologies, their cooperative spirit and their sense of commitment to democratic government. In short, there was 'a much greater degree of commitment to the restored republican system than had been the case in 1918'.[75] The new Austrian federation became a neutral country delicately poised between the East and the West.

Riker's explanation of the origins and formation of 'centralized federalism' in Austria traces it back to the 1860s, claiming that the creation of the Dual Monarchy vindicated his two conditions – the military condition and the expansion condition. Indeed, he reinforced this claim for the period 1918–20 when he added that 'the military-diplomatic reason for the federal bargain' among the quasi-independent provinces of Austria was 'abundantly clear'. Turning to the Second Republic, Riker argued that it, too, reflected 'something of the two conditions in a somewhat attenuated form'. Behind the federal bargain there always stood 'the fact of *Anschluss*, the ever-present fear of an aggressive Germany'.[76]

Dikshit challenged this interpretation in 1975 when he declared that 'in view of the trend of Austrian politics between 1918 and 1945' the German threat did 'not seem convincing'.[77] After all, even before the First Republic was instituted 'there was virtually unanimous agreement between the parties that Austria should join the German Reich'.[78] Dikshit's observations have been confirmed in the mainstream literature on Austrian political history and his conclusion that 'attributing the post-1945 federal structure of Austria to the fear of Germany would appear contrary to the facts of the case' is correct.[79] Once again we can confirm that Riker's insistence on the essentially military origins of federation appears 'excessive'.[80]

Germany

Rather like Austria, federal ideas and forms in Germany can be traced back to the Holy Roman Empire and can be found in the German Bund (1815–66) and in what in 1871 was the 'imperial federation' of Prussia and the surrounding German principalities that formed the German Empire until 1918. Many commentators on Germany also acknowledge the democratic federal credentials of the Weimar Republic (1919–33) as a federal precursor to the Federal Republic of West Germany constructed in 1949.

The main stumbling block to placating the consistent sceptics of Germany's federal tradition has been the weakness – or complete absence – of liberal democratic roots. Dikshit noted that federal practices 'hardly ever existed in the country till the victorious Allies virtually "imposed" it in 1949'.[81] Riker, too, joined the mass ranks of political scientists and historians who simplified the post-war events and circumstances of 1945–49 by asserting that constitution-making in Germany was 'dominated by American occupation forces who wished to impose federalism both as an alternative to the Morgenthau Plan of Balkanizing Germany and as an expression of their provincial conviction that federalism was a "good thing"'.[82] In fairness, Riker did concede that the federal nature of *Das Grundgesetz* (the Basic Law) owed much to 'a deeper political circumstance: the hope and expectation of reuniting West and East Germany'.[83] Nevertheless, it remains the case that too many interpretations of the formation of the *Bundesrepublik* consistently underestimate the indigenous contribution of German political elites to the construction of the federation. It is perfectly true that it was fashioned under the auspices of Allied occupation, with all of the military and political pressures that that entailed, but this should not be allowed either to overlook or obscure the peculiarly German impress upon what emerged in 1948–49. Nevil Johnson emphasised this point when he remarked that although the Allies 'provided instructions', these were 'only of the most general nature'.[84]

In the mainstream historical literature the chronology of events is clear. What later became West Germany was already divided up into eleven states based upon the western Allied zones of control so that 'the process was begun gradually from the lower to the upper levels'.[85] Although in theory political continuity was to be the guiding principle, so that the former *lander* would be reconstituted wherever possible, in practice there was plenty of scope for adding or subtracting to territorial boundaries that had to conform to zonal limits or other integrative pressures. The result was something of a hotchpotch of eleven constituent units, varying enormously in size and historical lineage, that eventually came to form the basis of the new federation. Consequently the *lander* of Hamburg, Bremen and Bavaria were familiar to the German federal tradition, while North Rhine–Westphalia, Baden–Württemberg and Rhineland–Palatinate were artificial constructs that ably illustrated the surgical propensities of the Allied forces.

The key point concerning the post-war federal reconstruction of West Germany is that once the plan for creating a united West Germany was accepted, the division of the area into eleven states was already an established fact. Dikshit's emphasis upon the indigenous contribution of the German elites is worth stating at length:

> The Parliamentary Council that assembled to draft the Constitution consisted of leaders and delegates from the existing eleven states that were by now enjoying virtual self-government. This in itself made a federal political organization of the State almost imperative, for the very existence of the Lander as organic political units before the rise of the united nation helped to create vested interests among the regional leaders, most of whom could not hope to have much say at the national level.[86]

What, then, are we to make of Riker's claim that federation in West Germany was in essence 'a proposed bargain in the face of the Soviet military threat'?[87] Dikshit's response was to describe Riker's military hypothesis as 'excessive at least in the case of the West German example' and in the light of 'the demilitarized and helpless state of Germany' he construed the claim to be 'overstated'.[88] In emphasising the military hegemony of the Allied occupation force, and especially the American military and political reality, in western Europe, Riker had unwittingly undermined his own case because their very presence would have 'taken much force out of this motivation'.[89] This objection to Riker's short defence of the federal bargain in West Germany must have reached him because he responded, albeit briefly, to Dikshit's criticisms in his 1975 survey of the subject. In this he retorted, rather waspishly, that since the necessary conditions were satisfied (by reason of the Soviet threat) 'there is no point to arguing about degrees of relevance of various influences'. For Riker, 'the universality of the conditions is proved by their satisfaction in this case, even though they may not be historically the most "important" force'.[90]

There is a clear sense of retreat in Riker's defence. We must remember that he had made great claims for his 'federal bargain' and that his military and expansion conditions – '*always* present in the federal bargain' – constituted the bedrock of his 'hypothesis of necessity'.[91] But the German case study reveals once again the highly contested nature of his historical interpretation and his need to be rescued by a resort to arbitrariness.

A theory of circumstantial causation

This chapter has reassessed and reappraised Riker's putative political theory of federalism. In reality it was not a political theory at all, but an analytical framework based upon a dual hypothesis about the primary purpose of federations. It presaged a fully developed theory of the origins and formation of federations that was never constructed. But it is important to remind ourselves of the immensity of the task that Riker set himself. He did not claim that his hypothesis was a *sufficient* condition for the creation of federation since he did not have enough information to prove sufficiency, but he did claim that it was a *necessary* condition for federal states. Our survey, however, has shown that even this more modest claim, while not completely unfounded, has very little theoretical significance. Indeed, we have demonstrated that the hypothesis of the military and expansion conditions necessary to the origins and formation of federations is at best exaggerated and at worst erroneous. To claim that both military and expansion predispositions are *always* present in the federal bargain is both crass and trivial. As we have discussed above, it tells us very little about the origins and formation of federations and does not enable us to make any precise distinctions between federal and non-federal unions.

Despite the shortcomings of Riker's analytical framework, his overall contribution to the intellectual debate about federation remains significant in the mainstream Anglo-American literature and his place in the pantheon of scholars of federalism is assured. But we have paid a price for the resilience of the Rikerian legacy regarding federalism in at least one important respect. His flawed analysis of the origins and formation of federations has served to perpetuate a misunderstanding of the nature, meaning and significance of this particular kind of state. Scholars who have followed in his footsteps have invariably accepted the basic assumptions and arguments upon which his work is founded with an equanimity that has bordered upon complacency. Consequently much of our understanding of why and how federations are formed has been the result of a benign neglect. Even today, forty years after his original work on federalism was first published, some scholars continue to build upon a conceptual foundation that is fundamentally unsafe. For example, David McKay has recently referred to the Rikerian perspective on the creation of federation as 'the most analytically powerful of those theories devoted to the subject'.[92] Similarly Alfred Stepan, whose recent reference to 'some key analytic, historical, normative and policy dimensions' that are either 'not found, or are misleading, in the Rikerian framework', nonetheless insists that Riker's argument for the USA and Switzerland remains 'powerful'.[93]

Our survey suggests that enough evidence has now been gathered to underline the deficiencies inherent in the Rikerian approach to understanding the origins and formation of federation as an analytically distinct form of state. What I propose here is a theory of circumstantial causation that takes into account a whole host of internal and external factors that have contributed to the creation of federation, taking into account important historical changes and the huge variations that have characterised the origins and formation of different federations. The construction of this theoretical framework is built upon the following four assumptions:

1   That federation as a conceptual and analytical category is founded upon the notion of a liberal democratic constitutional state.
2   That the *origins* of federation must be distinguished from the *formation* of federation.
3   That both the origins and formation of federation are predicated upon two distinct historical processes that constitute different points of departure, namely, aggregation and/or disaggregation, devolution and decentralisation.
4   That we must distinguish between different democratic credentials for the origins or 'founding moments' of those federations that were formed in the late eighteenth, nineteenth and early twentieth centuries and those created since the end of the Second World War.

Let us explore briefly the implications of these four assumptions. The first assumption enables us usefully to omit non-democratic, authoritarian, military states that do not facilitate authentic local/regional autonomy with constitutional guarantees for the constituent units of federations. This allows us effectively to rule out the old Soviet Union and Argentina, Brazil and Nigeria when they suffered intermittent periods of military government. Such coercive unions certainly exhibited federalism but they were not real federations. Federations are voluntary unions based firmly upon liberal democratic notions of constitutional government.

Second, the distinction between the *origins* and the *formation* of federation is important for reasons of historical accuracy, conceptual clarity and comparative analysis. It assists us towards a much clearer understanding of the nature, meaning and significance of federation. Third, the distinction between two historical processes in the origins and formation of federation helps us both to understand the different purposes of federation in different contexts and to have a more subtle appreciation of their subsequent evolution. Finally, it is important for us to recognise the nature and impact of the different kinds of contemporary pressures that impinge upon federations that are emergent (for example, the European Union) or have only emerged relatively recently (for example, Belgium) compared to the challenges that confronted those federations established during the years between 1789 and 1945. We cannot utilise the same Rikerian criteria that have been applied to the creation of the USA (1789), Switzerland (1848), Canada (1867), Australia (1901) and Austria (1920) in order to explain the Belgian, Spanish and EU cases. Indeed, we have already revealed the shortcomings of Riker's model in the cases of West Germany (1949), India (1950) and Malaysia (1963).

What I propose here, then, is a set of historical factors that pertain in various ways to every modern federation in its origins and formation and that contain sufficient scope and flexibility to facilitate, in each case study, a different hierarchy of causes. In some cases Riker's military and expansion conditions will be highly pertinent and will perhaps rank as the two overriding motives for union among others (as in the USA), while in other cases they will be present but either clearly subordinated or ranked only equal in significance to rival motives (as in Australia, West Germany and India). There is plenty of research still to be done in this area of comparative federal studies and it would assist enormously toward a better understanding of how and why federations are formed.

In some ways this proposal echoes the approach taken by Ronald Watts forty years ago. We have already referred in Chapter 1 to his magisterial *New Federations: Experiments in the Commonwealth* in which he identified a series of 'motives for union' and concluded that most of them were 'present to some degree' in each case but that the 'relative importance of different factors has varied with each federation'.[94] For our purposes, the point is that Watts was not reductionist: he did not try to reduce and refine his analysis to two overriding variables that Riker called the military and the expansion conditions. Consequently Watts' comparative survey was quite prescient in its formal acknowledgement of the complex realities involved even if its empirical scope was narrower than that of Riker and its theoretical concerns much less ambitious. It is, however, prudent for us to recognise the enduring value of previous scholarship in this area and to present a new synthesis of earlier major contributions that looked at the origins and formation of federation.

Mindful of these earlier comparative excursions, a tentative start might be made here by acknowledging what can broadly be alluded to as two principal factors, namely, perceived common interests and real or imagined external and/or internal threats. Here I shall take into account the received wisdom of the earlier standard commentaries on this subject: Wheare (1946), Deutsch (1957), Riker (1964), Birch (1966) and Watts (1966). The combination of these works might produce a list of constitutive elements of these two broad categories that could be formulated in the following way:

Common Interests	*External and/or Internal Threats*
a) Shared political values.	a) A sense of military insecurity
b) Expectations of stronger economic	real or imagined.
ties and associated benefits.	b) A sense of economic insecurity
c) A multiplicity of ranges of communica-	real or imagined.
tions and transactions.	c) A sense of cultural insecurity
d) The desire for political independence.	real or imagined.
e) Prior political association.	d) A perceived threat to the
f) Strategic (territorial) considerations.	stability of the existing political
g) Geographical proximity.	order.
h) Common cultural-ideological factors, such as nationalism, religion and inherited traditions and customs.	
i) Political leadership and a broadening of the political elite.	
j) Similarity of social and political institutions.	
k) The appeal of federal models.	
l) The culmination of historical processes that were founded upon prior political commitments.	

This list of factors that spans both common interests and external and/or internal threats furnishes the basis for the accommodation of every modern federation since 1789 and allows us to take account of the relative importance of different factors that have varied with each federation, as Watts put it. In this schema of circumstantial causation it is possible effectively to accommodate both Belgium and the EU as well as the more familiar federal case studies. In short, it is possible to establish a hierarchy of causes for each federation examined so that both historical specificity and analytical complexity are acknowledged. We can also observe that the Rikerian criteria have been suitably accommodated in this framework but that their conceptual validity has been appropriately adjusted.

Conclusion

In this chapter we have explored the origins and formation of federation as a distinct form of state. In pursuit of conceptual and theoretical clarity, we have investigated the framework of analysis established by William Riker and found it wanting in several important respects, not least the assumptions upon which it was based. Moreover, the historical analyses of Riker's case studies were found to be fundamentally flawed and his reductionist propositions were exposed as both trivial and crass. Clearly it is not sufficient simply to state, as Riker did, that historically two principal factors were *always* present in the federal bargain and to infer from this that they therefore constitute a sound theoretical basis of explanation for the origins and formation of federation. Closer historical analysis of our case studies has demonstrated that a complex amalgam of socio-economic, historical and political variables were also present at the creation. As McKay has correctly stated, 'where Riker can be faulted is in the quality of his empirical investigations'.[95] This conclusion, then, serves both as a plea for further research into circumstantial causation and as an intention to recast the continuing theoretical debate about federalism and federation in a new light in order the better to accommodate that most difficult of tasks, namely, 'change and development' in federal studies.

It is now time to move away from our concerns with the genesis of federations – the historical process of state-building – and look instead at another problem in comparative federal studies, namely, the question of national integration or nation-building. This will enable us to take another step in our overall quest to explain the contemporary nature and meaning of federalism and federation.

4 Federalism, nationalism and the national state

Legitimacy and the problem of national identity

Introduction

Until recently the question of nationalism has not been the subject of detailed investigation in the mainstream literature on federalism and federation. Where it has appeared in this literature, it has usually been referred to either as the by-product of a related subject or as a case study of a particular federation. Consequently genuine comparative surveys are few and far between.[1]

In this chapter I want to reaffirm the conceptual distinction between federalism and federation in order principally to locate nationalism in the former category while situating the national state in the latter one. This means that for the purposes of this chapter I shall construe nationalism as the federalism – the cultural-ideological component – in federation. Federalism, we are reminded, is the animating force of federation and it can take many different forms: historical, intellectual, cultural-ideological, socio-economic, territorial and non-territorial, philosophical and legal. It is, in essence, a multidimensional concept. Nationalism is itself a complex phenomenon and it is important that our survey not only recognises its inherent complexities, but that it is also sensitive to its many different manifestations in different federations. Context is therefore the defining feature of nationalism because it alone takes account of historical specificity above and beyond the intellectual generalities that characterise the subject. Terms such as 'nation', 'nationalism', 'nationality' and 'national identity' are in practice part of a highly charged political discourse and have to be handled with extreme care.

These preliminary cautions having been stated, I do not wish to immerse myself in the huge scholarly literature that exists on the subject of nationalism. This is not my purpose. Instead I want to explore the relationship between federalism as nationalism and federation as the national state. Since we still live in a world of states and most of those states are commonly referred to as *nation states* in the sense that the state has been *nationalised* (referring politically to a single people), I prefer to use Anthony Smith's terminology that refers to the historical processes of state-building and national integration so that we can utilise the term 'national state'.[2] This is not meant to imply the assimilation of all distinct cultures and identities into a single cultural homogeneity. There is no such thing

as a nation state. Rather it construes the national state as a kind of constitutional, political and legal framework, part of whose purpose is to shelter these
diversities from the pressures of cultural standardisation, providing them, via the
politics of accommodation, with discrete, autonomous policy spaces in which to
determine themselves. Accordingly, this broad umbrella term implies that we can
subsume within it a range of different meanings. For example, the term 'nation'
sits uneasily in Canada, Switzerland and Belgium where it is commonly understood to be a *political nationality*, that is, a broad instrumental term used to
describe what is essentially a political rather than a cultural identity.

Consequently these are multinational and/or multicultural federations that
individually must become, in the words of the Canadian historian W.L.
Morton, 'a community of political allegiance alone'.[3] They cannot afford to
allow their multiple identities and multiple allegiances – their distinct federalisms – to fragment and polarise around narrow, visceral, cultural-ideological
loyalties whose effect would be fissiparous. This would create enormous constitutional and political instability and could even result in the break-up of
federations via secession. Instead, as essentially political communities, these
federations have been compelled to ensure that claims of citizenship are fundamentally compatible with other sub-state loyalties, be they religious, linguistic,
nationalist or territorial.

These considerations mean that the principal focus of this chapter will be
multinational federations in comparative perspective. It is important in a book
like this for us to understand and appreciate more clearly than we do how far
sub-state nationalism (as federalism) can be accommodated successfully in federation. What sorts of stresses, strains and tensions exist; how are they expressed;
and what forms of representation are utilised to accommodate them? Before we
explore this relationship, however, it is also important for our purposes to look at
the way that nation, nationality and nationalism have traditionally been
construed in the mainstream literature and we will begin by providing a very
brief overview of the extant literature derived in part from Chapter 1.

Federalism, federation and nationalism

Among the major contributions to our conceptual and methodological review of
federalism and federation in the nineteenth century, one of the most memorable
statements was Edward Freeman's famous description of federation as 'the most
finished and the most artificial production of political ingenuity'.[4] This reference
to the 'artificiality' of federations was what James Bryce called 'the sentiment of
nationality' in such states, derived from an appreciation of the complex coexistence of both 'aggregative and segregative' forces that corresponded to the
interaction of centripetal and centrifugal pressures in the state.[5] In other words,
the prospects of success for any federation rested upon a kind of balance or
equilibrium between two broad sets of opposing forces, one comprising 'long-
established particularity' and the other oriented towards 'nation-statehood'.[6]
Federation was a 'political contrivance' designed to create a 'legal habit in the

mind of the nation'; it was a plan or device that was in some sense an improvisation, something that had the quality of expediency about it.[7] Following this line of reasoning, then, federations were conscious rational attempts or experiments designed to create and foster a sense of belonging to what, at least initially, was an artificial political community – a political contrivance – with an overarching political authority that encompassed, institutionalised, accommodated and gave official recognition to those identities that were politically salient.

One conceptual and theoretical implication of this predicament is that not all federations have become national states in the sense of establishing a relative cultural homogeneity like the nations of Australia, Austria and Germany. Clearly, if all federations began their lives as political contrivances, then at least in respect of nationhood and national identity, some federations are more political contrivances than others. The presumption here is that the historical processes of state-building and national integration would foster and cultivate loyalties that would lead eventually to a new identity formation, namely, the national state. The key question was whether the new (artificial) national identity would evolve *alongside* those national identities that already existed at the formation of the federation or whether it would effectively suffocate and ultimately assimilate them via a combination of malicious indifference, wilful neglect or genuine absent-mindedness. Furthermore, in circumstances in which a national majority successfully – even if subconsciously – equated *itself* with the overarching federal political nationality, the effect would be to displace and marginalise distinct minority nationalisms. In Canada, for example, the historical propensity for some anglophone Canadians to regard English-speaking Canada as synonymous with Canadian national identity – with being Canadian – effectively rendered Quebecois invisible. And it is important to remember that there need be no deliberate concerted conspiracy by the national majority to achieve this; mere neglect in policy or principle is sufficient to undermine and enfeeble minority nationalisms.

When we consider the problem of minority nationalism in the context of federalism and federation it is abundantly clear that we are really dealing with the relationship between a set of concerns that revolve around competing identities related to national loyalties and nationhood and a cluster of issues linked to the prerequisites of liberal democracy. It is also clear that what has emerged from contemporary studies of this intriguing but inherently complex and difficult relationship has been a lively scholarly debate centred upon normative empirical theory. Put simply, the kernel of the conceptual and theoretical problem is how far questions of national identity, nationhood, nationality, patriotism and the repercussions of national, ethnic or cultural belonging, as well as the feasibility of multiculturalism, are compatible with liberal political values.[8] Moreover, it is to be expected that the theoretical debate about particularistic attachments, such as nationalism, and their relationship to the liberal democratic state should entail a search for historical precedents and traditions of thought. As Georgios Varouxakis has recently put it, there has been a marked tendency for political theorists to 'invoke a long pedigree for their respective prescriptions' leading to 'a compulsion to endow their theories and recommendations concerning the appropriate attitude towards nationhood with a 'liberal descent' and in consequence many of them 'feel obliged to turn to nineteenth century debates on nationality'.[9]

In this brief section on federalism, federation and nationalism, the figure of John Stuart Mill looms much larger than either Freeman or Bryce in the contemporary debate that seeks to reconcile 'some kind of national attachment to liberal values'.[10] In particular, Mill's *Considerations on Representative Government*, with its two separate essays respectively entitled 'Of Nationality, as Connected with Representative Government' and 'Of Federal Representative Governments', remains 'the starting point of relevant discussions today'.[11] It will be recalled that we have already included Mill in our conceptual and methodological review in Chapter 1 where we noted that his principal contribution to federal studies included the preconditions of federation and the significance of representation in federal states, as well as some remarks about the 'common sympathies' of 'race, language, religion, and, above all, of political institutions'.[12] On first glance, it might appear that Mill had a one-eyed view of federalism that construed 'common sympathies' to mean a national federation with a single nationality suggesting cultural homogeneity, but closer analysis indicates that he actually acknowledged both the desirability and feasibility of multinational and/or multicultural federations. His reference to the strength of religious differences in Switzerland confirms this, but so do the following statements:

> The question then is, whether the different parts of the nation require to be governed in a way so essentially different that it is not probable the same Legislature, and the same ministry or administrative body, will give satisfaction to them all. ... there needs seldom be any difficulty in not only preserving these diversities, but giving them the guarantee of a constitutional provision against any attempt at assimilation, except by the voluntary act of those who would be affected by that change.[13]

Without wishing to engage the current theoretical debate about Mill's various pronouncements on nationality and their competing interpretations, it is clear from these statements that there was a place in mid-nineteenth-century English liberal thought for the reconciliation of liberalism and nationalism.[14] And this is certainly evident in the writings of recent contributors to the debate, such as Yael Tamir and David Miller.[15] It was also evident in the famous essay by Lord Acton entitled 'Nationality', first published in the *Home and Foreign Review* in July 1862, in which he argued that 'liberty provokes diversity, and diversity preserves liberty by supplying the means of organisation'.[16] Acton's political analysis of 'the theory of nationality' took as its fulcrum the 'spirit of English liberty' and developed what was essentially an early pluralist claim for the balancing of 'interests, multiplying associations, and giving to the subject the restraint and support of a combined opinion'.[17] This echoed the classic liberal position of providing bulwarks against the excessive power of the state that 'a union of nations' and a 'community which is the vastest' could conceivably furnish.[18] Consequently, his intellectual and practical predispositions were the same: 'the coexistence of several nations under the same state is a test, as well as the best security of its freedom'.[19] This critique of the sort of national unity espoused by the modern liberalism of the mid-nineteenth century led Acton to eulogise 'the purely political nationality of Switzerland' whose 'political capacity' and self-government guaranteed its political liberty. Acton's relevance to our survey of nationalism as the federalism in federation can perhaps best be conveyed in the following way:

> A state which is incompetent to satisfy different races condemns itself; a state which labours to neutralise, to absorb, or to expel them, destroys its own vitality; a state which does not include them is destitute of the chief basis of self-government. The theory of nationality, therefore, is a retrograde step in history.[20]

These excerpts from Acton's essay underline his belief in the futility of the idea that every nation should, by virtue of its self-definition, have its own independent state, but it also enables us to understand why scholars conventionally have portrayed Mill and Acton as representing two opposing schools of thought on nationality. Our short survey of their views on nationalism and multinationalism, however, suggests that they were not that far apart. Indeed, Varouxakis has argued that 'they were much closer to each other' than existing scholarship would have us believe.[21]

If we follow the line of thinking evident in the works of Freeman, Bryce, Mill and Acton referred to above we can easily appreciate how far the federations of Canada, Belgium and Switzerland are national states only in the sense that they are communities of political allegiance. They are not nation-states. And this applies also to some other contemporary federations, such as India and Malaysia. As Tamir has remarked, the conventional wisdom is that modern nation-states 'have attempted to blur the fact that they are composed of different national groups by fostering a liberal-democratic definition of the nation'. This has allowed them to claim that 'all those who inhabit a particular territory and live under the rule of the same government are members of the same nation' when in fact historical experience has 'time and again refuted the claim that citizenship and membership in a nation are one and the same'. 'No amount of conceptual manipulation', she has observed, 'could do away with the problems aroused by the presence of minorities'.[22] One significant implication of this reasoning is that we must separate the nation from the state. It is no longer acceptable for citizenship to be an instrument of cultural-ideological uniformity and standardisation. Claims of citizenship in modern welfare states entailed identification with the state and its central institutions, but today the suggestion that it should also involve identification with 'the culture of the ruling nation' is clearly antediluvian.[23]

Tamir's argument that, while it would be difficult in practical terms for every nation to have its own state, 'all nations are entitled to a public sphere in which they constitute the majority' brings us back to the purpose of this chapter.[24] Nationalism as the federalism in federation raises questions about the origins and formation of federations as well as issues concerning their subsequent evolution and continuing legitimacy. If the principal *raison d'être* of a federation is its continuing capacity to protect, promote and preserve one or more sub-state nationalisms, as it is in Canada and Belgium, and in a similar vein in India and Malaysia, then its primary purpose will be subject to persistent scrutiny. The federal government, as the agent of the federal state and keeper of its federal conscience, will always be the object of what Acton might have called a 'healthy scepticism' that entails endless complaint and criticism in the pursuit of accountability from its constituent units or partners. In this respect, federations are perennially frustrating polities. This is precisely because federal government is always, in Daniel Elazar's memorable words, 'a continuing seminar in governance'.[25]

Adjustment and adaptation in the evolution of federations means that, periodically, new bargains have to be negotiated which sometimes involve changes to territorial boundaries, as they did in 1978 in Switzerland with the creation of the Jura canton and in 2000 in India on the occasion of the formal constitutional recognition of the three brand new states, Chhattisgarh, Uttaranchal and Jharkhand, which emerged from the truncation of Uttar Pradesh. We should also note the elevation in 1999 of Inuit self-government with the creation of Nunavut – the new territorial government in the eastern Arctic – in Canada that compels us to revise and reassess the federation as bilingual, multicultural and multinational.[26] These three cases are classic examples of territorial reorganisation in established federations in pursuit of the formal political recognition of communal identities. They are contemporary examples of Tamir's important emphasis upon the need for public spheres where national minorities can express themselves, for some specific purposes, as majorities. As we shall see, this is precisely what makes federation, in certain circumstances, an appropriate structural, institutional and procedural response as a particular kind of state. Let us turn now to look in more detail at the main focus of this chapter.

Multinational federations in comparative perspective

The question that is central to our concerns in this chapter can be clearly stated: how far can federations successfully reconcile competing national visions and aspirations? Furthermore, what lessons can be learned from particular case studies?

Recently Will Kymlicka has made the following series of claims:

> On any reasonable criteria, democratic federations have been surprisingly successful in accommodating minority nationalisms. ... democratic multi-nation federations have succeeded in taming the force of nationalism. ... It is difficult to imagine any other political system that can make the same claim. ... [W]e are currently witnessing yet another burst of interest in federalism in multination countries.[27]

This optimistic outlook on the success of federations in furnishing the basis for political order, stability and legitimacy in the potentially difficult and unpromising conditions of multinationalism was substantiated by reference to contemporary change and developments: Belgium and Russia had both adopted fully fledged federation in the early 1990s while Spain had implemented federal arrangements since 1978 and South Africa had also incorporated strong federal elements in its constitution. Indeed, Kymlicka also claimed that 'it is quite natural that multinational countries should adopt federal systems' because 'one would expect countries that are formed through a federation of peoples to adopt some form of political federation'.[28]

Let us explore the grounds for such optimism. Today there is a well-developed contemporary theoretical literature on liberal multiculturalism with firm evidence of a lively convergence of scholarly opinion on some of the essential moral bases and goals concerning the pursuit of justice in the democratic polity, but much less attention has been paid to the related subject of liberal multinationalism.[29] Clearly many of the conceptual and theoretical arguments and debates on liberal multiculturalism spill over into the related question of liberal multinationalism, but they are not the same subject. Both deal with issues that focus largely upon identity questions but the empirical problems associated with each of them are different. The main empirical focus of multinational federations is *ipso facto* sub-state nationalism, that is, the collective needs and requirements of the nation or nations that coexist within the larger, overarching political nationality of the federation taken as a whole. Consequently, to speak about multicultural issues in Canada is not synonymous with multinational questions. Instead of looking at the latter debate through the conceptual lenses of the liberal theorists, let us channel our subject via a different route. In the mainstream theoretical literature on federalism and federation (such as it is), there is an established conceptual debate about the relationship between a 'federal society' and a 'federal state'. It is usually construed in terms of the juxtaposition between 'social homogeneity' versus 'social heterogeneity', and it pits the former category of federations such as Australia, Austria and Germany against the latter one that includes Canada, Belgium, India, Malaysia and Switzerland. As we saw in Chapter 1, the debate can be traced back at least to William Livingston's seminal paper entitled 'A Note on the Nature of Federalism' that was first published in *Political Quarterly* in 1952 and which remains a source of considerable scholarly debate.[30] Brian Galligan, a noted scholar of the Australian federation, continues to dismiss what he calls 'the sociological fallacy' and remains convinced that federation is ultimately well suited not to the sort of social heterogeneity endemic in multinational issues but rather to the relative social homogeneity characteristic of Australia:

> Federalism is a function not of societal differences but of institutional arrangements and political communities. Obviously, as has been the case of Australia, these can be formed and supported by people without distinct societal features that are regionally based. ... Federalism requires political

sophistication rather than ethnically diverse regions and works quite well for countries like Australia that are broadly homogeneous.[31]

Galligan claims that the continuing vitality of federalism in the Australian federation owes nothing to 'underlying sociological factors, such as significant regional differences in language or culture', and that it appears to be a puzzle to its detractors precisely because 'it has no such roots'. His reply to the critics who wondered aloud why Australians bothered with a federal system, however, was to portray them as having 'misunderstood or distorted the character of federalism and Australia's federal Constitution'.[32] For Galligan, the federalism in Australia's federation can be summarised as 'democratic republican values' in established local communities; all of the rest is 'spurious sociological and political economy analysis' that is the result of 'bad theorising about federalism'.[33]

In hindsight Galligan's somewhat sweeping generalisation about the putative sociological fallacy in federal theorising was understandable: he was responding to a battery of attacks on Australian federalism and federation that questioned its authenticity. His response was, not unnaturally, one that bore traces of indignation. But the case that he made for the suitability of federation in conditions of social homogeneity was also buttressed by his reference to the failure of 'hastily contrived federations' in 'multicultural and multitribal territories as the European powers withdrew from colonial empires in the postwar decades'.[34] These remarks and assessments about the prerequisites of federation in the post-war imperial retreat could not really be gainsaid, but they had no necessary implications for *every* federation whose principal characteristic was social heterogeneity.

Clearly this debate is sterile if we try to draw firm theoretical conclusions from it for the simple reason that the reality is much more complex than such a debate would allow. Both historical experience and contemporary social reality demonstrate that context is crucial to this debate. Galligan had ignored the fact that political elites engaged in conflict-management and seeking the sort of liberal democratic order and stability in multinational states that only legitimacy could bring had to operate in very different conditions than those that pertained to Australia. Our brief reappraisal of the origins and formation of federation in Canada, India and Malaysia in Chapter 3 perfectly illustrates the point: in the making of federations political elites must work with the grain. They have to work with the materials that they have at hand. Federation is appropriate only at certain times and in certain circumstances. It is a theory of circumstantial causation. Indeed, the contingent nature of these circumstances in respect of nationality was recognised as far back as 1946 when Kenneth Wheare first observed that the desire to unite to form the federations of Canada and Switzerland 'arose in spite of differences of language and race ... of religion ... and of nationality'. These were examples of the desire for union among peoples who differed 'in all these important particulars'. Consequently 'the desire ... for federal union was directly produced by these differences'.[35] And Wheare also openly acknowledged the complex nature of multinational federations and the crucial role played by 'political nationality' when he confessed that:

although it is possible for a state which differs in race, religion, language, nationality and the like to form a union and although such differences provide a good basis for a federal union, it is also desirable that some feeling of common attachment to the new general government should be developed. ... Citizens (of the United States, Switzerland and Canada) came to feel a sense of double nationality. ... Nationality in a federal state means something more complicated than it does in a unitary state. And one of the factors which produce in states the capacity to work a federal union is the growth of this sense of a new common nationality *over and above but not instead of* their sense of separate nationality.[36]

The evidence suggests therefore that it is simply not tenable to claim that federation works better in conditions of relative social homogeneity than in circumstances of social heterogeneity because history indicates that it can work either well or badly under both sets of conditions. Certainly there is a different dynamic at work in multinational federations than in those, like Australia, that sustain a relative social homogeneity, but this tells us little about their prospects for either success or failure. The fact remains that it is difficult to envisage what the alternatives to federal arrangements (allied to consociational procedures) might be in countries such as Canada, India, Belgium, Switzerland and Malaysia. Critics of the concept of multinational federation must therefore make a strong case for a viable alternative.

Federation is certainly no panacea for the problem of relative autonomy and self-determination sought by distinct, self-conscious nations living together in the same state. We can already appreciate the limitations of federation in these circumstances if we think of the chequered track records of Nigeria, Malaya, the Central African Federation, the West Indies Federation, Yugoslavia, Czechoslovakia and the Soviet Union, taking into account the absence of liberal democracy in the last three cases. The vicissitudes of fortune evident in such cases tells us that federation *qua* federation might sometimes have to give way to new forms of federal-type relationships that involve a lesser formal status than federation *per se* but include a huge variety of flexible arrangements such as those identified by Elazar as 'associated states, federacies and condominiums'.[37]

The point about such flexible arrangements that allow for internal autonomy either within the state (the Inuits of Nunavut in Canada) or between states (Puerto Rico and the USA) is that it is possible to promote practical proposals only if we are prepared to work with the grain. Once again, we can work only with the materials at hand. Historical legacies, ideological predispositions and vested interests constitute serious obstacles to federal construction and reconstruction. In some cases – as in Cyprus and Sri Lanka – it has so far proved impossible to bring together two distinct cultural communities as a dyadic federation, and even in the case of federal Belgium, which has been highly successful, it has been notoriously difficult to prevent an ingeniously contrived multifocal federation from drifting back towards what is an inherently bipolar federal polity.

Working with the grain, then, means that practitioners must be able to identify the limits and possibilities of negotiating often largely intractable cultural-ideological conflicts that are highly charged precisely because they go to the very heart of what constitutes self-definition. In short, they engage sensitive questions of identity. Let us probe a little further and explore the empirical and theoretical implications of how multinational federations work.

National identity and legitimacy in multinational federations

Let us begin by looking at the fundamental question of individual self-definition in multinational federations. In terms of the national state – the overarching political nationality that we identified above – we can speak of a *demos* in the narrow political sense of a single people, but the problem with this conventional conception is that it is predicated upon a liberal democratic definition of the nation, one that obscures national minorities and, indeed, identifies all collective identities as part of the same nation. In effect, it presupposes the existence of the nation state. Where this definition operates in circumstances of relative cultural homogeneity it has the possibility happily to coincide with a social reality that is expressive of political reality. This reflects the position adopted by Galligan above when referring to Australia. But in states that are sociologically diverse such a definition is highly problematic. We have already seen in the work of Tamir that this particular conception of the state leads to the marginalisation, suffocation and alienation of stateless nations:

> The nation-state was not only assigned administrative, economic and strategic functions, but also adopted a particular cultural and national identity. Consequently, in order to be considered full-fledged citizens, individuals had to identify not only with the state and its institutions but also with the culture of the ruling nation. State involvement in cultural issues deeply affected the self-image of national minorities, which came to feel that the effort to shape all the citizens of the state into one homogeneous nation destined them for erosion.[38]

In a famous essay entitled 'Why do Nations have to Become States?', Charles Taylor had also arrived at the same conclusion as Tamir, specifically in respect of the place of Quebec in Canada, but the theoretical implications of his analysis extended further than this narrow empirical context.[39] The essay clearly possessed a direct relevance to multinational federations in general. The individual who is part of a minority national culture that lives in but does not identify wholly with the dominant national culture – however liberal it is – has a problem in terms of self-determination. How far can such an individual live a life that has real meaning in terms of his or her own cultural values, beliefs and attitudes? Taylor's point is that 'the claim about identity is particularized' because:

outside of the reference points of this culture I could not begin to put to myself, let alone answer, those questions of ultimate significance that are peculiarly in the repertory of the human subject. Outside this culture, I would not know who I was as a human subject. So this culture helps to identify me.[40]

One major consequence of this defence of collective identity is the recognition that 'cultural differences are part and parcel of the political reality rather than merely private matters' that can be conveniently compartmentalised and insulated from the dominant national culture. Correspondingly, what Tamir has called 'the illusion of neutrality' resident in the claim that a liberal state could be 'nationally and culturally neutral' prompted her to advocate a liberal nationalism capable of 'taking cultural and national differences into account'.[41] This liberal conception of the national state differed from 'the traditional liberal entity' because it introduced 'culture as a crucial dimension of political life'.[42]

The contributions of Kymlicka, Tamir and Taylor to the contemporary theoretical debate about liberalism, nationalism and the problem of multinational and multicultural democracies constitute, for our purposes, a representative sample of the current broad convergence of contemporary liberal political thought. But it is important to note that this burgeoning literature also contains within it a very interesting line of reasoning with potentially significant theoretical implications. Recent writers have noted the reappraisal of established political concepts and structures such as federalism, consociationalism and different forms of decentralisation, autonomy and self-government that has 'resulted in more elaborate arguments, not only of an empirical or comparative tendency, but also normative', and that they have been 'strongly influenced' by the pressing problems of what Ramon Maiz has called two political logics: 'the logic of democracy and the logic of nationalism'.[43] In short, there has been a discernible shift in thinking about the nature and meaning of multinational democracies. Maiz claims that the normative basis for the comparative analysis of multinational federations is both lucid and simple:

> when considering national problems from the perspective of encouraging democracy, we have again found that it makes little sense to separate the analysis of what *is* and its causal explanations from the analysis of what *should* be and its philosophical-political and moral fundamentals.[44]

Alain Gagnon has also acknowledged the combination of contemporary political events and experience and changing theoretical perspectives as a potent analytical cocktail destined to undermine received liberal thinking derived from the basic tenets of individualism and homogeneity.[45] His understanding of normative political theory with regard to multinational federations lies in what he calls the 'varying assumptions about what is good or valuable in a society', so that the 'normative dimension' resides in 'different conceptions of the good'.[46] Both Maiz and Gagnon, it should be noted, acknowledge the convergence of three distinct literatures that are relevant to the comparative survey of multi-national federations, namely, democratic theory, comparative federalism and federation and studies of nationalism. What is called for here is a meeting of minds, where the empirical and theoretical worlds meet the normative world. Maiz puts it thus:

> Something has taken place in this field of study, which seems to indicate that we are moving slowly towards a perspective finally capable of overcoming the traditional limited duality of nationalism and statism, heads and tails of the same obsolete and reductionist vision of the problem. ... the theory of democracy has generated a revision, which ... points towards a viewpoint that is not merely 'expressive' of democratic politics, but is also constructive or, so to speak, 'performative' concerning preferences, interests and identities'.[47]

It is important to underline the purpose of this recent trend towards what we might legitimately call 'the normative political theory of multinational federations'. Maiz's intention is clearly to promote 'the renewal of normative and institutional analysis of multinational states, thus in turn facilitating their complex democratic viability', and it leads him in precisely the same direction as Gagnon.[48] The destination of these two recent studies is asymmetrical federalism, whereby *de facto* sub-state national minorities can be successfully accommodated by *de jure* constitutional, political and legal recognition in the federation.[49] But in recognising the sociological character of sub-state nationalism and national identity as a political reality in multinational federations, there is also something more at stake. This is the federal spirit – also known as *Bundestreue* (federal comity) – that brings us back to Gagnon's different conceptions of what is good or valuable in a society. Briefly, federal spirit refers to the bonds that unite the political community – the reconciliation of individual and collective needs that bind the political community. And the terms embedded in the discourse of *Bundestreue* include faith, mutual trust, partnership, dignity, friendship, loyalty, consent, consultation, compromise, reciprocity, tolerance and respect that together form the moral foundation of the federation and are the animating force of its evolution.[50] Indeed, we might claim with good reason that it is the federal spirit that serves as the ubiquitous operative principle in the overall quest for justice, equity and equality in all federations.

We will return to the issue of asymmetrical federalism in Chapter 8, but suffice it to add here that there is another underlying principle that serves to buttress all federations – political legitimacy. In multinational federations, of course, legitimacy assumes a special significance. We are reminded of Wheare's telling remark that 'nationality in a federal state means something more complicated than it does in a unitary state'.[51] This implies that it is the very survival of a nation or the fate of a distinct culture, however small, that is at stake. Small wonder that sub-state national identities will accept the federation as legitimate only if they perceive it to be both sensitive and sympathetic to their own cultural-ideological preferences, interests and values. Accordingly, the purpose of the federation – literally its *raison d'être* – must never be in doubt. This was one of the criticisms that Taylor levelled at Canada. He claimed that it was the persistent denial of Quebec's own conception and understanding of Canada that had led to general disillusionment with the country. The fact that 'Canada never gelled as a nation for them', combined with the growth of specifically 'French power' inside Canada, resulted in the concerted demand that Quebec should be recognised as 'a crucial component of the country, as an entity whose survival and flourishing was one of the main purposes of Canada as a political society'. Consequently, what was missing was 'the clear recognition that this was part of our purpose as a federation'.[52]

Once again we can appreciate just how important the origins and formation of federations are for both academics and practitioners. Academics need to understand the complex motives for federal union in order to assess their implications for contemporary problems, while practitioners have a vested interest in defending and promoting their own particular historical interpretation in order to legitimise their contemporary conception of, and claims upon, the federation. This is the world in which national minorities and indigenous peoples have recourse to the political uses of history and can legitimise their constitutional, political and legal claims for formal recognition in the federation. It is also the world in which the federal spirit can be activated in what is ultimately at its core a moral discourse.

Liberal nationalism in multinational federation

In her impressive survey of the theoretical dimensions of liberal nationalism, Tamir brought her project to a close by acknowledging that in future it had to take cultural and national differences into account by recognising that members of national minorities had legitimate grievances that needed to be addressed.[53] Kymlicka, too, observed that secession would remain an ever-present threat in many multinational countries unless we learned to accommodate 'ethnocultural diversity'.[54] Taylor has also added his considerable intellectual weight to this debate by developing an argument for 'a new form of Canadian federation' that would formally recognise 'the duality that is basic to the country'.[55] All three liberal theorists espouse the cause of a normative, liberal democratic, political theory that would facilitate a 'politics of recognition' for national minorities in multinational states.

To this formidable list of political theorists we must now add James Tully, whose recent work on what I shall call the 'new constitutionalism' has served to refocus the theoretical debate towards a new constitutive question in contemporary constitutional discourse, namely, what kind of democratic framework can adequately facilitate the endless processes of mobilisation, negotiation and reconciliation that underpin the increasing claims made for national self-determination?[56] Tully's principal purpose is not so much to underscore the intrinsic values and principles that inhere in the politics of recognition, identity and difference as to emphasise the goal of freedom: the freedom, that is, 'of the members of an open society to change the constitutional rules of mutual recognition and association from time to time as their identities change'.[57] Assuming that such conflict management results neither in imperial domination nor secession but in the internal self-determination characteristic of multinational federation, the constitutional implications that follow are crystal clear:

> The meaningful exercise of the right of internal self-determination consists not only in the exercise of certain powers of political, economic, social and cultural development, by means of institutions of self-government, protection of distinctness, and federalism, but also in having a democratic say over what those powers are, how they relate to and are recognized by the other members of the multinational association, and to be able to amend them from time to time.[58]

Here the pursuit of justice, order and stability requires the reconceptualisation of constitutions and constitutional discourse so that there is an unending conversation and debate that allows for legitimate argument and reasonable disagreement. Constituent nations of the larger federal polity are empowered to 'engage freely in negotiations of reciprocal disclosure and acknowledgement as they develop and amend their modes of recognition and cooperation, in conjunction with the fair reconciliation of other forms of diversity'.[59]

Given the strong moral case that this theoretical consensus has made for the pursuit of a liberal nationalism in multinational states, what instruments, procedures and mechanisms are appropriate for this purpose? How far can constitutional and institutional design assist practitioners of reform and is it really possible effectively to tame nationalism? Let us look briefly at some case studies in order to draw some tentative conclusions about one of the most difficult problems of the new millennium. We will begin with the case of Belgium and then extend our focus to include Switzerland, Canada, India and Malaysia.

Belgium

Territorially Belgium is a small country in western Europe with a population of just over ten million people, but the territorial concentration of its two major linguistic communities are so tightly distributed that it continues to give credence to the claim made nearly a century ago that 'there are no Belgians … there are only Flemish and Walloons' living in the same state.[60] Flanders in the north constitutes only about 40 per cent of the total land mass, but with approximately 58 per cent of the Belgian population. Wallonia, on the other hand, occupies the lion's share of the territory but the Walloons constitute only 32 per cent of the total population. Meanwhile, a little less than 10 per cent of Belgians live in Brussels, which is located just inside the Flemish boundary with Wallonia. There are also about 67,000 German-speaking Belgians living inside Wallonia that are territorially concentrated in Eupen and Malmedy to the east.

This complex composition makes for an extremely difficult and divisive political culture for the purposes of government. The linguistic and territorial cleavages serve to reinforce each other while the socio-economic characteristics also assist in promoting fissiparous tendencies in the federation. And as with Canada–Quebec relations, there is more than one history that is vigorously kept alive. Historically Wallonia was the dominant economic force in Belgium, so that even the upper and middle classes in Flanders were francophone while the working classes and the poor were overwhelmingly Flemish, thus emphasising the reinforcing nature of the interrelationship between social class and the linguistic divisions in society. French was the language of the upper class and the bourgeoisie. In the twentieth century, however, the economic roles were gradually reversed, with Flanders having the vibrant 'high-tech post-industrial' economy while the outdated structure of Wallonia's economy was increasingly characterised by long-term industrial decline and structural unemployment.

The existence of Brussels further complicates the basic dynamic at work in the Belgian polity. In theory, Brussels is bilingual, but in practice it is a predominantly French-speaking incubus situated just inside Flanders. It is often remarked that a combination of just three unifying factors keeps the Belgian state in existence: the monarchy, membership of the EU and Brussels. But Brussels is also potentially a powder keg of an issue that has the possibility to explode in the future. Flemish resentment at the expansive tendencies of Brussels and the conspicuous encroachment of French-speakers into Flemish territory remains a constant source of anxiety and is a ready-made recipe available for political mobilisation.

How, then, does Belgium manage this seemingly intractable combination of cleavage patterns that is hardly very promising for legitimate and stable liberal democratic rule? And what might be the implications for other federations seeking to accommodate such sharp cultural-ideological fissures? The answers to these questions lie in a judicious combination of constitutional, legal and political procedures, mechanisms and devices that furnish a battery of checks and balances which guarantee respect for the integrity of entrenched cultural identities and protect minority rights. Examples of such mechanisms include the following:

1   The institutionalisation of the language divisions in the shape of two cultural councils (Flemish and francophone) together with a council for the German-speaking community, with law-making powers in cultural affairs.
2   The representation of Flanders, Wallonia and Brussels in regional councils with constitutionally assigned powers in the socio-economic field and each having its own parliament and executive.
3   Brussels is a special case: it maintains a peculiar relationship to both Flanders and Wallonia as a bilingual region with its own distinct institutional and socio-economic interests. It is a living example of non-territorial, personal federalism that guarantees minority Flemish representation in the regional government.

4   An 'alarm bell' procedure that gives two-thirds of a linguistic group the right temporarily to suspend the adoption of certain language laws.
5   Procedures that guarantee legislative approval via a 'double majority' so that laws require a two-thirds overall majority *and* a majority of each linguistic group in the Belgian Parliament.[61]

Apart from these territorial concessions to socio-economic and cultural differences, it is worth highlighting the non-territorial, personality principle at work in the structure of the Belgian federation, with particular reference to the Brussels Capital Region and the German-speaking linguistic community. With approximately one million inhabitants of whom only about 18 per cent are Dutch speakers, it is perhaps not surprising to discover that in practice the Flemish Community and Region have formally merged their institutions so that there is now only one Flemish government and parliament that deals with *both* regional and community competences for citizens living in the Flemish region and for those Dutch-speakers resident in Brussels.[62] This reflects both the distribution of the Flemish and Walloon populations and the inherent polarising pressures that continue to characterise Belgian politics.

The overall picture that emerges, then, is one of a multilingual federal polity that has an inherent propensity towards bipolarity. And if it is probably more accurate in social-science terms to construe Belgium as composed mainly of three distinct language communities rather than sub-state nations, each respective sense of composite identity displays a depth and range that is akin to nationality. The bipolar relations between the Dutch- and French-speakers reflect a political culture that is fundamentally antagonistic, rooted in a mutual political distrust which is largely offset by the countervailing weight of Brussels and the existence of the small German-speaking community. Bipolarity therefore coexists with strenuous attempts at multipolar responses, not least via the interaction of 'a triad of orders of government' (federal, regional and community) that implies 'that some policy areas will require cooperation between two orders of powers, others between all three'.[63] The upshot of the 'complex ambiguity' that constitutes the Belgian federation can be crisply summarised: while 'the logic of Belgian federalism is bipolar, several solutions designed to respond to different tensions are multipolar'.[64]

Switzerland

If we turn our attention to Switzerland we will see that these sorts of reassuring procedural guarantees are also characteristic of decision-making processes in what is a very different kind of federation. Switzerland is widely considered to be the role model of a federal polity in Europe largely because of its long history of order and stability underpinned by an evolving liberal democratic rule. As a tiny country of only seven million people situated in the heart of Europe, Switzerland's federal origins, as we saw in Chapter 3, stretch back to 1291 when the three minuscule communities of Uri, Schwyz and Unterwalden formed what in the German language was designated an *Eidgenossenschaft* (Oath-Fellowship). Based upon its more recent constitutional landmarks of 1803, 1815, 1848, 1874 and 1999, Switzerland evolved into the contemporary federation that it is today partly as a result of strong American influences but mainly due to its own practical experience of living together in a spirit of *Bundestreue* – of reciprocity, mutual trust and understanding, tolerance, dignity, partnership, and respect for and recognition of minorities – that values consensus, conciliation and compromise above crude majoritarian calculation.[65] As we noted in Chapter 3, the notion of *Eidgenossenschaft* refers to the idea of a covenant, a moral basis, to preserve and promote the politics of difference and diversity.

The combination of Switzerland's small size, geographical position and topography, and its conservative political culture has often been used as the main reason that explains its relative political order and stability. It is, after all, a model of federal stability. However, even a cursory glance at its multilingual, multicultural and historic multinational complexities allied to its complicated constellation of cross-cutting social-cleavage patterns would suggest that many more forces making for unity are at work than such simplistic references would initially imply. Switzerland's social make-up, like that of Belgium, appears at face value to furnish the most unpromising conditions for stable government. It has four recognised languages – German, French, Italian and Romansh – but only the first three are designated 'official' languages of the federation. Today taking into full account the 16 per cent of the population that are technically 'foreigners', about 68 per cent of Swiss citizens are German-speaking, 19 per cent are French-speaking, 8 per cent Italian-speaking, and 1 per cent (about 50,000) speak Romansh, a minor language descended from Latin and spoken only in a handful of Alpine areas in the south east of the country. On this reckoning, the existence of four different cultural systems based upon four different languages would seem to provide little basis for consensus politics, but a closer look at the interaction of the language cleavage with the religious factor helps to explain why hope springs eternal in the federation.[66]

The Swiss federal polity is characterised by a multiple structure of cleavages that is also a changing pattern of cross-cutting cleavages. Consequently the divisive impact of the linguistic cleavage in Swiss federal politics in practice has been significantly dampened down in part by the different religious identities of the 26 cantons so that language and religiosity do not reinforce each other but on the contrary have consistently had a decisive cross-cutting effect. For example, the 'natural' Swiss-German-speaking majority in the federation is divided by religion and the German-speaking Catholic cantons have been accustomed to forming coalitions with the 'Latin' cantons – some of the French-speaking cantons and Ticino, the only Italian-speaking canton – to resist the culturally stronger and more urbanised German-speaking Protestant cantons. In short, the linguistic minority and the religious minority can combine to block change.[67] In this respect, Switzerland is a federation composed of 'varied cultural, linguistic, religious, historical and political minority groups ... with practically no consistent majority'.[68] It is a country of minorities.

If we summarise the federalism in federation in Switzerland it would include the following features: language, religiosity, territoriality (cantonalism), social class, urban–rural contrasts and conservative traditionalism. Shifting our focus to the political institutions, procedures and mechanisms that constitute the federation in which this federalism is represented, we would include the following:

1   The federal structure: the Federal Assembly, including the National Council (lower house) and the Council of States (second chamber); the Federal Council (the executive) based upon the *collegial* principle; and the Federal Court *elected* by the Federal Assembly.
2   National elections every four years to the National Council based upon the party list version of proportional representation (PR) and equal elected representation of the 26 cantons (that set their own electoral rules) in the Council of States.
3   Direct democracy: cantonal and local communal democracy; the use of obligatory and optional referenda and popular initiatives; referenda for constitutional and legislative reform.
4   The principle of proportionality: power-sharing in small communities.
5   The principle of double majorities; citizens participating in the electoral politics of decision-making in their dual capacity as cantonal interests and identities and federal (national) interests and identities.
6   Cantonal autonomy and strong local powers and competences.
7   Administrative (interlocking) federal practice whereby the 26 constituent units implement most federal legislation.

These seven major characteristics of the Swiss federation by themselves portray neither the subtleties nor the complexities of precisely how the system works. The symbiotic relationship between federalism and federation could hardly be better illustrated than to investigate the Swiss model from the particular standpoint of representation, but even here there is the sense of only scratching the surface. Political analysis must be combined with a strong historical perspective together with both an institutional and a structural approach in order fully to grasp these subtleties and complexities.

Our brief focus upon Switzerland suggests that it is the long historical process that has socialised mass publics into consensus-seeking political animals. The fact that up until 1789 the Swiss Confederation was composed of only German cantons is particularly relevant. The absence of linguistic diversity early on in the development of the polity meant that 'by the time that the Confederation first faced the implications of emergent linguistic nationalism, its members had more than five centuries of experience in the settling of other types of disputes through well-developed techniques of neutrality, mediation and decentralisation'.[69] Consequently the famous 'politics of accommodation' is achieved by a system of broad consultation, negotiation and bargaining that decreases the potential political polarisation of Swiss society by prior consultation of the political parties, administrations, experts and the cantons. Consensus results from the deeply rooted liberal democratic political culture that furnishes a framework of tolerance, reciprocity, respect and trust to facilitate successful elite negotiations in a long, meticulous federal process.

In summary, political order and stability in Switzerland seem somewhat para-doxical. Swiss political stability and legitimacy are rooted in difference and diversity, the very characteristics that are the source of such stresses, strains and tensions in Belgium, Canada, India and Malaysia. Clearly its peculiar form of federal unity can be ascribed to a combination of the federal political system allied to a consensus-seeking political culture that is historically rooted in propor-tionality, pluralism, wide-ranging consultation, conciliation and negotiation and minority representation, all appropriately encapsulated in the 'politics of accom-modation'. But we should also remember that in our understandable admiration of the Swiss federal model, its federal system is 'at odds with much political theory and with mainstream political thought'.[70]

Before we leave this thumbnail sketch of Switzerland, it is important for us finally to acknowledge certain conceptual ambiguities that pertain to the social heterogeneity of this classic federation. Even a cursory glance at the Swiss federal model would persuade many analysts to describe it as multinational mainly because of the broad coexistence of language and territoriality. However, the integrity of French-, German- and Italian-speaking cantons does not mean that they are living, breathing, self-conscious nations, nor should we assume that conflict-management techniques and procedures in the federal polity are built upon sub-state nationalism. They are not. The two most salient identities in Switzerland are the cantonal identity and the Swiss identity itself.[71] In the main-stream literature these ambiguities boil down to a broad agreement that Switzerland is not a multinational federation. Rather, it is a multicultural, multi-lingual federal state.[72] Kymlicka refers to it as a 'historical multination federation' while Stepan claims that Switzerland is 'the most difficult to classify as to whether it is actually multinational or not'.[73] Nonetheless, the self-proclaimed determination of this complex mosaic of moving, shifting minorities to live its 'diversity in unity respecting one another' in a federal polity is sufficient reason for us to include it in a comparative survey of multinational federations.[74]

Canada

Canada is a multicultural, multinational, bilingual federation. Its bilingualism at federal level originated in the Canadian Constitution (the British North America Act, now known as the Canada Act, 1867), its multiculturalism derives from the Canadian Multiculturalism Act, 1971 and much more recently its multination-alism was officially consecrated when the boundaries of the North-West Territories were redrawn in 1999 to accommodate the Inuit peoples in a new nationality-based territorial unit called Nunavut. As a result, Aboriginal self-government has been established in Canada with the Inuit, like the Quebecois, a permanent minority in the federation as a whole but a self-conscious majority within their own territorial jurisdiction.

Today there are 60–80 self-styled Aboriginal 'nations' and over 600 Aboriginal communities living in Canada that function alongside Quebec as an official legal recognition of its undeniable social diversity having political salience. Even from this brief glance at the new Canadian mosaic, it is clear that several important questions emerge which have enormous implications for the idea of multinational federations.

The first is the issue of 'nation' itself. Clearly we cannot use the category 'nation' in the same way to compare these communities with that of Quebec. The realities are very different. Second, many of these self-definitions are simply incapable of sustaining themselves as national governments in terms not only of their cultural attributes but also in respect of their material resources, their capacity to deal with the daily routine of managing scarcity. It might therefore be both more realistic and more practical to classify them as cultural identities that can be subsumed into the larger, more encompassing, notion of Aboriginal nation.

This 'deep diversity', to borrow Charles Taylor's engaging terminology, demonstrates the complexity of Canada's contemporary political culture and underlines an admirable political will in formally recognising and reintegrating Aboriginal identities in the federal polity.[75] But it has still not come to terms with precisely how to accommodate Quebec successfully in the Constitution. Quebec as a nation of approximately 7 million people out of a total Canadian population of 31 million remains formally unrecognised. Its own cultural and historical specificity has no special status in Canada above and beyond a series of parliamentary resolutions that have only a limited symbolism. The problem for Quebecois – 83 per cent of whom are French-speaking (francophones) and 10 per cent English-speaking (anglophones) – has been ably summarised by André Laurendeau, one of the architects of the report published by the Royal Commission on Bilingualism and Biculturalism (1967), who couched the problem of being a permanent national minority in the federation in the following way:

> We began to formulate for ourselves an understanding of the situation we were observing; that is, a multiculturalism that is an undeniable fact and must be taken into account, but which manifests itself differently according to locality. Over and above it is the great problem of English–French relations in Canada. How can we get across the point that an 'ethnic group', even one that is relatively large provincially, but only represents 3 per cent of the total Canadian population, is not at all the same thing as an organised society like Quebec, with a large population, its own institutions, and a long and specific history?'[76]

We can see from this statement how far Quebec nationalists have had well-founded suspicions of multiculturalism as an anglophone policy preference designed to deflect the eye away from Quebec's legitimate claims to be a founding national partner of the federation in the 1860s. René Levesque, the erstwhile leader of the Parti Quebecois (PQ) in the 1960s and 1970s remarked rather waspishly that it was 'a red herring' devised to obscure 'the Quebec business', to give an impression 'that we are all ethnics and do not have to worry about special status for Quebec'.[77] For many separatists, multiculturalism in Canada has in principle reduced the 'Quebec fact' to a merely 'ethnic phenomenon'.

Today the constitutional order in Canada, based upon the Constitution Act (1982), remains a source of great consternation and controversy in Quebec and is obstinately impervious to formal change. It has fossilised a particular conception of Canada that no longer accurately reflects contemporary social and political realities.

From the particular standpoint of Quebec nationalists, it is largely the Charter of Rights and Freedoms that is the main bone of contention because in its insistence upon entrenching the rights of Canadian citizens as individuals wherever they live in the federation it has effectively rendered Quebec's specificity invisible. This predominantly anglophone conception of Canada has left a bitter legacy in Quebec where successive provincial governments have striven to promote the politics of recognition. The classic collision of collective versus individual rights lies at the heart of this quarrel and it reflects two competing conceptions of Canada. And the fact that the Charter formally recognised Aboriginal rights as the collective rights of a distinct people further inflamed Quebec's sensitivities. Consequently, the answer to the question 'What does Quebec want?' is simple: it wants its historical-cultural specificity formally recognised by being incorporated in the Constitution.

This is the fundamental dilemma for Quebec and this is precisely why Quebecois will continue to mistrust federal government in Ottawa and rely instead principally upon their own provincial government in Quebec City. The Quebec predicament is one where – as a minority nation within a larger (multi)national state – it finds itself incessantly exposed to predominantly anglophone policy preferences that are frankly corrosive to Quebec's francophone identity and constantly invade its social, economic and political space. Small wonder that Quebec's struggle to resist the ubiquitous infiltration of anglophone values, beliefs and socio-economic mores into its francophone identity has served to sour its relations with the 'rest of Canada' (ROC). And small wonder, indeed, that its watchword has been '*la survivance*'.

This brief cameo of Canada as a case study of a multinational federation at work is necessarily superficial. It ignores the nature and role of the anglophone ROC (sometimes called 'Canada outside of Quebec', COQ) – the predominantly English-speaking majority of Canadians – who tend to identify overwhelmingly with the Canadian nation at large, and it also overlooks the complexities and subtleties that characterise the identity of anglophone Quebecois.[78] But it does suggest that the Canadian case has several implications for the larger question of how such unions can succeed or fail. Canada is usually held up as one of the great success stories as a multinational federation and, rather like Switzerland and Belgium, we can only admire the way that it has managed to accommodate its complex diversities that have political salience. As we shall see, it compels us to rethink and revise our assumptions and preconceptions about the very concept of the multinational federation. However, before we examine some of these implications for the study of multinational federations, let us look at two further cases, namely, those of India and Malaysia.

India

India is a multilingual, multicultural, multinational federation whose population of just over one billion makes it the world's largest liberal democratic federation. The sheer scale of its diversity can be fully appreciated if we consider that its major religions include Hindus (82 per cent), Muslims (12 per cent), Christians (2.3 per cent), Sikhs (1.94 per cent) and Buddhists (0.76 per cent) while its most prominent languages comprise Hindi (40 per cent), Bengali (8 per cent), Telegu (7 per cent), Marathi (7 per cent), Tamil (6 per cent), Urdu (5 per cent) and Gujarati (4 per cent).

Language combined with regional identity has proved to be the most significant characteristic of ethnic self-definition, and among the 28 constituent territorial units that constitute India today, the Sikhs in Punjab, the Tamils in Tamil Nadu, the Bengalis in West Bengal and the Nagas in Nagaland are a good representative sample of the strong sense of sub-state nationhood that exists.

India's constitution dates only from 1950 but its origins and evolution stretch back to the days of the British Raj and to specific British legal acts that were designed to devolve power to different administrative units at different levels. As we saw in Chapter 3, the India Councils Act (1892) and successive Government of India Acts in 1909, 1919 and 1935 represented the most significant milestones in the long piecemeal process by which India arrived at its final federal destination. The British imperial legacy of centralised administrative control combined with the traumatic experience of partition in 1947, Nehru's socialist beliefs in centralised economic planning and widespread anxieties about the possible disintegration of a nascent independent India compelled political elites to accept the idea of a strong centre. Consequently, the federation of India possessed at the outset such a strong centre with concomitantly weak constituent units that Wheare was able to describe it as 'quasi-federal'.[79] Indeed, the term 'federal' was not used at all in the constitution.

The nature of these circumstances, that should also include evidence from the Constituent Assembly debates of the late 1940s, explains conclusively why many commentators have been reluctant to describe India as a federal polity. The term 'federal' was suspect from the start. However, after Nehru's death in 1964 there was a conspicuous resurgence of regional political parties that began to challenge the hegemony of the Congress Party and questioned the dominant role of the central federal government in New Delhi. Increasing resistance to the Union's use of emergency powers (known as President's Rule) together with a marked dissatisfaction with the distribution of powers between the Union and the constituent units and a growing desire for enhanced regional autonomy, culminated collectively in what we might interpret as pressure to reassert the federal character of the constitution.[80] And there is no doubt that the Indian Constitution had what Balveer Arora has called 'a remarkable degree of flexibility and pragmatism' in which 'the virtues of asymmetry in bringing about and maintaining union' were evident:

> It also took cognizance of the layering of socio-political realities and the importance of local self-government. In a social system characterized by … 'asymmetrical obligations among unequals', special status and multilevel arrangements encountered no conceptual objections. In the ongoing search for new modes of adaptation to the pressures generated by democratic development, these elements of flexibility were significant. They were designed to make the federal system more responsive.[81]

One major challenge that emerged during the 1980s was pressure emanating from 'resurgent identities at the sub-state level' that had to be accommodated without compromising the territorial integrity of the states, and this led to a clear shift of attitude evident in the willingness 'to rediscover and explore flexible federalism'.[82] Examples of the procedures and mechanisms that constituted this so-called 'flexible federalism' were tantamount in many cases to the liberal nationalism in multinational federation. And a brief survey of recent trends in federalism and federation in India strongly suggests that the overall impact has been to accentuate different forms of asymmetrical federalism. The battery of devices has included the following practices: more effective intergovernmental concertation that refocused decision-making towards 'executive federalism', a greater willingness to activate procedures for redefining internal boundaries between constituent units along 'ethno-linguistic' lines, the extension of preferential treatment in the allocation and distribution of financial grants and resources to 'special category states', periodical reassessments of the efficacy and validity of claims for special status and support for the genuine decentralisation of politico-administrative structures (including councils for self-government in autonomous districts) at the sub-state level and the introduction of a third tier of government – the panchayats – enjoying formal constitutional recognition as an autonomous governmental form in its own right. In most cases the sort of experimentation with asymmetrical provisions and multilevel institutional arrangements that have been introduced has facilitated the democratic development of India as a unity without uniformity.

Arora's observation that the Indian Constitution started with the assumption of asymmetry in the special status accorded to Jammu and Kashmir in Article 370 – according it an autonomy that distinguished it from all other states – is a salutary reminder of the essentially moral and practical case for federations to meet specific needs and requirements as part of their original design from the beginning. India as a case study of a multinational and multicultural federation has demonstrated a remarkable flexibility in constitutional design and amendment, legal interpretation and political versatility in accommodating its profoundly complex and subtle social diversity typically expressed as overlapping ethnic, regional, tribal, communal and religious as well as sub-state national identities. Consequently, it is not difficult to find concrete evidence of such flexible adjustment and adaptation to changing needs and demands, and not only in the more familiar problems of Assam, Kashmir and Punjab. Other examples where the federal spirit can also be seen at work are in the cases of Nagaland (Article 371A) with protection of its own pre-existing laws, protection of its local identity via restrictions on immigration and a preferential financial regime, in Sikkim (Article 371) with the reservation of seats on the basis of community and religion in the state assembly and judicial recognition of its special status, in Mizoram (Article 371G) with protection for Mizo customary law and religious-social practices, and in Assam (Article 371B) and Manipur (Article 371C) with flexibility for special needs provided by committees of the state legislatures. The list of such cases in India is voluminous and it is important to emphasise the adaptive capacity of the federation in managing and defusing sub-state national, ethnic and tribal conflicts.[83]

The delicate constitutional and political balance to be struck in such a huge country as India between constituent cultural-ideological identities, the territorial integrity of the constituent units themselves and the larger unity of the federation can therefore be viewed as 'an extended discovery of the minimum degree of uniformity necessary for maintaining a coherent union'.[84] And just as it is certain that the progressive maturation of Indian federal democracy will bring with it new challenges in the form of unrest in socio-political movements for the protection of language and culture, fresh demands for greater state autonomy and new pressures for the formation of new states or autonomous regions and tribal councils, so will its innovative capacities evolve to accommodate new multilevel forms of local autonomy, governance and statehood.

Malaysia

Even the briefest of glances at federalism and federation in Malaysia tells us that the outstanding feature of the constitutional system is its centralisation. In this particular respect it is constitutionally and legally similar to India. But politically its liberal democratic credentials are much less convincing. Put simply, the Malaysian federation is not only 'tilted in the direction of an overweening executive arm of government' but, indeed, 'the fine line between constitutional government and outright authoritarian rule has become even finer'.[85] Rather like the Indian federation, however, Malaysia has to be understood largely in terms of its overriding concern for order, stability and national unity in a society that can be described as multiethnic, multiracial, multilingual, multicultural and multinational.

As outlined in Chapter 3, the federation of Malaysia is a union of thirteen states: eleven constituent units in peninsular Malaysia (Johore, Kelantan, Kedah, Malacca, Negeri Sembilan, Pahang, Penang, Perak, Perlis, Selangor and Terengganu) and two in the northern part of Borneo, namely, Sabah and Sarawak, which are separated by about 400 miles from the peninsular by the

South China Sea. Most studies of Malaysia acknowledge that the survival of its federal form of government, dating back to the Federation of Malaya Agreement (1948), has been due in no small measure to 'the communal character of its population, and to the insistence of the Malays, and later also the indigenous peoples of Borneo, that their special position be assured'.[86] As in the case of India, it is common practice to construe political conflicts related to social diversity in terms of 'communal politics', although Malaysia's constituent units were not constructed along communal lines so that its territorial boundaries do not coincide (as they largely do in India) with linguistic, religious or ethnic social cleavages.

Malaysia's population comprises approximately 20 million people of whom the Malays and other indigenous peoples constitute approximately 59 per cent, Chinese 32 per cent and Indians 9 per cent, but this broad social composition of the federation conceals a series of distinct political conflicts that can be examined from three different perspectives: first, that between the *Bumiputras* (meaning literally 'sons of the soil') who comprise the Malays and other indigenous or native peoples, and the non-Malays largely based in peninsular Malaysia; second, conflicts among Malay Muslims in peninsular Malaysia, particularly between fundamentalist Muslims who want to create an Islamic state and moderate Muslims who prefer the *status quo*; and, third, conflicts within the *Bumiputras* between Muslims (largely peninsular Malays) and non-Muslims (natives) of Sarawak and Sabah. This conflict within *Bumiputras* must also be seen in terms both of Malay hegemony, which was perceived by the non-Muslims of Sarawak and Sabah as a pernicious 'Malayanisation' and 'Islamisation' of their cultural and religious freedom, and distinct divisions between the majority Kadazan Dusun and other natives in Sabah, and the majority Iban and other natives in Sarawak.

The federal constitution affords the Malays and indigenous peoples of Sabah and Sarawak special recognition and status in the federation. Despite the claim stated in Article 8(2) that 'there shall be no discrimination against citizens on the ground only of religion, race, descent, place of birth or gender in any law', this right is subject to other provisions of the constitution that expressly authorise discrimination. Article 153(1), for example, allows discrimination on grounds of race by providing that the head of state (the *yang di-pertuan agong*, or king) shall 'safeguard the special position of the Malays and natives of any of the States of Sabah and Sarawak and the legitimate interests of other communities', and the remaining nine clauses of that Article serve to buttress the privileges of these 'sons of the soil' by protecting and promoting their interests in the following four main areas: reservation land, quotas for admission to certain sectors of the federal public service, the issuing of licences and permits for the operation of certain businesses and the provision of scholarships and other forms of educational assistance.[87]

In order to understand why such a 'special position' was incorporated in the Malaysian Constitution, it is necessary to appreciate the historical background to these circumstances. The short answer to this question is that it emerged as a result of a series of arrangements made by the British with the Malay rulers for the conferment of special rights and privileges dating back at least to the Federation of Malaya Agreement (1948). In other words, special status was an imperial legacy and existed long before Malaya gained independence in 1957.[88] Consequently, much of what remains in the Constitution today regarding formal recognition of the diversity of the population of Malaysia can be traced back to the Independent Constitutional Commission appointed in 1956 to provide for full self-government and independence for the Federation of Malaya in 1957. The Report of the Independent Constitutional Commission (known as the Reid Commission Report, named after Lord Reid, the Chairman of the Commission) made various recommendations concerning the highly sensitive issues of religion, race, citizenship and the official language of Malay that contained sunset clauses designed either to be phased out or periodically reviewed in the future. An extract from the report illustrates precisely what their intentions were:

> We are of opinion that in present circumstances it is necessary to continue these preferences. The Malays would be at a serious and unfair disadvantage compared with other communities if they were suddenly withdrawn. But, with the integration of the various communities into a *common nationality* which we trust will gradually come about, the need for these preferences will gradually disappear. Our recommendations are made on the footing that the Malays should be assured that the present position will continue for a substantial period, but that in due course the present preferences should be reduced and should ultimately cease so that there should then be no discrimination between races or communities.[89]

Their stipulation of a time limit of fifteen years for the continuance of these privileges, however, was not adopted in the final constitutional proposal and it was considered preferable that, in the interests of the country as a whole, as well as of the Malays themselves, the *yang di-pertuan agong* would become responsible for activating a periodic review of any revised proposals. One consequence of this decision has been particularly unfortunate: an erroneous perception developed in the minds of some observers and critics that Article 153 provided safeguards of the privileges of only the *Bumiputras* by the head of state when in fact this was an incorrect reading of the purpose of the article. The Malaysian Constitution, we are reminded, actually stipulates in Article 8(2) that 'there shall be no discrimination against citizens on the ground only of religion, race, descent, place of birth or gender in any law' so that in practice the special status of the *Bumiputras* is limited to the four specific areas identified above and therefore it follows that in all other matters not covered by the constitution there can be no discrimination either in favour of or against any particular race.

Finally, let us mention briefly the issues of language and religion. These have both aroused much controversy in Malaysia where Malay, English, Chinese and Tamil are live languages that coexist with many tribal dialects and where Islam, Buddhism, Christianity and Hindu mingle with animists and other traditional indigenous beliefs. Both constitutional purpose and judicial interpretation ensured that Article 152(1) was worded in the following way: 'the national language shall be the Malay language and shall be in such script as Parliament may by law provide'. In hindsight, it is fair to state that this form of words betrayed a particular preconception of the role and purpose of language in such a diverse, multifaceted society as Malaysia. Given the nature of its origins and formation, the priority of the federation in its early days was unequivocal: to promote both internal order and stability and the external security of the state. Consequently the government of the country considered that it needed to integrate the multicultural mosaic into a federal form of national unity in which language would play a pivotal role. The mode of linguistic accommodation was therefore determined by historical and pragmatic considerations.

The thinking that lay behind the Malaysian model of language policy was always clear: its primary purpose was to integrate the many different races and cultures into a multiethnic nation but one in which the Malay language would become the most prominent and widely spoken. The process of nation-building was one in which both the official language and religion of the federation would reflect those of the Malay majority. This did not prohibit the other languages from being actively cultivated and used in both private and public discourse, but judicial interpretation of the phrase 'official purpose' in Article 152(6) meant in practice that they could not be used in the conduct of business with the government or any other administrative body.[90] Compared to the case of Canada, this kind of linguistic compromise appears much less liberal and enlightened, but the constellation of cleavage patterns in respect of language and territory in the two federations is very different, and the Malaysian Constitution does make special provisions for the use of English and native languages in Sabah and Sarawak.[91]

At first glance, the statement in Article 3(1) that 'Islam is the religion of the Federation' gives the understandable impression that Malaysia is an Islamic nation and that it could pave the way for a Muslim theocracy. The reality is that Islam is formally the religion of the state but Article 3(1) also acknowledges that 'other religions may be practised in peace and harmony in any part of the Federation' while Article 11, entitled 'Freedom of Religion', clearly establishes the fundamental right of every person to profess, practise and (subject to legal provisos) propagate his or her own religion. Clearly the official position of Islam, according to the constitution, is elevated in the specific context of an understanding and formal recognition of the constitutional rights of minorities to practise their own religions. Islam remains the religion of the majority in Malaysia but it does not seek either to suffocate or extinguish minority religious practices. As one Malaysian lawyer has put it, 'quite apart from the declaration that Islam is the religion of the federation, Malaysia remains a secular state'.[92] Once again, then, what appears initially to be a somewhat rigid, authoritarian constitutional fiat in theory turns out in practice to be a passive liberal predisposition.

In retrospect, race, language and religion were couched in the specific constitutional formalities of cultural guarantees because of what the Malays construed as a serious economic imbalance that existed between them and the non-Malays. They were deliberately designed to redress this imbalance by formally recognising, protecting and preserving Malay cultural identity against the perceived threat of economic power wielded, in particular, by the Chinese community. The existence of special privileges therefore was really the result of communal political bargaining between the Malays and the mainly Chinese and Indian immigrant populations that had arrived during former British rule. This kind of constitutional asymmetry was the result of a trade-off between special status for *Bumiputras* and a liberal citizenship for Chinese and Indians.[93] Accordingly, the nature of this constitutional elevation appears today more as a defensive insurance policy than some kind of illiberal device to consecrate Malay majoritarianism. This should not, however, be allowed to obscure the fact that some non-Malays remain highly critical of special constitutional preferences for the *Bumiputras* and continue to entertain certain anxieties and resentments about the threat to their own distinctive cultural identities posed by what they perceive as both 'Malayanisation' and 'Islamisation'.

Conclusion

In this chapter we have explored the relationship between federalism, federation and nationalism by focusing principally upon historical perspectives, emergent normative empirical theory and comparative case studies of constitutional, institutional and procedural responses. We have shown that federation in the formal sense of a particular kind of liberal democratic state that embraces and celebrates social diversity via constitutional entrenchment, together with 'federal-type' arrangements in formally non-federal states, are likely to be the most successful institutional response to nationality claims for recognition in multinational democracies. But we have also acknowledged that the satisfaction of such lived and felt needs, which can take many forms, ultimately rests upon a combination of historical specificities, contemporary contextual peculiarities, political legitimacy and the force of a moral discourse embedded in normative empirical liberal democratic theory. There is clearly a complex dynamic at work in such states where the constitutional and political accommodation of nations revolves around notions of internal self-determination and public-policy spaces. Federation, it is clear, is no panacea for such deep-rooted, visceral claims, but it alone displays the hallmark of a constitutional commitment not so much to tame nationalism (as Kymlicka has put it) but to channel and canalise it in forms of peaceful, deliberative discourse where claims can be put on the table, recognised, examined, discussed, negotiated and ultimately answered. This is the continuing seminar in governance, the continuing referendum on first principles.

Our exploration also confirms Taylor's claim that we are in 'an age of identity awakening' where more and more groups in the world 'which could legitimately construe themselves as nations' are 'making demands for recognition'. But is he correct to refer to 'multinational' states as a legitimate category of classification?[94] And is Tully's repeated use of the phrases 'multinational societies' and 'multinational democracies' accurate?[95] There is clear evidence of some genuine intellectual discomfort about this use of terminology and its accuracy in portraying different kinds of nationalism.[96] In a thought-provoking article, published in 2001, entitled 'Canada and the Multinational State', Kenneth McRoberts has questioned the 'new phrase', observing that it is 'not the most fortuitous of terms' because it has 'far too many other meanings'.[97] The conceptual gist of McRoberts' argument is that while we can speak about the presence of multiple nations in a so-called 'multinational state', this is far from claiming that 'the state should itself be multinational'. In other words, it is one thing to speak about a multinational society but it is quite another to base 'the multi-national state itself wholly or in part on the multiple nations it contains'. McRoberts' principal argument is telling: 'very few states that are "multi-national" in their composition are actually "multinational" in their functioning'.[98]

This is precisely where the emerging normative liberal theory of multinationalism outlined in this chapter has already engaged the mainstream intellectual debate on nationalism. Gagnon and Tully – together with Taylor, Kymlicka and other Canadian scholars – have followed a line of thought and reasoning that has evolved in the last decade to include *inter alia* Tamir, Miller, Maiz and Keating.[99] McRoberts is right: multinationalism has become 'no less than an important and influential Canadian school of political thought'. But the intellectual debate must also engage with social and political reality and be translated into the practical language of a public debate if it is to have what Margaret Canovan calls 'some purchase on the world and some relevance for political activity'.[100] Clearly, the largest obstacle to Canada becoming a genuine multinational federation would seem to be the dominant anglophone mindset, with indelible preconceptions, that remains stubbornly resilient about an overarching 'Canadian state nationalism'.[101]

Nonetheless, McRoberts' article has raised important conceptual issues that continue to surround multinational federation, not least the problem of rival conceptions of nation that, at least in Canada, are 'fundamentally opposed'. This argument brings us back full circle to a problem that has long been recognised by writers on nationalism, namely, competing conceptions of what constitutes a nation. It is imperative to clarify this matter in different contexts and social settings if the 'discourse of equality and nation-to-nation negotiation' is to hold.[102] Currently these considerations leave us with a category of multinational federations that unequivocally includes the following: Belgium, India and Malaysia. They also suggest that Canada is a multinational society but is neither organised nor functions as a multinational state. It is therefore a multinational society in a bilingual, multicultural federation. Switzerland, on the other hand, qualifies as neither a multinational society nor a multinational state. It is therefore a multicultural, multilingual federation.

Before we leave the complex subject of this chapter, it is instructive to recall the underlying theoretical thread that connects notions of nations, nationhood and nationality to comparative federalism and federation, namely, liberal democracy itself. At its core we have been surveying what Canovan soberly construes as the reconciliation of 'the universalist aspirations of liberal democratic theory with its particularistic underpinnings'. In other words, we have placed the microscope upon the tensions between 'universal principles and particular solidarities'.[103] It is important not to forget the scale of the problem that we are dealing with here and Canovan's scepticism serves as a salutary warning not only of the dangers of an overly optimistic liberal cosmopolitan persuasion that sees problems of nationalism as ultimately capable of political management, but also as a reminder of the real limits of practical, constitutional and political engineering and design. We have to be aware that there is an alternative school of thought that embraces a consistent scepticism about the matters discussed in this chapter. It is one that challenges the assumptions of a neo-Kantian universalist cosmopolitanism and urges us to confront the realities of power and the distribution of collective power when dealing with contemporary nationality or nationhood.

With these parsimonious remarks and their theoretical implications for multinational federations clearly spelled out, we can conveniently bring the chapter to a close. We are reminded that our empirical focus has been limited to multinational federations and that there are equally interesting multinational states, such as Spain and the United Kingdom, that are not formally federations but which manage their multiple nationalities with admirable success. Different forms of autonomy, devolution and consociational techniques and procedures exist to accommodate sub-state nationalism and, as Simeon and Conway have emphasised, 'by themselves, federal institutions are no guarantee of either success or failure'. The political scientist is confronted by a variety of different federal models together with huge differences in the societal conditions in which federal constitutions and political institutions are meant to operate. This makes it virtually impossible to construct broad generalisations about the effectiveness of federation in multinational societies. Most commentators seem to agree however that one fact remains incontestable: if federation does not guarantee success, it is hard to see any form of successful accommodation of multiple nations within a single state that does not include some form of federal arrangement.[104]

In sounding this practical note of optimism we leave the basic conceptual questions and issues behind us and turn instead in Part II of the book to five chapters that shift the empirical focus to the bases for comparative analysis. We will begin in Chapter 5 with the comparative study of federal political systems that serves as a methodological route map for those students who contemplate different approaches to the subject.

Part II

Bases for comparative analysis

5 The comparative study of federal political systems

Introduction

In 1964 William Riker observed that 'general works on federalism are few in number and spotty in quality', but he nevertheless lamented his own refusal to attempt a comparative study of modern federalism.[1] His overriding concern to assist the general development of political science by providing testable and tested generalisations about comparative federalism was, so he thought, vitiated by the sheer scale of the enterprise. It seemed there were far too many imponderables to make the exercise feasible. According to Riker, these uncertainties could be reduced to the need for 'information about history, the sensitivity to culture and the linguistic competence to examine all these societies' that claimed to be federal – a task well beyond the ability of the 'isolated scholar'.[2] Instead only a 'semi-comparative' study of federalism was deemed practicable, although Riker believed it had the undoubted merit of improving considerably upon what then conventionally passed for 'comparative government'. This meant that it at least went beyond mere description to political analysis.

However, that was in 1964. Forty years later – and after a series of professorial revisions to the traditional approaches to the subject that we outlined in Chapter 1 – can we now be more optimistic about the comparative study of federal political systems? At the outset it is only right and proper for us to acknowledge Kenneth Wheare's classic study entitled *Federal Government*, published originally in 1946, as the first genuinely comparative study of federal political systems (despite its title).[3] Riker dismissed it as 'highly legalistic in tone', claiming that it displayed 'very little understanding of political realities', but his consternation in the 1960s really reflected the intellectual debate in the USA concerning the so-called 'behavioural revolution' in the social sciences.[4] Since then political scientists have developed new classificatory concepts that today are much more capable of eliciting extensive information which is sufficiently precise to be compared. We have already traced the conceptual and methodological evolution of federalism and federation in Chapter 1 and we have seen how far the intellectual debate has enabled us successfully to 'compare like with like'.

In this chapter I want to examine five principal bases for the comparative study of federal political systems. These bases act as conceptual lenses or prisms through which the political scientist can identify and explore both the similarities and differences between distinct federal systems. The five bases are as follows: the structure of federations; the sociological bases of federations, the political economy of federations that explains the bases of ideology, political parties and party systems and constitutional reform and judicial review. Each of these provides an insight into different aspects and dimensions of a variety of federal systems that enhances our understanding and appreciation of how they work, what their priorities are and why they vary, and how they adapt to change and development. In this way the student of federal political systems can choose to follow different pathways into the subject that each reveal a particular feature of the federal whole and can offer clues pointing to at least partial answers to research questions. Let us begin our comparative examination in the order in which we have just identified them.

The structure of federations

Most studies of federations recognise three broad types: the Westminster model, the republican-presidential model and a hybrid mixture of both types. The Westminster model, based on representative and responsible parliamentary government, applies in particular to Canada, Australia and India – as former parts of the British Empire – while the republican-presidential model is most closely associated with the USA. Hybrid examples that combine various elements of these two models include Germany, Austria and Switzerland while Belgium with its constitutional monarchy and cabinet government responsible to a lower house, the Chamber of Deputies, might be considered closer to the Westminster model than the republican-presidential type. These groups of comparisons work well from the standpoint of internal structures, but we also have to consider how they would change if we adopted another perspective, namely, the question of the distribution of powers in federations.

This viewpoint, as Ronald Watts has recently demonstrated, alters the kaleidoscope of comparison in significant ways.[5] As Watts has pointed out, the basic design of all federations is to express what Daniel Elazar called 'self-rule plus shared rule' via the constitutional distribution of powers between those assigned to the federal government for common purposes and those assigned to the constituent units for purposes of local autonomy and the preservation of specific identities and interests.[6] And it should be noted that the division of powers and competences can be organised on a territorial *and* a non-territorial basis. In federal systems there are always at least two orders of government, whose existence is firmly entrenched in a written constitution that is subject to specific amendment procedures and judicial review. And the specific form and allocation of the distribution of powers have always varied according to the specific circumstances of each federation.

Watts has claimed that, for example, 'the more the degree of homogeneity in a society the greater the powers that have been allocated to the federal government, and the more the degree of diversity the greater the powers that have been assigned to the constituent units of government'.[7] However, this (as he admits) is a broad generalisation and it has not always been quite so simple in the highly diversified societies of India and Malaysia. The existence of the Emergency Provisions that comprise the nine Articles 352–360 of Part XVIII of the Indian Constitution and the eighteen-month period of Emergency rule during 1975–77 testify to the potential power resources available to the federal government. Indeed, where the President considers that a state of emergency exists either because of external aggression or internal disturbance, 'the distribution of powers can be so drastically altered that the Constitution becomes unitary rather than federal'.[8] Moreover, while it is true that India approximates to the Westminster parliamentary federal model it is not an exact replica of either Canada or Australia. The Constituent Assembly that produced the draft constitution was able to draw upon the experience of a wide variety of federations so that what ultimately emerged and has since been much modified and amended was a new federal model tailored to the peculiar needs of India and 'the exigencies of the times'.[9]

In Malaysia, too, there is clear evidence of a distribution of powers that can be and has been altered to suit the tastes of the federal government in Kuala Lumpur. Article 75 of the Federal Constitution clearly establishes federal supremacy in the event of state law being inconsistent with federal law. This article is of paramount importance in the event of conflict between state and federal governments because it effectively allows the federal government to interfere in state legislation on virtually any matter. Article 76 also allows the federal government to encroach upon state competences (as enumerated in the State List) in pursuit of the uniformity of law with the exception of Sabah and Sarawak. Powers to cope with emergencies are embodied in Article 150 of the Constitution, which the *yang di-pertuan agong* can interpret to issue a Proclamation of Emergency granting both the parliament and/or the federal government virtually unlimited powers. These powers have been invoked on several occasions to meet various crises that have occurred in the life of the federation, including the confrontation with Indonesia in 1964, the constitutional impasse in Sarawak in 1966, the racial riots of 1969 and the political crisis in Kelantan in 1977, not to mention the subsequent extensions of central (federal) powers in the Constitution (Amendment) Act (1981) that gave 'unbridled power to the executive to declare an emergency at will and to perpetuate emergency rule' that contains the potential for authoritarian rule to be introduced at 'the stroke of a pen'.[10] Indeed, one authority on the Federal Constitution has claimed that Malaysia's undoubted economic and social prosperity and political stability have been bought at the expense of constitutionalism and the rule of law:

> A historical survey of constitutional amendments since 1957 gives credence to the view that the Constitution is treated in a somewhat cavalier fashion. Often the amendments are effected to achieve short-term political gains or to facilitate long-term expansion of executive powers. There appears to be an obsession with the need to control at least two-thirds of the seats of the Federal Parliament. ... The fine line between constitutional government and outright authoritarian rule has become even finer.[11]

This pattern of relations between the federal centre and the constituent units in Malaysia is clearly an historical relic, a legacy of British rule. We can easily trace this legacy from the Malayan Union (1946), the Federation of Malaya (1948), the Federation of Malaya (1957) and the Federation of Malaysia (1963) to see that strong federal government has resulted in the highly centralised federation that exists today. In both India and Malaysia, then, the priority of state security – of internal order and external threat – has shaped the structure of the federation. And it has been the overriding objective that has served in practice to enhance the growth of executive power over and above increasing concerns for liberal democratic constitutionalism. But if we shift our attention away from the formal distribution of powers and look instead at a different perspective, namely, 'administrative-executive' procedures in federations, we alter the kaleidoscope of comparison still further.

From this perspective, the legislative process enables the constituent state governments to administer federal legislation, giving them policy influence and latitude in how it is implemented in different parts of the federation. Germany, Austria and Switzerland constitute an obvious basis for comparison in this respect, but a shift of focus towards the study of 'intergovernmental relations' in federations could conceivably facilitate valid comparisons not only between, say, Canada and the USA but also between Canada and Germany, where a more precisely defined 'executive federalism' underlining the key role of governments could be employed. The interlocking relationship between the federal and *lander* governments in Germany is in some respects unique, but there is sufficient similarity with the Canadian case to warrant a comparative focus that could provide insight. Moreover, federal–provincial relations in Canada have evolved in similar, although not identical, ways to Australia and even to the German model, involving, for example, regular formal meetings between federal and provincial ministers and their respective civil servants that suggest a symbiotic association in both legislative and public policy terms along the lines stipulated in their constitutions.[12]

These considerations about the structure of federations raise many important questions in the comparative study of federal systems that we cannot address here. However, it is appropriate to call attention to one issue in particular that is extremely complex and retains its contemporary significance, namely, the question concerning the design of federations. Put simply, does constitutional and institutional design matter in federations? The real complexity of the question can be more fully appreciated if we acknowledge at least two preliminary considerations: first, the origins and formation of each federation; and, second, the relationship between each federation's complex of institutions and its social context. The former consideration gives us some idea of the primary purpose(s) of each federation – its principal *raison d'être* – while the latter compels us to examine in detail the interaction between each federation and the social context in which it is embedded. For Roger Gibbins the departure point of analysis is that 'some rough initial symmetry will exist between the nature of the underlying society and that of the new federal institutions'. Indeed, to some extent 'federal institutions will "reflect" the nature of the society'.[13] This is what earlier writers meant when they alluded broadly to 'federal state' and 'federal society', and it is also what Preston King meant when he claimed that 'if we understand the problems, the understanding of structure more clearly follows'.[14] These contributors reinforce the point that both of these factors – the origins and formation of each federation and federal state–society relations – require detailed analysis before any answer can be forthcoming about institutional design.[15]

Clearly the role of political elites in constructing federations is one focus of research – identifying who they were and what were their motives – but the interaction between constitutions and political institutions and the society in which they operate requires a developmental approach over a long period of time. This reminds us of what Maurice Vile once claimed when comparing federal systems: the most difficult question is that of change and development.[16] But the question of how to conceptualise change and development is itself predicated upon the kinds of distinctions that we draw between different social diversities. Everything depends on the character of the diversity and its political salience. The pertinent point to be made about investigations into traditional state–society relations, then, is that there are many conceptual and empirical imponderables which make it virtually impossible to make anything other than broad generalisations about whether or not institutional design matters.

In a recent survey that looked at the conditions under which a federal political system is likely to be successful, Richard Simeon and Daniel-Patrick Conway concluded on a note of cautious optimism: institutional design *did* matter but 'by themselves, federal institutions are no guarantee of either success or failure'.[17] They needed to be reinforced by other societal, procedural and institutional factors. Simeon's and Conway's research strongly suggests that to be successful institutional design would have to be based *at a minimum* upon the following preconditions:

1   A coexistence between local–regional community sub-state identities, values and loyalties and significant elements of shared, overarching identities and values in the federation at large.
2   These dual values, identities and loyalties must be reflected in the central institutions of the federation so that different forms of representation facilitate the expression of different interests on different policy matters.
3   Additional to the central institutional framework, a series of consociational techniques and procedures related to decision-making and the overarching accommodation of elite interests must be introduced.
4. Attention should be paid to the changing character of the social diversities that express political salience in order to adapt and adjust both to the new, as well as to a reawakening of the old, identities, values and loyalties.

Let us turn now to the second of our conceptual lenses through which we can compare federal systems, namely, the sociological bases of federations.

The sociological bases of federations

This focus for our comparative survey of federal political systems takes us back to the controversies that continue to surround the debate about a 'federal society'. We have already referred in Chapter 4 to the 'sociological fallacy', a phrase coined by Brian Galligan to dismiss the arguments advanced by those who advocate the federal idea specifically for countries with a high degree of social heterogeneity, but the kernel of the argument stretches back to William Livingston's seminal article entitled 'A Note on the Nature of Federalism', first published in the *Political Science Quarterly* in 1952.[18]

Livingston's famous declaration that 'the essence of federalism (sic federation) lies not in the institutional or constitutional structure but in the society itself' has been the source of a lively scholarly debate that continues today to permeate public affairs in federal states. Given that the conceptual and empirical focus of this perspective is the sociological bases of federation, it is rooted in the following social cleavages that, broadly speaking, have different levels of political salience in different federations at different times: sub-state nationalism, linguistic diversities, territorial identities, religious differences, indigenous peoples and communal tradition. It is important to note that it is not the mere existence of a particular social cleavage that matters in a federation so much as the constellation of cleavage patterns having political salience. How the variety of social cleavages is territorially distributed throughout the federal state and how far this distribution changes is crucial to the stability of the constitutional and political order. And in the terms used in this book, we are reminded that these cleavage patterns represent the *federalism* in federation.

We have already looked in detail at the complex composition and significance of nationalism in federation in Chapter 4 and we have seen that both the character and territorial distribution of sub-state nationalism are key factors in determining the nature of this relationship. It has to be assessed according to the circumstances of each individual case. Similarly with the category of linguistic diversities: the way that language is spoken throughout the federation is crucial to its political significance in different federations. For example, the potentially divisive politics of language in Switzerland is mediated by the cross-cutting cleavages of religion, custom and territory that tend to damp down social conflict while these have the opposite impact of reinforcing conflict and competition between the dominant linguistic communities in Belgium. It is sometimes difficult for the social scientist to determine for analytical purposes whether or not a distinct linguistic community has become, or sees itself as, a distinct nation, but few would dispute this in Quebec, Catalonia, Euzkadi, Punjab, Sabah and Sarawak, and there are many minority voices that would also claim this status for Flanders, Wallonia, Kashmir, Assam, Malaya and francophone Acadia inside established (multinational) federations.

Territoriality is also a key factor when dealing with sociological variables. It is a very complex phenomenon that is often glossed over by political scientists who have sometimes confused it with geography and have in consequence impoverished the concept. In one particular sense, preconceptions of territoriality as a rather one-dimensional, if oversimplified, cleavage in federations are to be entirely expected. This is because federations are *ipso facto* composed of clearly demarcated constituent units that are territorial units, that is, they are to do with space, place and political processes. The German *lander*, the Swiss cantons and the Canadian provinces are all territorially bounded communities that represent the political organisation of space in the occupation of the territorial state. And in most, although not all, examples of federation, territoriality – the sense of place – plays a significant role in their self-definition.

A survey of territoriality in the mainstream literature on federalism and federation strongly suggests an uncritical and excessive reliance upon the concept.[19] In practice the notion of territory has been utilised as both a dependent and an independent variable in social-science analysis. But it is in reality a composite term that incorporates an amalgam of socio-economic and cultural elements encapsulated in a spatial organisation. It is therefore wrong to construe territoriality as if it is something akin to an empty container that stands in its own right as an independent variable set apart from other patterns of social cleavages having political salience. Territorial identity cannot be construed in isolation from other social cleavages that interact with it to forge distinct identities, that is, a strong sense of self. The reality, as usual, is more complex. To appreciate the proper significance of territoriality in federal systems, it must be viewed as part of the *federalism* in federation: it is, in short, part of the larger conception of the politics of difference that inheres in discussions of federalism. In practice, territoriality interacts with a variety of intervening social variables to produce complex forms of political identity.

Territoriality, then, is considerably more complex than the contributors to the early intellectual debate seemed to suggest. The nebulous and shifting nature of territory is perhaps best illuminated by adapting Frank Trager's claim: territoriality is not a fixed point on a map.[20] A proper analysis of the social, economic, political and cultural-ideological forces involved in the processes of decision-making would demonstrate that the composition of the so-called 'territorial aggregate' – and consequently its concerns – varies from one policy issue to the next. Territoriality is therefore a dynamic not a static concept in political science that means much more than the notion of constituent regional units in federations. In terms of *federalism* the focus of the survey shifts to the interaction of a wide range of socio-economic and cultural-ideological factors that interact to produce a distinct sense of territorial identification. This means that 'territoriality' should not be oversimplified, nor should it be referred to in absolute terms. Unless we are referring specifically to the administrative machinery of the state, it is advisable to construe territoriality as at best an intervening variable that can be extrapolated by the social scientist only in abstract terms.

Before we leave territoriality as a social cleavage, it is appropriate to make a passing reference to the notion of non-territorial federalism already mentioned in the case of Belgium in Chapter 4. We must not to forget that the idea of the territorial state, originating in the principle of *ius soli*, and having exclusive power over all the people living within its boundaries, is relatively recent. Prior to the emergence of the modern sovereign state in sixteenth-century Europe, the competing principle of *ius sanguinis*, based upon the idea of personality, furnished the basis for a viable alternative model of state organisation that had thrived in medieval Europe and in the Holy Roman Empire.

This model suggested that human relationships need not be territorially based at all. Indeed, as John Ruggie has noted, systems of rule existed whereby spatial extension was demarcated on the basis of kinship and it was only the shift from consanguinity to contiguity as the relevant spatial parameter that elevated territoriality to a new organisational level. In practice both territorial and non-territorial forms of human association and political organisation coexisted in sixteenth-, seventeenth- and eighteenth-century Europe. In other words, certain rights, duties and obligations criss-crossed territorial boundaries in medieval Europe because 'authority was both personalized and parcelized within and across territorial formations and for which inclusive bases of legitimation prevailed'.[21] We are reminded that a version of this non-territorial federalism surfaced during the last days of the Austro-Hungarian Empire when Karl Renner and Otto Bauer proposed novel forms of association to resolve the nationalities question. This non-territorial or corporate federalism combined the principles of personal autonomy (or the principle of personality) and national and ethnic unity so that no nationality possessed a special claim to a fixed territory and autonomous status applied to the individual not to a territory.[22]

Traditionally religious differences as a social cleavage having political salience in federations have been a potent and highly divisive source of both violent and non-violent conflict. This is because religion is a cultural-ideological cleavage that is extremely difficult to engage for the purpose of negotiation. Religion is what political scientists call a non-bargainable issue. It is not something that can be traded as a public good because it entails metaphysical issues about faith and the human spirit that are non-negotiable. This means in practice that religious differences are tantamount to a zero-sum conflict: what one actor gains the other one loses. But religion is rarely viewed in isolation. Rather it is usually construed as part of a larger cultural identity and, once again, its political significance depends mainly upon its relationship to a range of other distinct sociological variables. It is, after all, perfectly possible to accommodate religious differences in non-federal states using legal and constitutional means to protect and preserve distinct identities. The example of British Muslims demonstrates the existence of an ethnic group with a distinct set of cultural values and a shared language that pursues no territorial claims and lacks an intrinsically political identity. In other words, Islamic identity does not necessarily imply the need for political autonomy in a clearly demarcated territorial unit.

Religious differences, then, must be identified and located as part of the larger constellation of cleavage patterns in a federation. Historically the conflict between the Roman Catholic and the Protestant cantons that came to a head in the *Sonderbund* Civil War in 1847 in Switzerland has been softened by the modernising forces of secularisation and the cross-cutting nature of the religious cleavage with those of language and territory so that there are French-speaking Protestant cantons as well as German-speaking Catholic cantons.[23] Roman Catholicism constituted a significant part of the identity of francophone Quebecois up until the 'Quiet Revolution' of the 1960s and it continues to play more than a passive role in the *lander* of Bavaria and Baden-Württemberg in southern Germany while the impact of Hispanic culture has served to increase the use of the Spanish language and boost the strength of the Roman Catholic Church in the USA. In India 82 per cent of the population are Hindus, but the existence of Muslims (12 per cent), Christians (2.5 per cent), Sikhs (2 per cent) and Buddhists (1 per cent) has created a veritable social mosaic where religious differences interact with regionalism, territoriality, language, the caste system and a plurality of beliefs and practices while Malaysia, despite its official promotion of Islam in the Federal Constitution, also exemplifies a multi-religious federation including Hindus, Christians, Buddhists, Taoists and native animists.[24] And once again the characteristic feature of these multi-religious federations is the cross-cutting nature of the religious cleavage. It is true that religion and ethnic identity, broadly speaking, reinforce each other in Malaysia, but the territorial distribution of the Chinese and Indian non-Malays, the conflicts within the *Bumiputera* (the native 'sons of the soil') between Malays and non-Malays and tensions among Malay Muslims in peninsular Malaysia caused by differences about the need for an Islamic state have served to produce a kind of *modus operandi* that has allowed for peaceful coexistence and cooperation in religious affairs.[25]

Religion as an intrinsically intractable cultural-ideological cleavage in political affairs has been commonly perceived in the late twentieth-century Western world to be in retreat in the face of the secularising forces of modernisation, but it is now clear in the new millennium that this perception is outdated. The revival and resurgence of the Islamic faith has compelled social scientists in general to reassess and reappraise the role of religion in public affairs and it may conceivably exert a renewed pressure on multi-ethnic and multicultural federations in the foreseeable future. So, too, might the challenge of indigenous or native peoples, sometimes referred to also as Aboriginal Peoples and First Nations.

It is no exaggeration to state that the late twentieth century witnessed a worldwide reawakening and mobilisation of indigenous peoples in several states, including the federations of Canada, the USA, Australia and Malaysia. The terminology and labels used to identify these communities vary according to each country, but the basic thrust of a constitutional and political assertion of human rights, freedom, justice and collective identity is unmistakable. Given that the hallmark of federations is recognition of and respect for diversity and difference in its many forms, it is only to be expected that they should be well disposed to accommodating the interests of these new territorial and non-territorial political actors. And they are symptomatic of the dynamic relationship that exists between federalism and federation. Aboriginal politics is yet another example of the federalism in federation. Whether or not these collective identities will be successfully accommodated on the basis of equality as new partners in the federation or afforded a subordinate constitutional status will doubtless vary according to the kaleidoscope of organised political forces that mobilise around the issue in each federal state, and it is clear from the contrasting constitutional outcomes in Canada and Australia that different federations will respond to the situation in different ways.[26]

The creation of Nunavut in 1999 in Canada is a good example of how federations adjust and adapt to contemporary change. New actors appear on the political terrain representing new challenges to the federation so that new bargains have to be struck in order to address new claims for justice and renew the legitimacy of existing federal polity. This once again is reminiscent of Daniel Elazar's famous reference to the appearance of constitutional demands as providing both governors and governed in federal polities with 'a continuing seminar in governance' in which they must constantly ask the questions: Is it possible? Is it right?[27] And these questions have at their core a tension and tussle between what are undoubtedly moral judgments and the realities of power resources.

The brief consideration of Aboriginal claims, then, brings our list of the sociological bases of federations to an appropriate close. It is clear that the debate triggered by Livingston in the early 1950s about the sociological bases of federation and which confirmed the idea of a federal society remains a part of the scholarly discourse but his conceptual analysis was flawed. The easy assumption that the mere existence of sociological bases necessarily implied a federal society was tautological. It remains unclear just what a federal society looks like or should look like. Today it is probably much more accurate to acknowledge the significance of sociological bases, where they exist, but to resist the temptation to designate federal states *ipso facto* as having federal societies.

Having already touched upon socio-economic factors in federations, let us now focus more sharply on political economy as a conceptual approach to the comparative study of federal systems. Here we will encounter the direct interaction between politics and economics that shapes the underlying constitutional and political agendas of federal and provincial governments in federations.

Political economy: the bases of ideology

The political economy approach to the understanding of federal states is predicated upon the dynamic relationship between the changing structure of national, regional and local economies and the political system(s) in which they operate. Clearly if federations are founded upon the principles of difference and diversity that engender the territorial dispersion of power in a variety of ways, it is important to examine precisely how the federal constitution and the political process relate to the nature and distribution of economic power and resources in the state. Since the end of the Cold War, signalled by the collapse of the Soviet and East European communist regimes, it is perfectly reasonable to assume that our empirical focus is liberal democratic states in which constitutionalism and the rule of law are based upon the capitalist mode of production. Federations therefore are rooted in capitalism. There is still room for both Marxist and non-Marxist liberal analyses of political economy, but the dominant economic paradigm today remains the market model.

In one particular sense the adoption of this kind of approach is quite revealing: it underscores capitalism as an economic ideology. Once we accept that capitalism is the economic base of federation, it logically follows that federations, in turn, are liberal democratic capitalist states based upon capitalist values, beliefs and goals. And if the primary purpose of capitalism is the accumulation of capital in its many forms, this conceptual lens must be riveted upon how far federal systems are structured and restructured to serve this overall objective. In this light, federations 'move and change' (to use Preston King's terms) in a manner that reflects purpose, and since 'some form of federalism is always implicit in any given federation at any given time' we shall regard the purpose of capital accumulation identified here as essentially ideological. Federalism, then, is inherently ideological.[28]

The political economy approach is useful for the way that it goes to the very heart of the relationship between economics and politics and enables us to focus sharply upon the way that federalism and federation function in order principally to maximise economic profitability and welfare in its broadest sense. Accordingly, political debates and arguments about constitutional reform, fiscal federalism, regional resources and the division of powers that address the distribution of competences in federal states can be construed in terms of the nature of economic power and the relations between government(s) and key corporate actors. Viewed from this perspective, federalism and federation can be relegated to the conceptual status of dependent variables in social-science analysis. And federal systems become mere instruments of vested capitalist interests. However, it is important that we do not go too far in this direction. Political economy is not mere 'economic determinism'. We must not disregard the force of human agency and the relative autonomy of political and cultural life. This is why Wallace Clement's definition of political economy is suitable for our purposes here:

> While the economic provides the context, it is the political and the cultural/ideological that write the text of history, the particularities of each nation, and the possibilities for the future. The script is one in which human actors have significant freedom of action.[29]

Clearly this is an extremely complex relationship that is customarily located at the local, regional, national and continental levels and has now been extended to include globalisation so that the comparative study of federal systems appears to underline three distinct dimensions: the scope of the analysis, the interconnectedness of the phenomena under scrutiny and the notion of linkage. Let us look first at Canada, where the political economy of federalism and federation can be used to help to explain important shifts in the constitutional, political and public-policy agenda.

Here scope, interconnectedness and linkage are brought into sharp relief. Scope refers to the location of government and public affairs in general within a wide framework that encompasses local, provincial, national and international imperatives. Interconnectedness is used to emphasise that 'political economy makes the connection between the economic, political and cultural/ideological moments of social life in a holistic way'.[30] Public-policy issues therefore cannot be portrayed and examined as a discrete phenomenon divorced from their material bases. They can never be agnostic towards power relations. Indeed, if we investigate the constitutional reform agenda in Canada during the last half-century we can see that it is purposive and designed to reflect and accommodate changing power structures. Finally the notion of linkage stresses the quintessentially interdisciplinary nature of the political-economy tradition. Here the significance attached to constitutional reform is determined by the particular standpoint from which it is viewed. In other words, we would need to examine in detail how far economic policy impinges upon constitutional affairs and *vice versa*. This would entail a thorough investigation into the nature of the relationship between economic policy at both provincial and national levels and constitutional politics in general.[31]

The political economy of constitutional reform in Canada suggests that the combination of scope, interconnectedness and linkage politics identified above are responsible for the coexistence of conflict and consensus manifested in the struggle to achieve a constitutional settlement. The changing political economy has been both the cause and the explanation of conflict and consensus in Canada. The form might change – sometimes conflict, sometimes consensus – but the content remains the same. Richard Simeon put it thus:

> Levels of interregional and intergovernmental conflict, cooperation or competition are not primarily a matter of constitutions or of intergovernmental machinery. They are a function of the underlying political economy, the issues that arise, the mobilization of interests and the ambitions of federal and provincial leaders.[32]

In Canada the regional structure of the national economy combines with the federal structure of the state to produce intermittent trends in favour of the centralisation and/or the decentralisation of economic and political power resources. In some instances there is a strong tide in some provinces for Ottawa to take charge of economic policy while in other cases there is a distinct trend in favour of strengthening provincial economic powers. In a famous essay entitled 'Federalism and the Political Economy of the Canadian State', published in 1977, Garth Stevenson adapted insights derived from Marxist writings on the capitalist state to the peculiar circumstances of what he saw as Canada's decentralised federation.[33] In this essay he demonstrated how far the changing nature of the Canadian economy over time placed great strains on the federal structure. The defence of vested economic interests in Montreal and Winnipeg that required a strong central (federal) government in Ottawa gradually gave way after the First World War to new strongholds of economic power in Toronto, Vancouver and, later, Calgary, that had less need of Ottawa than their predecessors, but whose interests necessitated much more control of the provincial states.

This explained the growing pressure for a marked decentralisation of power that accelerated after the Second World War. Provincial jurisdiction over resources made control over the provincial state apparatus important to certain sections of the capitalist class, and gave them the incentive to push for a strengthening of the provinces that enabled them to 'assume new functions and acquire new assets'.[34] Apart from the hegemony of American economic imperial interests, the overall conclusion to this study clearly demonstrated the way that shifting economic power resources impinge upon federal–provincial relations. These relations, in turn, have a significant impact upon the larger questions of constitutional reform and the strength of Quebec sub-state nationalism and separatism.[35]

The links between the political economy and constitutional reform agendas – or the reform of the state structure – in federations could hardly be more explicit than in Germany. Processes of European integration and German unification combined in the 1990s to put enormous pressure on the federal state to reassess and reappraise many of its basic internal structures and socio-economic values, interests and public policies. The constitutional reform agenda was bulging with proposals that involved *inter alia* the rationalisation of constituent units in the federation, a new formula for fiscal federal relations, changes in both the composition and decision-making processes of the Bundesrat and new forms of representation in the EU. But political economy had also been at the heart of these pressures for change in Germany even before the convulsive decade of the 1990s. Already in the 1980s pressure for change was beginning to mount as the north–south divide between the wealthy *lander*, such as Bavaria and Baden–Württemberg, in the south and the relatively poor *lander*, such as Bremen and Saarland, in the north furnished the basis for increasing political conflict and confrontation.[36]

One legacy of the double movement of unification, on the one hand, and closer European integration, on the other, has been the intensification of the constitutional reform debate and a heightened tension about the role of the *lander* in the federation. The old north–south fault line characteristic of the national political economy dating back to the Basic Law of 1949 has been superseded by an east–west divide that in economic terms has pitted the five new eastern *lander* of Berlin, Saxony-Anhalt, Thuringia, Mecklenberg-Western Pomerania and Brandenburg against the original 11 *lander* of West Germany. Unification has placed new economic burdens on the fiscal base of the German federal system and this has given rise to much discontent in the western *lander* that are having to shoulder most of the costs of fiscal equalisation and redistribution. As a result the earlier strains and tensions that were already an established feature of the north–south divide before 1990 have been dwarfed by the huge economic costs of a unification that has served to exacerbate the regional patterns of economic development.[37] During the past decade, therefore, Germany and the Germans have been concentrating their efforts on absorbing these new members of the federation in terms of the 'uniform' (now 'equivalency') 'living conditions' originally enshrined in Section 72(2) of the Basic Law.

The political economy of a new Germany, with 16 constituent *lander* having highly variegated local economies grouped into areas with large regional disparities, seems likely to dominate domestic politics for at least another decade and provides a useful and interesting comparative case study.

Notable in both Canada and Germany is a fundamental constitutional commitment concerning the distribution of economic resources and financial capacities between the federation and the constituent units. Article 72(2) of the Basic Law in Germany is equivalent to Canada's guarantee in Section 36(2) of the Constitution Act (1982) to 'provide reasonably comparable levels of public services at reasonably comparable levels of taxation'.[38] In practice a variety of both constitutional and non-constitutional arrangements exist in federations to enable federal governments to allocate resources. In some cases, as in Australia and India, the federal government is the dominant player in both revenue-raising and expenditure activities while in others there is evidence of a much more balanced arrangement between revenue and spending powers, as in Canada, Switzerland and Germany. The relationship between revenue-raising and expenditure powers, vertical and horizontal imbalances, and fiscal equalisation and transfers is broadly designed to ensure that constituent units do not fall below what are deemed national standards in the provision of public services.[39] India, for example, has had a formal commitment to planning since 1950 that has been pivotal in its economic development, enabling the centralised Planning Commission to take an overall view of the needs and resources of the country. The Indian Constitution also provided for independent Finance Commissions that report at five-year intervals on the distribution of tax revenues between the Union and the constituent states, Union grants-in-aid to the states, and basic transfers to the states, the panchayats and the municipalities. Together the Planning Commission and the 11 Finance Commissions to date have sought to strike a balance between the competing and sometimes conflicting pressures of national and regional economic development and central–state relations.[40]

The shift in the 1990s in the structure of the national political economy in India from a huge public sector in basic, heavy industries towards the private sector and economic deregulation has signalled a new era in centre–state relations.[41] Currently the federation is attempting to find a *modus operandi* between developmental planning, market development and fiscal decentralisation. Already the prosperous states of Andhra Pradesh, Gujarat, Maharashtra and Tamil Nadu find themselves in precisely the same position in India as the wealthy *lander* of Bavaria and Baden–Württemberg in Germany or the well-to-do provinces of British Columbia and Alberta in Canada, while the Flemish in Belgium increasingly complain at having to cushion the economic impact of industrial decline in Wallonia.

Fiscal federalism, then, is in many ways a function of the national political economy and it serves to highlight several fundamental features of federation that are worth more than a moment's glance. Indeed, for those interested in how federations change and develop or more specifically how different federations exhibit centralising and/or decentralising trends, the study of fiscal federalism is illuminating to the point of being a veritable litmus test of what we might call 'federality'. It is understandable therefore if some students of comparative federalism and federation use fiscal federal relations as their main yardstick to measure just how *federal* federations are. Clearly fiscal federalism has a direct bearing upon how federations work, not only in economic terms but also in terms of government and politics. It is a source of both conflict and consensus in federal–state relations, but its significance stretches much further than just this. It can also help to determine the political legitimacy, relative political stability and even the future of the federation itself. For some, it is no exaggeration to claim that fiscal federalism takes us to the very heart of what makes federation tick.[42]

Today fiscal federalism is no longer an object of study that is reserved for economists alone.[43] It remains a highly specialised field of enquiry, but it is one that requires the active cooperation of economists *and* political scientists working together to produce well-rounded explanations of how and why federations operate as they do. In a recent short survey of comparative research in this subject, Ronald Watts put it thus:

> I would argue that in considering the dynamics of federal and intergovernmental relations it is *also* important to consider the broader social and political context within which these financial relations operate. In virtually all federal and intergovernmental systems, financial relations have invariably constituted an important, indeed crucial, aspect of their *political* operation. ... This political significance places financial relations between central and constituent-unit governments at the heart of the processes of intergovernmental relations. Intergovernmental financial arrangements are therefore not simply technical adjustments but inevitably the result of *political* compromises.[44]

One conclusion is clear and irrefutable: when investigating how federations work, the basic principles at stake cannot be reduced simply to the economic concepts of efficiency and equity. The basic economic functions of modern government comprise the allocation of resources, stabilisation and redistribution but the efficient, effective and equitable running of the national economy in federations cannot be explained solely in these terms. A detailed explanation of the function and role of fiscal federalism would also require us to take into account the constitutional and political dimensions of federal systems. These include the constitutional assumptions entrenched in each and every federation, the nature of the federal political system, the role of the federal and constituent state party systems and the durability of federal values inherent in the federal spirit.[45] Comparative surveys of fiscal federalism, then, should be construed as part of the larger study of the political economy of federations.

Political parties and party systems

The significance of political parties and party systems for the comparative study of federalism and federation is well established. It has been the subject of some considerable attention and debate in the Anglo-American literature since at least the early 1960s. Kenneth Wheare devoted only four pages to parties and party systems in his classic study entitled *Federal Government*, first published in 1946, but David B. Truman's oft-quoted 'Federalism and the Party System' appeared in 1955, while William Riker in 1964 and Aaron Wildavsky in 1967 both emphasised the significance of parties and the structure and organisation of party systems in federations.[46] Indeed, we will recall that for Riker it was the structure of the party system that was 'the main variable intervening between the background social conditions and the specific nature of the federal bargain'.[47]

The main focus of the intellectual debate about the role of political parties in federations has been how far their internal organisation and the structure of party systems have impinged upon the operation and maintenance of federal systems. This is an intricate relationship that requires close and careful examination since it involves a whole host of factors that are interrelated in complex fashion. Political parties are vehicles and instruments of organised, vested interests that express particular values, beliefs and aspirations, and these interests and values change over time so that parties are able to channel and canalise them through the various structures and institutions of the state. In federations this means that parties and party systems can function as a kind of prism through which the social scientist can effectively track their impact upon different parts of the political system. It is in this sense that we can understand why Riker chose parties and party systems as a route into 'the measurement of federalism' first in 1964 and then again later in 1975.[48] Let us look briefly at his approach to the relationship between parties, party systems and the maintenance of federal systems.

Riker began this exploration by looking at the kind of party organisations that operated at the two main levels of government in federations. This focus prompted him to claim that a fairly consistent relationship existed that could be accurately summarised in the following well-known proposition:

> The federal relationship is centralized according to the degree to which the parties organized to operate the central government control the parties organized to operate the constituent governments. This amounts to the assertion that the proximate cause of variations in the degree of centralization (or peripheralization) in the constitutional structure of a federalism is the variation in degree of party centralization. ... There are strong *a priori* arguments for the validity of this assertion of a causal connection.[49]

Riker's conclusion was that empirical evidence existed to support the notion that the degree of partisan unity between the constituent and central governments was 'closely related to changes in the federal relationship' and that 'to a very high degree variations in the federal relationship, especially variations in the ability of constituent governments to conflict with the central government', depended on 'variations in partisan relationships between the two levels'.[50] He exported these conclusions into his later extended essay on federalism that

appeared in 1975 and it enabled him once again to call attention to the relationship between types of party system and degrees of political centralisation in
federal systems. His own research into the contemporary mainstream literature
suggested that there was a correlation between decentralised parties and relatively decentralised federations by which he meant that many significant political
decisions were still made by constituent state governments. And at the other end
of the spectrum, it also seemed clear that this correlation applied in reverse.
Thus the examples of the Soviet Union, Yugoslavia and Mexico as highly
centralised federations with highly centralised party systems seemed to confirm
the hypothesis. However, while it was impossible to state either that particular
federal structures and institutions (federation) *caused* the decentralisation of
parties or that the decentralisation of parties *sustained* a relatively decentralised
federation, there was a high probability that 'the two things go along together in
a relation of reciprocal reinforcement'.[51] The empirical evidence appeared to
support this carefully measured statement.

Riker arrived at the following destination: in a variety of federal governments
the structure of parties parallels the structure of federations so that when parties
are centralised so is the federation and when they are 'somewhat decentralised'
then federation is also relatively decentralised. He was therefore able to reiterate
his earlier claim, originally made in 1964, that 'one can measure federalism by
measuring parties'. His overall conclusion was consequently unequivocal: 'the
structure of parties is thus a surrogate for the structure of the whole constitution'. What mattered, then, was 'the degree to which the party in control of the
central government controls the constituent governments'.[52] And he had already
devised his so-called 'index of disharmony' (or 'index of state–party independence') almost twenty years earlier as a practical way of using this particular
measure. Riker believed that he had taken the necessary steps to reach sound,
empirically verifiable, social science conclusions about the comparative study of
federal systems.

He had hoped that this index might be compiled for a variety of federations
because he believed that it would provide 'a solution to many puzzling problems
of federalism and comparative government'. Indeed, he even claimed that it
would 'make possible a truly comparative study of federalism for the first time'.[53]
There is certainly enough empirical evidence to support part of Riker's position
and several scholars have subsequently come to acknowledge the significance of
his work. Where there is a political party 'symmetry' between the federal
(central) government and the governments of the constituent states of the federation we can expect the relative partisan harmony to have a binding impact
upon the federation. Conversely where there is a notable and resilient 'asymmetry' between the central authorities and the local party elites and
organisations the resulting differences of interest may have a centrifugal effect
leading to political mobilisation for decentralist reforms.[54] As far as it goes, then,
Riker's hypothesis holds up. And in his brief summary of the role of political
parties in federal systems, the Australian scholar of comparative federalism
Geoffrey Sawer confirmed that they could act as a counterweight to economic

centralisation: 'national political parties are forced by the mere existence of the federal system to take on a federal shape and be influenced by the vested interests of region governments in their own existence'.[55]

Elazar had also arrived at the same conclusion. He acknowledged that recent studies had shown that the existence of a 'non-centralized party system is perhaps the most important single element in the maintenance of federal non-centralization'. He also traced the development of these 'non-centralized parties' back to the constitutional arrangements originating in the federal compact, pointing out that once they had come into existence they tended to be self-perpetuating and to function as decentralising forces in their own right.[56] The USA and Canada served his illustrative purpose by representing two contrasting models of highly decentralised federal polities (what he called 'non-centralized' party systems), the former a republican presidential system and the latter a parliamentary form of government based upon the Westminster model. In reality, the nationwide two-party system in the USA comprised coalitions of the several state parties with a high degree of organisational autonomy while Canada exhibited more party cohesiveness but its federal parties were internally divided along provincial lines with each provincial organisation more or less autonomous as in the USA. The main difference in the Canadian case was the periodic domination of the provinces by regional parties, such as the Parti Quebecois in Quebec, which sent only a few representatives to the national legislature, and the existence of strong party discipline in the House of Commons that is absent in Congress. But if symmetry characterises the two-party system in the USA in the sense that the Democrats and Republicans dominate political activity at both state and national levels, Canada's propensity for regional parties at both federal and provincial levels (such as the Bloc Quebecois and the Canadian Alliance in the former case and the Parti Quebecois and Social Credit in the latter) clearly makes for an asymmetrical party system. In the USA a combination of the separation of powers, weak party discipline, flimsy national parties and strong local state autonomy help to account for the decentralised nature of the federation.[57] And in this putative symmetrical party system there is still plenty of scope for party–state dissonance regarding presidential, congressional, gubernatorial and local state elections and representation.

According to Elazar, those federal systems in which parliamentary government was the norm resembled the Canadian model and included Australia and Switzerland, with West Germany showing traces of it and India offering a centralised variation of the same pattern but with significant factionalisation at state level.[58] This interpretation certainly reflected the circumstances prevailing in Australia, where a scholarly consensus stressed the autonomy of state-level party organisation. However, while it remains true that in each party 'it is the state organization that counts most' and 'even at the federal level a party is continually affected by state differences and pressures', it is also the case that 'politics *within* each party (is) as important as those *between* them'.[59] The existence of divisions within each party at federal and state levels therefore serves to challenge, although not completely to discredit, Riker's hypothesis about party symmetry and asymmetry in federations. This is presumably what he meant by reference to the 'index of state–party independence'. The key issue that continues to merit further exploration is the relationship between different degrees and levels of partisanship and different traditions of state autonomy. As J.D.B. Miller put it fifty years ago, when referring to Australian party organisation, 'any generalization about an Australian political party must always be examined to see whether it applies only at the Federal level, or to only one State, or to most States but not to all'.[60]

The Federation of Malaysia is also worth more than a moment's reflection because it too falls into the category of parliamentary government along the lines of the Westminster model. However, it has many unique features that make it unusually interesting for comparative purposes. The federal system is dominated by a powerful centralised federal government that is controlled by the Barisan Nasional (National Front), a national coalition of three major partners: the United Malays National Organisation (UMNO), the Malayan Chinese Association (MCA) and the Malayan Indian Congress (MIC). These three political parties reflect the dominant communal cleavages having political salience in Malaysia, but the largest partisan component of the national coalition and the most influential in the federal government is UMNO. Put simply, then, the Malaysian federal system is characterised by three leading features, namely, communal cleavages, regionally based parties and the inter-communal executive hegemony of a single national coalition of three parties.

A measure of the dominance of the Barisan Nasional in Malaysia can be appreciated when we consider that it has managed to maintain a parliamentary majority ever since independence in 1957. This hegemony, reflected in party congruence at federal and state levels for long periods, was largely responsible for the relatively cordial and stable federal–state relations that came to characterise Malaysian politics. Recently, however, the challenges to the centralisation of executive power in Kuala Lumpur, which have always been present, have grown and intensified in the form of regional party representation in several of the thirteen constituent states of the federation. In the 1990s the electoral success of opposition parties in the peninsular states of Kelantan and Terengganu and in Sabah in north Borneo, introduced new strains and tensions in federal–state relations while conflicts also emerged within UNMO itself as the interests of the federal government (dominated by UMNO) clashed with those of the state government of Pahang (also controlled by the UMNO).[61] In recent times therefore the Malaysian federal system has oscillated between party symmetry and asymmetry in some parts of the federation leading to federal government intervention in the affairs of the constituent states.[62]

The constitutional primacy given to the federal government has afforded it sufficient powers effectively to control the constituent states and steer them towards federal goals, while the instruments at its disposal include both the coopting and disciplining of state political leaders, administrative pressures, financial incentives, the use of police powers, media control and, ultimately, direct intervention by the declaration of a state of emergency that cannot be challenged in court.[63] Indeed, the whole structure and apparatus of federal government bureaucracy in Malaysia is oriented towards strong central government. With regard to Riker's party-symmetry hypothesis, it is clear that 'national leaders were basically unwilling to accept the fact that a state was under the control of a party which was not an integral part of the ruling Barisan Nasional coalition'. Consequently the federal government 'sometimes behaved in a manner going beyond the bounds of federal principles by using whatever powers they had at their disposal to undermine a state government'.[64] The centralisation of the federal party system is further enhanced by the peculiar role of UMNO, whose leader is traditionally chosen as both the President of Barisan Nasional and the Prime Minister. It is the Prime Minster that approves the appointment of the Chief Minister of each Barisan Nasional-controlled state:

> The Prime Minister from the UMNO has considerable powers within the *Barisan Nasional*, that is, he may veto the candidate for election proposed by any constituent party, is empowered to allocate seats between the various parties, and retains the right to nominate the Chief Minister or *Menteri Besar* in any state controlled by a component party.[65]

Moreover, the role of the Central Executive Committee of the Barisan Nasional is pivotal in the selection of candidates deemed suitable to contest elections for both the national legislature and the state legislative assemblies and this power extends to the removal of a Chief Minister deemed unsuitable in any state led by a component party of the national coalition. Clearly the dominant characteristic of the Malaysian party system is that it is highly centralised: party discipline is very strong; the selection of candidates is subject to central control; communal allegiance is paramount; patronage is endemic; and there is a huge concentration of financial resources in the hands of the Barisan Nasional.

This brief outline of the circumstances that typify party politics and the party system in Malaysia brings into sharp focus the conflicting priorities of federal democracy and national integration. For all of its unseemly features, the overwhelming centralisation of power in the hands of the Barisan Nasional, and UMNO in particular, must be set against the backdrop of Malaysia's turbulent history and its overriding concern for internal and external security that places a premium on the priorities of public law and order and development planning in a federation commonly referred to as multiracial, multilingual, multi-ethnic and multinational. UMNO's underlying priority is the national project, a quiet determination to integrate multinational Malaysia around the central core of Malay culture.[66] But party competition is increasing in different parts of the federal polity, aided by the revival of Islamic fundamentalism and a growing concern for states' rights, and if Riker's basic hypothesis that party congruence between the federal and state levels of government induces centralisation seems to be borne out in the case of Malaysia, it is much more accurate to state that this congruence has actually served to reinforce, rather than create, a centralisation of federal power that already existed as a legacy of the British imperial experience.

One lesson to be learned from the application of Riker's hypothesis to Malaysia is that the enduring combination of party congruence in federal–state relations, together with strong constitutional powers, control of the media, police and army, and a huge concentration of fiscal resources and revenues in the hands of the federal government, seriously calls into question the federal credentials of the federation. For comparative purposes this is a remarkable example of a federal model the main defining feature of which is not so much the imprimatur of centralisation as the doubts about its authenticity.

In conclusion, the specific issue that Riker raised concerning the relationship between the party structure and organisation and differing degrees of political centralisation and/or decentralisation in federations remains a tantalising question. But this question is really part of the much larger and more all-encompassing issue of the overall role that parties and party systems play both in promoting national integration and in sustaining federation *qua* federation. In retrospect, Riker's claim to have discovered a method of 'measuring federalism' now seems somewhat optimistic. In practice, it is just one indicator in what is a highly complex relationship. Federal–state fiscal relations could just as easily be used as an index of political centralisation/decentralisation. But we must remember that Riker was part of that generation of scholars associated with the so-called 'behavioural revolution' in the social sciences in the USA during the 1950s and 1960s and he was 'one of the intellectual founders of rational choice theory in political science' so that this academic background predisposed him to utilise theoretical rigour and scientific investigation in the search for 'testable and tested generalizations'.[67]

Today we retain the need in political science to pursue theoretical rigour and to look for empirically verifiable connecting links that assist towards conceptual refinement, terminological precision, analytical prowess and thoughtful reflection, but this kind of intellectual activity occurs in a much more relaxed post-behavioural atmosphere. Our current intellectual expectations do not necessarily lend themselves to the scientific measurement of all political phenomena. In the case of parties and party systems in federations, it is obvious that there are many imponderables that are simply incapable of any but the crudest form of measurement. Nonetheless, Riker's contribution to this particular subject is massive, even if it leaves many questions unanswered. Among the assortment of important outstanding research questions that his work has inspired are the following:

1   What is the nature of the relationship between structures and institutions and the particular societal diversities that exist in each federation?
2   How far do divisions within the same political party at federal and state levels serve to undermine the notions of symmetry and asymmetry in federations?
3   What are the correlates of political centralisation and decentralisation?
4   Can a valid distinction be made between constitutional structure and practice in federations?

Let us turn now to our fifth and final basis for the comparative study of federal political systems.

Constitutional reform and judicial review

Constitutional reform in any state is a particularly difficult and highly sensitive project involving a variety of entrenched socio-economic and cultural interests, but these difficulties are magnified in federations precisely because of the nature of the state. Federations are not accidents of history; they are the product of deliberate, conscious and purposive acts of human agency. They are the result of a series of bargains, agreements and compromises emanating from the interaction of political elites. To use Elazar's terminology, they are 'federal covenants' or 'federal compacts' while Riker referred to them as 'rational political bargains'. These covenants, compacts and bargains are binding agreements that enshrine certain values, beliefs, assumptions and expectations that are formally incorporated in written constitutions and represent, so to speak, the birth certificate of the federation. And even if the federal destination is the result of a long evolutionary process of adaptation and adjustment between distinctive communities, as it was in Belgium, Spain, Switzerland, Malaysia and Canada, this does not alter the fact that constitutional accord and ratification represent 'a formalised transaction of a moment in the history of a particular community'.[68]

Federations emerge, then, because of the imperative to structure and institutionalise difference and diversity. Their genius lies in their capacity, via constitutional entrenchment, to accommodate and reconcile different forms of unity with different forms of diversity. Consequently political elites can engage mass publics in order to mobilise them for major constitutional change precisely because the very *raison d'être* of the federal state – its original purpose – can sometimes be challenged. In such circumstances, organised groups, assorted collectivities and vested interests will jostle for position in the public debate about how to protect and promote certain cherished values, beliefs and interests. And this means that they can hardly avoid returning to fundamentals. In a sense they revisit their origins and formation and reinterpret their history. Constitutional reform, then, is *ipso facto* an extremely daunting challenge for federations. The attempt to reform a federal constitution highlights the significance of the relationship between that country's constitution and its society, in this case a federal society.

There is an important preliminary point to be made here concerning the motives for wanting to reform federal constitutions. All constitutions change over time simply because the broad socio-economic and political context in which they were originally embedded itself changes, but it was Ivo Duchacek who put his finger on what remains the essential hallmark characteristic of constitutional reform in federations:

> There is only an agreement to try to agree at a later date *again* (that is, there is a commitment to add, if possible, new federal bargains to the initial

bargain). Federalism is by definition an unfinished business because many issues can be neither foreseen nor immediately solved; at the time of the initial bargain, some issues may not have yet crystallized and other issues may have already proven too controversial (too hot) to try to solve immediately. But this is the whole point and the political merit of a federal formula. It is based on a wise recognition that in politics many issues cannot be solved now or ever. With its seemingly precise and elaborate articles defining the way in which authority is divided between the two or more sets of different jurisdiction, a federal constitution is misleading: like any other political system it creates an impression of finality and accuracy in a context that leaves – and must leave – so many issues to future improvisation.[69]

This extract from Duchacek's classic work in which he emphasised the binding commitment among all the parties to the federal bargain to 'seek accommodation without outvoting the minority and without the use of force' underlines the moral basis of the federal spirit.[70] Constitutional reform in federations is firmly predicated on the legitimate assumption and expectation that basic federal values will be respected and protected. Preston King acknowledged that 'federations move, they change, and this movement is equally reflected in the views of those who operate and study them', but if it is true that 'the normative orientation will change over time within each federation and will vary as between them all', this does not automatically imply the abandonment of the promises and commitments originally made when the federation was first formed.[71] Constitutions, we are reminded, bear the hallmarks of the circumstances in which they were created. Governments and citizens, however, cannot be made prisoners of the past and federal constitutions will inevitably evolve in response to new pressures and accommodate themselves to a variety of needs and changing demands, but their evolutionary nature does not mean that they should lose their federal character. They are therefore 'living constitutions', that is, they are 'continuous creations' that enable successive generations to contribute to their evolution, but it is also a contribution that builds upon a living legacy.[72]

The subject of constitutional change in federations is necessarily predicated upon the distinction between the *process* and the *substance* of reform. The former focuses on the formal procedures by which a constitution is amended while the latter deals with the actual content of the reform. But each is related to the other in a complex manner so that a proper understanding and appreciation of this complexity would include historical, philosophical, political, socio-economic, cultural-ideological and legal dimensions of analysis. Procedurally there are wide variations in how constitutions are amended in different federations. However, it stands to reason that since the written constitution represents the birth certificate of every federation, those aspects that establish its fundamental federal character should not be unilaterally amendable by just one order of government because that would render the other level of government subordinate to it. This means in practice that approval of amendments to those portions of the constitution relating to the distribution of powers and the integrity of the constituent units usually requires approval in both houses of the federal legislature. In addition, such amendments require either approval by a special majority of the constituent state legislatures, as in Canada and in the USA, or a majority of state legislatures, as in India. Indeed, in some federations formal approval necessitates a referendum requiring a double majority consisting of an overall majority and majorities in a majority of constituent states, as is the procedure in Switzerland and Australia.[73]

These procedural similarities and differences in constitutional reform cannot be separated from the substance of reform. Citizens' perceptions of changing the constitution are shaped by the interaction of these two facets of constitutional amendment such that their preconceptions of the one will determine their reactions to the other. This occurred in the epic public debate about constitutional reform in Canada during 1987–90 over the Meech Lake Accord. Serious doubts about the democratic nature of the constitutional reform process had important consequences for the fate of the substantive reform package. Richard Simeon summarised it very well in his brief to the Ontario Select Committee on Constitutional Reform:

> I suppose it is true that one's attitudes about process depend entirely on one's attitude about content and *vice versa*, so my worries about the process might be a lot greater if I were more worried about the substance of the accord. What Meech Lake does is ... to reaffirm our federal character. ... It seems to me that we must make modest demands on our Constitution. We must see it as being, at any given time, a somewhat awkward balance which is politically acceptable at that time. We must see it therefore as a continuous matter of unfinished business.[74]

Given the pivotal significance of the division and distribution of powers between two or more orders of government enshrined in written constitutions in all modern federations, it stands to reason that constitutional supremacy is one of the hallmarks of this kind of state. Indeed, Ronald Watts stipulates two distinct features as 'prerequisites for the effective operation of a federation': first, explicit and/or implicit recognition of the supremacy of the constitution over all orders of government and, second, a political culture that emphasises the fundamental importance of respect for constitutionality.[75] Constitutional supremacy therefore means that all governmental authority is rooted in and derives from the sovereign written document which is subject to independent and impartial judicial interpretation.

There is, then, a powerful role to be played by the law courts, and in particular supreme courts and constitutional courts in all federations. Consequently the role of judges as impartial umpires and the significance of judicial review both as process and substance must be included in any assessment of constitutional change and development in comparative federalism and federation. Formal constitutional amendment is complemented by informal judicial review. Watts identifies three main functions of the adjudicating role of these courts: (1)

impartial constitutional interpretation; (2) adaptation of the constitution to changing circumstances; and (3) the resolution of intergovernmental conflicts.[76] However, because it is essentially incremental and is often couched in the formal technicalities of legal realism, judicial review has a much lower public profile than formal constitutional amendment which directly engages public debate. Generally speaking, then, mass publics have less awareness of what judges say and do and some scholars see in judicial review genuine danger for federal polities. Elazar, in particular, viewed judicial activism with great concern because general compliance with Supreme Court decisions in the USA had such a nationalising impact that it altered the character of the federation, undermining it as a 'matrix of larger and smaller arenas' and tilting it in the direction of a hierarchical system.[77]

Similar concerns about judicial activism have been expressed in Canada, Germany, Australia and Switzerland. In Canada the introduction of a Charter of Rights and Freedoms in the Constitution Act (1982) has had the overall effect of nationalising the federal polity in ways that have brought it much closer to the federal model of the USA.[78] Needless to say, the centralising impact of judicial decisions has caused particular concern in Quebec, where the Canadian Supreme Court is still perceived as a predominantly anglophone central institution, despite three of its nine judges originating from Quebec.[79] In Germany, too, the tension between the federal models of hierarchy and partnership has been an ever-present theme in the debate about the role of the courts, and this tension is still reflected in the persistence of federal comity (*Bundestreues Verhalten*) in relation to cooperative federalism, executive–administrative entanglement (*Politikverflectung*) and Bund-*lander* relations in the context of German membership of the EU.[80] Australia has also exhibited pronounced centralist features but it is different from Germany in that its High Court has a broader mandate than being just a constitutional court. The High Court of Australia is also a superior appellate court for all Australian common law and statutory interpretation and in this respect is closer in exercising judicial review to both the Canadian (since 1982) and the US models. Judicial nationalism, according to Brian Galligan, has certainly been the predominant historical trend in the High Court's judgments but 'the centralist interpretation of Australian federalism while generally true has nevertheless been exaggerated'.[81]

Switzerland is an interesting case for comparative purposes because the introduction (in April 1999) and subsequent ratification (in March 2000) of the new Federal Constitution has left both the Federal Supreme Court as an institution and the role of the judges in the federal system in a curious state of ambiguity. Articles 188–91 of the Federal Constitution declare the Federal Supreme Court as 'the highest federal judicial authority' and establish its jurisdiction to include complaints against the following violations: of constitutional rights, of the autonomy of the municipalities and other public corporate bodies, of federal law, international law and inter-cantonal law and conflicts between cantons as well as between a canton, or several cantons, and the federal government.[82] Moreover, while Article 190 does not actually forbid the Federal Supreme Court from issuing its opinion regarding the constitutionality of federal laws, it does oblige it and other bodies to apply federal laws, even if such laws are considered to be unconstitutional.[83] The picture of ambiguity that emerges from these circumstances is that 'the Court has been willing to review federal laws in the sense that it states its opinions on their constitutionality, without the consequence of not applying the law or even nullifying it'.[84] Whether or not Switzerland will eventually introduce full constitutional review in the future remains to be seen, but it is important to emphasise that the combination of the Swiss political culture based upon a consensual style of decision-making, the tradition of parliamentary supremacy, popular sovereignty as expressed in procedures of direct democracy and the political homogeneity between the judges and the governmental political parties tends to channel conflict-management into the traditional political forums and arenas and away from the courts. Consequently disputes are diffused, managed and resolved via political rather than legal routes.

In summary, it would appear that one of the greatest challenges to the *federal* character of federations lies in the threat of judicial activism that can lead, and in many cases has led, to the centralisation of political authority and the uniformity, standardisation and nationalisation of socio-economic and legal policy preferences desired by the majority. In other words, both formal constitutional amendment and non-constitutional reform can pose serious problems for federal states. They can conceivably alter the character of federations in ways that might have unintended consequences. Clearly these circumstances reflect the in-built tension between the conflicting pressures of what has been called 'uniformity versus multiformity' in all federations, but the persistence of this tension is a salutary reminder that 'a federal system whose people and leaders consider multiformity to be a nuisance will sooner or later be transformed into a unitary system'.[85] Certainly it does not take much imagination to foresee the real danger that judicial activism coupled with 'a positivistic view of jurisprudence' could present to the federality of federations.[86]

Conclusion: the comparative study of federal political systems

These five conceptual lenses furnish the bases for a series of comparative studies of federal political systems. They underline significant similarities and differences in a variety of ways that point up the interaction between governments and societies, between economic and political systems, and between institutions and policies. They also allow us to investigate the philosophical and ideological foundations of federalist practice – what makes federations tick, why there are such wide variations on a basic theme and how they change and develop. And once again they remind us of the indelible stamp of history. While it is true that all federations 'can only be a formalised transaction of a moment in the history of a particular community', the comparative study of federal political systems can help us to understand how and why it is that this particular kind of state structure continues to survive and thrive in the new millennium.[87]

Having looked in some considerable detail at the comparative study of federal political systems, it is now appropriate for us to turn our attention to another important dimension of our subject that broadly complements this study. This is the comparative survey of two distinct political traditions of federalism and federation, namely, the Anglo-American and the Continental European. Together these two traditions incorporate important historical, philosophical and ideological assumptions, values and beliefs that serve to buttress our overall picture of comparative federalism and federation in theory and practice.

6 The Anglo-American and Continental European federal political traditions

Introduction

In this chapter I take the notion of a political tradition to refer principally to the origins and evolution of what I shall call a 'family' of political ideas about the nature and structure of the state and society in the modern historical epoch that dates from around the late sixteenth and early seventeenth centuries in Europe. It is my main purpose to sketch out the political, philosophical and theological contours of two quite distinct traditions of federal thought that can be identified as the Continental European and the Anglo-American strands of federalism and federation. This purpose is not meant to render invisible the existence of other federal political traditions that have also evolved in Latin America, Africa, Asia and the Middle East. It is merely to focus upon the two oldest known, mainstream, federal political traditions that have their philosophical and empirical bases in the emergence of the modern state.

In pursuit of this goal it is important for us to consider some preliminary conceptual and methodological problems that have to be set in their respective historical and philosophical contexts. In order to understand the contemporary significance of these two political traditions and their complex interrelationship, we must clear the ground of ambiguity and imprecision. One of the most basic of these problems is the extent to which we can establish something that can legitimately be called 'Continental European' or 'Anglo-American' federal political thought. Clearly there are many pitfalls involved in this exercise. To use the labels 'Continental European' and 'Anglo-American' is to suggest that there exists something which is meaningful in a classificatory sense; a relatively coherent set of federal ideas and principles that is both intellectually accessible and conveniently identifiable as a distinctive body of federal political thought. Consequently, to point to the 'Continental European' federal political tradition is to presuppose that it possesses composite characteristics that mark it off as quite distinct from its 'Anglo-American' counterpart. However, we have to be very careful when we shift from the language of political thought to the discourse of political tradition. A political tradition suggests the combination of thought and practice; it suggests a coherent body of ideas that informs behaviour – the way that people live their lives.

Thinking about thought and tradition reminds us that such intellectual labels are almost always the product of hindsight. They are attributed retrospectively and may therefore be oversimplifications. They may also be the product of unacknowledged motives and intentions. Scholarly historical analysis must be distinguished from the political uses of history. As Francis H. Hinsley remarked: 'People often study history less for what they might learn than for what they want to prove'.[1] It is in this sense of concealed ideological purpose that the epithets 'Continental European' and 'Anglo- American' must be used with caution. Finally, the terms 'Continental European' and 'Anglo-American' may be contentious from a different standpoint. They both suggest a continuity of thought and practice about federalism and federation which is at once conscious and purposive in broadly defined political contexts. However, it may be more accurate for the sake of historical specificity to refer to both the Germanic and the French federal traditions in the case of Europe, while it could conceivably be argued that there are two quite separate federal political discourses or traditions, namely, the British and the American, in the Anglo-American category. What I think might be a plausible response to this apparent conundrum is to construe the Continental European and the Anglo-American federal political traditions as broad-brush conceptions of federalism and federation that have a distinct shape but within which there are several subcategories that can be examined closely and distilled to produce further conceptual refinements. It really boils down, as Sartori once remarked, to how fine the comparative analysis needs to be.[2]

These, then, are some of the precautions that we must take when accepting the notion of a 'Continental European' and an 'Anglo-American' corpus of philosophical and political thought about federalism and federation in the early period of conceptual formation. They certainly prompt us to take account of the prevailing mainstream historical and philosophical background contexts within which federal thought first appeared and they serve as a salutary warning not to assume what needs to be proved. With these reflective and sobering remarks uppermost in our minds, let us turn now to look in more detail at the two distinct federal traditions that form the basis of the chapter. We will examine the Continental European federal tradition and its implications for comparative analysis before shifting our attention to the Anglo-American tradition that follows it.

The Continental European federal tradition

The Continental European federal political tradition is the product of several centuries of thought and practice. Modern European *federations* may owe something to the American federal model in the way that they structure multiple identities and diversities and establish firm links between the state and its citizens, but European *federalism* antedates the New World revelation by two centuries. Its roots are medieval and feudal as well as modern.

The rise of the modern state in Renaissance Europe during the sixteenth and early seventeenth centuries went hand in hand with the emergence of sovereignty as a conceptual instrument for the organisation of power in the state.

The modern state is an historical phenomenon but it is also analytically a distinct political institution developed by society, a particular means of organising political power. Through its evolution the state came to be seen as 'public' power while society was equated with 'private' activities related to the ordinary day-to-day practice of living. The seventeenth and eighteenth centuries witnessed the gradual development and consolidation of the modern territorial state as the sole legitimate source of public order and political authority. And the state was 'sovereign' in the sense that it admitted no rival or competing authority within its own territorially demarcated boundaries. The modern territorial sovereign nation state was predicated upon the assumption that there was a final and absolute political authority in the political community. In Weber's terms, it possessed the legitimate monopoly of the means of physical coercion in a given territory. The internal face of sovereignty was understood to be the source of the legal sanctions governing the use of physical coercion while the external face of sovereignty – international relations – confronted a world of similarly sovereign states in which elite actors recognised no authority higher than their own except for treaty commitments that they could revoke.

It is in this sense that Hinsley referred to the origins and history of the state and sovereignty as indissolubly connected. The origin and history of sovereignty are intimately linked to the nature, origin and history of the modern state.[3] In the turbulence of sixteenth-century Europe, in an era of sustained dynastic and civil wars, religious schisms and a Holy Roman Empire in decay, the case for 'sovereignty' was made most forcibly by the French scholar Jean Bodin. His *Les six Livres de la republique* was first published in 1576 and became the classic rationalisation of the unitary monarchical state.[4] Bodin constructed his major work principally as a prescription for the achievement of order, stability and security for France in a dangerous uncertain world, but his recommendation also served the established interests of the hereditary nobility and medieval constitutional authorities. *La Republique* distilled the need for an undisputed sovereign authority into a simple formula: first, the authority of the state should be centralised, absolute and indivisible; and, second, the supreme sovereign power should reside in a monarch answerable only to God and natural law. Unless royal authority was endowed with supreme and indivisible authority, anarchy and civil war would result. Particular interests were elevated to universal prescription. However, it is also true that Bodin was saying something much more profound than mere recommendation. *La Republique* stood as a bridge between the medieval, feudal period and the early modern epoch in the extent to which it recognised the existence of a natural order of things together with the new requirement that authority must henceforth be based upon legitimacy and consent. This reflected the shift from the divine rule of God to the notion of human will – the idea that human beings 'will' authority into existence via consent.

The Bodinian conception of the state and sovereignty was extremely rigid. The equation of order and stability with centralised, indivisible and notionally unlimited power yielded a strict hierarchical structure – a single, basic pyramid of command and obedience. But if the triumph of the secular, monarchic, sovereign nation state – the state in which there was only one master – became the dominant political reality of this historical epoch, it was not without its critics and opponents from the very beginning. Indeed, the fundamental principles of political authority and the true attributes of sovereignty established by Bodin gave rise to much intellectual argument and speculation that culminated in the following century in the emergence of social contract theory as the major philosophical challenge to the Bodinian state.

The significance of Bodin for the emergence of federal ideas about the organisation of the state resided in the imperative to refute his rigid conception of the state and sovereignty. By defining the state in such exclusivist terms he compelled his critics to come to terms either with his formulation of the concept or its application to particular cases. As S. Rufus Davis observed, it might initially seem paradoxical to include Bodin in a study of federal ideas but to omit him completely would actually be 'a grave error', for 'whether by the force of repulsion or resistance, his catalytic influence on federal theory cannot be ignored. … other jurists could no more evade Bodin than successive generations of political jurists could free themselves from the questions – who commands and how many masters can there be in a stable state, one, two, three, or more?'[5]

Bodin's legacy was enduring. In the two centuries after *La Republique* was published the debate about the nature of the state and sovereignty continued to shape the philosophical climate. In seventeenth-century Germany, the rigid Bodinian view of federation was perpetuated by Samuel Pufendorf, whose *De Jure Naturae et Gentium* reinforced ideas of the indivisibility of sovereignty and insisted upon the supremacy of state authority. Federal ideas were therefore indissolubly tied to notions of alliance, pact and treaty in the world of interstate relations so that any deviation from this norm was deemed either 'irregular' or 'monstrous'.[6] And in the great pantheon of British political thinkers who also helped to mould this new philosophical environment the names of Thomas Hobbes, Algernon Sydney, John Locke and David Hume loom large. Hobbes' *Leviathan* (1651) stands in a direct line of descent to Bodin's *La Republique* as a theory of sovereignty. But Hobbes, who continued the work that Bodin had begun, must also be set in the context of 'social contract' theory, which 'opened the door to a restatement of the classical notion of the popular basis of sovereignty'.[7] Along with Locke's *Second Treatise on Civil Government* (1690), the idea of the social contract epitomised the shift from absolutism and the divine right of kings to the subversive ideas of consent – the notion of a compact or contract (or even covenant) freely entered into – and limited government. Whereas Hobbes was agnostic about where the sovereign power should logically reside (although his sneaking preference was for monarchy), Locke's reasoning catapulted him in the direction of the rights of man and representative parliamentary government.

It is important to note that neither Hobbes nor Locke donated anything directly to the modern federal idea, but in helping to shape a climate of intense speculation and debate in which old, encrusted assumptions about authority and obligation were gradually discredited they contributed the fundamental philosophical basis to it. Political theorists trace a fairly consistent line of thought grounded in social contract, natural rights, popular consent, the justification of resistance to authority, and utilitarianism, which brings into question the very essence of sovereign power. And the same observation may be made regarding the particular contributions of Jean-Jacques Rousseau and Baron de Montesquieu. Montesquieu's *L'Esprit des lois* (1748) and Rousseau's *Contrat social* (1762) both addressed fundamental philosophical questions that were germane to a political climate in which notions of popular sovereignty, individual liberty, limited government and the separation of powers could flourish.[8] Here, as we shall see, the French influence from the Continental European federal tradition intrudes into the Anglo-American federal literature, thus confirming the philosophical cross-currents endemic in every political discourse and tradition. These influences, it should be noted, do not constitute impurities in another political tradition; they merely underline the fact that some elements in one tradition are more heavily emphasised than in another. Moreover, Montesquieu and Rousseau could equally legitimately be linked philosophically with Immanuel Kant's essay 'Perpetual Peace' (1795) in those aspects of their works that addressed the world of international relations and the pursuit of a lasting peace.[9]

In seeking to understand the philosophical and empirical origins of the Continental European federal political tradition, then, there is an important link to be made between federal theory as it pertained to internal authority *within* the domestic politics of the modern state and that which related to external authority in the relations *between* states – the realm of international relations. Here we can do no better than to return to two seminal articles published by Patrick Riley in the 1970s that furnish us with invaluable insights into the complex origins of this historical and philosophical tradition.[10] Riley's chief concern was to underline the importance of an accurate historical understanding of the evolution of European federal ideas. He deemed it essential for the student of federal ideas to know their intellectual history. Many of the complexities and oddities that continue to reside in federal theory can be explained by the way that the modern (national) federal state broke out of the received mainstream federal tradition that had been essentially a theory of international relations, that is, of treaties and alliances. We will recall that the original Latin term *foedus* meant simply treaty, compact and alliance, so that 'federal' unions were 'always thought to be formed and governed according to principles of international relations, rather than principles of national statehood'.[11] For our purposes here, Riley's important contribution to understanding the origins of federal theory lies in his historical and philosophical analysis of the relationship between these two types of federal ideas – national and international. His reminder that 'the strict modern division of politics into "national" and "international" was not made before the eighteenth century' helps to explain precisely why federalism has been so variously interpreted.[12] There have been, in short, many different kinds of federalism – before the emergence of the modern federal state – that fall within the broad spectrum of the 'medievalist' federalism of corporate and regional prerogatives and the international federalism of peace leagues and unions of states.

This curious historical legacy has produced both clarity and confusion. But in any case the main intellectual inspiration for the Continental European federal tradition did not derive from the largely secular liberal Enlightenment thinkers identified above, but from a much less well-known political theological source. In an instructive research paper delivered in May 1994 to the International Committee for the Study of the Development of Political Science, Michael Stein referred to a group of mainly 'theological-political, collectivist, corporatist thinkers of a social Catholic and Protestant Reformist (particularly Calvinist) background, beginning with Althusius', that projected a common and distinctive pattern of federal ideas.[13] This research was founded upon what was already a well-established understanding and appreciation of a distinct European tradition of federalism and federation – rooted in medievalism, feudal residues, corporatist perspectives and Christian socio-religious principles and values such as personalism, subsidiarity and solidarism – that antedated the American federal model of 1787–89 by two centuries. Indeed, Charles Pentland acknowledged this indigenous tradition in 1973, believing it to be:

> quite different, tracing its origins to medieval European society and denying the federal principle its more familiar associations with the legal constitution of a territorial state. This tradition of thought ... is ... abstract and philosophical ... its analytic bias is toward small groups and sociological variables and its prescriptive bias is towards fundamental social reorganisation both below and beyond national boundaries.[14]

Many of these ideas and perspectives about a *European* tradition of federalism were immanent in Western political science discourse, but they existed largely in fragmentary form and had not been systematically analysed, collected and collated. It is in this sense that Stein could claim with some accuracy that 'the notion of a distinct European tradition of federalism is a relatively recent one in the theoretical literature'.[15] Cognate research on Christian democracy in western Europe, for example, served to highlight the philosophical connections between Roman Catholic social theory, subsidiarity and federalism, as well as the revival of the political ideas of Althusius in the Protestant (Calvinist) tradition, but it was not always obvious to those who studied these subjects that they were part of a larger, distinct tradition of European federalism. This lacuna in our knowledge about European federal ideas has now been filled.[16] In this chapter therefore we will focus upon three broad strands of federal thought that together enable us to define a Continental European federal tradition that is both distinct and accessible. These three elements that criss-cross to form its intellectual basis are the political thought of Johannes Althusius in the German tradition, the theoretical contribution of Pierre-Joseph Proudhon in the French tradition and the significance of Roman Catholic social theory.

Before we look in more detail at the family of social and political ideas that together constitute the Continental European federal tradition, let us return briefly to the historical context within which these ideas gradually emerged.

Since some of the most characteristic features of political ideas and institutions are functions of the peculiarities of their historical development, there is an interesting empirical basis to the intellectual ferment of European federal ideas in the form of both the Holy Roman Empire and the Habsburg Empire that suggests a complex interaction between thought and practice that is well worth more than a moment's reflection. The gist of what is tantamount to a revisionist reappraisal of the character of the Holy Roman Empire is rooted in a major reassessment of the concept of sovereignty and a series of preconceptions about the unified sovereign nation state. Indeed, one scholar, Andreas Osiander, has claimed that 'only relatively recently has the empire been 'rediscovered' by historians.[17] His research into the nature of the Holy Roman Empire leaves little doubt that its operational characteristics were markedly federal:

> If the European system as a whole can be called a loose, informal regime with few institutions, ... the empire was essentially a more developed regime with more elaborate institutions, providing a system of governance for matters of common interest while leaving internal government to each of the participating actors individually. With the military strength of most estates of the empire negligible or indeed nonexistent, evidently their actor-hood was exclusively ascriptive: based on rules, not power. They, as well as the collective entity they made up, existed exclusively because of collective and mutual empowerment, which in turn was based on a shared, rather elaborate code of structural and procedural legitimacy.[18]

It should come as no surprise to learn that the contemporary EU has frequently been referred to as a neo-medieval federal model. But it is also true that the evolution from medieval to modern European society made several alternative models of political order available. Along with the territorial nation state there were, for example, the city states and city leagues that flourished in Germany and Italy.[19] And one important characteristic of medieval Europe underlined by John Ruggie is of particular relevance to the Continental European federal tradition:

> The archetype of nonexclusive territorial rule, of course, is medieval Europe, with its patchwork of overlapping and incomplete rights of government, which were inextricably superimposed and tangled, and in which different juridical instances were geographically interwoven and stratified, and plural allegiances, asymmetrical suzerainties and anomalous enclaves abounded. The difference between the medieval and modern worlds is striking in this respect.[20]

The extracts chosen above constitute evidence of a forgotten socio-economic and political reality that has enabled interested scholars to rethink and re-conceptualise contemporary international politics. One major implication of this recent research is that notions of political organisation and power-sharing need not necessarily be wedded to the state. Past experience suggests that federal ideas and practices come in many different forms that are inherently flexible and have the capacity to extend beyond the conventional limits of the national state. Consequently contemporary speculation about the notion of an emergent post-statist political order in Europe since the collapse of the Berlin Wall in 1989 has provided the intellectual inspiration for a renewed interest in and rediscovery of earlier forms of human association and political organisation. For the political scientist, the intellectual impact is particularly evident in both the mainstream international relations (IR) and European integration (EI) literatures where *inter alia* attention has been riveted on sovereignty, the Westphalian state and the re-conceptualisation of boundaries, frontiers and territoriality.[21] And while it remains unclear precisely where this revisiting of old, established conventional wisdoms will ultimately lead scholars, it seems certain that at the very least it will stimulate a radical rethinking of future possibilities of institutionalised cooperation and constitutional design.

We can see, then, that the Continental European federal tradition has a strong, if hitherto neglected, socio-economic and political heritage *in practice*. Medieval Europe was a veritable hotchpotch of random, highly variegated organisational and associational relations in which both territorial and non-territorial functional contexts existed alongside each other. And parallel to this practical reality there also emerged a distinctive family of political ideas that evolved over 500 years to constitute a rich political tradition. It is to this body of thought that we now return.

Pentland, quoted above, referred to the European federal tradition as a distinctive form of social federalism, with its primary focus upon small groups and sociological variables and a prescriptive bias towards social reorganisation *both below and beyond national boundaries*. What does this mean? His position that federalism is a principle of social organisation clearly finds its way quite easily into theories of pluralism. The various schools of pluralism draw their inspiration from 'the social life of citizens as it manifests itself in the family, the church, the sporting or cultural group and the civic association'.[22] Pluralism is concerned, in short, with the daily routine and practice of social life – how people live their lives – and it construes political authority and organisation in terms that should accurately reflect the natural diversity of society. Accordingly, some writers and intellectuals equate pluralism with federalism and we can see why they might do so. But closer analysis suggests that pluralism cannot be equated with federalism because it does not possess the same conceptual status. Daniel Elazar clarified the nature of this relationship in the most unequivocal way:

> Federalism differs from pluralism because it bases its efforts to deal with the realities of human nature on a firm constitutional structure … pluralism in one form or another may indeed be a safeguard of liberty, but … it cannot be relied upon by itself unless properly institutionalised constitutionally … The existence of federalism (in the United States) allowed the development of a variety of forms of pluralism side by side within the same civil society.[23]

Put simply, pluralism is a descriptive, largely sociological, concept that has a normative political basis for some scholars but its relationship to federalism and federation can be appropriately summarised in one simple observation: there is no such thing as a pluralist state.[24]

Leaving this debate aside, it is clear from this line of thought that social differentiation springs from freely formed bodies, institutions and associations of citizens that do not owe their existence to the state. In Continental Europe we can identify a philosophical tradition rooted in these assumptions and values that dates back at least four centuries. Indeed, many writers and intellectuals in the pluralist school of thought have drawn on this tradition, which is widely acknowledged to have begun with the ideas of Johannes Althusius, a German Calvinist scholar and political magistrate. His famous *Politica Methodice Digesta,* now often referred to as 'The Politics', was first published in 1603 and his federal ideas evolved in the third edition of the *Politica,* published in 1614, to encompass what most students of European federalism today regard as the hallmark of his work, namely, a theory of society based upon natural law whereby individuals freely organised themselves into associations, both religious and secular, that were the fundamental essence of the state.[25] These associations, or intermediate bodies, were a complex amalgamation of religious groups, guilds, communes, corporations, leagues of towns and cities, merchant associations and many other local organisations that antedated the modern state and owed nothing to it for their existence. They constituted the living practice of society. Althusius accordingly identified the family, private and public associations, the commune, the province, and ultimately the state as a kind of rising hierarchical nexus of complex social institutions that together created the state, were incorporated within it and effectively intervened between it and the individual. Althusius therefore formulated what Elazar referred to as essentially 'a theory of polity-building based on the polity as a compound political association established by its citizens through their primary associations on the basis of consent'.[26] Mogi claimed that Althusius 'went further into the question of federal union than any other thinkers or jurists' and that his greatest intellectual merit was his theory of the corporation. Interestingly he also observed that Althusius formulated the federal idea 'on the basis of both *actuality* and his religious and political doctrines', thus confirming federalism as social reality.[27] Small wonder that Althusius is now widely recognised as the intellectual 'father' of Continental European federalism and federation.[28]

There is one particular aspect of the *Politics* that requires us briefly to pause and reflect upon its contemporary implications and significance. This concerns the opening paragraph of the treatise (1614 edition) and is worth quoting here:

> Politics is the art of associating (*consociandi*) men for the purpose of establishing, cultivating, and conserving social life among them. Whence it is called 'symbiotics'. The subject matter of politics is therefore association (*consociatio*), in which the symbiotes pledge themselves each to the other, by explicit or tacit agreement, to mutual communication of whatever is useful and necessary for the harmonious exercise of social life.[29]

As we have already stated above, Althusius construes his federal political system as a compound polity being based upon private and public associations composed not of individuals but, in ascending order, of families, corporations comprising villages, estates, towns, cities and provinces and, ultimately, of groups of provinces, cities and regions. This federal polity, grounded in natural-law theory, grows from the bottom up so that the larger associations are not only the product of the lesser ones but are also subsidiary to them. This means that 'the people' in its collective associational capacity is prior to and superior to its governors: 'For however great is the power that is conceded to another, it is always less than the power of the one who makes the concession, and in it the pre-eminence and superiority of the conceder is understood to be reserved'.[30] Today we can fully appreciate how far Althusian notions of contract and consent readily apply to the EU and indeed how far his conception of sovereignty might resonate both in the principle of 'conferral' and in the role of judicial power evident in the current public debate about the EU Constitution. We are also reminded of the etymological derivation of the contemporary notion of consociational democracy – or overarching elite accommodation – that has frequently been related to federal arrangements in many countries, such as Belgium, Switzerland, Austria and the Netherlands.[31] Conceptually it is yet another form of *association*.

On reflection, it is also worth noting that these ideas may have lain dormant, lost in history, had they not been resurrected during the late nineteenth century by the German jurist and legal historian Otto von Gierke, who thereby rescued Althusius from two centuries of obscurity. The idea that the various communes, guilds, corporations and other local associations were independent of the state (as were individuals), yet of the same nature, was thus already deeply rooted in the Continental European federal tradition of political thought by the time that Gierke revived it. As Stanislaw Ehrlich has emphasised in his impressive work on pluralism, the towns and various other associations had developed the conception of their own distinct personality long before the modern centralising state first emerged. Their origins and activities did not depend on their being endowed with the status of legal persons by the state. They were 'really existing autonomous bodies which, relative to the state, were capable of self-government and were self-governing in fact'. Alluding to Gierke's views, 'groups, whatever their organisation, and hence legal persons, too, were ... real entities in which (there existed) a sphere of freedom other than that which can be obtained within the framework of the state'.[32]

If we take the anti-absolutist ideas of Althusius and Gierke to be in the intellectual mainstream of a strong European philosophical tradition that sees groups, associations and collectivities as the basic social unit of the body politic, we can understand why many contemporary writers might continue to regard pluralism as historically and philosophically more comprehensive than federalism. After all, Althusius and Gierke did not seek to invent a new theory of associations: they sought instead to revive the role of free associations, dignify them as collective personalities and furnish the basis of a comprehensive theory that would effectively prevent their absorption and suffocation by the modern state. In other words, their prescriptions were founded upon an already existing social reality or, in Mogi's terms, *actuality*.

Given our limited purposes in this chapter, it is important for us to identify the key defining features of Althusius' theory of federalism rather than to provide a detailed examination of his system of political organisation and we will return to summarise these essential characteristics a little later. For the moment let us turn briefly to another important intellectual contributor to the European federal tradition whose *Du Principe fédératif* was first published in 1863, namely, Pierre-Joseph Proudhon.[33] Proudhon constitutes our second strand of federal thought and is probably best known as the father of anarchism and libertarian socialism, but he is also part and parcel of the European federal tradition. Indeed, there are some interesting similarities in the federal political thought of Proudhon and Althusius in the way, for example, that both focus upon collectivities, functional and territorial representation, the organic conception of state and society based on corporatism and subsidiarity, and the emphasis on the whole person rather than the isolated, atomistic individual. But Proudhon was really concerned with what he called a system of 'mutualist' exchange developed on the basis of the free economic association of producer groups intended to replace the capitalist state.[34]

According to Richard Vernon, Proudhon regarded federalism as 'a philosophy of political life, ... a philosophy of history,' rooted not in utopian thought but on the contrary arising from 'the practical tensions and inconsistencies essential to politics'. Indeed, Vernon claims that 'his is a theory which takes as its point of departure a practical contradiction' that construes liberty and authority as irreconcilable.[35] These opposing forces constitute Proudhon's theoretical conundrum, which is why Vernon aptly portrays his position as standing at the intersection between federalism and anarchism. And the model of human liberation that Proudhon sought to recommend was therefore founded upon 'the non-political relations of civil society', specifically those of economic exchange, a system whereby the horizontal relations of exchange would replace the vertical hierarchy of power relations in the state so that matters customarily directed from above would be 'placed in the hands of autonomous agents who manage them by mutual agreements' based upon the principle of fairness.[36]

Du Principe fédératif is clearly many things. Its composite character includes basic normative and empirical political and economic theory, political philosophy, historical interpretation and ideological imperative. In a nutshell, Proudhon's federal vision, despite its conspicuous ambiguities and incomplete propositions, anticipated a polity – composite in nature – founded upon both territorial and functional (non-territorial) communities that would enter into multiple contractual arrangements intended to be part of an unending series of negotiated agreements. It would be a new kind of polity rooted in the federal spirit of bargaining and arranging rather than commanding and coercing, one in which top-down hierarchical relations would give way to different levels of organisation based upon bottom-up consent. And the essentially contractual nature of the federal polity meant that the negotiating partners would delegate powers upwards to the next higher level on terms that were both amendable and revocable, affording it a confederal rather than a federal character.

There remain many contested views about Proudhon's federal formulation, some emphasising its utopian air and others pointing to its failure to adequately explain the precise relationship between socio-economic and political variables.[37] But for our limited purposes here we can already see that Proudhon's version of federalism contains several key constituent elements – notions of contractual bargain, freely formed associations, corporatism, subsidiarity and consent – typical of what we would expect to find in the Althusian federal conception. In particular, his highly normative conception of federalism construed human beings as both social and moral persons rather than as mere isolated, atomised individuals; they were 'whole' persons in the sense that their liberty and autonomy were achieved only by their interaction with and responsibility to other humans. However, the conspicuous Proudhonian emphasis upon socio-economic aspects of federalism understandably brings his contribution to the European federal tradition closer to anarchist, socialist and anarcho-syndicalist ideas and it should come as little surprise to learn that his political thought was particularly influential in late-nineteenth-century Spain as well as in France.[38]

Despite the general impression conveyed here about the rather blurred and fuzzy nature of some of Proudhon's federal ideas, it is remarkable how they managed to resurface later in the interwar years of the twentieth century in France, Belgium, Italy and Germany, extending into the period between the closing years of the Second World War and its immediate aftermath. Variously labelled 'integral', 'personalist' and Proudhonian, these federal ideas first emerged in France during the 1930s and were developed and expounded in the two organisations known as *L'Ordre Nouveau* and *Esprit*. The personalists were originally led by a small group of highly influential philosophers among whom Alexander Marc, Robert Aron, Emmanuel Mounier, Daniel Rops and Denis de Rougemont were the most important. They were joined, after the end of the Second World War, by Henri Brugmans, whose own wartime experience in the Resistance had converted him to personalism.[39]

Derived mainly from the philosophical writings of these intellectual thinkers, personalist ideas were based upon a set of underlying assumptions that revolve around the dignity of the human person. These principles are premised upon a searching critique of the modern capitalist state the mass society of which, in cutting man off from his family, his neighbours and his local associations, has reduced him to the isolation of anonymity in a monist world where he finds himself confronted directly by global society. As an isolated individual, man is ultimately cut off from himself. Put simply, personalism seeks to restore man as a whole person who is in close touch with his own social life and with himself. Logically, then, personalism is a perception of the world that is societal rather than state-based and is concerned to bring political authority back to human beings as complex, responsible members of society.

Most, although not all, of this group of internationalist thinkers were Roman Catholics, and it is easy to appreciate how their Christian beliefs and values might link the temporal and the spiritual dimensions of man in this way. The focus upon Roman Catholicism, however, is also appropriate here because it enables us to turn to our third strand of federal political thought that constitutes the larger Continental European federal tradition, namely, Roman Catholic social theory. This dates from the late nineteenth century and is properly located in 'political Catholicism', which existed to defend both the spiritual and material interests of the Church. Catholic social thought was spelled out in a series of important papal encyclicals which spanned the decades between the 1880s and the 1930s. For our purposes the key encyclicals are *Rerum Novarum* (About New Matters) enunciated in 1891, *Quadragesimo Anno* which appeared in 1931 and marked the fortieth anniversary of the previous encyclical, and more recently *Pacem in Terris* promulgated in 1963.[40] Together, these doctrinal pronouncements constituted a philosophy of man and society that was rooted in pluralism, personalism, solidarism and subsidiarity. The Church did not formally address itself to federalism per se in these papal encyclicals, but in propounding a peculiarly organic view of society and its ethical-religious implications, it gave ecclesiastical authority to the central concepts that formed the basis of federal thought and action.[41] The papal encyclicals therefore incorporated a set of assumptions and principles about man, the state and society which yielded a particular brand of Continental European federalism that remains firmly integrated into the latter-day Christian democratic conception of European integration.[42]

Catholic social theory was predicated upon the notion of the organic community in which people were united by profound social bonds, such as religion, inherited from the past and the continuing source of their vitality and creativity. The significance of *Rerum Novarum* lay in its formal adoption of 'Social Catholicism' and in the way that it defined the direction of Catholic social teaching. Solidarism, then (sometimes called mutualism), referred to the socially interactive citizen who assumed responsibility not only for his own welfare, but also for the welfare of other members of the community, thereby emphasising the collectivist spirit and commitment to the whole. But *Rerum Novarum* was also important for the firm assumptions that it made about the nature of man and society. These assumptions had far-reaching political implications. They coalesced in a pluralist conception of society that acknowledged man's innate propensity to enter into a multitude of relations with his fellow beings. These relations produced a veritable host of groups, associations, communities and societies extending from the family to international society. And it is also important to stress here that they were freely formed associations which existed independently of the state and owed nothing to it for their creation. As with the Althusian, Proudhonian and pluralist conceptions of society identified above, Roman Catholic theory construed these entities as the very living practice of society, forming part of an immense network of complex and diverse social institutions reflective of man's multiple identities and capacities.

In 1931 Pope Pius XI published the encyclical *Quadragesimo Anno* in which he summarised previous Catholic social teaching and extended it under the impact of changing social and economic conditions. Here he outlined the changes that had occurred in both capitalism and socialism since *Rerum Novarum* in 1891, and attacked them for neglecting spiritual values. In order to limit both state power and the growth of government, while simultaneously demanding that public authority be used to regulate the economy and protect the working class by just legislation, Pius XI invoked the ancient social 'principle of subsidiarity' against excessive centralisation. This principle, which was derived from the experience and vision of an essentially organic society, was defined thus:

> It is a fundamental principle of social philosophy, fixed and unchangeable, that one should not withdraw from individuals and commit to the community what they can accomplish by their own enterprise and industry. So, too, it is an injustice and at the same time a grave evil and a disturbance of right order, to transfer to the larger and higher collectivity functions which can be performed and provided for by lesser and subordinate bodies. In as much as every social activity should, by its very nature, prove a help to members of the body social, it should never destroy or absorb them.[43]

Today this principle has become much more widely known, having been formally incorporated in the Treaty on European Union (TEU) – popularly dubbed the Maastricht Treaty – that was officially ratified in 1993. Since then, what was originally invoked as a theological response to the emergent modern liberal society of the late nineteenth century and the secular forces of unbridled *laissez-faire* capitalism and collectivist socialism – and defended by the Catholic Church as essentially a moral principle – has become, in Hydra-like fashion, a legal, constitutional and political principle. In the EU, it is worth adding, it has also become a highly contested and contestable concept.

Subsidiarity first entered the modern world of practical politics via post-war Christian democracy in Western Europe, but it is important to note that it had already been part and parcel of nineteenth-century 'political Catholicism', which was gradually superseded by Christian democracy in the immediate aftermath of the Second World War. Consequently many of the core traditional political and philosophical values of Roman Catholicism were simply carried over, or woven into the broader spectrum of Christian democratic ideas and beliefs.[44] The key to understanding the link between subsidiarity and federalism, then, lies in the uniquely Christian democratic approach to power and authority. Theirs is essentially a pluralist conception that favours the dispersion of power both territorially and functionally. Taking its cue from Catholic doctrine, man is a member of certain natural groups – the family, the craftsmen, the profession, the commune, the region, the neighbourhood – which are natural law entities whose autonomy should be protected by the state.

Since the main danger in modern society is defined by Christian democrat thought as the development of an all-powerful state, the idea of federation that emerges is a political order which seeks to accommodate the greatest possible number of communities and societies, primary and intermediate, without destroying them. Accordingly, federation is construed as a living pluralist order that builds itself from the ground upwards, constructing its tiers of authority and decision-making according to the principle of subsidiarity. It is, in short, the reverse of a centralised state; it is a state based upon the territorial and functional dispersal of power with limited centralisation. In the specific context of the EU, then, we can appreciate from this brief outline of Christian Democratic social and political thought that their conception of federalism and, by implication, European integration is both multidimensional and organic. It is largely a societal concept of federalism, but one that has enormous constitutional and political implications. Federation in this sense constitutes the only form of the state that can logically satisfy the requirements of the social order described above. Consequently, if subsidiarity is to be applied to the entire social order, the federal principle of dividing powers and competences between different levels of authority is its logical complement.

Originally the principle of subsidiarity appeared to be related principally to the role and structure of the state. It did not seem to have any particular significance for international relations until *Pacem in Terris* was enunciated in 1963. In this papal encyclical the principle of subsidiarity was formally elevated to the discussion of international relations and world order. Here the Catholic conception of the world community, having as its fundamental objective 'the recognition, respect, safeguarding and promotion of the rights of the human person', requires that modern states acknowledge their interdependence in solving major problems. Subsidiarity applied to relations between the world community and modern states is expressed thus:

> The public authority of the world community is not intended to limit the sphere of action of the public authority of the individual political community, much less take its place. On the contrary, its purpose is to create, on a world basis, an environment in which the public authorities of each political community, its citizens and intermediate associations, can carry out their tasks, fulfil their duties and exercise their rights with greater security.[45]

There is, then, an essentially continuous, unbroken link between the citizen, associated groups, the state and the international community. Subsidiarity is a principle which is universal.

Our brief investigation into the composition of Roman Catholic social theory brings us to the end of our broad survey of the Continental European federal tradition. How, then, do we summarise this complex federal tradition? What are the fundamental elements that characterise it as a distinct tradition? The hallmark of this federal tradition would seem to be its overwhelming emphasis upon 'society' and societal perspectives. Pentland was therefore unquestionably correct to emphasise its focus upon small groups and sociological variables, and its implications for relations between states and citizens. There is certainly a very close affinity with pluralism and many of its assumptions and principles are identical to those schools of thought that regard socio-economic groups, local communities and public associations as primary building blocks of the polity. This, of course, gives rise to notions of the organic nature of society and the structures that comprise it. Nonetheless, it is worth emphasising here that none of this makes it any easier for the political scientist to utilise the term 'federal society' with very much analytical confidence.

Another characteristic feature of this federal tradition is its recognition of both territorial and non-territorial, functional dimensions of representation. We have already noted in Chapter 5, for example, the existence of the personality principle originally proposed by Karl Renner and Otto Bauer as a basis for their multinational federal state, and this principle continues to operate today in the Brussels Capital Region in Belgium. There can also be little doubt that the Continental European federal tradition, rooted in a moral imperative based on the dignity and fellowship of human beings, is a highly normative and ethical political tradition. The federal idea therefore cannot be reduced to mere instrumentalism or to the mechanics of political organisation. It is not something that one merely observes as an objective reality. On the contrary, it embraces the moral values of partnership, mutual reciprocity, comity, human dignity, tolerance, respect and recognition. Together these values constitute the moral imperative appropriately encapsulated in the German term *Bundestreue* (federal comity) that implies socially interactive citizens. Consequently, there is a strong emphasis upon the socially interactive citizen as a whole person rather than the isolated atomistic individual cut adrift from his or her family and community.

What stands out in this complex federal tradition is the way that particular themes, values and assumptions are so heavily interwoven across four centuries of tumultuous historical change in Europe that what looms large in the Germanic political theology of Althusius reappears in modified form in the French secular anarchist-socialist thought of Proudhon and yet again in universalist Roman Catholic social theory. In retrospect, it is no surprise that medieval corporatism, Roman Catholic theology, Protestant Reformism, the Swiss experience and the quasi-federal organisation of first the Holy Roman Empire and later the Habsburg Empire were the historical sources of fertile federal ideas. It was, as we have emphasised in our survey, a combination of thought and practice.

The Anglo-American federal tradition

The historical and philosophical origins of the Anglo-American federal tradition are much older and much more complex than is often acknowledged in the mainstream literature. Drawing on 'The Antecedents of American Federalism' in Chapter 2, it is possible to identify three principal strands that have interacted to form the basis of a distinct federal tradition.[46] These are the following: first, the covenantal tradition; second, British and American federal ideas and experience; and, finally, the enduring legacy of *The Federalist Papers*. Before we turn to the first of our antecedents, however, let us introduce our subject with some general remarks about the philosophical context of late-eighteenth-century colonial America. We will sketch in the historical background on a broad canvas.

Most commentators on the American federal tradition would concede that its philosophical roots lie in the gradual emergence of social contract theory in the seventeenth and eighteenth centuries in England and France. This means that the federal idea evolved *pari passu* with changing conceptions of the state and sovereignty so that we must look to some of the major political thinkers of the time – Hobbes, Locke, Rousseau and Montesquieu – for the philosophical configuration of the political discourse of the age. In 1776, the year that the leading colonial revolutionaries drafted and issued the Declaration of Independence, it is clear that the underlying political theory in the American colonies was largely identical to that of the seventeenth century in England. The belief in the state of nature, the conception of natural rights, the idea of consent and the notion of government on the firm basis of contract infused the Declaration and legitimised the twin ideas of limited government and the right of resistance against arbitrary power. But there seems little doubt in conventional mainstream American political thought that the overriding influence upon an emergent, if embryonic, late eighteenth-century republican political culture was the towering figure of John Locke. To this day there remains an intermittently lively intellectual debate about Lockean conceptions of individualism, property rights and constitutionalism but it has never been possible completely to shake off the Lockean influences that continue to fall like a shadow across the American federal experience.[47]

This much is widely accepted in the mainstream literature. American federalism grew out of the complex interaction of theory and practice, but its theoretical basis did not lie in any elaborate, abstract constructs about liberty and equality. Rather it evolved from the experience of practical affairs gained by generation after generation of English colonists, along with German and Dutch neighbours, who, even at the time of the American Revolution, were not discontented with their own political institutions. Indeed, the consequence of the War of Independence (1776–83) meant casting off their allegiance to the British monarchy, not the abolition of their own governmental systems which suited their local needs and which in general they were happy to retain. Consequently they did not have to exercise their political ingenuity by creating any fundamentally new institutions. Indeed, many of their constitutions, based upon seventeenth-century charters granted by the British monarchy, remained in force until long after the Revolution and the essentially English ideas of the suffrage, the distribution of representation, the qualifications for office-holders and the legislative, executive and judicial institutions of old English origin survived without many radical alterations. Here, then, we have sketched out very briefly the broad philosophical context of eighteenth-century colonial America within which the colonial experience of local government, grounded in practical circumstances, must be firmly located. Let us turn now to the first of our antecedents of the Anglo-American federal tradition.

Recent research on the origins of Anglo-American federalism demonstrates the existence of a competing, almost shadowy, tradition of federal thought unknown to most scholars of federalism until now. It shows that alongside the conventional mainstream philosophical tradition of secular Enlightenment thinking derived from Hobbes, Locke and Montesquieu there exists another different political-theological tradition that is located in covenant theory. This rival tradition of federalism is best described as the Biblical-Reformed-Puritan-ethical-religious strand of Anglo-American federalism and its intellectual origins stretch back to Heinrich Bullinger, a Swiss theologian-philosopher of the sixteenth century. We will return to this political-theological dimension to our subject later but let us first look at the idea of the covenantal tradition for which we prepared the ground in the conclusion to Chapter 1.

In modern times covenantal theory is most closely associated with the contributions to federal scholarship of Vincent Ostrom, Daniel J. Elazar and John Kincaid. It is, above all, a biblical perspective of federalism. According to this perspective, the concept of covenantal federalism embodies a set of normative principles that bind partners together in a moral contract or agreement of trust. The act of coming together remains a 'political bargain', but it is more than just this; it is also based upon mutual recognition, trust, toleration, respect, obligation and responsibility. Indeed, Elazar refers to the genesis of such an arrangement in the original relationship between God and man which descends from the Bible. Michael Stein has recently underscored this:

> In the religious compact there is supposed to be a set of tacit moral obligations mutually acceptable by the Deity and those who adopt his code of law and its moral precepts. The same covenant is supposed to commit the individual members of the covenanting group to appropriate moral behaviour in their relations with each other.[48]

As we noted earlier in Chapter 1, Elazar's own research on American federalism arrived at the conclusion that a major source of the covenantal idea was both *The Federalist Papers* of Hamilton, Jay and Madison and the American Constitution (1789) itself.[49] The journey to this destination was assisted by Ostrom's pioneering work on the interpretation of late eighteenth-century American political debates and constitutional negotiations in terms of these normative and covenantal principles.[50] This scholarship has firmly established the link between federal theology and federal politics. Covenantal theory is clearly central to a particular perspective of and approach to the study of modern federalism and modern federal political systems. However, in 1991 two academic specialists in theology, Charles McCoy and J. Wayne Baker, published their revisionist monograph entitled *Fountainhead of Federalism: Heinrich Bullinger and the Covenantal Tradition*.[51] This revealing survey of Bullinger's own intellectual contribution to federal theory serves to confirm the latter-day positions of both Elazar and Ostrom in the covenantal tradition and it also underlines how far this tradition antedates that of the conventional Western liberal individualism of Hobbes, Locke and Montesquieu. But it is also of great significance for the assertion of a distinct Anglo-American tradition of federalism. Let us take a closer look at the contribution of Bullinger to this tradition.

Like Elazar and Ostrom, McCoy and Baker are unequivocal in their belief that 'the terms "federal" and "covenantal" are closely related and, when carefully examined, virtually inter-changeable'.[52] This argument of course is not restricted to American intellectual debate. In 1978 the Australian scholar of federalism, S. Rufus Davis, acknowledged precisely the same point:

> Somewhere near the beginning of it all is the idea of 'foedus', ... And the lexicographic association of foedus with covenant, and of its cognate 'fides' with faith and trust, provide us with the first crucial clue. Because in the idea of covenant, and the synonymous ideas of promise, commitment, undertaking, or obligation, vowing and plighting one's word to a course of conduct in relation to others, we come upon a vital bonding device of civilisation, ... the idea of covenant ... involves the idea of cooperation, reciprocity, mutuality, and it implies the recognition of entities – whether it be persons, a people, or a divine being.[53]

To McCoy and Baker, then, the term '"federal" derives from the Latin "foedus", which means covenant. A covenantal order is federal. A federal order is covenantal'.[54]

But what role does Bullinger play in the unfolding revelation of the Anglo-American tradition of federalism? The key to understanding Bullinger's contribution to this tradition is to realise that academic specialisation has separated the terms 'federal' and 'covenantal'. McCoy and Baker claim that what has been forgotten as academic disciplines have tended to isolate themselves from one another is that 'federal terminology is used by theological and political writers, as also is the language of covenant, compact and contract':

> In the 16th, 17th and 18th centuries, the era when the institutions of the modern world were taking shape, federal theologians dealt with political as well as ecclesiastical issues and political philosophers concerned with societal covenants dealt also with religious issues.[55]

Bullinger's 1534 treatise entitled *The One and Eternal Testament or Covenant of God*, according to these commentators, is the fountainhead of federalism in the specific sense that it is a basic source of federal thought among theologians, political philosophers and practising leaders in church and state. Bullinger was the leader of the Reformed Church of Zurich between 1531 and 1575 so that the *Testament* became a major theological and political influence upon the Reformed tradition in the sixteenth century. McCoy and Baker claim that the *Testament* is important for three principal reasons: first, because its influence was 'direct in the century following its publication and indirect during later times'; second, because in both theological and philosophical terms it established the formal link between federalism and covenant; and, third, because it recognised the significance of primary social entities – such as families, congregations, occupational guilds and commercial organisations – and their relationships as essentially 'federal'.[56] Additional reasons for its continuing significance are the emphasis (long before Montesquieu) upon the division of powers, the need to construe federalism in dynamic terms as a pattern of changing relations and, finally, the belief in humanity and history as both developmental and progressive.

In the *Testament*, Bullinger regarded the covenant as the divine framework for human life, both religious and civil. The Scripture in its entirety taught the covenant and its conditions; the moral law was a restatement of these conditions and the Magistrate had been designated to enforce the covenant's condition among God's people. In short, the divine covenant between God and his people was to be replaced on earth as the very essence of human organisation and civil society. Bullinger's *Testament* therefore became a hallmark of the Reformed tradition in Continental Europe and in England and Scotland by the end of the sixteenth century. McCoy and Baker claim that at this time federal theology and political philosophy were 'evolving into the forms that permeate modern democratic societies' and, crucially for our purposes, that it was 'this federal tradition, with explicit theological, ethical and political dimensions, that was taken to the new world by the Puritans and used as a model for the colonies of New England'.[57]

Bullinger's *Testament* has now been rescued from obscurity and stands as a distinct branch of the larger Reformed tradition that has tended to be equated solely with Calvinism and thus oversimplified. This relatively recent research reminds us that it is difficult if not impossible to separate theological from political federalism in the sixteenth century and it is only later in the following century that the two elements can in practice be separated. However, if for the purposes of academic convenience we do separate the development of theological federalism from the evolution of political federalism, it becomes clear how the first fully developed, systematic articulation of federal political philosophy emerged in 1603 in the form of *Politica Methodice Digesta* written by Johannes Althusius. It is important therefore to situate Althusius' federalism in the context of the Reformed tradition: 'Althusius is immersed in Reformed faith, in the political thought of the Reformed communities, and in the biblical and theological scholarship of the Reformed tradition'.[58] The argument here, then, is that Althusius' intellectual development was shaped and moulded by a religious, political and philosophical environment which already expressed admittedly embryonic elements of a federal tradition.

Before we bring this aspect of our survey to a close, it is important for us to emphasise the intellectual links that were made across the generations in different countries. The transmission of Bullinger's 'theological-political' federalism appears to have been pervasive. According to McCoy and Baker, federal political thought spread rapidly throughout the seventeenth and eighteenth centuries and was brought to America by early settlers in the British colonies – the Anglicans in Virginia, the Puritans in New England in particular, and by the Presbyterians in the Middle Colonies. Furthermore, it was taught in the colonial colleges, one of the most striking examples being John Witherspoon, a Scottish federal theologian and political philosopher at the College of New Jersey, who taught James Madison. Small wonder, then, that the federal tradition of the American colonies should have influenced the formation of colonial charters and, later, the state constitutions. 'It gathered strength during the colonial period and acquired the characteristics that identify a distinctively American federal tradition'.[59]

This recent research, then, is important in a number of respects. It is especially important to the establishment of an Anglo-American federal tradition. But it is also vital that we do not exaggerate its significance. Donald S. Lutz, a leading scholar in the field of historical and political analysis of American federalism, has already acknowledged that 'most state constitutions can be seen as reflecting a direct link with religious covenants traced through the compacts written by colonists during the seventeenth century'.[60] However, his historical research into 'the colonial portion of American political thought' also reveals the deep complexity of the subject: covenants, compacts and contracts meant different things to different people at different times in different colonial political communities. The civil covenant, for example, was not the same as the religious covenant. There was, in other words, 'a plethora of terms'.[61]

McCoy and Baker's comment upon this scrupulously detailed analysis of the early American colonial documents and their sources would presumably be that 'as with theological federalism, political federalism' developed 'beyond Bullinger's views'. However, 'later expansions only demonstrate that he is the primary source of the movement'.[62] The transmission of political ideas across time and space are, to repeat, often extremely difficult to determine.

The second of our antecedents – as identified in Chapter 2 – refers to British and American federal ideas and experience. Here we are dealing with concrete constitutional and political experience. We will recall that the idea of a British federal discourse during this historical era seems initially paradoxical, given the Anglo-American imperial experience. After all, the constitutional and political relationship between the mother country and her American colonies was unequivocally one of the superordinate and the subordinate. However, the British were not averse to constitutional and political experimentation and adjustment when it was deemed necessary to the order, stability and integrity of the state. Nor were they averse to various forms of constitutional innovation in order to maintain the integrity of the empire. The legislative union between England and Scotland in 1707 is one obvious example of the former but British imperial relations during the seventeenth and eighteenth centuries was also a fertile area for a variety of different political relationships. The irony is that these evolving forms of colonial autonomy ultimately failed to prevent the rupture of 1776 and the subsequent loss of the American colonies.

The federal idea surfaced intermittently in a series of 'empire federalist ideas' of which the most persistent was colonial representation in the British Parliament.[63] First urged for Barbados in 1652, colonial representation was one way of incorporating the constituent parts of the empire into the central institutional framework. Adam Smith had recommended it in his enormously influential *The Wealth of Nations*, first published in 1776, and in 1778 the British peace mission to the rebellious American colonies led by Lord Carlisle was authorised to offer representation in Parliament to them along with the acknowledgement of the practical supremacy of Congress in American affairs. Moreover, as the British Empire evolved during the eighteenth and nineteenth centuries, the concomitant development of local colonial autonomy was sometimes construed as akin to some form of shadowy federal relationship. Much of this was assumed and unspoken: 'a division between central and local powers, even when the latter are delegated and theoretically revocable, will work in a federal sense and come to be thought of in that way'.[64] The British imperial–colonial relationship, we are reminded, was a fertile policy arena for many different federal and quasi-federal political ideas. And, it should be noted, they were practical suggestions to perceived problems of that evolving relationship, especially once the American colonies had left the empire.

Turning now to the indigenous political ideas and the practical local governmental experience of the American colonies, it is clear that this, too, is an important dimension to Anglo-American federal political thought. Lutz has already remarked that political relationships in colonial America potentially had three levels: the intracolonial, the intercolonial and, finally, the colony–mother country. And, he observed, 'it is interesting that in the first and third instances, the solution tended to be federalism'. Taking his cue from Tocqueville, Lutz noted that it was 'a federalism that was unconscious, was not derived from theory, and had no name to describe it'.[65] Tocqueville himself had remarked that the federal government was 'the last to take shape in the United States; the political principles on which it was based were spread throughout society *before* its time, existed independently of it, and only had to be modified to form the republic'.[66] The colonies, Lutz reminded us, were each a collection of towns or counties rather than a single, undifferentiated entity. Plymouth Colony, for example, was eventually composed of seven towns, each with its own town meeting. But since the charters establishing the colonies, and signed under the royal seal, the highest civil authority, recognised only a single entity – a colony – the various constituent parts of the colonies responded by writing federal documents, such as the Fundamental Orders of Connecticut (1639) and the Acts and Orders of Rhode Island (1647). These created 'a common colony-wide government with limited powers while preserving town governments to operate in their own sphere of competence'. Lutz also noted that 'both town and colony governments were often derived in form and substance from covenants', and that even when they did not derive from covenants 'colonial governments functioned effectively as federal polities, having been built up from below'.[67]

The early seventeenth-century American colonists were permitted to form and operate their own governments provided that the laws which they passed did not conflict with those laws passed by the English Parliament. And England had good reasons to grant charters to the colonies. Given the difficulties of travelling between the colonies and England – a minimum two-month round trip – the mother country could not realistically administer them. Added to her preoccupation with the Civil War and the threat of French expansionism in the New

World, the imperial power found it convenient to encourage local self-government and administration. This was based largely upon the 'obvious needs of practicality': the relationship between colony and mother country was 'federal in operation, although not federal by design'.[68]

In its obsession with the Philadelphia Convention and the subsequent ratification of the American Constitution in 1789, political science analysis has often overlooked this aspect of American constitutional development. But it is vital to appreciate that by the time of the Declaration of Independence in 1776, the colonies had already been in existence as functioning polities, with varying levels of autonomy, for over a century and a half. As Lutz has emphasised, the evolution of state constitutions were the culmination of a long development: 'Americans wrote and evolved protoconstitutions containing all the elements later to be found in state and national constitutions'.[69] In this sense the rudiments of Anglo-American federal political thought must be traced back to those documents which established local self-government on American shores during the early seventeenth century.

Looking at inter-colonialism, Lutz noted that there was a distinct lack of interest among the early English colonists in uniting their colonies under either region-wide confederations or a continent-wide government. As we have seen, his explanation for this indifference lay in early Whig political thought – 'the American Whig devotion to local control made the Whigs highly resistant to confederations larger than a single state'. Preference for local control over political unions 'at a distance' also fuelled a suspicion that 'any continental government would be a source of danger' even if it used 'standard Whig institutions'.[70] But this is not to say that such schemes and plans did not exist. On the contrary, there were a considerable number of plans. Among the most prominent of these were the following: the New England Confederation (1643) created by the colonists, the Commission of the Council for Foreign Plantations (1660) devised in England, William Penn's Plan of Union (1696), the Report of the Board of Trade on the union of New York with other colonies (1696), the plan of the Lords of Trade (1721) and the Albany Plan of Union (1754) written by Benjamin Franklin.[71] According to Lutz, the last of these – the Albany Plan – was 'one of the first serious designs for an intercolonial government' and it came 'much closer to a federal system' than did the later Articles of Confederation'.[72]

As we noted in Chapter 2, it is abundantly clear from this brief survey of British and American federal ideas and experience that the origins of American constitutional history stretch back almost two centuries, long before the more familiar landmarks of 1776, 1787 and 1789. Lutz's research has demonstrated that the only way to arrive at a proper appreciation of the Anglo-American federal political tradition – and the peculiarly American dimension to it – is to investigate what occurred much earlier than the late eighteenth century. And McCoy and Baker concurred: 'Though ignored by most historians of the Constitution, there is a tradition of federalism that pervaded the entire colonial era, developed in distinctive ways apart from European thinkers, and formed the background of experience upon which the leaders of the Revolution and new nation relied as they shaped the institutions of what became the United States of America'.[73]

Clearly the key to understanding this aspect of the Anglo-American federal tradition is 'political experience'; it was the actual practice of local colonial self-government and administration over many years that helped to mould a distinct federal political culture. This relatively recent research shows that if we are prepared very carefully to study and analyse the constitutional history of the early colonial and state documents, it is possible to see a continuous, unbroken tradition of federal political thought and practice that is indigenous to Americans. While those who shaped the social institutions of colonial America, carried out the Revolution and produced the US Constitution might have had 'some indirect or direct influence on them from European thinkers', these American leaders were 'primarily persons who relied on their immediate context, the tradition in which they were trained, and the experience accumulated on American soil'.[74] In retrospect, it is hardly surprising that both Alexander Hamilton and James Madison could describe the advantages of the extended republic in the language of David Hume with great equanimity in *The Federalist Papers*.[75]

This leaves us with the third and final of our antecedents, namely, *The Federalist Papers*. It is impossible to overestimate the enduring significance of this remarkable composite document that is tantamount to an American theoretical and philosophical treatise on constitutional government. Clinton Rossiter alluded to its 'exposition of certain timeless truths about constitutional government', acknowledging that it had 'converted federalism from an expedient into an article of faith, from an occasional accident of history to an enduring expression of the principles of constitutionalism'.[76] The compound republic was founded upon the idea of a popular sovereignty that was rooted in the written constitution with political authority both divided and shared between different levels of government in separate territorial spheres. And because the American federal experience became the archetypical model of what a federation should be and look like, it is hardly surprising that subsequent commentators and observers should have looked upon it as the yardstick by which to assess the authenticity of those federal experiments that came after it. This predisposition is clearly reflected in Kenneth Wheare's famous remark that 'the modern idea of what federal government is has been determined by the United States of America'. Consequently 'any definition of federal government which failed to include the United States would be ... condemned as unreal'.[77] But if this narrow perspective served merely to impoverish the federal idea, confining it to the conceptual straitjacket of Anglo-American values and beliefs, it also lent the impression that federalism was really only about formal constitutional and legal rules and political institutions. It was, in short, very much a constitutional-institutional model that reflected the liberal-rational design of the Founding Fathers of the American Constitution. Part of the historical legacy of *The Federalist Papers* therefore has been the general perception that federalism is a somewhat instrumental, pragmatic kind of constitutional-legal formalism based largely upon Lockean notions of Western liberal individualism. We will return to this legacy in the conclusion to the chapter. For the moment, let us turn away from the Anglo-American federal tradition and look instead at an interesting case study that brings together the two political traditions identified above in an unusual and unexpected way.

Quebec federalism revisited

In this short section I want to call attention to the existence of a tradition of federalism in the province of Quebec in Canada that serves to point up the way that different federal influences from seemingly discrete political experiences can infiltrate and impinge upon other federations. The case of Quebec federalism is especially interesting in this respect because its historical, philosophical and ideological roots in the Canadian federation correspond much more closely with the Continental European tradition of federalism than with the Anglo-American federal tradition.

Quebec's place in the Canadian federation has been the subject of interminable public debate and political controversy both within and without Quebec for well over forty years since the modernising period of the 1960s, widely known as the 'Quiet Revolution'. This decade witnessed huge changes in the state, economy and society of Quebec and is often regarded as a watershed between two very different eras in Quebec's modern history. The Quebec that we see today is both a self-assertive nation and a self-confident province in Canada that has pushed back the frontiers in technology, research and socio-economic development in ways that have become a veritable model for the rest of Canada. Today francophone capital structures are highly sophisticated and widely respected throughout North America, illustrating how far the new Quebec has successfully adapted and adjusted to the contemporary challenges of economic competition, international trade and globalisation. Quebec would seem, then, to fit comfortably into the Anglo-American federal tradition with its contemporary liberal political values, economic wealth and prosperity, and modern secular tastes. But if we search beneath the surface of contemporary politics and government to look at the philosophical and ideological roots of federalism in Quebec, we stumble upon a rich vein of values and beliefs that are distilled in Catholic social theory.

Historically, the roots of Quebec federalism reveal a markedly different political tradition from that characteristic of mainstream North America. They hark back to part of the Continental European federal tradition that surfaced briefly with the publication of the Tremblay Report in the 1950s. This report, which was published in 1956, emphasised the preservation of regionally based particularisms and offered up a moral and philosophical enquiry into the justification of a culturally distinct French-Canadian society. As David Kwavnick acknowledged, the immediate objective of the Tremblay Report was 'to shore up the claim of the Quebec provincial government to provincial primacy in the field of direct taxation'.[78] Without legal support, however, it was deemed expedient to utilise historical, sociological and cultural arguments to buttress a provincial fiscal autonomy. This at least is what received wisdom would have us believe. The detailed moral and philosophical edifice constructed by the Tremblay Commission is usually presented by its critics as a mere contrivance designed to defend what were already archaic values and beliefs abandoned by Quebec society in the throes of modernisation. We will return to this assertion a little later in the section.

The Tremblay Report comprises five large volumes and we shall focus upon only one of these, namely, one chapter taken from the second part of Volume II of the report and entitled 'Federalism as a System of Social Organisation'.[79] The report identifies and explains four philosophical and sociological bases fundamental to its essentially organic conception of society: the Christian concept of man and society; the fact of social life's variety and complexity; the idea of a common good; and the principle of subsidiarity in every community. Together these four basic elements gave French-Canadian society its distinctive characteristics and explained its peculiar brand of federalism. They arose out of a corpus of Roman Catholic teachings derived from two main papal encyclicals: *Rerum Novarum* (1891) and *Quadragesimo Anno* (1931). In other words, Quebec federalism was rooted in Catholic social theory.

The Christian concept of man and society drew upon the notion of personalism which emphasised, above all, man's spiritual being. Man cannot be reduced to, in essence, the material universe, but on the contrary is endowed with an immortal soul and must perforce be free to develop his own personality; society must be regulated for him in order that he may fulfil his spiritual and moral potential. It thus follows from this concept that federalism must recognise man as a developing personality and social being whose participation in social organisation is guaranteed to preserve, protect and promote his unique self-fulfilment in a society of persons. The fact of social life's variety and complexity alluded to man's innate propensity to enter into a multitude of relations with his fellow beings that yielded a host of groups, associations, communities and societies. These, it should be noted, could extend from the family to international society. Federalism here, it followed, had to be based upon a pluralist conception of society that was designed to nourish and foster these freely organised associations that constituted the living practice of society. And these associations formed part of an immense network of complex and diverse social institutions reflecting man's multiple identities and capacities. They furnished him with spheres of freedom other than those that could be obtained within the framework of the state.

The third defining feature of Quebec federalism – the idea of a common good – was also intimately linked to the two previous characteristics. Here the common good was not some kind of unidimensional monolith built upon majoritarian precepts. Quite the reverse. It had to mirror the very complexity and variety of social life itself. There could therefore never be one single common good but only a myriad of common goods. Since man places himself in multiple groupings, each one corresponding to different aspects of his nature, the common good had to be conceived in the multitude of diverse associations 'as a whole, organised in concentric circles around the human personality and reaching from the family to international society, while realising itself by degrees, by stages, by levels'. Federalism, according to this emphasis, had to prevent the state from suffocating and ultimately absorbing the natural social activities of freely formed associations by ensuring that it accommodated and sustained the particular 'common goods' emanating from them, whether they were families, professional groups, cities or provinces. Finally, the principle of subsidiarity in every community was proposed as an organising principle designed to entrench and guarantee the autonomy of each part of this vast plurality of associations stretching from the family to international society. It was the logical complement of the three previous defining features of Quebec federalism.

It requires very little thought and imagination to appreciate how far this distinctive organic brand of federalism was at odds with the dominant Anglo-American model of Canadian federalism championed by Ottawa. Clearly, Canada had no other federalism within the federation to rival such a deep-rooted ideological-cultural identity as that of Quebec. Indeed, the way that this social federalism was to be translated into political institutional forms and constitutional meaning was certain to provoke another Quebec–Ottawa confrontation. The political implications – founded upon pluralism, increased decentralisation, the juridical recognition of local and regional autonomies, and the union of national groups rather than their unification – were so far-reaching in the mid-1950s as to call into question the very survival of the Canadian federation itself.

Even if we acknowledge the disputed circumstances that surrounded the appointment of the Tremblay Commission in 1953 and its subsequent report three years later, there is no doubt that Quebec is historically and culturally linked to a federal tradition that does not exist elsewhere in Canada. And even if we concede that the report promoted a series of social and political values that were already outdated at the time they were published, this does not detract from their historical and political significance in terms of Quebec's cultural identity in the 1950s and 1960s. If Catholic social theory was used merely as an instrument – part of a political strategy – to challenge the dominant anglophone conception of federalism resident in Ottawa, this cannot alter the fact that such a federal tradition was available to French-Canadians if only as a political resource.

In retrospect, the Tremblay Report was the product of confused and confusing circumstances. Today few Canadians are aware of it outside the intellectual confines of university life. But it nonetheless continues to offer a rival conception of Canadian federalism that underlines the legitimacy of Quebec's unique culture and ideology within the Canadian federation. Kwavnick described it as 'one of the most remarkable government documents in Canadian history'. The Tremblay Report was 'nothing less than an examination in depth of the philosophical and moral basis of French-Canadian society and a restatement of its *raison d'être*.[80] Alexander Brady claimed that English-speaking Canadians could have 'little excuse for misunderstanding the position of their French-speaking compatriots ... (it was) a landmark in the literature of federalism': it described and explained 'more fully than any other public document the position and anxieties of Quebec in the federal state'.[81] And William Coleman noted that what was usually ignored was that the political programme of the report became 'the basis, the cornerstone, of political strategy by the government of Quebec throughout the 1960s and into the 1970s'. Indeed, he observed that 'the various movements for independence and for renewed federalism that have emerged since are all variations on the Tremblay theme'.[82]

In summary, it is tempting to downgrade the significance of Catholic social theory in the wake of the waning influence of the Catholic Church in Quebec society and the challenge of modernisation, but the assumption that old values and beliefs are quickly swept away and automatically replaced by new urban secular attitudes and social practices requires careful analysis. Old values and beliefs are often adjusted and adapted, and gradually absorbed into political tradition, rather than summarily dissolved. As Gingras and Nevitte noted in the 1980s, 'it is unlikely that the changes of the 1960s were as complete or as sudden as many interpretations of the Quiet Revolution would have us believe'. They claimed that 'a residue of traditional values remains lodged in a significant portion of Quebec society and that the coexistence of traditional and modern orientations provides a diverse context for the expression of contemporary Quebec nationalism'.[83] Garth Stevenson, however, adopted a different stance, claiming that 'an ideological view of federalism was invented' in the Tremblay Report in order to justify the ambiguous position of the Quebec government concerning federal grants and subsidies.[84] These conflicting interpretations certainly raised serious questions about the authenticity of the federal ideas enshrined in the report so that their status today as an accurate portrayal of the sociological and philosophical bases to Quebec's cultural identity during these years probably remains both contested and contestable.

The Tremblay Report, then, appears to have been utilised by Quebec to achieve four main interrelated objectives: to strengthen provincial authority over fiscal policy, to buttress its own unique cultural identity in Canada, to underline its special position *vis-à-vis* the other overwhelmingly anglophone provinces, and to give its own history and development a new intellectual legitimacy. For our purposes here, however, the real significance of the case study of Quebec federalism is to demonstrate how certain features of the Continental European tradition of federalism have infiltrated and influenced the Anglo-American federal tradition of which Quebec-in-Canada is obviously an integral part.

Conclusion: the convergence of two federal traditions

This chapter has confirmed the existence of two distinct traditions of federalism and federation, namely, the Continental European and the Anglo-American. Our brief focus upon Quebec federalism has also revealed evidence of a certain intermingling of some of the elements of both traditions, underlining the philosophical cross-currents endemic in every political discourse and tradition. This serves to remind us that all political traditions are derivative. They draw upon sources that are often surprising and highly variegated. If we look back far enough into the American colonial past and into British imperial experience, it is possible to discover a veritable myriad of philosophical sources that overlap and intermingle in such complex ways that sometimes it is impossible to separate them. And this complexity is as it should be. Lutz has already remarked that no single idea or tradition has monopolised American political thought.

This much, then, should not surprise us, but recent research has improved our understanding of modern federalism in suggesting that there is a distinctively 'American' federal tradition that is much more indigenous than might have previously been appreciated. The specifically 'American' sources are especially apparent if we study the early colonial documents and institutions. And this conclusion is corroborated by McCoy and Baker, who have also acknowledged that 'the major sources of federalism in America were the federal theology, the federal political philosophy and the federal practice in societal institutions brought by groups coming from Europe to establish colonies and developed in distinctive ways in the 180 years from Jamestown to Philadelphia'.[85]

The significance of Bullinger and the covenantal dimension to the Anglo-American federal political tradition is clearly indisputable. It is another piece in the overall jigsaw of a distinct political tradition. But the religious aspect to the covenantal tradition should not be exaggerated in its impact upon modern American political thought. It is logically much more visible in the seventeenth and eighteenth centuries than it is today. It is perhaps the secular or 'civil' covenant, based upon voluntary consent and reflecting the spirit of the community, that is integral to modern American federalism. This point has been endorsed by McCoy and Baker, who claim that 'human covenants and federal perspectives occupy so central and pervasive a place in the experience and actions of persons in contemporary societies that federalism has become invisible to those who dwell in [a] covenantal culture'. But, then, 'people who wear spectacles do not look at the glasses but see everything through them'.[86]

The Anglo-American tradition of federalism, then, is much more distinctive and complex than might previously have been appreciated by scholars of modern federalism. Indeed, in many ways it is just as complicated in its historical origins, philosophical antecedents and social practices as its putative forerunner. This conclusion suggests that much more research is still required if we are more fully to understand this federal tradition. Certainly it is a much richer tradition than most commentators have hitherto realised. Consequently the general perception of it as mainly Lockean individualism must now give way to the recognition of a much more normative, communitarian and pluralistic conception of federalism. This view brings it much closer to the Continental European federal tradition than might originally have been anticipated. Given the relatively recent research focus on Bullinger and Althusius, it is now clear that these two intellectual pioneers of early modern federal political thought have had a pervasive influence upon both American and Continental European federal traditions. To this extent, their philosophical contributions to the theory and practice of modern federalism might conceivably serve to bring the two separate federal political traditions closer together as a basis for comparative analysis in the future.

In hindsight, Sobei Mogi was quite correct to refer in 1931 to Anglo-American and Continental European federalism, but in bringing this chapter to an appropriate close it is worth reflecting upon just how prophetic his own concluding remarks were:

> Anglo-American federalism has been far more elaborate and has contributed by its ideas and schemes more to progress than has continental federalism, but at the same time continental federalism is much more inclined to the legal interpretation and the legal form of federalism than the Anglo-American.... The contribution of the French thinkers towards federal ideas is novel and suggestive, but rather of a general than of a detailed nature. No realisation of the new federalism can be attained unless these two forms of thought – the Anglo-American and the continental federalism – harmonise and form a synthesis of the best that is contained in both sets of ideas.[87]

7 The concept of representation in federalism and federation

Introduction

In the conceptual world of federalism and federation the question of representation is fundamental. It goes to the very heart of federal democracy and has enormous theoretical, philosophical, historical and empirical implications that pull us into the wider spectrum of the study of government and politics. Our specific focus upon federal states means that the concept of representation serves to open up the relationship between federalism and federation in a way that compels us to reexamine some very basic, elemental issues and assumptions that are usually taken for granted. Accordingly, there are two questions that underpin the structure of the chapter: 'Who or what is represented in federations and how are they represented?'

In response to these two questions it is not necessary for us to traverse territory that would involve us in a detailed investigation of the variety of approaches to representation and its historical origins in the Middle Ages. Instead we shall keep to the path that connects us to the 'democratic revolution' of the late eighteenth century and in particular to the problems – real practical problems – that confronted the Founding Fathers of the young American Republic. The federal form of liberal democracy is rooted in the established principles of representative and constitutional democracy that inform all federal states as quintessentially liberal democratic states. In short, we want to identify, examine and explain the different kinds of representation evident in different kinds of federations. Our approach, we are reminded, is firmly predicated upon the conceptual distinction between federalism and federation principally because it allows us more accurately to locate the variety of different identities and interests that furnish the impulses, rhythms and the underlying impetus that has shaped particular forms of representation characteristic of different federations. Put simply, federalism determines who or what is represented in federation.

The simple question who or what is represented in federation is deceptively difficult to answer. As Hanna Pitkin wrote in her classic study entitled *The Concept of Representation*, first published in 1967, 'Questions about what representation is, or is like, are not fully separable from the question of what "representation" means'.[1] Indeed, a detailed investigation would have to include not only the context in which the concept operated but also its theoretical and philosophical assumptions. Its empirical dimension would perforce involve an analysis of numerous linkages peculiar to each individual federation before any significant conclusions could be drawn. These linkages would include *inter alia* the origins and early evolution of the federal state together with an examination of its institutional framework and associated democratic legitimacy as well as its sources of political stability and instability. Potentially therefore representation is a huge subject.

We will begin our exploration with a brief survey of what we take the basic concept of representation to be. This partly conceptual and partly empirical survey is the *sine qua non* to a comparative focus upon the various forms of representation that inhere in federations and to which we shall subsequently turn. But it is worth repeating here that virtually all of the difficult and awkward problems wrought by the perplexing conundrum of representation that are obvious to us all today had already been addressed by the late eighteenth-century pioneers of American federalism. A detailed exegesis of *The Federalist Papers* reveals a veritable conceptual wrestling match of contending positions. Let us look first, then, at the concept of representation and its implications for the comparative study of federal states.

The concept of representation

Pitkin claimed that considering the undisputed significance of the concept of representation, and the frequency with which it was used by writers on politics, there had been 'surprisingly little discussion or analysis of its meaning'. She remarked that it was perhaps 'one of those fundamental ideas so much taken for granted that they themselves escape close scrutiny'. Worse still, its complexity might actually have 'discouraged analysis'.[2] Today this claim cannot be sustained. In the comparative analysis of federal political systems, the concept of representation is ubiquitous. It looms large as one of the most significant factors that underpin the claims for consent and legitimacy in modern federal democracy. In a later essay, Pitkin arrived at the halting conclusion that the concept of representation had 'a number of quite different – though related – uses, each with its own characteristic context, assumptions and implications'. It was, in short, 'a sort of uneasy combination of all these uses'. But the central core meaning of 're-presentation' was 'a making present of something absent' while 'not making it literally present'.[3]

Representation, then, meant 'making present indirectly', via an intermediary, but it could take many forms so that the concept and its uses were 'complex and multiple'.[4] We can already see from this brief cameo of representation that we are trespassing on difficult and dangerous ground where there are many pitfalls. To the question 'Who or what is represented?' we might add 'How are they represented?' or 'What form(s) does representation take?' But our purpose, we must remember, is not to engage the main theoretical and/or philosophical debate about representation, but to look at it in the specific context of federalism and federation. This is why it is convenient for us to take as our point of departure the American federal experience of the late eighteenth century wherein many of these pitfalls were confronted and overcome for the purpose of establishing that 'more perfect union'.

At the dawn of the age of mass democracy in the late eighteenth-century United States, the concept of representation was central to the building of the new compound republic. In the Federal Convention of 1787 in Philadelphia, it is clear that the Founding Fathers of what eventually became the consolidated national government of the new American Republic virtually had to perform conceptual somersaults in order to achieve agreement about 'the principle of representation' while James Madison, Alexander Hamilton and John Jay regarded it in *The Federalist Papers* as fundamental to the very nature of republican government, what Madison famously referred to as the 'extended republic'.[5] We have already touched upon this aspect of the American federal experience in Chapter 2, but it is now time to return to it in order to sharpen our focus upon the concept of representation. In hindsight, it is clear that in the great debate about the nature and character of modern federal government conducted in the pages of *The Federalist* we can identify the following four main elements: first, the broad question about what interests should be represented; second, the issue of the extension of territory; third, the idea of equality of representation; and, finally, the notion of representation as numbers, or, as it were, how 'representative' representation can be. In practice, these four separate elements of representation are inextricably intertwined but we will look at each of them in turn.

The representation of interests

Both Hamilton and Madison addressed themselves to the first question about what particular interests should be represented. Clearly government was instituted for 'persons and property'. As Madison put it in *Federalist* 54, 'the one as well as the other ... may be considered as represented by those who are charged with the government', but it was important to note that the rights of property were 'committed into the same hands with the personal rights'.[6] This was Madison's answer to the thorny question of representation with respect to slavery and the vested interests of the southern states in the union. It revolved around whether or not slaves should be treated as either property or persons having rights of representation and was resolved by Madison in a way that implied a subtle shift in emphasis upon states as unitary actors in the decision-making process of the union to that of individual citizens as the unit of analysis in the larger federal legislature based upon majority voting.

Accordingly, the *confederal* union of states was to become a much more consolidated *federal* union of citizens and states. This reflected, in short, the shift from pre-1789 confederation to post-1789 federation. The difference between the old confederal (treaty) constitution and the new federal constitution in terms of representation, then, lay in the process of internalising what had previously been externalities. States were no longer independent unitary actors but were instead represented in the larger body politic according to aggregate numbers, with the overall effect that, as Madison put it, 'each vote, whether proceeding from a larger or a smaller state, or a state more or less wealthy or powerful, will have an equal weight and efficacy'.[7] Persons and property would therefore be appropriately represented in the federal union as tangible 'interests' but in a new, restructured, constitutional order.

The extended federal republic

The issue of the extension of territory arose indirectly from Madison's anxieties in *Federalist* 10 about the dangers of faction and the threat of 'some common impulse of passion, or of interest, adverse to the rights of other citizens, or to the permanent and aggregate interests of the community'.[8] Ironically it was the very virtues of liberty – that which nurtured 'diversity in the faculties of men' – that produced the threat of faction. But Madison's cure for the ensuing division of society into different and often competing interests and parties, as we may recall from Chapter 2, was firmly predicated upon his clear distinction between a democracy and a republic:

> The two great points of difference between a democracy and a republic are: first, the delegation of the government, in the latter, to a small number of citizens elected by the rest; second, the greater number of citizens and greater sphere of country over which the latter may be extended.[9]

The answer to this conceptual dilemma resided, in a nutshell, in the combination of the principle of representation with the extension of territory. Consequently extensive republics were to be preferred to small republics: 'extend the sphere and you take in a greater variety of parties and interests', and make it 'less probable that a majority of the whole will have a common motive to invade the rights of other citizens'.[10] The medium of an elected body of representatives combined with the territorial dispersion of power among federal and state institutions, as we noted in Chapter 2, was tantamount to what Madison called 'a republican remedy for the diseases most incident to republican government'.[11]

The equality of representation

The idea of an equality of representation was addressed by Madison in *Federalist* 62, and since it focused mainly upon the Senate – the second chamber of legislative decision-making – can be dealt with speedily – as Madison did. We must remember that up until the seventeenth amendment to the Constitution of the USA, ratified as recently as 1913, the Senate was appointed by the state legislatures. Madison viewed the notion of the equality of representation in 1787, once again, in terms of the shift from what had formerly been a union of states to a union of both states and citizens. Consequently he construed the idea in terms of the new 'compound republic, partaking both of the national and federal character', that produced 'a mixture of the principles of proportional and equal representation'.[12] In retrospect, his justification for conceding what at that time appeared to be inevitable seems like an apology:

> The equality ought to be no less acceptable to the large than to the small states; since they are not less solicitous to guard, by every possible expedient, against an improper consolidation of the states into one simple republic. ... Another advantage ... is the additional impediment it must prove against improper acts of legislation. No law or resolution can now be passed without the concurrence, first, of a majority of the people, and then a majority of the states.[13]

Madison's final rhetorical flourish was to anticipate the objections of his adversaries by reminding them that the new constitution was not the result of theory but of 'a spirit of amity, and ... mutual deference and concession'. In other words, theoretical propriety was once again sacrificed to practical requirements. Equality of representation was ultimately a circumstantial compromise.[14]

Representation as numbers

The fourth and final element of representation that we have identified in the epic public debate about the new federal constitution of 1787 is the question of representation as numbers and the implication that this had for just how 'representative' the new federal political system was likely to be. Both Hamilton and Madison looked closely in *Federalist* 52–62 at the elective principle, the structure of the federal government and, in particular, 'the number most convenient for a representative legislature'. Madison began his defence of the proposed House of Representatives – the lower chamber of legislative decision-making – in *Federalist* 55 with an unequivocal statement: 'Nothing can be more fallacious than to found our political calculations on arithmetical principles'.[15] His comparative survey of the representative principle at work in the various states of the union was revealing: there was no point on which the policies of the several states were more at variance. Whether one looked at the proportions that their legislative assemblies bore to the number of their constituents or compared the assemblies directly with each other, huge differences between the states were abundantly evident. There was, then, no fixed and finite political formula.

Clearly, Hamilton and Madison had arrived in this fourth element of representation at the heart of our current concern in this chapter. The basic question 'Who or what is represented in federal political systems?' was addressed by these two pioneers of modern American federalism as far back as the late eighteenth century. Since both their line of reasoning and their precise conclusions still resonate resoundingly in the twenty-first century, it is appropriate here simply to call attention to their main arguments in the following abbreviated form:

1   Would a small number of representatives pose a serious threat to the public interest? Madison in *Federalist* 55 pointed to the 'genius of the people of America, the spirit which actuates the state legislatures and the principles which are incorporated with the political character of every class of citizens' as the safeguard to 'the liberties of America'. Today we would construe Madison's heavy reliance upon already established popular values and beliefs as reflecting the political culture and socialisation processes characteristic of the federal polity.

2   Would a small number of representatives be able to possess a due knowledge of the interests of their constituents? Madison in *Federalist* 56 recognised the necessity of knowledge and information that a representative must possess and acquire in his federal and/or state roles(s). Once again, it was 'the objects of federal legislation' that would determine the nature and role of representation, which would itself be subject to an increase in size commensurate with 'a more advanced population'. The key to understanding Madison's argument here was to appreciate that time would have an assimilating effect upon the states acting in their federal capacity while having the opposite impact upon the internal affairs of the states so that local diversity would be preserved *vis-à-vis* other states in the union. Accordingly, representation would have a binding effect upon the union at federal level while simultaneously sustaining difference or diversity at the state level.

3   Would the small number of representatives really be 'representative' of the 'mass of the people'? Madison responded to this question in *Federalist* 57 with a conspicuous degree of incredulity. Clearly the safeguard of liberty resided *inter alia* in the elective principle and in the frequency of elections as well as in 'the genius of the whole system; the nature of just and constitutional laws'; and, above all, 'the vigilant and manly spirit' that enervated the mass of the American people. Hamilton in *Federalist* 35 also dealt summarily with this issue: 'the idea of an actual representation of all classes of the people by persons of each class is altogether visionary'. In *Federalist* 60 he conveyed his belief that there was 'sufficient diversity in the state of property, in the genius, manners and habits of the people of the different parts of the Union to occasion a material diversity of disposition in their representatives towards the different ranks and conditions in society'. His claim in *Federalist* 35 that the representative bodies could be composed overwhelmingly of 'landholders, merchants and men of the learned professions' would today be construed simply as democratic elitism – representation by political and economic elites. He concluded in *Federalist* 60 that the people would themselves have sufficient sense and virtue to elect 'men of sense and virtue'. Liberty therefore was protected by both the political virtue and experience of the American people and by 'the dissimilar modes of constituting the several component parts of the government'.

In summarising this section of the chapter, it is clear that the many practical problems encountered by *Publius* in addressing the concept of representation

could not realistically be divorced from their theoretical and philosophical implications. American federalism in the late eighteenth century was already rooted in
a particular form of representative liberal democracy that derived partly from
the received political ideas of the Enlightenment and partly from the practical
constitutional and political experience of colonial government in the New
World. The concept of representation therefore had a contextual dimension – as
Pitkin has stressed – related directly to the American Revolution, but it also had
a universal dimension in which it was part of the much larger 'democratic revolution' that for some was the logical culmination of late eighteenth-century
Enlightenment rationalism.

The democratic revolution: four developmental models

The United States of America

The modern element in the democratic revolution of the late eighteenth century
was the principle that individuals are the basic units in the constitutional order of
human societies, 'one of the most fundamental theorems in a political science'.[16]
This is also true for other societies that crossed the divide between pre-modern
and modern political structures, but only the USA managed successfully to
combine federalism and democracy. Even here, however, this combination did
not succeed immediately; it became a political reality only after the Civil War,
1861–65. Consequently federalism came to be associated with 'the accommodation of diversity' only after the threat of secession in the ten southern states had
been crushed by force in a bloody civil war.

From Tocqueville to the recent debates about changes of governance in the
National Performance Review, an important feature of the American federal
model is the fact that it is a system of government 'in which a serious effort has
been made to come to terms with the possibility that people might, in some
significant sense, "govern" and to avoid presuming that "the government"
governs'.[17] The USA is still more 'classically liberal (libertarian), distrustful of
government, and populist. It gives its citizens more power to influence their
governors than other democracies, which rely more heavily on unified governments fulfilling economic and welfare functions'.[18] It is this political culture that
allows it to sustain a strong, asymmetrical federal system with a weak representation of the states in the national decision-making process, a point to which we
shall return later.

Federal democracy was instrumental in strengthening citizen input while
simultaneously buttressing the system of checks and balances of a political
system united by the division of labour between federal, state and local levels of
government. Administration was originally implemented at state and local levels
while a weak vertical and horizontal cooperation among the states and between
them and the federal government gradually evolved. The classic federal political
system has therefore been essentially a non-centralised system.[19] And it also

furnished the basis for 'an alternative to a theory of sovereignty'.[20] This distinctive feature of American federalism, however, gradually gave way in the light of pressing economic and social problems to national solutions that prompted the USA to develop a nationwide capacity for regulation that was sustained by new mandates, preemption and the emergence of a 'professional bureaucratic complex' as a form of representational federalism.[21]

Europe: France and Germany

While the feudal monarchies of France and England consolidated during the late medieval and early modern era into states with a high degree of political unity, the feudal system of Germany disintegrated into a loose association of states. 'The hard core of statehood in Germany over centuries was with the lander, regions and states'.[22]

This geopolitical pattern characteristic of Germany was interwoven with two principal features. First, the long-standing weakness of democratic forces (the so-called commercial or middle-class bourgeoisie) meant that Germany's late take-off on the path of modernity ensured that it would also be a latecomer to the liberal tradition of politics.[23] Second, the nation-building of 1871 (the Franco–Prussian War) resulted in a monarchical-hegemonic imperial federation that was not only highly asymmetrical but also failed to combine federalism with democracy or republicanism as it had in the USA. In consequence, the political system was based upon an executive federalism without strong legislatures but with procedures and institutions that facilitated the processing of outputs between the powerful bureaucracies of the constituent states and the empire.[24]

The German path to modern federalism therefore ensured that the discussion of the federal structure would follow the lines of weak democratic institutions and strong administration in a setting in which nationalist values had a strong impact on state and society. After the end of the imperial federation of the First World War, the relatively short interlude of the Weimar Republic, 1919–33 and the centralised dictatorship of the Third Reich, 1933–45 , the concepts of federalism and federation were among the prime features of the new post-war West Germany and were institutionalised in the Basic Law (*Das Grundgesetz*) in 1949. Three components in particular formed the structural basis to the new federation (*Bundesstaat*):

1   The distribution of tasks was delineated along with the new competences.
2   The second chamber (*Bundesrat*) represented the *lander* governments that had in consequence a powerful position in the central (federal) decision-making process.
3   The *Bundesstaat* incorporated a strong vertical and horizontal cooperation.

Although much criticised, the German federal system worked effectively even during periods in which different majorities controlled the lower chamber (*Bundestag*) and the second chamber (*Bundesrat*).

A different path to modernity was followed by France, where a strong absolutism had already curbed the powers of the estates and intermediate governments. When representation became an issue it occurred within the framework of the nation(al) state. Based upon the concept of sovereignty developed by Jean Bodin in his *Les six Livres de la republique*, first published in 1576, its meaning was encapsulated thus: '*Republique est un droit gouvernement avec puissance souveraine*'.[25]

A comparison of the Virginia Bill of Rights (1776) and the French Declaration *des droit de l'homme et du citoyen* of 1789 underlined the difference between American and Continental European concepts. The former was a document intended to restrict the power of government while the latter lacked any such distrust of governmental power. The nation '*une et indivisible*' was the repository of sovereignty and the law as an expression of the *volonté générale* limited the freedom of the individual who was construed not so much as an individual *qua* individual but rather as a member of the *corps social*. And it was more than by pure chance that the Abbé Sièyes not only expressed the national claim of the Third Estate in his famous treatise entitled *Qu'est-ce que le tiers état?* (What is the Third Estate?) in 1789, but also played an influential role in the creation of the departments as the organised infrastructure of the centralised French Republic.[26] The abolition of the old *pays d'états* was justified by the 'irresistible power of reason' and there was no means more powerful 'to create without unrest from the different parts of France a whole and from it a divided people as a single nation'.[27] And what was this nation? It was 'A body whose members live under one common law and who are represented by the very same lawgiving assembly'.[28] The law was the expression of the general will – the *volonté générale* – and the representative system was instrumental in recognising the common weal. In contrast to the Anglo-American tradition, it was not a mere reflection of competing interests but a self-evident fact that had to be recognised by the *Assemblée nationale*.

The Swiss model

This rational concept of national centralist representation finds a strong contrast in Switzerland. Historically the *Confederatio Helvetius* is referred to by German-speaking Swiss as an *Eidgenossenschaft* (oath-fellowship), the non-hierarchical elements in it constituting an association bound together by reciprocal oaths. *Genosse* is an equal, a comrade, a covenanter. Typically Bodin referred in 1576 to the obvious lack of a sovereign supreme power and drew the inevitable conclusion that the *Eidgenossenschaft* was not actually a *Staat* at all.

The consolidation of Switzerland into a federation in 1848 – after the example of the USA – followed the *Sonderbund* Civil War of 1847 in which the Catholic cantons were defeated by their Protestant neighbours and was itself consolidated in the general constitutional revision of 1874. One notable hallmark of the federal constitution was to leave sovereignty with the cantons but within the framework of the federal constitution, a feature that prompted

Christopher Hughes to describe Swiss federalism as 'cantonalism'.[29] Other significant cantonal traditions are their republicanism, participatory (direct) democracy and the voluntarism of the *Milizsystem* (citizen militia system) that together are still to this day tied to a strong sense of territorial identity buttressed by linguistic distinctiveness.[30] One further dimension that is so characteristic of the Swiss model of federalism and federation is its highly developed mechanisms and procedures of consociationalism as a mode of socio-political consensus creation, known generally as the *konkordanz* (concordance) system, aligned with the power-sharing enshrined in the federation. This is very similar to the highly interwoven German system of 'cooperative federalism', especially since the constitution leaves the federal government largely dependent upon the cantons for the administration of most of its legislation.[31] In consequence, Germany, Austria and Switzerland furnish the empirical basis for a comparative study of the Germanic tradition of federalism and federation in western Europe with a sharp focus upon administrative-executive structures.[32]

The Westminster model

The emergence in the nineteenth century of so-called 'parliamentary federalism' had its origins much earlier in the British imperial tradition which stretched back to the eighteenth century. The first country to introduce what later came to be known as the 'Westminster model' of federation was Canada in 1867 followed by Australia in 1900 and India in 1950. In each case the formation of parliamentary federalism occurred as part of the larger process of British imperial decentralisation, later described as decolonisation, and was an attempt to reconcile the seventeenth-century notion of 'parliamentary sovereignty', involving a fusion of executive and legislative powers, with the idea of a basic territorial dispersion of power. The model has worked effectively in Canada and Australia, furnishing the basis for stable and responsible government, but it is flawed in the extent to which its adversarial nature and majoritarian thrust can equally serve to exclude territorial minorities, leading in the case of Canada–Quebec relations to dissonance and even de-legitimisation. The problem of representation therefore has been the source of many different and largely unsuccessful attempts at constitutional reform including the electoral system, the Senate and the constitutional amendment procedures themselves.[33]

In some significant respects the Westminster model falls somewhere between the American and the Continental European versions of democratisation. While the American federal experience emphasised the sovereignty of the people rooted in the written constitution and the Continental European federal tradition identified it with the state, the British (often mistakenly called Anglo-Saxon) tradition channelled it through Parliament. Moreover, the Westminster model emerged from a British political tradition in which local elites forged pragmatic alliances with the central authority in London and were able successfully to retain considerable relative autonomy. This was also one reason why London never built up a strong administrative base very early on in the state-building process to implement and enforce central imperatives. Territorial management of the periphery was essentially cooperative and consensual.

If we now summarise the discernible patterns of representation that emerge from our four developmental models, we can identify the following broad trends:

1   The modern concept of representation is very closely interwoven with the representation of individuals and the expression of a national authority by and through the representatives of the people. This basic feature is shared by all four models.

2   The concept of sovereignty in the Continental European federal tradition is identified with the state, in the USA with the sovereignty of the people in the written constitution, and in the Westminster model in Parliament.

3   The framework of the nation(al) state, so decisive for the modern theory of representation, presses for a solution to the nation-building process that is centralist (Jacobin–Marxist), unitarian with strong intergovernmental structures such as in Germany and Canada, or a 'polyarchy' as in the USA.

This shortlist also underlines what we might call a 'path dependency' of federations. More than any other socio-political concept formation, federalism and federation are replete with historical irregularities and do not conform to the more conventional geometric view of politics, political development and spatial relations. If we look at the big picture in the USA, the line of evolution is, roughly speaking, first, democracy (popular representation), then industrialisation (common market) and, in turn, bureaucracy (regulatory/interventionist national state). In Continental Europe, by way of contrast, it is bureaucracy that is the departure point followed by democracy in France and also much later in Germany. The delineation of our four models points up the very different historical processes of state-building and national integration that help to explain how and why the concept of representation evolved in different ways in different federal traditions. Let us now look briefly at the concept of representation from the perspective of different levels of representation and in so doing return to the complex relationship between individual and community that we first addressed in Chapter 2.

National and sub-national levels in federations

In *The Federalist Papers* Hamilton had, at least theoretically, resolved the 'insufficiency of the present Confederation to the preservation of the Union'. We will recall from Chapter 2 that he related to it in the following way:

> The great and radical vice in the construction of the existing Confederation is in the principle of LEGISLATION for STATES or GOVERNMENTS, in their CORPORATE or COLLECTIVE CAPACITIES, and as contradistinguished from the INDIVIDUALS of whom they consist.[34]

But Madison had also underlined the virtues of federalism as an instrumentality of the division of power:

> In the compound republic of America, the power surrendered by the people is first divided between two distinct governments, and then the portion allotted to each subdivided among distinct and separate departments.[35]

The political reality, however, was not so simple and straightforward. The debate about nullification, states' rights and state sovereignty in the first half of the nineteenth century riveted attention once again upon the question whether or not the USA was 'a Government in which all the people are represented, which operates directly on the people individually, not upon the states'.[36] Standing against this national interpretation was the rival position expressed most notably by John C. Calhoun that the 'whole system' was federal and democratic:

> 'Federal', on the one hand, in contradistinction to 'national' and, on the other, to a 'confederacy'. ... To express it more concisely, it is federal and not national because it is the government of a community of states, and not the government of a single state or nation.[37]

Calhoun's doctrine of the concurrent majority, which preferred consensus to conflict, however, had no political future, especially in view of the deep moral cleavage that underpinned it, namely, the exclusivist system of slavery that denied both human and civil rights to a large section of American society. Although the Civil War effectively ended the secession of the South by force, fears of its potential for secession lingered for many years afterwards and were frequently debated up until the mid-1960s.[38]

The problem that Hamilton, Madison and Calhoun wrestled with concerning relations between the federal (central) government and the constituent state governments, the impact of federal authority upon individuals as distinct from state governments, and the general complexities of divided government – in short, relations between the national and the subnational levels – continue to resonate two centuries later in the USA, but are brought into sharp relief when we shift our attention to contemporary Europe and the EU. The parallels between the two projects are in several important respects quite remarkable.[39] In the shift from one form of confederal union to the new, much more consolidated, federal state the United States clearly broke new conceptual ground and forged over the following seventy years an empirical reality that has evolved into a nation(al) state in which its citizens enjoy multiple political representation.

In the EU, which is clearly developing into something much more binding and regulated than Calhoun's 'community of states', similar arguments, debates and anxieties have been articulated among both elites and mass publics in the established member states of the EU. The recent exchanges after the famous

Berlin address of 12 May 2000 by the German Foreign Minister Joschka Fischer, and his counterpart Hubert Vedrine in France, testify to the sense that the EU is breaking new ground in relations with its citizens. Indeed, since the Treaty on European Union (TEU) was formally ratified by the then twelve member states in November 1993 and accepted by the three new members – Austria, Finland and Sweden – in 1995, the EU has strengthened the federal elements that coexist with its confederal heritage and in consequence engaged the public debate about political representation. Fischer saw the remedy for the recent enlargement of the Union from 15 constituent units to 25 in the 'transition from the confederacy of the Union towards a fully parliamentarised European Federation'. And he added that in the light of the importance of the nation(al) state for citizens' identity the completion of European integration would be successful only if it happened 'on the basis of a division of sovereignty between Europe and the national state'.[40] The French Foreign Minister in his reply stressed the importance of a clear demarcation of jurisdictions between the federation and the member states. Indeed, 'this delimitation', in his view, was 'essential'.[41] Vedrine also emphasised that a model of European integration that sustained the integrity of the member states would become increasingly opaque. At least four levels of government and governance would have to interact and cooperate for it to function effectively: first, the local and regional level; second, the national state level; third, the level of the federation itself; and, finally, the enlarged EU with its new member states. It comes as little surprise to learn that public concern for transparency, accountability and legitimacy in the EU has recently condensed into a general anxiety about the so-called 'democratic deficit'. Madison would have recognised and understood this very well. But this shift of focus in the public debate about the character of European integration is in one sense not at all new. Indeed, it is a very old debate: 'Is it possible to "federalise" the Community significantly while retaining a key policy-making role for national governments?'[42] Clearly the EU is an excellent example to highlight the contemporary significance of the question 'Who or what is represented in a federal Europe?' Is it EU citizens, national governments, regional and local governments or organised minority interests and identities?

Second chambers and the problem of double representation

The status and role of second chambers in federations has always been a kind of identity bracelet for this kind of state. Put simply, every federation must have a second chamber in the legislature for it to be an authentic federal state. This much is self-evident. But this still leaves plenty of scope for huge variations in composition, powers and functions, and it is important to note that this question is not simply one of institutional arrangements alone. Both France and the United Kingdom, for example, are cases of bicameral systems in non-federal states, the former based upon indirect elections in the *departments* and with mostly a suspensive veto power and the latter an essentially pre-modern relic recently reorganised along purely functional lines. This distinction refers to the important difference between functional divisions of authority (e.g., the separation of powers and checks and balances) and the territorial distribution of authority which today is the predominant pedigree of federation.[43]

To accommodate and placate the fears of the smaller states concerned about the potential hegemony of the larger states in the union was one of the central problems confronting the Founding Fathers at Philadelphia. But the USA Constitution as a working instrument also safeguarded the corrosive impact on the states of the national decision-making process. The great compromise in Article 5 of the constitution awarded each state two votes in the Senate, enshrined in the words' that no state, without its consent, shall be deprived of its equal suffrage in the Senate'.

The Senate that Madison regarded as 'the great anchor of the Government' is based upon equal representation. But this is the exception rather than the rule in modern federations, as Watts has confirmed in his recent comparative study. Indeed, in only two of the ten federal second chambers studied were the constituent states equally represented, that is, in the USA and Australia.[44] In all other cases the population – the 'democratic' factor – is an intervening variable. And the examples are many and varied. Switzerland and Germany are both federations, but in the former there are basically two types of representation predicated on the narrow category of full and half-cantons while the latter distributes the *lander* representation in a continuous pattern. The result is that Switzerland has twenty cantons with two representatives and six half-cantons with just one each while in Germany account is taken of the size of the population of each *land* so that representation in the *Bundesrat* rises from three to six votes according to democratic size, including minors and foreigners, which is in marked contrast to the national representation based on German citizenship as a prerequisite to cast a vote in the lower chamber, the *Bundestag*. In other federations the range of constituent state representation is much wider and mostly with a conspicuous bias toward the smaller constituent units.

The theoretical problem at the heart of representation here is that the participation of the constituent states in the legislative decision-making of the federation always conflicts with the democratic principle of 'one person, one vote'. The paradox inherent in federal systems is that the constituent units – *lander*, cantons, states or provinces – both enlarge and extend the possibilities of citizen input in the polity as voters as well as lobbyists and interest activists, but in an age of globalisation with its attendant 'debordering' the secular trends of modern industrial/post-industrial societies strongly suggest that territorial representation is fast becoming less and less effective to the point of de-legitimation, 'for the representation of the individual voter has come to dominate notions about democracy and therefore has much greater legitimacy than does the representation of territorial government as an institution'.[45]

Linked to this already complex problem is the sort of elemental question posed at the beginning of the chapter, namely, 'Who should speak for the constituent states in their capacity as members of the nation(al) state or federation?'

Should it be the population as voters, as we find in the USA since the Seventeenth Amendment in 1913 or the democratically legitimised constituent state government of the federation? Equal representation in the USA Senate leads to the curiosity that a single vote in Wyoming counts sixty-five times more than its equivalent in California. The same is true in the case of Germany where a vote in the city state of Bremen counts thirteen times more than an equivalent vote in North Rhine–Westphalia.[46] Preston King has already pointed out that such a logical conundrum, immanent in federations, confirms that, theoretically, 'federal democracy is universally incomplete'.[47]

If we look at the institutional arrangements for the German *Bundesrat* model we can see that they much more clearly represent the aggregated interests of the territorial dimension of politics, even if the consequences of 'executive-administrative' federalism that led to the joint decision trap are obvious.[48] On the other hand, in the USA 'the states have primarily to rely upon *ad hoc* political instruments to influence the responsible national institutions and the systemic changes induced by such shifts'.[49] The overall impression conveyed by this short survey of second chambers with respect to the principle of representation, then, is that the grass-roots vitality – the subnational polity as 'demos' – in federal systems with popular representation such as the USA and Switzerland is very strong. The acceptance of territorially based asymmetries and the fact that there are no serious territorial reform debates in these two federations would seem to indicate that the democratic foundations of federalism and federation are both strong and stable.

Conclusion: compounded representation for a compound republic

This chapter suggests that the theory and practice of representation in federations is clearly complex. But it also suggests that, with only a few exceptions, we search in vain for logical principles, general tidiness and comfortable regularities. They are conspicuous by their absence, reflecting in practice an untidy reality and one that often defies our expectations. Does it matter that the German *Bundesrat* facilitates the (indirectly elected) representation of the *lander* governments rather than the (directly elected) individual representative of party–state interests who sits in the USA Senate or the minority activism that is characteristic of the (directly elected) Australian Senate?[50] What are we to make of the prime-ministerial patronage powers when appointing members of the Canadian Senate where party interests and regional groupings determine the size and character of the second chamber? What, in short, is being represented, and whose organised interests are being promoted in these federations?[51]

The different federalisms in each federation are represented in a variety of ways that confound many of the assumptions that underpin traditional democratic theory. Ultimately representation in federations is so variable because of the uniqueness of each federation; because their respective origins and evolution differ so markedly from each other. The historical path dependency identified in this chapter is certainly not deterministic but it has nonetheless pushed second chambers in particular directions. As our four models outlined here demonstrate, the nature of their historical origins and political development matters. And we should remember that it was Pitkin who first reminded us that 'to understand how the concept of representation moved into the realms of agency and political activity, we must keep in mind the historical development of institutions [and] the corresponding development in interpretive thought about those institutions'.[52] This chapter confirms Pitkin's observation. For the answer to the question 'Who or what is represented in federal states?' we must perforce return to the origins and formation of federations that we surveyed in Chapter 3. Only in this way can we understand the motives for federation, the principal actors involved in its formation and then take account of the developmental character of each federation as it has evolved. Put simply, the concept of representation reflects historical specificity and comparative political development in the modern democratic era. There is a certain fascination in the way that the structure and operation of federations impinge directly and indirectly upon the concept of representation and *vice versa*. The concept of representation embraces both change and continuity.

If we look at recent research on this important and difficult question we will note that it, too, has confirmed that representation varies considerably across federations and that 'the relationship between federalism and representation is not a one-way street. Representation can also affect federalism'.[53] Consequently, the emergence of the concept 'compounded representation' is a novel development that is important because it has some interesting theoretical and empirical implications for the comparative study of federalism and federation:

> Compounded representation is ... a special type of interest organization that results from formally divided but overlapping government authorities. ... [I]t is an attempt to capture the essence of the linkage between federalism and representation. ... Compounded representation entails the situation where the number of choices and the amount of competition among potential agents vary according to the nature and degree of federalism's jurisdictional overlap. ... federalism has important implications for political representation and, in fact, produces a special type of representation – compounded representation.[54]

A fresh look at the relationship between federalism and representation is long overdue and it is indeed puzzling why scholars of comparative federalism and federation have neglected it for quite so long. After all, if the relationship between difference and diversity (federalism) and its institutional expression (federation) has always been – if often only implicitly so – at the heart of this particular subject, it is obvious that the principle of representation should be the conceptual ligament or linkage that ties them together. We have already emphasised the pivotal attention accorded this relationship by Hamilton and Madison in Philadelphia, but it is essential for an accurate and up-to-date understanding of federal political systems that we sustain a research interest in compounded representation. On reflection, it should not surprise us if Madison's compound republic, which was firmly rooted in the fundamental principle of a compounded representation, should now have a much sharper intellectual focus to reflect its contemporary significance.

8 Asymmetrical federalism and federation

Introduction

The notion of asymmetry in federalism and federation is not a novel idea. It has been implicit in the mainstream literature in studies of individual federations, such as Canada, Germany, Belgium and India, as well as in comparative surveys of federalism and federation, for many years. References to the differential status and rights among the constituent units of federations and between them individually and the federation as a whole have appeared sporadically in this literature without attracting much scholarly attention, let alone controversy. Indeed, scholars of federal studies have been quite relaxed and dispassionate about this area of enquiry, treating it very much as a mere matter of fact, or as a neutral concept of sound social-science enquiry.[1]

Today, this calm, almost perfunctory, approach to the question of asymmetry has given way to a much more sustained intellectual enquiry into its philosophical, theoretical and empirical foundations that has led scholars to dig deeper into the basic assumptions, values and beliefs that underpin its conceptual utility. As we shall see in this chapter, it has in practice become Janus-faced, being perceived by some as a positive instrument designed to buttress and sustain federal values and structures while simultaneously inducing fears and anxieties in others who construe it very much as a dangerous threat to the stability and integrity of the state. Either way, there is no doubt that asymmetry has now become a prominent feature of the language and discourse of federalism and federation.

The purpose of this chapter is to provide an up-to-date comparative survey of asymmetrical federalism and federation. As the title suggests, it consistently applies the conceptual distinction between federalism and federation as the foundation of the comparative exploration in order once again to point up the essentially symbiotic relationship between these two analytical constructs. In pursuit of this goal, we will first sketch out the important preliminary background to the emergence of the concept of asymmetry, followed immediately by a detailed textual exegesis of the relationship between symmetry and asymmetry in federal relationships that can be found in the first major study of the subject. We will then take a closer look at some of the significant comparative features that can be found in Belgium, Canada, Switzerland, Germany, India and

Malaysia. This will bring us to our final section that will address the issue of asymmetry as normative theory in multinational federations. Finally we will conclude with some reflections about the future significance of asymmetry in federalism and federation that might have important implications for contemporary problems in Cyprus, Sri Lanka and Iraq. Let us begin with some key background information about the gradual emergence of the concept of asymmetry in comparative federal studies.

The emergence of the concept of asymmetry

The term 'asymmetrical federalism' has appeared in the mainstream literature at regular intervals but only in a fragmentary manner. A re-examination of William Livingston's famous article entitled 'A Note on the Nature of Federalism', first published in 1952 in the *Political Science Quarterly*, shows that he certainly alluded to asymmetry when discussing the range of social diversities that gave rise to federalism, but he neither specified the word nor did he use the phrase.[2] In contrast, Ivo Duchacek referred to it in 1970 when he devoted a whole chapter to its meaning and implications in his classic text entitled *Comparative Federalism: The Territorial Dimension of Politics*.[3] Duchacek's approach was to identify huge disparities in what he called 'power ingredients' among the component units of federations which could be highly politicised if their territorial boundaries coincided with significant linguistic, ethnic, racial or religious differences or, to the contrary, if they overlapped and were not formally recognised in the federation, could even add 'an explosive dimension ... to the tensions caused by the disparities in power and attachment to the federal system'.[4] Ronald L. Watts also referred to asymmetry in 1970 in his contribution to the studies for the Royal Commission on Bilingualism and Biculturalism in Canada and had already made passing references to it in his classic study entitled *New Federations: Experiments in the Commonwealth*, first published in 1966.[5]

In 1977 R. Michael Stevens conducted a comparative study of some twenty 'federacy' types of vertical arrangements, defining them as joining separate distinct communities of disproportionate size and resources in a political association designed to maintain the integrity of the smaller community. Federacy, on this reckoning, was simply a form of political association that enabled smaller communities to preserve their distinct identities and separate political organisations while retaining economic, political and military links with the larger national state.[6] More recently, Max Frenkel identified 'Asymmetrical' as a distinctive type of federalism in his 'Alphabet of Federalisms' in 1986 and Daniel Elazar included a small section on 'Asymmetrical Federal Arrangements' in his *Exploring Federalism* that appeared in 1987.[7] Today, however, there is a burgeoning literature on the subject of asymmetrical federalism that seems suddenly to have come of age.[8] Part of the explanation for this is the nature and character of contemporary international change that can conveniently be summarised as a combination of increasing global and regional economic and political cooperation and integration. The general impact of this change has been twofold: it has led to new forms of political association *between* states in the international world and it has triggered a simultaneous process of decentralisation *within* states. In consequence, constitutional and political relationships both between and within contemporary states in many parts of the world are now increasingly contested and complex.

Formal recognition of this significant development in comparative federal studies was evident in the creation of two panels of scholars who met under the auspices of the Comparative Federalism and Federation Research Committee of the International Political Science Association (IPSA) in South Africa in 1993 to discuss both the concept and the empirical implications of asymmetrical federalism. Further research papers were formally presented at the World Congress of IPSA in Berlin in 1994 and were subsequently published in 1999 in a volume of essays edited by Robert Agranoff and entitled *Accommodating Diversity: Asymmetry in Federal States*.[9] Even a cursory glance at these essays makes it clear that the intellectual point of departure for these scholars was a then little-known article published in 1965 that was devoted to the conceptual utility of symmetry and asymmetry in federalism. In that year the article written by Charles D. Tarlton entitled 'Symmetry and Asymmetry as Elements of Federalism: A Theoretical Speculation' was published in the *Journal of Politics*.[10] Forty years later, as we have seen, it has acquired an unexpected significance for those scholars studying federalism and federation. Today, then, it has a new relevance. It also has a new audience.

The concepts of symmetry and asymmetry explored

The principal purpose of our conceptual exploration in this section of the chapter is to provide a springboard to further conceptual and empirical investigation. It is therefore necessary for us to revisit Tarlton's article to examine the concepts of symmetry and asymmetry afresh. After all, it is the conceptual and empirical analysis that will furnish the basis for what lies at the very heart of our comparative survey in this book, namely, the accommodation of diversity.

Tarlton's article appeared in 1965 at a time of great intellectual turbulence in political science. It was a period known as 'the behavioural revolution' in the social sciences in general. In political science in particular, there was a serious attempt to ask new questions about human behaviour, posit new hypotheses, construct new concepts and test them in order to determine their intellectual validity. The fundamental quest was to explain human behaviour. Consequently, Tarlton's analysis must be situated in the context of its time. It was an attempt not only to expose the complexities of federalism and federation, but also to look at the subject from what was then an unusual perspective. In the context of the mid-1960s, his 'theoretical speculation' encouraged scholars to consider, so to speak, the anatomy of federal systems in all of their complex dimensions. In practice, this meant 'a consideration of the diverse ways in which each member state in a federal system is able to relate to the system as a whole, the central authority, and each other member state'.[11] In a nutshell, he invited them to contemplate the obvious fact that 'a federal system may be more or less federal throughout its parts'.[12]

In this broad objective, Tarlton's endeavours came close to the arguments of Livingston, mentioned above, whose contribution to the study of federalism he acknowledged in the article. Tarlton did not adopt Livingston's conceptual framework but he did recognise that 'quality and levels of federalism present in the relationship between the central government and each component government considered separately may vary in significant ways throughout the system'.[13] This enabled him to forge a link between Livingston's societal approach to the subject – that all societies are composed of elements that feel themselves to be different from the other elements in varying degrees and demand varying degrees of self-expression – and his own concern for symmetry and asymmetry. He concluded that the 'federalism' of the system is 'likely to be variegated and disparate among all the essential units'.[14] With hindsight, this exercise corresponds to an early, if unwitting, meeting of minds about federalism and federation.

Let us look in more detail at the basic premises of Tarlton's 'theoretical speculation'. He referred to 'symmetry' as 'the extent to which component states share in the conditions and thereby the concerns more or less common to the federal system as a whole'.[15] This preliminary reference was later developed into a much more elaborate and complete definition: 'the level of conformity and commonality in the relations of each separate political unit of the system to both the system as a whole and to the other component units'. In fact, 'the overall extent to which the federal system is characterised by a harmonious pattern of states partaking of the general features of the federal nation is at the core of the symmetry of federalism'.[16] The symbiotic relationship between federalism and federation could hardly be made more explicit. In Livingstonian terms, Tarlton believed that 'the specific elements' and 'the degree of symmetry' in the relations of a single member state 'to the system and to other states and in the total pattern of federalism throughout the system' are equally important in assessing 'the quality of federalism'.[17] In the ideal symmetrical system, each of the separate political units would be 'miniature reflections' of the important aspects of the whole system and 'no significant social, economic or political peculiarities would exist which might demand special forms of representation or protection'.[18]

Why, in the model symmetrical system, would federation be justified at all? In the complete absence of 'significant differences' between the component states of the federation, it would seem to be superfluous. Tarlton anticipated this objection: the basic justification would be found in 'the completeness and integral character of the various political sub-systems'. 'Separate political existence', he claimed, rapidly became a 'self-justifying arrangement as political loyalties granted to local governments become permanent features of the prevailing political ideology'.[19] There is much here that merits further discussion and we will return to the concept of symmetry later. Now, however, we must turn our attention to the concept of 'asymmetry'.

According to Tarlton, the concept of 'asymmetry' expressed the extent to which component states do not share in the conditions and concerns common to the federal system as a whole. The ideal asymmetrical federal system would be one 'composed of political units corresponding to differences of interest, character and makeup that exist within the whole society'.[20] Again, the shadow of Livingston loomed large. The diversities in 'the larger society find political expression through local governments possessed of varying degrees of autonomy and power'. In short, the political institutions correspond to 'the real social "federalism" beneath them'.[21] And, in summary, in the model asymmetrical federal system, each component unit would have about it a unique feature or set of features which would separate its interests in important ways from those of any other state or the system considered as a whole. 'Clear lines of division would be necessary and jealously guarded insofar as these unique interests were concerned'.[22]

We have briefly sketched and clarified Tarlton's definitions of 'symmetry' and 'asymmetry'. However, it is important at this juncture for us to challenge some of his views and assertions before we proceed any further with our textual exegesis. We will identify four principal objections to his 'theoretical speculation'. First, there is the claim he makes regarding the asymmetrical model: 'it would be difficult (if not impossible) to discern interests that could be clearly considered mutual or national in scope (short of those pertaining to national existence *per se*). This is surely an exaggeration. It is reminiscent of the sort of 'national federalism' championed by American scholars such as William Riker and Samuel Beer.[23] The quality of asymmetry is not dependent upon this wide-ranging criterion. To accept this statement at face value would be dangerous and misleading because it imports into asymmetry a kind of stigma of disloyalty to the larger national interest. It is possible in practice to find many examples of public-policy issues where the 'mutuality' of interests has coincided and where the scope of interests was 'national'. Tarlton referred to 'each component unit' but it is obvious that these circumstances would vary over time and between different units or groups of units. There would in reality be a constantly shifting pattern of overlapping interests and concerns. This characteristic of federations is, after all, what secures their legitimacy and, ultimately, their overall political stability.

second, we must look again at Tarlton's assertion that 'the degree of harmony or conflict within a federal system can be thought of as a function of the symmetrical or asymmetrical pattern prevailing within the system'. Indeed, 'federal–state conflict is a likelihood … where that asymmetry is characteristic only of a few of the states in their relation to the whole'. Tarlton admitted that 'most real federal states' would actually be 'somewhere between the complete harmony symmetrical model and the complete conflict potential of the asymmetrical model'.[24] Here Tarlton reveals both positive and negative views. But is it a helpful assertion for genuine analytical purposes? Conflicts derived from asymmetrical factors can conceivably spread throughout the whole system, but many imponderables remain. What, for example, did he mean by 'only a few of the states in their relation to the whole'? Quebec's capacity to challenge the Canadian federation is much greater in relative terms as a single component unit than, say, either Texas or Wisconsin in the USA. The total number of component units in the federation is related in a complex way to political stability. Furthermore, we would need to know more about the exact nature of the conflicts involved. We would need to know, for example, which kinds of conflicts were generated by which particular constellations of asymmetry.

third, it is necessary to question Tarlton's belief that where the 'elements of diversity predominate' a 'unitary and centralized system would be better'. He claimed that 'meaningful participation' in national affairs most often necessitated 'compulsion'. It is not precisely clear what he meant by this statement. He may have intended simply to emphasise the coercive nature of the state in difficult circumstances but he seems to have suggested that a unitary and centralised political system was infinitely preferable to a federal system in conditions of predominant asymmetry. If so, it would be a quite remarkable preference in the new millennium.

Finally, I would like to draw attention to Tarlton's prescription for 'relieving the tensions and discord often attendant upon asymmetrical systems'. In an astonishing statement, even for its time, he rejected the politics of recognition. Instead, he believed that 'increased coordination and coercion from the centralizing authorities in the system 'was' appropriate'. This led him to conclude with a note of scepticism about 'the feasibility of using federalism' as a means of political organisation: 'diversity tends really to necessitate increased central authority if the system is to continue operating as a system'.[25] Although they are only implicit in his article, there is no doubt that the dual concepts of 'legitimacy' and 'political stability' represent an undercurrent to Tarlton's main analysis. The four criticisms outlined above, however, lead us to question whether he gave them serious consideration. But Tarlton, we must remember, was very much an American author writing from a particular perspective. His overriding concern was with the so-called 'secession-potential' inherent – as he saw it – in federations. This was a concern clearly revealed in the following statement: 'If the entire United States reflected relationships like those typical of the states in the Deep South, then federalism in the United States would long since have perished'.[26] Tarlton's own position, then, was far from that of a neutral observer; he was anything but an advocate of states' rights. On the contrary, rather like Riker and Beer, his was a 'national' view of federalism in the USA. He favoured a strong federal, national government. Yet even as he wrote circumstances were changing. The early 1960s were a time of far-reaching social, economic, legal and political change in the USA. A series of celebrated Supreme Court judgments during this decade enhanced civil rights and culminated in 1965 in the Voting Rights Act which strengthened the citizenship basis of the USA federation. In short, these events served to buttress the central legal and political bases of the union and thereby removed many of the fears and anxieties expressed in Tarlton's article. In this respect, the article was overtaken by events.

We will return to some of these related issues later in the chapter. Our purpose in raising these points here is merely to prevent Tarlton's otherwise admirable 'theoretical speculation' from becoming some kind of intellectual yardstick. His article raised many important questions about federal political systems and it continues to this day to reward close analysis. However, it is now forty years old and reflects its age. Indeed, as we have already seen, it appears also to be both flawed and highly tendentious in several important respects. Let us now turn to what Tarlton called 'the level, nature and distribution' of the federal system's asymmetry. Here it is important to make a distinction between the conditions that lead to asymmetry and its actual relations or outcomes. We will look first at the preconditions of asymmetry.

The preconditions of asymmetry

This section reaffirms the conceptual distinction between federalism and federation, and identifies two broad types of preconditions of asymmetry: the socio-economic and the cultural-ideological.[27] They are, it should be noted, objective empirical criteria. In short, they are what actually exists. The two sets of preconditions correspond with Livingston's societal criteria and, in contemporary research terms, with 'federalism'. Within each of these two broad preconditions of asymmetry there are many important distinctions to be made. In addition, since reality is always more complex than even the most sophisticated of social-science distinctions, I have identified the following specific empirical preconditions of asymmetry for purely illustrative purposes:

Federalism

Political cultures and traditions

These terms refer in a general sense to what we might call habits, customs and conventions reflective of particular cultures and traditions. They are social predispositions or propensities that characterise the polity and form part of its received traditions. They are evident in every federation and are significant for the way in which they inform differential philosophical, political, legal and constitutional discourses. For example, John C. Calhoun regarding the American South, and Constantin Franz and his critique of Prussian domination of the German Empire (or imperial federation), represented competing perspectives of their respective unions that challenged the dominant discourse. A more modern example would be the Germanic tradition of 'executive federalism' and Article 72(3) of the Basic Law (*Das Grundgesetz*) which referred to 'uniform living conditions' (changed recently to 'equivalence of living conditions'). In Canada, Article 36 of the Canada Act (1982) has a similar cultural implication related to redistribution that refers to 'equalisation and regional disparities'.[28] Both the German and Canadian federations are committed to the provision of essential public services and minimal living standards which confirm an underlying culture and tradition of citizen welfare extending beyond territoriality to the individual person.

Social cleavages

The focus here is on those social cleavages that have political salience. They are what we would broadly categorise as 'cultural' factors and are accommodated in the spectrum of religious, linguistic and ethno-nationalist pluralism. This 'social pluralism' varies enormously among federations: the constellation of cleavage patterns is a constantly moving, shifting matrix of complex interlinkages. The interplay of these cleavages has a variable impact upon both legitimacy and the overall political stability of the federation itself.

Territoriality

We have already encountered territoriality both conceptually and empirically in Chapters 4 and 5. Here this rubric refers to spatial concepts in political science analysis which have as their principal focus the territorial basis of politics space, place and politics. The predominant cleavage pattern is territorially based and would include centre–periphery relationships, urban–rural contrasts and the strains and tensions associated with metropolitan developments. Clearly these sorts of divisions interact closely with the non-territorial social cleavages already identified above. Two obvious examples are Quebec in Canada and Jura in Switzerland where territory has combined with language, religion and history to produce a set of cleavage patterns that required the politics of recognition.

Socio-economic factors

This precondition is isolated here for academic convenience. In reality, it is intimately interlocked with both social cleavages and territoriality. It refers in particular to large regional economic disparities that lead inevitably to differential demands and expectations within federations. Another way of looking at socio-economic factors as a precondition is to adopt a political economy perspective of federation. We have already done so in Chapter 5. This is an approach which has an all-embracing focus: it takes into account the structure of the national economy and its underlying socio-political features. In consequence, it exposes the structural strengths and weaknesses of constituent state economies in their relationship both to each other and to the larger national economy, thus furnishing the basis for asymmetrical perceptions and behaviour. In simple terms, each federal national economy has the apparatus to intervene using a variety of fiscal federal equalisation and revenue-sharing mechanisms or to resist intervention and leave constituent state economies to self-help. These regional disparities, where poor constituent state economies have to rely upon federal fiscal redistribution, abound in federations: examples include the five new eastern *lander* in Germany, Newfoundland and the Maritime provinces in Canada, and Wallonia in Belgium.

Demographic patterns

When looking at population as a precondition of asymmetry, it is important to emphasise two initial points. First, demographic patterns are often a function of national and constituent state economies; and, second, population should be construed as an objective factor in the sense that it happens to be where it is. A variety of complex factors conspire to make territories either heavily or sparsely populated. But it is also important to note that asymmetrical percep- tions and behaviour are determined as much by the composition and nature of the population as by its size. This precondition brings us back to Tarlton's argument about the issue of representation. In the USA, as we have already noted in Chapter 7, the strict equality of state representation in the Senate creates a necessary inequality of representation between citizens throughout the federation. A further consideration is that American senators, while elected as territorial representatives of states, actually perceive their role as representing individual constituents in their states rather than relating in any direct way to their state governments as governments.[29] The asymmetrical implications of demography are also highlighted when we consider issues such as fertility rates, immigration patterns and labour market structures. The problem of low fertility rates in Quebec and the growing influx of immigrants in the south-west and south-east of the USA have to be accommodated in any analysis of asymmetry in these two countries.

Asymmetrical outcomes

When our analysis shifts from the preconditions of asymmetry to asymmet- rical outcomes, it corresponds to the conceptual shift from federalism to federation. Consequently, when we turn our attention to federation it is important to determine how far, if at all, the preconditions of asymmetrical federalism identified above are actually reflected in federation. We are reminded that the *preconditions* of asymmetry must not be confused with the asymmetrical *outcomes* that derive from them and are the principal focus of the chapter. We must not confuse the fish with the water that they swim in. Moreover, it is also important for us to make some further conceptual distinc- tions before we proceed with our analysis. First, it is necessary to acknowledge different kinds of asymmetrical relations and different degrees of asymmet- rical outcomes. Second, it is important to distinguish between two types of asymmetry that occur in federal systems, namely, *de facto* and *de jure*. The former refers to asymmetrical practice or relationships which result from the impact of the socio-economic and cultural-ideological preconditions already outlined above, while the latter is formally entrenched in constitutional and legal processes so that constituent state units are treated differently under the law. Third, the principal empirical focus is 'horizontal' asymmetry, which originates in Tarlton's concern to look at how different constituent state units in federations relate to one another, the central authority and the federal system as a whole. Let us look first at *de facto* asymmetries, which are reflected in federal–state relations and general political practice:

Federation

De facto asymmetries

THE CONSTITUENT STATE UNITS

In every federation there are huge variations in territorial and population size, just as there are enormous differences in wealth between the constituent state units. In his own comparative analysis of asymmetrical federalism, first published in 1970, Duchacek referred to the 'disparity of power ingredients' and noted that 'there is no federal system in the world in which all the component units are even approximately equal in size, population, political power, administrative skills, wealth, economic development, climatic conditions, predominance of either urban or rural interests, social structure, traditions, or relative geographic location'.[30] Consequently he observed that the constituent state units varied in their attachment to the federation, in their willingness to contribute to or abide by federal programmes and in their insistence on the scope of territorial autonomy.

Examples of *de facto* asymmetries exist in Canada, where the combined population of Quebec and Ontario constitutes 62 per cent of the total population of ten provinces, two territories and the recent territorial unit of Aboriginal self-government called Nunavut, and in Australia, where the combined population of New South Wales and Victoria represents some 60 per cent of the total population of six states and two territories. A similar situation exists in Germany, where three constituent units, namely, North Rhine–Westphalia, Bavaria and Baden–Württemberg contain roughly 50 per cent of the population of the 16 *lander* of the federation. This kind of dominance, if it is reflected in 'power ingredients', can of course lead the most prosperous component units to resent federation if the perceived economic benefits of union are not commensurate with their financial contributions. In fact, perception – as Duchacek correctly observed – is of fundamental importance when dealing with such *de facto* asymmetries. Consequently these power disparities also have to be seen from the standpoint of the smallest, and inevitably the weakest, units in federations. The fears and anxieties of the weakest units such as tiny Prince Edward Island in Canada or Bremen in Germany have to be construed in terms of relative powerlessness and the danger of 'dissatisfaction and resistance to the federal way of life'.[31] Ultimately it is impossible to translate asymmetrical perceptions into real power relations. The constituent state units, as Duchacek remarked, may perceive 'the objective facts of disparity of power either correctly or incorrectly', but both can have real consequences.[32]

FISCAL POWER AND AUTONOMY

One of the most common indicators of 'power ingredients' and 'relative autonomy' is fiscal capacity in federal–state relations. Given the huge variations in population size, constituent state units, *ipso facto*, vary enormously in their taxing capacity and in their general financial resources. It is clearly very difficult to establish a firm relationship between the political economy of constituent state units or groups of units and their political behaviour. There can be little doubt that large, wealthy component units, such as California in the USA or Ontario in Canada, have both the power resources and political influence to assert their relative autonomy in the federation. But the converse assumption that economic dependence upon fiscal federal transfer payments leads ineluctably to a docile political compliance on the part of poor component states is an oversimplification. It has already been demonstrated in Canada, for example, that no such constitutional dependency exists in the relations of the Atlantic provinces with Ottawa. There is very little empirical evidence to suggest that the relatively poor Atlantic regional political economy has resulted in a stereotypical constitutional dependency.[33] The general notion of powerlessness does not necessarily mean that economically weak or poor constituent units in a federation are completely lacking in power resources. Tarlton, after all, noted that in the asymmetrical model there would be 'varying degrees of autonomy and power'.[34] The ability of weak units to react differently depending upon the particular policy issues at stake suggests that their relations with the federal centre are likely to be much more complicated than might initially be assumed. Clearly this kind of *de facto* asymmetry has to be examined very carefully. The relationship between asymmetrical perceptions and behaviour, as Duchacek warned, is neither simple nor straightforward.

REPRESENTATION AND PROTECTION IN FEDERATIONS

As we concluded in Chapter 7, the question of representation is fundamental in federations. It emerges from the asymmetrical model that the accommodation of diversity can take many different forms and the representation, expression and protection of what Tarlton called a 'unique feature or set of features' is crucial to the legitimacy and, indeed, the very survival of the federal system itself. Federations obviously provide electoral representation for individual citizens and constituent states, governments and legislatures. The former are represented, as we have seen, in lower chambers where seats are determined according to population size while the latter are incorporated, either symmetrically or asymmetrically, in various types of second chambers. In Canada the combined population of the two provinces of Ontario and Quebec enjoy a *de facto* asymmetrical representation of 178 seats out of a total of 301 in the House of Commons, but the 'regional' principle in the non-elected Senate has had the effect of counterbalancing their combined dominance in the lower chamber. In the Senate, Quebec and Ontario each have 24 seats as regions rather than as provinces.

Yet this *de facto* asymmetrical representation obscures the vulnerable position of Quebec in the federation. In reality, Quebec's 75 seats in the House of Commons pits its predominantly francophone population against a nominal 226 anglophone representatives from the 'rest of Canada' (ROC), while its 24 seats in the Senate mean that it is easily outnumbered by the remaining 81 nominally anglophone representatives. Consequently, even if most of the major legislative policy issues in the Federal Parliament are not in practice decided along the simple anglophone–francophone divide, the minoritarian perception nonetheless endures in Quebec. This means that Quebec must find other ways to protect and promote its unique identity in Canada.[35] Conventional parliamentary representation by itself is insufficient. Since its own distinct identity corresponds with provincial territorial boundaries and statehood, it can defend its interests in the established processes of intergovernmental relations, or 'federal–provincial diplomacy' as it is sometimes called in Canada. But even here the limitations are once again apparent.

Representation facilitates expression and protection but the protection of difference can be achieved in many different asymmetrical forms. We are compelled, once again, to return to the question that we asked in Chapter 7, namely, 'Who or what is being represented?' Is it the individual citizen? Is it simply the constituent state unit? Is it a distinct political community or is it another form of collective identity? Moreover, are these differences territorial or non-territorial? Tarlton never spelled them out.

POLITICAL PARTIES AND PARTY SYSTEMS

One form of representation that constitutes a distinct type of *de facto* asymmetry is the role and nature of political parties in federations. Logically, parties express difference. They are vehicles of diversity. They are partisan, representing particular constellations of cleavage patterns and vested interests. In this case, the role of regional parties expressing territorial diversities is part and parcel of an asymmetrical party system.[36] Examples where this is the common practice are the Christian Social Union (CSU) in Bavaria and the Parti Quebecois (PQ) in Quebec. Neither party ventures outside of its own regional domain and both reflect deep-seated territorial–cultural differences in the German and Canadian federations. However, it is worth adding here that the CSU is in practice very closely allied to the Christian Democratic Union (CDU), a national federal party contesting federal elections everywhere else in Germany outside of Bavaria, while the PQ is closely linked to the Bloc Quebecois (BQ), also Quebec-based but which contests federal elections for representation in the Canadian House of Commons. Both Germany and Canada are 'parliamentary federations' but Canada can be differentiated from Germany by having a much more pronounced provincial party system that is organisationally quite distinct from the federal party system. Political parties, then, are institutional structures that express, defend and promote difference, and as such are a function of both symmetry and asymmetry.

De jure asymmetries

CONSTITUTIONS AND CONSTITUTIONAL REFORM

The most obvious forms of *de jure* asymmetry reside in both constitutional and legal processes where constituent state units are treated differently under the law and the constitution. These two arenas have become the most visible and popular contemporary responses to the reality of asymmetry. But while the politics of difference is usually expressed in the constituent state units, it can also be constitutionally protected via other methods. Tarlton did not elaborate on these processes in his short article but he did assume that a federal constitution enshrining *de jure* relationships would be based on the symmetrical model: 'Whether a state can function harmoniously with a federal constitution will … be a result of the level of symmetry within it'.[37] His mistake was to assume that symmetry equals harmony while asymmetry automatically produces discord in federations. In practice, asymmetry reflects difference; it does not create it. Asymmetrical outcomes are designed to achieve flexibility in the pursuit of legitimacy and overall federal political stability.

Asymmetry can be entrenched in federal constitutions in several ways which can vary in imagination. Typically it can be accommodated in the formal distribution of legislative and executive jurisdiction, but it can also be formalised in the entrenchment of a Bill of Rights, in the formal processes of constitutional amendment, in the role of constitutional courts and in the overall evolution of the constitution via judicial review. Different federations implement what we might call the 'politics of recognition' in these various ways and we must remember that federal constitutions always bear the hallmarks of their origins and formation. Accordingly, they invariably reflect the *raison d'être* of the federation at its inception and this always implies some kind of entrenched guarantee of difference, whatever form it might take. For our purposes here, some of the most well-known examples of *de jure* asymmetries, besides Quebec and Nunavut in Canada and Bavaria in Germany, are Sabah and Sarawak in Malaysia, Jammu and Kashmir, and Punjab in India, the German-speaking language community in Belgium, and Catalonia, Euzkadi and Galicia in Spain (if Spain is deemed a federation). Tarlton's approach to this aspect of symmetry and asymmetry was undoubtedly one-eyed. His overriding concern with the 'secession-potential' of asymmetrical relationships led him seriously to underestimate the capacity of federal constitutions successfully to accommodate the politics of difference. Yet a detailed comparative study of federal constitutions would reveal a myriad of novel principles and distinctions facilitating asymmetrical outcomes.

THE LAW AND LEGAL PROCESSES

If we followed Tarlton's logic in the arenas of federal and constituent state law we would doubtlessly arrive once again at an asymmetrical destination. However, there is no automatic convergence between federal and constituent state law and legal processes in federations. In Germany, for example, there is a basic uniformity between federal and state (land) law, but this is not the case in the USA where very different rules of application prevail. Moreover, in Canada, Quebec has a quite distinct body of civil law that originated in the French Civil Code and, along with the appointment of three Supreme Court judges (out of a total of nine), has become an integral feature of Quebec's specificity and unique identity.

Asymmetrical relations today

What are we to make of asymmetrical relations today? Of what practical use are they and what do they tell us about federalisms and federations in the new millennium? Clearly this analysis, having taken Tarlton as its departure point, is optimistic about both the continuing need for asymmetry and its practical value as a device for managing different kinds of conflicts and tensions within federations. In its most basic form, asymmetry constitutes the formal politics of recognition. It is rooted in respect for, and toleration of, difference.

Both symmetry and asymmetry are ideal types in political science analysis. There is no perfectly symmetrical or asymmetrical federation in the world. Consequently, it is better to see in asymmetrical federation an instrumental device for accommodating difference in a way that adds to the overall political stability of federations. Both *de facto* and *de jure* asymmetries suggest flexibility in federations in the general search for consensus among political elites and mass publics. Consensus is not something that can be taken for granted; it is something that is forged via hard bargaining and negotiations between competing and sometimes conflicting elites.

Asymmetrical relations have enormous significance for federal polities especially with regard to legitimacy, individual citizen and collective group participation and governmental stability, leading ultimately to overall system maintenance. In those federations where it has been applied in different ways and in varying degrees, success has itself been variable. We have already noted that it has been particularly successful in keeping Quebec in Canada, and that in Europe it has also successfully accommodated Jura in Switzerland. Other European examples where asymmetrical federation has been used successfully are Belgium and Germany, while Spain, although not yet a formal federation, has also put these mechanisms and techniques to good effect.[38] In 1993 the constitutional entrenchment of the regions and communities in the new federation of Belgium enabled the tiny German-speaking linguistic community of Eupen and Malmedy to find its own institutional and policy spaces while the special arrangements for the bilingual Brussels Capital Region – combining territorial and non-territorial federal elements – is yet another testament to the political acumen and imagination of Belgian constitutional design.[39] Asymmetrical experiments have also been introduced in Germany where the Danish minority in Schleswig-Holstein and the cultural identity of the Sorbs in Brandenburg have both been formally accommodated in the respective constituent state constitutional and legal processes.[40] Elsewhere we have seen that asymmetrical practices have also been successful in Malaysia where the two Borneo states of Sabah and Sarawak have enjoyed constitutional asymmetry since 1963 when the new federal constitution was introduced. Its success in Jammu and Kashmir and the Punjab in India may perhaps have to be interpreted more cautiously however. Nonetheless there can be no doubt at all that, notwithstanding separatist movements and intermittent violent conflict, the Indian federation, currently comprising 28 constituent state units and seven

Union Territories, has a remarkable record of constitutional and political stability given its colossal size and the complexity of its political culture.

In order more fully to appreciate these successes of asymmetrical federation they must be set against those examples of federations that have failed either through peaceful secession or outright civil war. The former socialist federations of the USSR and Czechoslovakia effectively imploded in the early 1990s after the fall of the Berlin Wall in 1989 that witnessed the subsequent emergence of the Russian Federation as a new, centralised federal system and the Czech Republic and Slovakia as independent national states, while Yugoslavia was ripped apart by a long, protracted civil war that ended only in 1995 and resulted in 2003 in the loose federal arrangement between the two Republics of Serbia and Montenegro, now bordered by Croatia, Slovenia, the Former Yugoslav Republic of Macedonia (FYROM), Bosnia and Herzegovina, Albania and Vojvodina. But these are examples of particular kinds of federal unions that utilised a variety of coercive techniques to ensure compliance from those constituent units with central demands; they were not liberal democracies. In the sense that we have defined federations as liberal democratic constitutional states in this book, they cannot therefore be classified as authentic federations. The implications for comparative analysis are consequently very limited. Today, the Russian Federation may ultimately have to utilise asymmetrical arrangements in some form in Chechnya to guarantee an enduring political stability and territorial integrity, while the future of the federal idea in the Balkans remains uncertain.

If we want to consider the future possibilities of asymmetrical federation in the light of the failures identified above, one clear lesson to be learned is that federation by itself is no panacea for all the ills of ethnic and sub-state nationalist conflicts. Its practical relevance will always depend upon contextual circumstances. What works in one context might not be successful in another. But the failures above do point to one minimal criterion for success: that future federal experiments must be firmly founded upon liberal democratic preconditions that entrench basic human rights and freedoms in a written constitution formally protected by an independent judiciary and based upon the rule of law, a free press, regular competitive elections by secret ballot and the right legally to change the government. Three contemporary conflicts that might yet be amenable to asymmetrical arrangements based upon these criteria are Iraq, Sri Lanka and Cyprus. Today these preconditions have yet to be established in Iraq, but it seems fairly clear that the social diversity having political salience which already exists there – given the predominance of the three main Shia, Sunni and Kurdish identities largely but not solely territorially based – will render a centralised unitary state highly inappropriate. A variety of federal arrangements might, in consequence, be deemed feasible in the near future.

Very different circumstances pertain to Sri Lanka, with the main conflict essentially of a bi-communal nature between the Sinhalese majority and the Tamil minority, but once again the way forward could conceivably be some form of asymmetrical federal arrangement. The likely alternative is an endless, violent and bloody stalemate. In Cyprus the circumstances are also bi-communal but very different from those that characterise Sri Lanka. The formal membership of Greek-dominated southern Cyprus in the EU in 2004 has further complicated an already complex constitutional, political and legal conundrum. Since the illegal military occupation and subsequent partition of the island in 1974 by Turkey, several attempts by the United Nations (UN) to resolve the problem have failed to bring the Turkish Cypriot minority and the Greek Cypriot majority together to reunite the divided polity. Both federal and confederal ideas have frequently surfaced and resurfaced during the past thirty years in the struggle to achieve a new *modus vivendi*, but without success. Ironically the 1960 Constitution enshrined asymmetrical arrangements at the outset in order to try to make bi-communalism work on the basis of political equality between two distinct communities. Consequently, asymmetry has a chequered history in Cyprus and it has not been assisted by opposing views of federalism and confederalism espoused by the two rival communities.[41] Nonetheless, contemporary circumstances have altered the dynamic between the north and the south so that some new form of asymmetrical federation or confederation could conceivably be part of the new agenda for constitutional change in the near future.

Conclusion: towards a normative theory of federalism and federation?

This chapter has provided a conceptual review of symmetry and asymmetry by analysing and exploring the work of Tarlton, Livingston and Duchacek. Its principal focus, however, has been asymmetrical federalism and federation. We have used Tarlton as our point of departure for this analysis and exploration, and we have shown that although his 'theoretical speculation' was both flawed and tendentious in 1965 it continues nonetheless to repay close attention. After forty years many of his arguments and assertions are obviously dated and often indefensible, but his belief that federal studies should attempt to investigate 'the diverse ways in which each member state in a federal system is able to relate to the system as a whole, the central authority and each other member state' remains instructive.[42] His work was an early attempt to explore the anatomy of federalism and federation.

The combined contribution of Tarlton, Livingston and Duchacek to the conceptual literature on symmetry and asymmetry has enabled us to enrich our understanding of federalism and federation in many ways. Duchacek claimed that Tarlton had introduced a new approach to 'the study of the reasons for which some federations fail to be established or, when established, dissolve again into their components'.[43] The main reason for the failure of federation, according to this view, was the presence of asymmetrical federalism. What Tarlton termed the 'secession-potential' of federal–state conflict was determined ultimately by 'the shared goals, aspirations and expectations of the elements constituting the federal union'. Without wishing to rekindle what would now be a sterile debate, it seems clear that Tarlton was railing against too much asymmetry in federal systems. He was concerned that diversity could be so great as to render the federation inadequate as a basis for 'unification under a single political authority'. This concern led him to conclude that 'the higher the level of symmetry' the greater the likelihood that federation would be a 'suitable form of governmental organization'.[44] This conclusion remains of great interest to scholars of federalism and federation. Its contemporary relevance to federal studies is well illustrated by the theoretical reflections of Brian Galligan in his magisterial survey of the Australian Federal Republic: 'federalism is a function not of societal differences but of institutional arrangements and political communities ... [it] is more likely to thrive in societies where regionally based societal differences are not extreme'. Accordingly, federation is 'unsuited for such situations'. However, it 'works quite well for countries like Australia that are broadly homogenous'.[45] The echoes of Tarlton are self-evident here.

Since 1965 Tarlton's 'theoretical speculation' has provided scholars of federalism and federation with new concepts in order to be able to appreciate more fully the many complexities of federal systems. If we discount his prejudices about symmetry and asymmetry, these novel routes of investigation can offer many fresh insights into the comparative study of federal systems. Today the term 'asymmetry' no longer possesses the negative connotations attributed to it by Tarlton. On the contrary, asymmetry is now regarded very much in a positive vein, bordering on virtue. It is ultimately linked to fundamental issues of legitimacy, participation and political stability. It is also related in a complex way to state–society relations and to the basic question of governance in federal polities. But it is vital to remember that 'diversity' in itself is not a sufficient basis for the existence of asymmetrical relations. It is necessary to examine both why and how the preconditions of asymmetry are translated into practical asymmetrical outcomes.

These theoretical reflections suggest that asymmetrical federalism and federation can be construed in two principal ways: first, as an analytical tool for the purpose of problem-solving in pursuit of federal political stability; and, second, as a normative or prescriptive predisposition reflecting particular, values, beliefs and interests. It can therefore be distilled as empirical political theory and as normative political theory.[46] And as we witnessed in Chapter 4, there do seem to be indications of a growing interest among some scholars to develop a fully fledged normative theory of federalism and federation. Clearly, a strong normative strand of political thought about federalism has always existed, especially if we consider the philosophical contributions of Althusius, Kant and Proudhon, but now there is a discernible contemporary intellectual trend towards building a composite normative theory of federalism that reflects changing perspectives of liberal democratic theory.[47]

Forty years later, then, Tarlton's 'theoretical speculation' has prompted considerable conceptual and empirical advances. We have made significant progress in understanding the symbiotic relationship between symmetry and asymmetry in federal systems. The focus in this chapter on asymmetrical federalism and federation, therefore, must not tempt us to overlook the fact that in theory and in practice symmetry and asymmetry are examples of complex interdependence: to change one is to alter the other.

9 The European Union as a federal model

Introduction

The theme of this chapter is a broad one: how far we can construe the EU as a new federal model. Daniel Elazar suggested that in the late twentieth century we were 'in the midst of a paradigm shift from a world of states, modelled after the ideal of the nation-state developed at the beginning of the modern epoch in the seventeenth century, to a world of diminished state sovereignty and increased interstate linkages of a constitutionalized federal character'.[1] He located the origins of the paradigm shift at the end of the Second World War, but claimed that its extensive and decisive character was not fully recognised until the disintegration of the Soviet Union during 1989–93. Indeed, even to most informed observers, it seemed to have 'crept up unawares'.[2] The reality of this momentous change is not that states are disappearing but that the state system is 'acquiring a new dimension' which is now beginning 'to overlay and, at least in some respects, to supersede the system that prevailed throughout the modern epoch'. Elazar's global conception of change construed this network of complex interactions as compelling states into various combinations of 'self-rule and shared rule', his own shorthand definition of modern federalism and federation.[3] And this 'federalist revolution' was not confined to modern federation but included a variety of looser federal arrangements designed to accommodate internal divisions. It also explained the emergence of the EU which, in his view, had developed into a 'new-style confederation ... designed to fit European realities'.[4]

Until recently it was possible to describe the EU as a classic example of federalism without federation. This meant that in its origins, formation and subsequent evolution and in its institutional framework and expanding policy output it had always been the repository of federal ideas, influences and strategies without actually transforming itself into a formal federation. In this chapter I want to suggest that the EU remains an intellectual puzzle because it is a conceptual enigma. But it is elusive, continuing to baffle and perplex observers and commentators on European integration, precisely because it is a new kind of federal model the like of which has never before been seen. Its metamorphosis has been slow, piecemeal and incremental, lending it a somewhat obscure, unobtrusive and even inscrutable quality, rather than being the result of a dramatic, providential moment in history like the Philadelphia Convention of 1787 in the United States of America. In this respect, the transformation of the EU from a *Community* into a *Union* with the ratification of the Treaty on European Union (TEU) in 1993 has, arguably, its American conceptual equivalent in the shift from confederation in 1781 to federation in 1789. We will return to some of these comparisons later in the chapter. For the moment let us focus upon European integration as a *process* of community-building rather than one of the state-building and national integration varieties that we have witnessed in conventional federations such as the USA, Canada, India and Australia. Clearly, there is much scope here for comparative analysis, but it also requires careful thought and reflection because there is also plenty of scope for what Giovanni Sartori once called 'comparative fallacies'.[5]

If we are to understand the contemporary EU as a federal model, it is vital that we are sensitised to the peculiarities and idiosyncrasies of European integration. This means that we must appreciate more fully the nature of the project that was launched with the Schuman Declaration of May 1950, for it is in this famous speech that the French Foreign Minister, Robert Schuman, revealed both the goal of a federal Europe and the strategy designed to achieve it:

> Europe will not be made all at once, or according to a single plan. It will be built through concrete achievements which first create a *de facto* solidarity. The coming together of the nations of Europe requires the elimination of the age-old opposition of France and Germany. Any action taken must in the first place concern these two countries. ... The pooling of coal and steel production should immediately provide for the setting up of common foundations for economic development as a *first step* in the *federation of Europe* ... [T]his proposal will lead to the realization of the *first concrete foundation of a European federation* indispensable to the preservation of peace.[6]

If we look very closely at what Schuman emphasised in his momentous speech we can immediately identify the incremental nature of European integration and the strategy designed to arrive at a federal destination. This much cannot be gainsaid. And what is important to understand for our purposes in this chapter is that the building of Europe would be unprecedented: the means would be economic but the underlying goal was unquestionably political. Europe would not be built in a day nor would it be constructed according to a federal blueprint. The genius of the strategy, as we shall see, lay in its simplicity. The European edifice, Schuman claimed, would be constructed only slowly, assembled brick by brick, so that its structure would rise up on the firm foundations of concrete economic performance based upon the convergence of national interest. The magnitude of the federal enterprise was bold and imaginative and the strategy designed to achieve it was unprecedented. The principal protagonist behind this post-war drive to lay the foundations of a federal Europe was Jean Monnet, who is widely acknowledged to have been the architect and builder of European integration.[7]

In order to set out the argument that will be used to clarify the thesis that the EU is a unique federal model, we shall structure the chapter in the following way: first, we will explore Monnet's conception of Europe and its political implications; second, we will reflect upon the relationship between history and theory, which brings into focus what I shall call 'intergovernmental revisionism' (IGR); third, we will look closely at the federal and confederal character of the contemporary EU; and, finally, we shall briefly address the question of the EU's Constitutional Treaty before concluding with a reassessment of some of the conceptual and empirical problems that confront political scientists today when seeking to define the empirical reality that is the EU. In particular, we will reflect upon some of the problems of comparison occasioned by the EU's remarkable evolution from its combined intergovernmental and supranational point of departure in 1950 to its current status as a new federal model. Now, however, let us turn to an exploration of Monnet's conception of Europe and examine its political implications.

Monnet's Europe and its political implications

Jean Monnet was born in Cognac, France in 1888 and is considered one of the founders of the European Community. Indeed, for many scholars of European integration Monnet is regarded as the principal protagonist in the drive to build Europe after the Second World War. Monnet's conception of Europe was rooted in his desire to remove forever the causes of war – what he regarded as a civil war – that periodically served to tear Europe apart. He sought, in an elemental sense, to identify the forces that drove Europeans to fight each other and, in contrast, to understand those forces that instilled in them a fundamental desire to cooperate with each other. In short, he wanted to persuade Europeans to channel and canalise their conflicts into a form of cooperation that would enable them to achieve their goals by seeking out and distilling their common interests. He believed that in every set of circumstances that might conceivably generate conflict there lurked a latent common interest that merely needed to be uncovered. It did not have to be invented; it was immanent in every condition of affairs. This meant that states, governments and citizens could be persuaded to transform their rivalries and animosities by changing the context in which these conflicts occurred. It was what he called the 'ECSC [European Coal and Steel Community] method' of establishing 'the greatest solidarity among peoples' so that 'gradually' other tasks and other people would become subject to the same common rules and institutions – or perhaps to new institutions – and this experience would 'gradually spread by osmosis'. No time limits were imposed on what was clearly deemed to be a long, slow, almost organic, process of economic and political integration:

> We believed in starting with limited achievements, establishing *de facto* solidarity, from which a federation would gradually emerge. I have never believed that one fine day Europe would be created by some great political

mutation, and I thought it wrong to consult the peoples of Europe about the structure of a Community of which they had no practical experience. It was another matter, however, to ensure that in their limited field the new institutions were thoroughly democratic; and in this direction there was still progress to be made … the pragmatic method we had adopted would … lead to a federation validated by the people's vote; but that federation would be the culmination of an existing economic and political reality, already put to the test … it was bringing together men and practical matters.[8]

This extract from Monnet's *Memoirs* throws the relationship between federalism, federation and European integration into sharp relief.[9] It underlines the interaction between economics and politics as the driving force behind integration and in explaining how Europe could be built by piecemeal, incremental steps – concrete achievements that were tried and tested – Monnet both confronted and confounded his contemporaries with the innovative idea of creating a federation by a hitherto unprecedented route. His federal Europe would not be the launching pad – the point of departure – for European integration. Rather, it would be something that constituted the *finalité politique*.

Changing the context of international relations in favour of the 'common interest' between states ensured that their energies were diverted from the competitive power politics that led to war into new areas of unity and cooperation that transcended the state. In consequence, the EU has introduced the rule of law into relations between European countries which, as François Duchene remarked, has 'cut off a whole dimension of destructive expectations in the minds of policy-makers'. It has in practice domesticated the balance of power so that the power politics of the so-called 'realist' school of international relations (IR) has been replaced by 'aspirations that come nearer to the "rights" and responsibilities which reign in domestic politics'.[10] In other words, Monnet's approach to the building of a federal Europe meant gradually internalising what previously were the externalities of the state. This, it hardly needs emphasising, was a major breakthrough in conventional inter-state relations. Nonetheless, in seeking to build a federal Europe principally by means of a series of economic steps, Monnet was attempting something that had no historical precedent. Indeed, the European Community (EC), and subsequently the EU, has evolved in a very different way to other federal models. To the extent that it has developed by the gradual 'aggregation' of previously separate political units, it is admittedly similar to the process by which the USA was consolidated during the years 1787–89. Here, however, the analogy ends. Past federations, as we have already seen in Chapter 3, were conscious acts of state-formation. They were constructed in rational Rikerian fashion as a result of treaty-like political negotiations that created a new federal constitution and government. Apart from the USA, this happened, for example, in Canada, Australia, India, Switzerland and Belgium. There is no historical precedent for the creation of a multinational, multicultural and multilingual federation or federal union composed of 15 – now

25 – national states, with mostly mature social, economic, political and legal systems. In this regard the contemporary EU is a colossal and original enterprise.

What, then, are the political implications of Monnet's Europe? How did he seek to transform his Europe by incremental economic steps into a federal Europe? And what sort of timescale did he envisage for this grand metamorphosis? The answers to these questions require us to return to some of the assumptions, already identified above, upon which his conception of Europe was originally based. If we recall Monnet's fervent belief in the significance of context and how it was possible to change the nature of problems by changing the context in which they were located, it was his own practical logic that compelled him to give that context a solid form. And it was institutional innovation that answered the call for new habits of thought and action.

The key to understanding the relationship between federalism, federation and European integration lies in the belief that by forging functional links between states in a way that does not directly challenge national sovereignty in a formal sense, the door to federation would gradually open. These so-called 'functional' links were primarily economic activities, and they were perfectly expressed in the ECSC initiative of the early 1950s. This innovative form of supranational organisation was to be the foundation of a European federation that would evolve only slowly to engage national elites in a process of mutual economic interest. These concrete benefits would gradually form that crucial solidarity – the common interest – which Monnet believed indispensable for the removal of physical and mental barriers.

Institutional innovation, then, was vital to the success of European integration. Europeans were limited only by their imagination. If they could develop the vision to look beyond the national state to solve what were actually common problems, they could forge new cooperative links and foster new habits of working together in novel institutions and circumstances. And novel institutions also implied novel decision-making processes and procedures to keep the wheels of integration turning. Monnet was convinced that nothing succeeds like success, and as long as the 'Community experiment' yielded results that furnished tangible benefits for its participants, their commitment, based upon their perceptions of the national interest, was assured.

The political implications of Monnet's conception of Europe were and remain far-reaching principally because his particular approach to European integration was the one that succeeded. But it is important to note that these political implications were and still are disputed. Moreover, Monnet was not without serious competitors in this quest and it is helpful for us to consider his approach from the standpoint of a much more conventional mainstream federalist perspective. If we put Monnet, as it were, face to face with his main federalist rival, namely, Altiero Spinelli, we can appreciate more fully the disputed political implications of his conception of Europe. Spinelli, who was born in Rome in 1906, had a turbulent life and an eventful political career as an adviser to the Italian government (1966–68), a European Commissioner (1970–76) and a Member of the European Parliament (1976–86), a position he held when he died.[11] As a leading activist in the federal cause in Europe, he was also widely regarded as the foremost champion of federalism via the parliamentary method that would engage the European citizenry in an act of political will to launch the federal convention. For our purposes, it is Spinelli's critique of what he called 'Monnet's Method' that is of primary concern and we will use his critique to explore what he considered its political implications to be.

The essence of the so-called 'Monnet Method' – his political strategy – for European integration was something that eventually came to constitute a major theoretical controversy about federalism, federation and European integration. It was also the crux of Spinelli's opposition. This was that Monnet's own method of piecemeal, cumulative integration whereby 'political' Europe would be the 'culminating point of a gradual process' contained the huge assumption that at some future undefined point a qualitative change would occur in the constitutional and political relations between states and peoples. But he believed that this would happen only when 'the force of necessity' made it 'seem natural in the eyes of Europeans'.[12] In short, Monnet's approach to federation rendered constitutionalism – the building of political Europe – contingent upon the cumulative effect of functional achievements.

It was precisely at this juncture – in the interaction between politics and economics – that Spinelli entered the theoretical debate. Spinelli argued that the fundamental weakness of the 'Monnet Method' lay in its failure to deal with the organisation of political power at the European level.[13] This meant that the political centre would remain weak and impotent, lacking the capacity to go much beyond what already existed. Spinelli's verdict on Monnet's conception of Europe can be succinctly summarised in the following way: it failed according to its own terms of reference. It simply did not possess that inherent sustaining dynamic which Monnet believed, at least initially, would evolve inexorably towards a union of peoples. The predicted shift from *quantity* to *quality* would not occur precisely because of Monnet's excessive reliance upon a functionalist or incrementalist logic. His confidence in such logic was misplaced because he failed to confront the realities of organised political power. Only strong independent central political institutions could provide European solutions to European problems. Without these institutions, national responses would prevail. Spinelli acknowledged that Monnet had made the first steps easier to achieve, but he had done so by making the later steps more difficult. The building of a 'political' Europe based upon economic performance criteria would not necessarily follow, according to Monnet's logic, and as a consequence Spinelli argued that Europe might very well remain little more than a 'Common Market'.

In retrospect, Spinelli's criticisms of Monnet seem in one sense to have been vindicated. The EC/EU's central political institutions have certainly grown in political influence, but their powers and competences remain weak in certain important respects. The powers of the European Parliament (EP), for example, have been significantly strengthened during the last decade, but it still has only very limited powers of accountability over the European Council/Council of Ministers, while its control over the budget remains only partial and the application of co-decision is not yet extensive.[14] These inter-institutional defects and deficiencies, however, are observations that rest on a conventional understanding of what federation is. Not everybody might wish to see the EP's powers, functions and role continue to grow exponentially. Indeed, some critics of the EP insist that its place in the institutional scheme of things in the EU is fundamentally ambiguous. Moreover, it could be argued that Spinelli underestimated the political will of the member states, invested in the European Council. In recent years the Council has taken several crucial steps forwards in strengthening the EP and in buttressing Qualified Majority Voting (QMV). Moreover, a series of intergovernmental conferences dating back to 1985 have produced the Single European Act (SEA), the TEU, the Treaty of Amsterdam (TA), the Treaty of Nice (TN) and the Constitutional Convention, each of which has contributed significantly to the building of a political Europe. Consequently, there remain certain grounds for optimism concerning Monnet's shift from *quantity* to *quality*. There is some evidence that we have witnessed *both* an expansion of quantity as well as a shift towards quality. In this respect, then, the political implications of Monnet's conception of Europe remain unclear.

If we move away from the institutional focus for a moment and turn our attention instead to policy matters, the profile of European integration becomes much more substantive and sophisticated. Here *quantity* has shifted unequivocally to *quality*. More and more policy matters that were formerly the exclusive domestic affairs of the member states have gradually been transferred to the EC and then the EU, so that Monnet's Europe has become a *de facto* polity with conspicuous policy outputs. The combination of an expanding policy arena increasingly subject to QMV and which is treaty-based has therefore corresponded to the transformation of a *Community* into a *Union* in which salient supranational, federal, confederal and inter-governmental features coexist, admittedly often uncomfortably, in permanent interplay and reciprocity.

In summary, the political implications of Monnet's conception of Europe harbour grounds for both optimism and pessimism. Much depends upon political leadership and the fortunes of two highly controversial enterprises, namely, the introduction of the euro in January 2002 and the ratification process of the new Constitutional Treaty during the next two years. The drive towards Economic and Monetary Union (EMU) is unquestionably a political imperative and constitutes yet another incremental step on the road towards a federal Europe while the Constitutional Treaty consolidates, clarifies and updates the European project. But in this short exploration of Monnet's Europe we must not overlook the existence of a lively scholarly controversy about the nature and meaning of European integration and its latest institutional manifestation, namely, the EU. In the next section therefore we will turn to consider the most recent theoretical broadside that has been fired across the bows of the federal cause in Europe. This latest challenge to the federal credentials of European integration is that which I shall call 'intergovernmental revisionism' (IGR).

History and theory

It is clear that recent theoretical perspectives which focus broadly on IGR have been founded largely upon a particular preconception of the origins and evolution of the EU. In other words, history – or at least a particular historical interpretation based upon shared assumptions about states and the role and motivations of states' elites – has become the basis for building a theoretical edifice that is tantamount to a self-fulfilling prophecy. Let us briefly survey the background to this mainstream literature in order first to underline its basic assumptions before we subsequently consider its fundamental flaws.

The following outline serves to call attention to the predominantly intergovernmental interpretation of the origins and causes of post-war West European integration that I have labelled IGR. This label embraces the major works of the two principal contributors to the theoretical debate about European integration, namely, Alan Milward and Andrew Moravcsik. We will look at their respective contributions to this debate in the order in which I have presented them. We will take as representative of the first branch of IGR the school of historical thought that I have dubbed 'Intergovernmental Historical Revisionism' (IHR), which includes the chief collected works of Alan Milward, whose impressive scholarly analyses have, until recently, stood the test of time. Milward's *The Reconstruction of Western Europe, 1945–51,* first published in 1984, set the scene for a remarkable consistency of scholarly purpose.[15] Put simply, his general conclusion was that the success of Western Europe's post-war reconstruction derived from 'the creation of its own pattern of institutionalised international economic interdependence'.[16] His book explained the way in which governments shaped this pattern to suit their own national objectives. Consequently, it was national governments and political and bureaucratic elites that were the pivotal actors in the process of increasing interdependence. The very limited extent of economic integration that did occur came about via the pursuit of the narrow national self-interests of what were still powerful nation-states. There was certainly no room here for what was variously called human idealism, idealisms and the higher ideals of men such as Konrad Adenauer, Robert Schuman, Paul-Henri Spaak and Jean Monnet. Milward claimed that previous accounts had failed to show precisely how such idealisms actually influenced governmental policy-making. Indeed, the empirical evidence indicated the very opposite: integration had been the bureaucratic result of 'the internal expression of national political interest' rather than that of the major statesmen who had implemented policy.[17]

Furthermore, the origins and early evolution of the European project were both 'relative and contingent' rather than expressive of fundamental principles that might be called 'universal and timeless'. European integration was not part of a grand federal design but had emerged merely to cope with certain historically specific economic and political problems. The ECSC and the Common Agricultural Policy (CAP), for example, were designed simply to resolve particular, limited – not generalised, universal – problems. They were only 'an arm of the nation state' and had no necessary implications for Europe's future. Above all, they had no destiny to supersede the nation-state.[18] There was, in short, no teleology which suggested that the emergent union of states had a predictable *finalité politique*.

Milward's second major contribution to the history and theory of the European project was entitled *The European Rescue of the Nation-State* and appeared in 1992.[19] The so-called 'rescue' of the nation-state hinged upon two main arguments. First, it was claimed that the evolution of the ECSC and the European Economic Community (EEC), along with the European Atomic Energy Community (EAEC), which together constituted the EC, had been an integral part of the reassertion of the nation-state since 1945; second, that the very process of European integration had been a necessary part of the post-war rescue of the nation-state. The main reason for the origins, early evolution and continued existence of the European project was that it was simply one more stage in the long evolution of the nation-state. And the economic historian in Milward could not resist the temptation to claim categorically that 'the true origins of the EC' were 'economic and social'.[20] Accordingly, the presumed antithesis between the EC and the nation-state was false; they could coexist perfectly well. And the evolution of the EC was principally state-directed: member-state governments were in control of the pace and direction of integration. Finally, in a ferocious attack upon the historical significance of the so-called 'European saints', Milward railed against the hagiographers, fabulists and theologians who had dominated the historiography of European integration and underlined what he took to be both colossal oversimplifications and absurd value judgments that purported to be accurate and objective historical accounts of the building of Europe by a small band of leading statesmen imbued with a shared, if grandiose, vision.

The third and final contribution to the historical debate that we shall highlight is probably the most significant for the political scientist, namely, Milward's *The Frontier of National Sovereignty: History and Theory, 1945–1992*, first published in 1993.[21] Here Milward and his fellow associates of the European University Institute (EUI) in Florence extended the historical analysis, somewhat boldly, from the 1950s into the 1990s. They sought to construct a theory of integration derived from empirical research into Europe's own history even while acknowledging that it was not yet 'susceptible to a full analysis'. Milward recognised their inability to predict the future nature of national policy choices based upon the evidence of contemporary events and circumstances, but he nonetheless claimed that 'the frontier of national sovereignty' based upon existing policy choices was 'essentially where it had been fixed in 1952 and 1957'.[22] They concluded that scholars had to descend from generalities to the detail of the relationship of each specific policy proposal in relation to the available international frameworks for advancing it. Even a cursory glance at the purpose of this type of research would demonstrate just how much of a tall order it was, but it nonetheless underlined the fundamental link between history and theory that remains at the core of all explanations of European integration.

Milward's journey had brought him safely to an inter-governmental destination. It was in many ways a predictable terminus. But if many of his conclusions can be construed as part of a self-fulfilling prophecy – the product of disputed assumptions and highly contestable preconceptions – there can be no doubt that his historical analyses have retained their practical relevance to the contemporary developments currently taking place in the EU. For example, Milward's historical interpretation of the recent shift of emphasis towards different aspects of the federal idea by some leading statesmen – such as the oft-quoted speech by Joschka Fischer, the German Foreign Minister, in May 2000 in Berlin's Humboldt University – would probably rationalise it by reference to the narrowing range of policy choices available to member states.[23] However, it would equally not detract from his basic premise that member-state governments remain in control of the EU, a very state-centric approach to European integration.

In many ways, Milward's broad historical interpretation of post-war European integration prepared the ground for the emergence in the 1990s of a much-trumpeted theoretical perspective dubbed 'Liberal Intergovernmentalism' (LI) that had the not inconsiderable merit of revitalising the theoretical debate about the European project for political scientists. In a series of seminal articles Andrew Moravcsik brought some of the intellectual baggage of IR theory with him in his impressive attempts to explain the conspicuous progress of European integration during the era of Jacques Delors, the President of the European Commission, that began with the inter-governmental agreement, forged in December 1985 in Luxembourg, to implement the SEA.[24] Moravcsik's single-minded determination to establish LI as the most convincing explanation of European integration had the immediate effect of rearranging the theoretical furniture in such a persuasive way that LI invaded both undergraduate and post-graduate university textbooks in the mainstream teaching of the EU in the United Kingdom and succeeded eventually in overshadowing nearly all of its putative rivals.

Without wishing to present a detailed survey of Moravcsik's contribution to history and theory, it is useful briefly to summarise some of the basic premises and conclusions of LI in the following way. LI is founded upon five basic principles: a critique of neo-functionalism, a liberal theory of national preference formation, the assumption of rational state behaviour that rejects path dependency, an inter-governmental analysis of inter-state negotiations and an account of international institutions as basically facilitators of domestic policy goals. It is further buttressed by a theoretical reliance upon regime theory and two-level games that help to explain the demand and supply functions necessary for international cooperation. Together these factors are used to account for the circumstances by which member states of the EU are intermittently prepared to delegate and pool purportedly sovereign powers that appear to reduce, but actually strengthen, their relative autonomy.[25]

Clearly the basic assumptions that underpin Moravcsik's explanation of European integration are rooted in the realist and neo-realist theories of IR that situate the state as the primary actor in international politics. The protection and promotion of member states' interests in the EU, in turn, means that it is national governments that are the principal agents of change and continuity in the pursuit of national self-interest. But as one commentator has remarked, it would be 'manifestly unfair to categorize Moravcsik's work as a realist or neo-realist' although it is 'decidedly intergovernmentalist'.[26] Transposed and modified to adjust to the institutional and policy arenas of the EU, LI has *en route*, been quite eclectic, absorbing comparative and international political economy in such a way that 'it can partly be understood as the feeding in of these debates into the discourse of EU Studies'.[27] LI, then, is a seductive explanation of what happens and why at the level of intergovernmental conferences (IGCs) and it helps us to appreciate the complex linkages that exist between the conceptually discrete realms of domestic politics and the EU arena. Moreover, since his early contribution to the theoretical debate in 1991, LI has become a much more developed and sophisticated model of how and why member-state governments say what they say and do what they do.[28]

This brief summary of the recent intellectual shift towards IGR encapsulated in Milward's IHR and Moravcsik's LI suggests that these are challenging explanatory models with interesting theoretical implications rather than new theories of European integration in their own right. What is notable about both models, however, is the absence of federalist perspectives and the conspicuous refusal to accommodate federalist explanations in their respective analyses. Milward, it is fair to say, confronted and rejected some of them in his historical interpretations, but Moravcsik did not even mention them until quite recently when he explained them *away* rather than explained them.[29] In view of this steely determination to avoid the 'f' word when putting a particular construction on the EU, let us turn now to address the question that lies at the heart of this chapter. It is time to confront the nature of the beast.[30]

Is the bottle half empty or half full?

What do we mean by a federal Europe? What will it look like and how will it be organised and constructed? One conclusion that we can draw from our short survey is that in the specific context of European integration, the evolving EU is a case of federalism without federation. Consequently, in this context federalism is a particular form of political integration. It is based upon a conception of Europe that implies 'self-rule and shared rule'. In other words, a federal Europe refers to a particular way that its advocates might prefer to organise Europe. The federal predisposition has certain obvious organisational and institutional implications for the building and design of Europe – a voluntary union, we are reminded, and one that is founded upon liberal democratic principles that recognise, respect and tolerate difference and diversity.

Logically, then, the construction of Europe is dependent upon how we wish to organise it. Given that federalists want to organise Europe according to federal principles that imply a contractually binding but limited form of union in which power is divided and shared between the component member states that created it, on the one hand, and the overarching central authority of the union, on the other, there are potentially an infinite number of institutional variations and jurisdictional permutations available. In practice, the EU has tended to rely upon institutional continuity. Today its central institutions, originally created by the Treaty of Rome (1957) to serve a small EC of six member states, remain largely the same for an EU of 25 constituent units. And as we shall see, the long-standing debate about institutional reform in the EU that has recently culminated in the proposed Constitutional Treaty has been tantamount to a rearranging of the existing institutional furniture in the EU house rather than a major house clearance.

Nonetheless, we are reminded of Spinelli's famous remark that we must begin with what has already been implemented. We cannot go back to the drawing board. And there are many commentators and interested observers who still claim that the current EU exhibits so many federal and confederal elements that we already have a federal Europe. Today these sorts of remarks are common-place in public discussions about the future of Europe. So is the bottle half empty or half full? Has the contemporary EU evolved to such an extent in social, economic, political, legal and constitutional terms that we can now make convincing claims to have a federal Europe?

In a recent essay that confronts precisely this question, Moravcsik describes the EU as 'an exceptionally weak federation'.[31] He is, however, clearly uncom-fortable with this description, adding that it might well be thought of as 'as something qualitatively different from existing federal systems' and much prefer-ring to refer to it as 'a particular sort of limited multi-level constitutional polity designed within a specific social and historical context'.[32] The reasoning that has led to what is for him a surprisingly equivocal conclusion derives from what he believes are the narrow range of policies that fall within the EU's ambit and the weakness of its institutions. We shall soon see that his discomfort is actually the result of failing to appreciate the significance of what we shall refer to as *empirical context* and the *point of departure*. For the moment, however, let us follow Moravcsik's argument. He claims that the contemporary EU is weak – indeed, so weak that it calls into question whether it is a federation at all. This is because of a battery of criticisms that includes the following areas of issue about which European voters care most: taxation, social welfare provision, defence, high foreign policy, policing, education, cultural policy, human rights, and small busi-ness policy. Correspondingly, he claims, the EU's central institutions are tightly constrained by supermajoritarian decision rules, a tiny administration; radical openness, stringent provisions for subsidiarity, a distinct professional ethos and the near-total absence of the power to tax and coerce. And he concludes solemnly: 'the EU constitutional order is not only barely a federal state; it is barely recognizable as a state at all'.[33] Viewed from this negative perspective, the bottle is clearly half empty.

But let us look a little more closely at Moravcsik's claims and let us first accen-tuate the positive rather than the negative attributes of the EU. If we approach the question of the EU's general powers and competences from a positive angle, we can see that its duties, obligations and responsibilities to EU citizens embrace the following: a Single European Market (SEM) for goods, persons, services and capital; an effective competition policy; a common external tariff; a common commercial policy; a single currency and a central bank serving 12 of the 25 member states with a monetary policy that operates from Frankfurt (with the additional ten new member states having just joined the EU also committed to EMU); common policies at varying stages of evolution in agriculture, transport, environment and fisheries; a range of functional and sectoral policies, where EU bodies share responsibilities with member-state governments, in steel, energy, research and technology; economic and social cohesion; industry, development and the social field; important new commitments in defence policy; and significant recent progress in common foreign and security arrangements that strengthen the capacity of the EU to speak with a single voice in external affairs and underline its role as 'a major world player in important policy spheres'.[34] On the institutional front the EU has three central supranational institutions – the European Commission, the EP and the European Court of Justice (ECJ) – whose functions, powers, influence and combined impact upon the policy- and decision-making processes and implementation procedures that impinge both directly and indirectly upon EU citizens, have grown enormously in the past two decades.

What emerges from this brief outline of EU policy competences and institutional capacity is the picture of an evolving, highly decentralised, federal union of states and citizens with limited but significant public duties, obligations and responsibilities that is built upon 'unity in diversity'. It is, in short, a voluntary democratic federal union based upon limited centralisation with unique state-like features and characteristics that is pointing in the direction ultimately of a European constitution with a charter of rights enshrining democratic values, human rights and fundamental freedoms. Even such a superficial survey as the one above amply demonstrates that the bottle is actually half full. Put simply, what Moravcsik has described is not inaccurate but it is selective by omission. It is the product of a particular parsimony, but the way that he has couched his description is somewhat disingenuous.

The reason for Moravcsik's evident discomfort, then, lies in what we have termed *empirical context* and the *point of departure* and is a classic example of the failure of some political scientists to see beyond the classic American federal model. They are either unable to step outside the conceptual confines of their own political culture or simply refuse to adopt comparative perspectives at all. However, it has been one of the fundamental premises of this book that there are many different types of federalisms and federations that must be compared and contrasted using a variety of different perspectives and approaches. Consequently, if it is still true that we must continue to draw upon the American historical and philosophical experience for meaningful contemporary comparative perspectives, this does not imply that such analyses must, of necessity, depend upon American yardsticks of definition. Indeed, this was the main problem with Duchacek's classic *Comparative Federalism: The Territorial Dimension of Politics:* its use of 'ten yardsticks of federalism' vitiated the exercise of definition at its source because the yardsticks were 'primarily based on the United States Constitution', which had acquired the 'reputation of a model'.[35] Clearly, to commit this error would blind us to the possibility that the EU is a new federal model. Indeed, it is worth remembering that Elazar was convinced that the evolving European model of confederal union had already replaced the classic American model of federation.

The point of departure, then, refers to Monnet's Europe, that is, how Europe has been built. We will recall that Monnet's approach to the building of Europe – a federal Europe – was unprecedented. His 'Method' – the point of departure – was a piecemeal, incremental construction that began with sectoral integration around coal and steel and shifted later to the larger goal of a common market. But the incorporation of broadly socio-economic objectives was underpinned by what was clearly a political imperative so that, at some undefined point in the future, the door to federation would open. There was neither deadline nor specific timetable for this shift from *functionalism* to *constitutionalism* (the building of political Europe), but the important implication for our argument about *empirical context* is that this peculiar approach to the building of Europe included certain risks for the federal project. One of the main dangers was that it left the central supranational institutions of the evolving EC/EU inherently weak – unable to go much beyond what existed – and it relied heavily upon concrete achievements to furnish the impetus for further cooperation and integration. In this light it is perfectly understandable why the LI model should relegate both the Commission and the EP to the sidelines of major treaty reform pushing integration forwards. These institutions have spent their whole existence struggling to insinuate themselves into policy- and decision-making processes wherein they were either excluded (by not being treaty-based) at the beginning or (even when they were treaty-based) were frequently challenged by member-state governments. And in the particular case of the EP, its struggle has been akin to that of an outsider fighting to become an insider. Small wonder, then, that these political institutions appear weak when compared to those of 'any extant national federation'.[36] In this respect we are not comparing 'like with like'. And this is also why it is easy to draw up a balance sheet that identifies policy and institutional deficiencies that lead to sceptical conclusions about a federal Europe. The EU is not a federation in the conventional sense that we have defined it in this book. It is not a state. But it is nonetheless a political union with strong federal and confederal elements and conspicuous policy outputs that broadly equate with the domestic policies of national states. It is, in other words, a new kind of federal–confederal union that we can classify either as a 'new confederation' or a new federal model.[37]

Empirical context also helps us to understand precisely why it is that the LI model can build such a convincing case against supranational institutions, like the Commission, as 'entrepreneurs'. They are an easy target because their peculiar role in the integration process has been determined by an institutional context unique in the world of states. They are propulsive forces for integration not just cooperation. This means that they have to be opportunists, expanding and even creating their own policy space by exploiting circumstances when they are deemed favourable to supranational progress. In a nutshell, the supranational institutions have also grown as part and parcel of the evolution of the 'ever closer union'. Consequently both empirical context and the point of departure for building a federal union are critical to a proper understanding of how the EU has evolved and how it works. IR-type models and theories of decision-making therefore are not as adaptable to European integration as some scholars would have us believe because the European project really is, in lawyer's terms, *sui generis*. To paraphrase Spinelli, the normative federalist imperative construes LI protagonists as highly skilful at explaining what exists but blind to what does not yet exist but must exist.

Intergovernmental conclusions about European integration are inevitably parsimonious, but parsimony, while a laudable analytical quality, does not tell the whole story. Neither IHR nor LI, for all their impressive detailed analyses, scholarly rigour and iconoclastic predispositions, have managed to produce models or partial theories sufficiently convincing to explain precisely why it is that European integration has evolved largely in the way that Monnet predicted. Indeed, it has now reached the point of evolution at which public debate about the EU's Constitutional Treaty reflects contemporary political realities.

The Constitutional Treaty

There is no doubt that something has been stirring in the EU since the public speech by Fischer in May 2000 at Berlin's Humboldt University. It was here that the German Foreign Minister first set out his vision for the future of Europe, a federal Europe, which signalled a flurry of activity in the inter-governmental world as one leading statesman after another added to the cacophony of sound about the destiny of the 'ever closer union'.[38] These visions, ideas and events were distilled in December 2000 at the IGC in Nice, France and culminated in December 2001 in the European Council decision in Laeken, Belgium to convene the 'Convention on the Future of Europe'. Chaired by Valéry Giscard d'Estaing, the former French President, the Convention was charged with the task of producing a report to be discussed at the subsequent IGC in 2004.

The building of Europe evident in the long journey from the Schuman Declaration in May 1950 to the Laeken Declaration in December 2001 has been a dynamic process characterised by a complex mixture of motives: domestic politics and policies, international imperatives, interest group motivations, personal conviction, political leadership, elite political vision and imagination, political opportunism and, not least, the pursuit of national self-interests. Moreover, since these motives are interwoven in such a complex fashion it should come as little surprise to us that no single all-embracing omnibus theory has emerged that can explain European integration. Certainly its complexities have continued to confound theorists from both the IR and Comparative Politics schools of thought in political science, neither of which have convincingly explained why it is that today a federal Europe, whether weak or not, confronts us as an empirical reality.[39]

Contemporary events and developments seem broadly to have confirmed different aspects of the rival European conceptions of Monnet and Spinelli. The Constitutional Treaty that emerged was entirely consistent with the teleology immanent in 'Monnet's Method' and was substantiated in 'political Europe' as the culminating point of a gradual process', while the very establishment of the Convention pointed in the direction of Spinelli's political strategy of the convention method of building Europe, albeit in the wake of Monnet's enduring legacy.[40] Given these circumstances, it was logical for the composition of the 105-strong Convention to have included the following participants: 15 representatives of the Heads of State or Government of the member states; 13 representatives of the Heads of State or Government of the candidate states (one per candidate state); 30 representatives of the national parliaments of the member states (two for each member state); 26 representatives of the national parliaments of the candidate states (two for each candidate state); 16 members of the European Parliament and two representatives of the European Commission with, in addition, three representatives of the Economic and Social Committee, six representatives of the Committee of the Regions, three representatives of the 'social partners' and the European Ombudsman invited to attend as an observer. Led by Giscard d'Estaing, as Chairman, and Guiliano Amato and Jean-Luc Dehaene as Vice-Chairmen, the Convention on the Future of Europe could hardly be considered Europe's equivalent to the Philadelphia Convention (1787) but it certainly represented the key players in the next stage of the European project.[41] Indeed, its composition was representative of a wide range of different institutions and interests, and embraced large sections of civil society.

In order for the debate about the future of Europe to be broadly based, the process of consultation necessarily involved the creation of a forum for organisations representing civil society, such as businesses, trade unions, universities, the legal profession and non-governmental organisations (NGOs). Public input into the debate was encouraged by regular information on the Convention's proceedings together with a series of public hearings which fed into the press, the media at large, political parties, interest groups, local meetings, written correspondence and the Internet, and was ultimately designed to pave the way for the Convention's formal proceedings that would draw conclusions to be incorporated in the final document, thus furnishing a starting point for discussions in the IGC. Beginning in February 2002, the process of public debate via the convention method ended in June 2003. This particular phase in the building of Europe was consistent with the federalist political strategy adopted by Spinelli during the period 1980–84 when he championed the draft treaty on the EU (later the European Union Treaty) in the EP which presaged the introduction of the SEA in 1986.[42] Twenty years later the 'Draft Treaty establishing a Constitution for Europe' developed by the Convention on the Future of Europe – having been modestly revised in October 2003 at the IGC in Rome, Italy – was formally adopted by the Brussels European Council in June 2004 and officially signed the following October by the enlarged (to 25) EU. At long last the intergovernmental consensus on a constitutional Europe, although fragile, had been cemented.

If we turn now to look at the skeletal structure of the Constitutional Treaty, it is first necessary for us to address the question of terminology. Despite echoes of the Philadelphia Convention (1787), the Constitutional Treaty is not a European version of the US Constitution. It is not a contract between a state and its citizens as a single people. It is a formal agreement or bargain between the member states of the EU to a treaty that formalises the EU with a single institutional foundation and a legal personality based upon conferred powers and competences that are divided and shared between the Union and its constituent units. Legally, then, it remains a treaty. However, the contemporary world of states and citizens does not always lend itself to neat and tidy legal definitions of reality. The EU has always been something of a legal and political hybrid, its evolution continuing to perplex both lawyers and political scientists alike with its tantalising conceptual and empirical ambiguities. Clearly much depends upon how the term 'constitution' is construed in this unique context. In some important respects the Constitutional Treaty might be regarded as akin to a federal constitution, especially in those areas that focus upon the individual citizen in relation to the EU as a whole. This brings us back to the principle of representation that we discussed in Chapter 7. For example, the principal constituent units of the EU are the 25 member states that are represented by national government ministers in the Council of Ministers and heads of state and government in the European Council, but they are not the only distinct entities represented in the Union. The individual citizen is also directly represented in the EP as a central institution of the EU and citizens are moreover indirectly represented at their sub-state local and regional capacities in the Committee of the Regions (COR), while individuals can also be represented in terms of the right to petition the EP as well as the redress of grievances in the office of the European Ombudsman. Furthermore, the entrenchment of a 'Charter of Fundamental Rights of the Union' – with rights judiciable in the ECJ – in the Constitutional Treaty firmly incorporates the individual citizen as a rights-bearing actor in the EU polity. In other words, the constitutional and political reality of the EU – if the Constitutional Treaty is formally ratified – expands and enriches the concept of citizenship so that in practice it embodies a multidimensional representation of individual citizens that will have enormous legal and political implications redolent of a constitution rather than a treaty.

The conceptual conundrum evident in the dispute about the status of the Constitutional Treaty typically reflects the intellectual puzzle that is the EU. It may be that in strict legal terms it remains a treaty while in other important respects it will function in practice as a constitution. Given the ambiguities inherent in the EU as a legal and political hybrid, it should not come as a surprise to learn that this has resulted in a somewhat enigmatic form of parchment governance. The Constitutional Treaty, after all, reflects largely what already exists. Consequently, this is a dilemma only to the extent that we allow ourselves to be imprisoned within the confines of old, outdated concepts. In short, it is an argument for reconceptualisation and redefinition. And it also strengthens the claim made here that we are dealing with a new federal model.

Let us look briefly at the anatomy of the curious hybrid that is the Constitutional Treaty.[43]

The Constitutional Treaty comprises four main parts: Part I defines the objectives, institutions, powers, competences and decision-making procedures of the EU; Part II establishes the Charter of Fundamental Rights of the Union; Part III focuses on the Union's polices and actions, including different legislative processes applying to different policy areas; and Part IV contains general and final provisions that include amendment procedures and entry into force. In size and structure, the Constitutional Treaty is a huge, unwieldy tome that remains, for the moment, a mystery to the vast majority of EU citizens, who are not yet properly engaged with the processes of constitution-building and ratification. A combination of popular ignorance and a general lack of awareness and interest in the European project in some member states makes ratification the most daunting of tasks for the national governments to accomplish during the next two years. Much will depend upon how effectively political leaders will be able to sell both the idea and the thing itself. And there is much at stake in the Constitutional Treaty. Let us look at the principal features of the new document.

Key elements relate to the following ten points of information:

1   The Constitutional Treaty is referred to as 'this Constitution' and sets out the definition and objectives of the EU in accordance with the values of respect for human dignity, freedom, democracy, equality, the rule of law and human rights, including the rights of persons belonging to minorities. These values, in turn, reflect those common to the member states in which pluralism, non-discrimination, tolerance, justice, solidarity and equality prevail. Designed to promote peace, liberal democratic values and welfare, the Union respects the equality of its member states as well as their national identities and their internal structures and territorial integrity.

2   The Charter of Fundamental Rights of the Union is entrenched and firmly establishes the protection of fundamental rights in the light of changes in society, social progress, and scientific and technological developments.

3   Clarification of the respective roles of the European Council, Council of Ministers, European Commission and the EP. In particular, the Commission's different roles – legislative initiative, executive capacity, external representative function and inter-institutional programming – are formally recognised and the co-decision procedure (henceforth to be called the legislative procedure) is extended to 95 per cent of EU legislation (adopted jointly by the EP and Council).

4   The main institutional innovation is the creation of the post of Union Minister of Foreign Affairs, the principal figure responsible for the representation of the EU in international affairs.

5   The establishment of the European Council as an institution, distinct from the Council of Ministers, that will be chaired by a President with limited powers who will be appointed for a period of two and a half years. The previous system of biennial rotation among the member states is retained but placed within a tripartite 'team presidency' of the different Council

formations (with the exception of the External Relations Council). The European Council, acting by QMV, can amend the new arrangement.

6   The definition of QMV is based upon the principle of the double majority of the member states and the people, thus confirming the Union's double legitimacy. QMV will require a majority of 55 per cent of the member states representing 65 per cent of the population to be activated. Two additional elements mean that a blocking minority of member states must consist of at least four governments (thus effectively preventing three large states from forming a blocking minority) while votes can be postponed to enable a broader consensus to be reached within the Council should a blocking minority of at least 75 per cent of the member states, whether by numbers or by total population figures, demand this.

7   The composition of the central institutions means that the EP will have a maximum of 750 seats allocated according to the principle of 'degressive proportionality', with a minimum of six and a maximum of 96 seats, the precise distribution of seats to each member state to be decided before the next European elections in 2009. The composition of the Commission in 2004 – one Commissioner for each member state – will be maintained until 2014. Thereafter it will comprise a number of Commissioners corresponding to two-thirds of the total number of member states. Following the Nice Treaty (ratified in 2002) Commission members will be chosen according to a system based on equal rotation among the member states.

8   The Constitutional Treaty builds upon existing Union competences so that it does not significantly increase its policy content but does update provisions in the field of Justice and Home Affairs in order to consolidate and improve the area of freedom, security and justice, placing most of them within the scope of QMV. The old distinction between common foreign and security policy and external relations is preserved, but the role of the new Union Minister of Foreign Affairs, together with the requirement for member states to cooperate more closely in the field of defence, is designed to buttress the credibility of the Union's foreign policy.

9   In general terms, there has been an overall extension of the scope of QMV and a huge expansion in co-decision that serves to reaffirm the double legitimacy of the Union via the Council (states) and the EP (citizens) and accordingly strengthens the roles of both the EP and the ECJ in the EU's affairs. However, unanimity is retained in the fields of taxation, although some inroads have been made in social policy and in common foreign and security policy, as well as in laws on 'own resources' and 'financial perspectives' and revisions of the Constitutional Treaty itself.

10   Overall, the Constitutional Treaty seeks to furnish the basis for a much greater democratic, accountable and transparent union of states and citizens. In furtherance of these goals it has introduced some novel procedures to bring EU institutions closer to the citizen: the right of citizens to invite the Commission to submit a proposal to the legislator if they can muster one million signatures in a significant number of member states, the proceedings

of the Council of Ministers, when exercising its legislative function, will be open to the public and national parliaments will be informed about all new Commission initiatives, with the proviso that if one-third of them consider that a proposal does not comply with the principle of subsidiarity, the Commission must review it. There are also new provisions on participatory democracy and good governance that promote public information, broad consultation and a regular dialogue with representative associations and civil society.

Even a cursory glance at these highlights of the Constitutional Treaty confirms institutional continuity as the departure point for this qualitative change in relations between member states and the Union. The EU is founded upon a fundamental recognition of the integrity of its component units, acknowledging the basic democratic duality of citizens and states, confirming a union citizenship that is additional to national citizenship and respecting Europe's cultural and linguistic diversity. Its official motto is clearly articulated in the phrase 'united in diversity'. It is, moreover, no accident that the ten features highlighted above incorporate in points six and ten familiar federal procedures and practices that are characteristic of established federations such as Australia, Belgium and Switzerland. These broad features, then, allow us to place the Constitutional Treaty in the category of a new federal model that builds largely upon what already exists.

The test of the Constitutional Treaty will be whether or not it can make the new enlarged Europe of 25 member states work effectively. Broadly speaking, its primary purpose is to redesign, clarify and simplify the process of European integration that has produced four main treaties – the SEA (1987), the TEU (1993), the AT (1999) and the NT (2002) – in the past twenty years. It can be seen therefore as an attempt to bring the EU closer to its 455 million citizens, partly by making it more democratic, accountable and transparent and partly by demonstrating its direct relevance to their immediate needs. It hardly needs to be added that the Constitutional Treaty is also symbolic of the new era of differentiated integration, of a Europe that is sufficiently flexible to accommodate the diverse requirements of what the *Financial Times* called 'a hybrid union of both states and peoples' and, more obscurely, a 'mix of states and peoples'.[44]

Conclusion: a new federal model

This chapter has demonstrated that both in its original conception and in its subsequent construction the EU has strong federal and confederal elements that coexist simultaneously with equally robust inter-governmental and supranational features. Each of these component parts of the European project were integral to the building of Europe throughout the past half century and have been the source of much theoretical dispute and disarray. If it is the purpose of theory to explain the world in which we live, it is clearly the case that the EU works in practice but not in theory. Today there is still no single, all-embracing omnibus theory of European integration that can explain the complex empirical reality that is the EU. It remains in many important respects an intellectual puzzle.

The main reason for this theoretical dilemma lies in two principal factors: first, the conceptual inadequacies of existing mainstream theories in IR and European integration, and, second, the novel manner in which the European project was originally conceived and constructed. As we have seen in Chapter 3, the origins and formation of most modern federations are typically the result of the combined historical processes of state-building and national integration. Their genesis and survival has been due to a series of complex circumstances that are characterised by a combination of common factors and historical specificity. But when we shift our attention from the world of intra-state relations – those matters that pertain to domestic politics *within* the state – to the inter-state world – those relations *between* states that we call IR – we confront the versatility of the federal idea and perforce we have to consider carefully how far its character and meaning can change from one context to another. A reconsideration of the federal idea in the world of IR necessarily brings us back to Patrick Riley's insistence that 'national federalism, in theory and practice, grew up out of international relations ideas and practices'. His position is worth more than a moment's reflection:

> It is essential, then, to study the development of national and international federal ideas together because national federalism is essentially an *internalization* of a form of external relations (a union of 'sovereign' states) while international federalism is essentially an *externalization* (world 'government') of a political form characteristic of the internal structure of a single state. Put another way, the development of federal ideas is the history of efforts to turn national government into international relations, and international relations into government. The characteristic ideas of national federalism – state sovereignty, the equality of states at the national level, rights of ratification, and (some would add) of secession – are really internalized international relations ideas; and the internalization of such ideas gives a peculiar instability to national federalism, insofar as international politics is less stable, less structured, less articulated than national politics.[45]

The problem that many scholars have with the EU, then, is that it exists in a kind of conceptual limbo between the two worlds described above by Riley. It appears to be neither fish nor fowl. In one particular sense – that of inter-state relations characterised by inter-governmentalism – the EU is clearly located in the world of IR that conventionally classifies it as a confederation while in another sense – that of supranationalism – the logic of European integration seems to portend the transcendence and transformation of the national state into a new, overarching, multinational federation. Here it would be a federation of existing, mainly mature, national states. Construed in this way, we can see that it is logically a new federal model, both in terms of its established component units and its unique combination of federal and confederal elements.

It is also novel, as we have seen, in its historical construction. Monnet's conception of Europe ensured that the question of a constitution for Europe was eschewed at the outset as redundant. It was never part of the official policy agenda of the EU member states simply because such a commitment was never required. The Schuman Declaration, we will recall, was silent about a European constitution. This was something that, if it occurred at all, would arrive in its own time as the logical result of a highly successful pioneering experiment in economic integration. Instead of beginning with a constitution for Europe, the inherent logic of 'Monnet's Method' suggested that it would be 'the culmination of an existing economic and political reality, already put to the test'.[46]

In phasing out the three pillars of the TEU that have served as rough boundary lines designating the competences of the Union and its constituent member states, the new Constitutional Treaty certainly clarifies what had grown into something of an institutional and policy thicket. It cannot be denied that one unwanted legacy of Monnet's Europe has been an evolving public perception of the EU as a cumbersome, often incompetent and insensitive, political contrivance. Public attitudes are therefore frequently characterised by confusion, controversy and misunderstanding. Consequently the constitutionalising of Europe's social, economic, political and legal reality is long overdue. It is time for the people(s) of Europe to make the EU a *constitutional* reality.

These considerations enable us to confirm that there is no need to decide whether or not the current Constitutional Treaty is either a treaty or a constitution. This is to pose the question in the wrong way. The effect is to simplify the answer by reducing it to two stark alternatives that cannot capture the complexity of what is going on in the EU. The question is frankly superfluous because the Constitutional Treaty is both of these things. We can conclude, then, that the current Constitutional Treaty is just that – a strange amalgamation of the formal language of treaty and the discourse of constitution. Consequently, if the EU remains something of an intellectual puzzle, we should hardly be surprised if the building of constitutional and political Europe generates yet another conceptual anomaly. Indeed, this odd appellation accurately captures the empirical reality of the EU and also reflects the conceptual enigma that is the EU.

The purpose of this chapter was to demonstrate that the EU is a new federal model in the world of states. We have shown that as a federal union of states and citizens it stands conceptually in a long line of descent stretching back at least to the 1781 Articles of Confederation in the USA, but we have also suggested that it is the harbinger of a distinctly new category of confederal-type unions.[47] In the course of this analysis the federal idea has navigated from the realm of domestic intra-state politics to the world of inter-state relations, underlining its versatility according to both context and the point of departure. It is now time to journey much further upstream by entering the world of globalisation and global governance with which some commentators might already associate the EU.

Part III
Lessons of experience

10 Federalism, democracy and the state in the era of globalisation

Introduction

The previous chapter examined the federal heritage of the EU and underlined the enduring federal and confederal features that continue to characterise it as a new federal model. We were also able to demonstrate the versatility of the federal idea as it moved from the realm of intrastate politics to the world of inter-state relations. Clearly meaning derives from context and in this chapter we turn our attention from the EU to a different, although intimately related, context. This is the relatively uncharted area of scholarly investigation that seeks to define the nature of the relationship between federalism and globalisation.

When thinking about the nature of this relationship we are compelled once again to draw together the conceptual and the empirical worlds of political science. Federalism in the context of globalisation engages a new conceptual challenge that requires a good deal of both intellectual enquiry and political imagination. Moving from the study of government and politics within the state to analyses of the relations between states has become something of an academic pastime for many political scientists, but the elevation of federal studies to the heady stratosphere of globalisation and its logical corollary, global governance, while enterprising, is nevertheless both daunting and speculative. It is a formidable conceptual and empirical challenge because it takes federalism into another research area that is already characterised by both academic and public controversy and confusion. While intriguing and fashionable, studies of globalisation are still surrounded by many conceptual and analytical imponderables that continue to give it a certain aura of the unknown and imprecise. There is, as yet, no established academic consensus about precisely what the term 'globalisation' means, let alone what are its socio-economic and political implications. Many rival perspectives are attached to the term and many different approaches have been used to try to understand and explain it.

In this chapter we will attempt to navigate a course through these uncertainties by linking federalism with the development of liberal democratic capitalism and the role of the modern state in the era of globalisation. As we shall see, part of this journey will take us into areas that encounter key elements of modern democratic theory while other parts will bring us back to the EU as a convenient and topical case study. We will begin, however, with the nature and meaning of globalisation.

Globalisation and global governance

In early December 1999 the projected World Trade Organisation (WTO) talks in Seattle, Washington, which had been organised to launch a trade liberalisation round for the new millennium, suffered a humiliating collapse. The world watched as thousands of people, many in organised groups that included workers, trade unionist activists, farmers representing small and medium-sized farms, environmentalists, students, and church and human rights groups, took to the streets to demonstrate and protest against what they perceived as more than just a growing uncertainty about global trade. The calamity in Seattle represented something much larger and much more disturbing to these people. The WTO talks served to distil and crystallise an emergent, if embryonic, international movement that mobilised both for and against an array of public issues that could easily be subsumed within the elastic term 'globalisation'.

In a nutshell the debacle in Seattle appears to have been a powerful symbolic backlash against globalisation. A general consensus seems to have developed among interested observers and commentators that the self-styled, progressive, international alliance that triumphed in Seattle was broadly representative of the interests and concerns of environmentalists, consumers, labour, agriculture, human rights and developing countries. And what the protestors shared was a dislike of the global market economy along with the creation and consolidation of potent, effective international institutions. These people were categorised, in short, as 'anti-globalisation' groups, and they were portrayed in the media as symptomatic of a largely 'anti-capitalist' international political movement that was vehemently opposed to the corporate domination of government and utterly disillusioned with the established political process. In hindsight this image seems to have been confirmed when Seattle was followed in the ensuing two years by similar orchestrated protests and demonstrations in a string of major cities across the world: Melbourne, Prague, Seoul, Barcelona, Nice, Washington DC, Genoa, Gothenburg and Quebec City.

From our vantage point five years later, it is now clear that we were witnessing the birth of an articulate, organised, international political movement that was able effectively to use the instruments of global technology in its crusade against corporate capitalism. But what are its political implications and what is its overall political significance? In his last 'State of the Union' address delivered in January 2000 in the Capitol Building in Washington DC, President Bill Clinton referred optimistically to 'the revolution that is tearing down barriers and building new networks among nations and individuals, and economies and cultures'. Globalisation was 'the central reality of our time', but it was about more than just economics; it was also about 'freedom and democracy and peace'.[1]

In this chapter we will address the relationship between three fundamental political concepts and Bill Clinton's 'central reality of our time'. Specifically, we will explore the complex relationship between federalism, democracy and the state in what I have called the 'era of globalisation'. So what do we mean by 'globalisation' and what are its far-reaching implications? In 1970 Ivo Duchacek referred to federalism in the following way:

> Federalism has now become one of those good echo words that evoke a positive response but that may mean all things to all men, like democracy, socialism, progress, constitution, justice or peace.[2]

Today this observation might appropriately be applied to the term 'globalisation' with the added caveat that it has become for many of its critics and adversaries, at least in Seattle, a bad echo word that evokes a negative response but may still mean all things to all men and women.

Among scholars of globalisation, two broad schools of thought can be identified. The first, reflected here in the writing of Herbert Schwartz, claims that globalisation understood as 'the increasing importance of global market pressures on daily life' is nothing new and has little effect upon local constellations of power and authority represented by states, while the second school of thought construes globalisation as 'an intrinsically new, irresistible force that will change all societies in a uniform way'.[3] The intellectual debate seems increasingly to have polarised between these two stark alternatives. Schwartz, however, warned us against the broad-brush oversimplifications that this polarised debate has engendered. It is the result of globalisation having become something of a 'buzzword'.[4] As is usual in these sorts of debates, the reality is much more complex and it hinges upon how the term is defined. Schwartz locates his definition of globalisation in the dynamic relations – a symbiosis – between states and markets and defines globalisation quite simply as linking 'the production of goods and services to markets for those goods, and to conflicts between states trying to create, enhance or subdue those markets'. Consequently, globalisation is 'nothing more than the re-emergence of markets that states temporarily suppressed in the aftermath of the Great Depression and World War II'.[5] In other words, it is nothing more than a return to the conditions that existed before the First World War. The world economy has simply recovered some of its earlier freedom. Accordingly, what needs to be explained is not so much the resurgence of contemporaneous global market pressures and patterns which, after all, existed before the Second World War, but the capacity of states to regulate their economies and subdue these markets in the forty-year interregnum after 1945.

It is clear, then, that the polar extremities of this debate are shaped and determined ultimately by the different ways of understanding and defining globalisation. Craig Murphy, in seeking to place the current era of globalisation in its historical context, has acknowledged that Europe, for example, is still in a position to exert significant 'adaptive pressure' on the rest of the world but can do so only 'within limits imposed by the historical trajectory of capitalist industrial society'.[6] In other words, a kind of path dependency exists which, while not deterministic, nonetheless enables the scholar to investigate earlier economic transactions or evidence of 'past moments' of globalisation. These investigations of earlier transactions from one industrial era to the next can, it is claimed, tell us 'something about the prospects for the current age'.[7]

The view that historical perspectives of globalisation can help us to understand the modalities of the contemporary era is endorsed by David Held. He has claimed that it is possible to distinguish different historical forms of globalisation in terms of: (1) the extensiveness of networks of relations and connections, (2) the intensity of flows and levels of activity within these networks, and (3) the impact of these phenomena on particular bounded communities. He summarised this aspect of the debate with both brevity and clarity:

> It is not a case of saying, as many do, that there was once no globalization, but there is now; rather, it is a case of recognizing that forms of globalization have changed over time and that these can be systematically understood by reference to points 1–3 above.[8]

The gist of Held's argument, then, is that globalisation must be construed as a relative not an absolute concept. Its meaning has changed over time so that its historical significance has varied considerably. Put another way, globalisation – its impact and the different ways that it has been perceived and understood – is rooted in an historical relativism. Its impact and meaning have been many-sided through both space and time.

Held's own definition of globalisation enables him successfully to accommodate historical context without sitting on the conceptual fence. He defines it as 'a set of processes which shift the spatial form of human organization and activity to transcontinental or interregional patterns of activity, interaction and the exercise of power'. But this involves 'a stretching and deepening of social relations and institutions across space and time' such that, as Anthony Giddens has put it, 'on the one hand, day-to-day activities are increasingly influenced by events happening on the other side of the globe and, on the other, the practices and decisions of local groups and communities can have significant global reverberations'.[9]

If we briefly summarise this section of the chapter, it is obvious that the meaning of globalisation varies according to different socio-economic, political and historical contexts. As Douglas Kellner has so aptly remarked: 'the conceptions of globalization deployed, the purposes for which the concept is used and the evaluations of the processes described by the concept vary wildly'. It remains a highly contested and contestable term. But it is used by journalists, academics, politicians, military elites and business executives to signify that something profound is happening, that the world is changing, 'that a new world economic, political and cultural order is emerging'.[10] There seems, then, to be a popular awareness of change; people clearly have a heightened sense of the 'immediacy' of change, that they are touched by forces and pressures that are simultaneously remote and close.

With these thoughts in mind it would seem that the key to understanding globalisation is to start with the assumption that it is essentially a multidimensional phenomenon. Indeed, Held has asserted this boldly:

> Globalization is neither a singular condition nor a linear process. Rather, it is best thought of as a multidimensional phenomenon involving domains of activity and interaction that include the economic, political, technological, military, legal, cultural and environmental. Each of these spheres involves different patterns of relations and activities.[11]

There is much common sense in this position. Globalisation is 'a complex and multidimensional phenomenon that involves different levels, flows, tensions and conflicts'. And Kellner is right when he emphasises that in a sense 'there is no such thing as globalization *per se*'. Instead 'the term is used as a cover concept for a heterogeneity of processes that need to be spelled out and articulated'.[12]

What, then, are these processes – these activities and relations – to which scholars of globalisation regularly refer? Judging by what appears broadly in the mainstream literature on globalisation, the most frequent references are to financial (capital) markets, information technology (IT), international trade and investment, and environmental issues and policy. In this world of global linkages states, governments and political systems have had to adjust and adapt to the presence of new actors engaged in worldwide activities with connections that form part of a complex bargaining process for resources wherein firms can provide them with instant access to capital and technology. And these circumstances immediately bring us into direct contact with the structure of the international political economy (IPE). In this fiercely competitive world we can see why Susan Strange should have referred to 'structural power' as the most important form of power in contemporary international relations. She claimed that structural power gave states the capacity to choose and to shape the IPE within which other states and their economic and political organisations and institutions were compelled to operate.[13] The implication of this analysis at least acknowledged that states still had a role to play in the globalisation game and that they had not, as some have argued, been superseded by new forms of capital, technology and production. Instead the evolutionary structural change in the IPE has been responsible for altering the notion of the state so that it is the character of the state and of the state system that has changed.

Before we shift our attention to the concept of 'governance' and subsequently to the disputed implications of globalisation, let us pause to reflect upon what all of this means. We have already seen that globalisation, like federalism, can be described positively and negatively depending upon subjective values, beliefs and interests. What sort of concept or phenomenon is it then? And what words do we usually associate with it? The terminology is important because it conveys the particular sense in which it is generally understood. Terms such as 'linkages', 'connections', 'interconnectedness', 'interdependence', and words such as 'permeation', 'interpenetration', and 'porousness' furnish the sense of a global network of multifarious, multilevel activities that exist independent of government, the state and the political system. Indeed, they seem powerless either to control or even exert significant influence upon them. And in turn citizens and mass publics appear increasingly distanced from and marginalised by the growing intensification of global forces.

Today the thinking citizen perceives a complex world of global/international organisations – the UN, the G7, the International Monetary Fund (IMF), the WTO and the World Bank – giant multinational corporations (MNCs), transnational social movements (for example, Greenpeace), international NGOs (such as Amnesty International), regional unions of states (the EU, the North American Free Trade Association (NAFTA) and the South American MERCOSUR (Mercado Comun del Sur or Common Market of the South)), international defence organisations like NATO, together with international arms manufacturers and international terrorists and drugs traffickers. It is a world in which the tentacles of international and global activities increasingly intervene and impinge upon the domestic politics of what they still construe as independent sovereign states. But what has been the nature of their impact upon states and citizens? More precisely what has been their impact upon liberal democracy and the much-vaunted nation-state? We will turn to address these questions in the next section, but before we do so let us first consider briefly the concept of governance.

Following the initiative of Willy Brandt immediately after the collapse of the Berlin Wall in 1989, Ingvar Carlsson and Sridath Ramphal were invited to co-chair the Commission on Global Governance – a group of twenty-eight state leaders – to suggest ways in which the global community 'could better manage its affairs in a new time in human history'. The Commission published its report in 1995 entitled *Our Global Neighbourhood* and since then there has been a huge outpouring of literature on global governance, both in theory and practice.[14] There seems to be a relatively recent consensus of opinion that the term 'governance' first emerged during the late 1980s in connection with the World Bank's description of public affairs on the African continent in general as a 'crisis in governance'. Since then the term has been 'widely, if not exclusively, associated with the politics of development and in particular with development in the post-colonial world'.[15] Clearly, we must make a distinction between the word and the concept. The word 'governance' has been used 'routinely over the course of many centuries to refer to the exercise of authority within a given sphere' and has been applied to 'many situations in which no formal political system can be found'.[16] Indeed, it has often been equated simply with 'governability' within individual states. But usage notwithstanding, it still implies the existence of a political process:

> 'governance' involves building consensus, or obtaining the consent or acquiescence necessary to carry out a programme, in an arena where many different interests are in play. ... The wide applicability of the term, its reference to basic problems of political order (including efficiency and

legitimacy), and its lack of any necessary relation to the state have made it useful to a growing number of participants in the development debate in the course of the last decade. ... Considering problems of 'governance' is relevant in strengthening civic cultures, promoting voluntary action and thus improving the societal bases for democracy. It is also increasingly important in considering how the international community can construct the institutions required to promote order and justice in the context of globalization.[17]

There is no doubt, then, that governance has been a convenient word or label used to convey the sense of political process – of decision-making activity and policy input, throughput and output – in areas in which the state either does not or cannot play a leading role, whether it be at a local or a supranational level. But the word has now given way to the concept and the concept of governance suggests something much more significant. Today it implies 'a new way of characterizing international relations that would involve not only states but also non-statal and avowedly non-political bodies'.[18] However, this characterisation does not appear to be rooted in values that are culturally neutral. In other words, 'governance' is being used by 'groups of very different ideological persuasion, for a number of different and often contradictory ends'.[19] Governance, in the words of Anthony Pagden, can best be understood as 'a bid to create a new rhetoric of international and interpersonal social and political relations, which now include a wide range of variables', but lead inexorably to only 'one social and political form of association', namely, 'liberal – or neo-liberal – democracy'.[20] Let us look at the ideological basis to global governance in particular and the disputed implications of globalisation in general.

Between integration and fragmentation

It is well known that the twin processes of state-building and national integration in Europe during the sixteenth and seventeenth centuries deposited a veritable mosaic of so-called 'nation-states' in the late eighteenth and nineteenth centuries wherein the conditions of state-building did not coincide with those of nation-building. In other words, there never was such a thing as a nation state. All states typically contained many nations, minority cultural communities or distinct identities, and not every self-conscious nation had its own state. This is why Anthony Smith's preference for the term 'national state' – the state that has been nationalised – makes more sense than the fallacy of the nation-state.[21]

The consolidation of the national state since the French Revolution in 1789 also meant that 'modern democratic theory and practice was constructed upon Westphalian foundations'.[22] The gradual emergence of liberal democracy in the late eighteenth and nineteenth centuries was therefore predicated upon the concept and reality of the national state. Slowly all of the familiar features of latter-day liberal democracy were grafted onto the sovereign national state, yielding representative and responsible government based upon popular consent, the rule of law, the constitution, the legitimacy of peaceful opposition, public accountability and a set of procedures and institutions designed to guarantee citizens' rights and provide a series of checks and balances against the threat of tyranny. And as Held has remarked, the cornerstone of modern democratic thought hinged upon liberalism, democracy and the national state:

> The vast majority of the theories of democracy, liberal and radical, assumed that the nature and possibilities of political community could be elaborated by reference to national structures and national possibilities, and that freedom, political equality and solidarity could be entrenched in and through the nation state. ... In the contemporary era the key principles and practices of liberal democracy are associated almost exclusively with the principles and institutions of the sovereign nation state.[23]

In this way democracy became 'liberal democracy' and the state became the 'national state', each wedded to the other. The issue that we must confront, then, is how to define the relationship between liberal democracy, the national state and globalisation. More specifically, we must examine the political implications of globalisation, and it is to this that we now turn.

Let us deal first with the conventional observation that is usually made concerning the political impact of globalisation. One notable contributor to this debate, Manuel Castells, has claimed that from the 1970s two fundamental transformations have taken place, one in the technology of information trans-missions and the other in the organisation of business and the global economy. These two processes have resulted in what amounts to a reconstruction of space: the nature of space, place and distance has been radically altered. Castells' belief is that a technological revolution – tantamount to a new technological paradigm – of historic proportions is transforming the basic dimensions of human life, namely, time and place.[24] Put briefly, this suggests that these two facets of global-isation – both a feature of the contemporary restructuring of the capitalist mode of production – are in essence a contradictory set of processes that are respon-sible for a double movement of integration and fragmentation. This means that the national state has been subjected to global forces and pressures that have propelled it in the direction of regional integration and cooperation, as exempli-fied by the EU and NAFTA, in the world of states while simultaneously generating new feelings of solidarity, new political linkages and new forms of political behaviour among its own citizens within the state. There has been therefore a notable propensity for states to come together to form new unions and to forge new economic and political arrangements at the same time as they have been confronted with new challenges from within by disgruntled social, economic and cultural groups and communities unhappy with their status and welfare. Let us consider briefly why this has occurred.

If we take as our principal case study the EU and some of its 25 constituent member states, we can examine briefly how this relationship between integration and fragmentation operates in practice. It is generally accepted that European integration is driven by conceptions of the national interest and that in pursuit of this the member states have pooled their power resources and decision-making capacities, which in consequence have been channelled and canalised upwards to Brussels. Member-state governments have acknowledged that by themselves they are no longer capable of national self-determination in an increasingly hostile and competitive world. Indeed, membership of the EU is construed by many precisely as a means of regaining their lost or declining state capacity. Consequently, statist terms such as 'sovereignty' and 'independence' can have no real meaning in a world in which the vast majority of national states simply do not have the economic and political resources to compete not only with other states but also with MNCs and the mobility of finance capital. They have not become mere ciphers in the era of globalisation, but they certainly cannot afford to ignore the harsh realities of another new age. In these ferociously competitive circumstances the best way to describe the position in which the national state finds itself is that of, at best, a 'relative autonomy' rather than a fictitious independence.

Power in this particular sense, then, has drifted upwards to Brussels. And an institutional structure has been created by member states in the EU the like of which has never before been seen, an institution that has generated much frustration and anxiety among the member-state governments and mass publics as well as remarkably innovative and progressive policy initiatives and departures. Looking back over the past half-century, the achievements of western European economic and political integration – of the European project – have been quite astonishing.

Indeed, it is a measure of its great success that it has been taken for granted by so many of its member states, governments and mass publics that another ten states have just become new members and that several other national states continue to form a queue to join this unique regional international organisation which we have construed here as a new federal model. This, then, is one side of the coin.

The other side of the coin represents the political implications of these developments, which have actually intensified since the Single European Act (SEA) was ratified in 1987. The jewel in the crown of the SEA was the Single European Market (SEM), which signalled the formal commitment of Europe's then 12 states to a comprehensive market model and strategy that would foster increased trade and capital flows, linked later in 1992 to an equally formal commitment to Economic and Monetary Union (EMU) in the Treaty on European Union (TEU) agreed at Maastricht. Both the SEM and EMU projects served to symbolise that fact that member-state governments' capacities to shape economic and monetary decisions had been seriously enfeebled. And as certain power resources and decision-making capacities have been gradually moving upwards to Brussels, the impact of this process has in a sense marginalised and marooned mass publics and the political institutions that represent them at the national level. They are further away from the sites where decisions that affect them directly are made. Small wonder that their self-perception is one of voices from the periphery. But this, it must be admitted, is also a perception of reality that needs to be carefully considered. After all, the sense that liberal democratic values, beliefs and institutional practices are being violated can be and often is exaggerated. It is a view that is predicated upon the assumption that conventions and practices such as parliamentary scrutiny, public accountability and transparency in decision-making already exist and are effective in the member states themselves, an assumption that might be construed as wildly optimistic in most of them. There is, then, an element of mild hypocrisy based upon double standards among such critics of the EU. They often apply standards of judgment to the EU that are much more stringent than those they apply to the liberal democratic member states that they themselves inhabit.

But the political impact of European integration does not end here. It is not just the national state – as a state – that has had to adapt and adjust to EU membership. It has become a veritable truism today to point out that integration also has an inherently political backlash against what are construed as the inexorable universalising forces of a dull, drab uniformity. The backlash, which can take many different forms and can be both violent and non-violent, has usually been triggered by a combination of factors that are perceived as being real: a recognised cultural identity is being suffocated; an established economic interest is being undermined; a distinct minority's rights are being transgressed; and a whole region's political status is simply being ignored. In the EU, particular steps have already been taken to try to accommodate this so-called 'political fragmentation' epitomised in the ubiquity of new social movements, the mobilisation of self-conscious regions, the assertion and reassertion of sub-state national identities and the assorted intra-state claims for social cohesion and structural funds to alleviate structural unemployment poverty. Nonetheless, it is within the states themselves rather than the EU that fragmentation has been most challenging. A large body of scholarly literature now exists that has chronicled the so-called threat to the national state from within as well as from without. Clearly the EU itself provides a convenient platform for these challenges to be played out but integral to the survival of the state is its capacity effectively to devolve power and decentralise decision-making down to lower levels of authority that can more directly engage these new challenges.

As this brief sketch outline demonstrates, there is manifestly a double movement of 'governance' both upwards beyond the national state and simultaneously downwards within the state that reflects the impact of new, largely economic, global forces. In reality it is of course a double movement of governance and government. But this movement can be portrayed as essentially contradictory only if these complex processes are viewed from a particular standpoint. In practice they are also complementary; they are two sides of the same coin, often giving the impression that the state is being squeezed to the point where its very *raison d'être* is brought into question. This is a mistaken impression. What it actually implies is that the state's position in world affairs and its relationship to its own citizens have both changed in a fundamental way rather than the somewhat facile but frequently voiced conclusion that it is now completely redundant and has already been supplanted.

Integration and fragmentation are therefore linked in an extremely complex way. But their relationship suggests that states are having to adjust and adapt imaginatively in order to create new constitutional and political spaces that will enable them successfully to reconcile the contemporary forces of global competitiveness (or economic prosperity) with the concomitant need for social solidarity (or social justice). We will return to the EU later in the chapter, but for now we will bring this section to a close by considering briefly the relationship between European integration and globalisation. It is vital that we do not assume, as many commentators do, that they are connected in a simple, almost causal, fashion.

Is European integration a response to globalisation? It is a seductive question that requires a carefully considered answer rather than an unthinking knee-jerk reply. The post-war origins of European integration can be traced back to a mixture of motives, not least the recovery and rehabilitation of the industrial economies of western European national states in a Cold War setting. It would seem, then, that the link between European integration and globalisation will be determined once again according to how the latter is defined. Certainly the integration of industries and legislative decision-making processes via the voluntary transfer of national sovereignty to supranational authorities meant that the evolving European project embraced many of the facets of globalisation, but member-state governments were hardly in a hurry to forfeit sovereignty in order to welcome global market principles. The economic integration of Europe was essentially a piecemeal, incremental affair that led ultimately to market deregulation, a single currency and the abolition of capital controls. In the early post-war years, regional integration was viewed as the best way in which to meet the challenge of both international and inter-European competition. In this sense, European integration can be seen as both creating the economic and political conditions to take advantage of global markets while simultaneously furnishing the basis for protection against their negative effects.

Since globalisation brings both benefits and costs that affect governments, citizens, businesses, workers, cultures and minorities in different ways at different times in different contexts, the global marketplace must be seen as essentially Janus-faced: it provides both opportunities and threats for domestic markets. George Ross has toyed with this question and boldly claimed that 'the origins of European integration may best be seen in the light of globalizing tendencies at work at the time, even if the word was not used at the time'.[25] This is a good example of just how elastic the meaning and interpretation of the term 'globalisation' can be. And the substitution of 'globalizing tendencies' for 'globalisation' invites suspicion of a good deal of conceptual stretching. But this also brings us back to a conspicuous conundrum: scholars have simply failed to agree upon a precise definition of globalisation and its implications also remain disputed.

Nonetheless the historical relativism claimed by Ross clearly chimes positively with Held's position outlined above: forms of globalisation have changed over time. Anthony Giddens, however, is probably on safer ground with his view that 'The EU began life essentially as a Cold War project, but it has to be seen today as a pioneering response to globalization'.[26] On this reckoning, then, the EU – as the current institutional and policy manifestation of European integration – must be construed, at least in part, as a regional reaction and response by the national state in Europe to essentially global pressures. However, the mode of thinking about the relationship is certainly not made any easier when others claim that 'European integration is difficult to distinguish from globalisation'.[27] A more convincing answer to the question posed might be that both European integration and globalisation – as processes – are moving targets: both have changed in meaning, theory and practice since 1945. During the early post-war years, European integration could be explained by a combination of internal factors specific to each participating state and external considerations located at both intra-and extra-European or international levels. From around the mid-1970s, however, its resilience and survival cannot be explained without reference to global factors and circumstances that simply did not exist during earlier decades.

This section has looked briefly at the relationship between liberal democracy, the national state, European integration and globalisation. It has utilised the twin concepts of integration and fragmentation to furnish an insight into the political implications of globalisation in Europe and also elsewhere that constitute such a huge, all-embracing challenge for the national state. Our concise discussion shows that everywhere the national state has begun to experience new economic, political, technological and environmental pressures, both qualitative and quantitative, that are unprecedented in their scope and intensity. It suggests that the single focus for citizens' loyalties and identities which the national state model has actively promoted with such great success until today has gradually been corroded and undermined but has not been replaced by any viable alternative focus for the forging of new identities and loyalties. In Europe the EU is actively seeking to develop a 'European identity', but one that is designed to sit alongside rather than replace the national state.

Meanwhile, on the other side of the Atlantic, relations between the states of North, Central and South America have recently moved in a direction that raises new questions about the response of the Americas to both globalisation and the obvious success of the European project. In April 2001 President George W. Bush led the United States and 33 leaders from the American hemisphere to sign up to the creation of the world's largest free trade zone, namely, the Free Trade Area of the Americas (FTAA), projected to come into existence in 2005. The Summit of the Americas that met in Quebec City constituted the new political impetus for the re-launching of the seven-year-old plan to create the FTAA, originally sponsored by President Bush's father, and reflected both American and Canadian determination to underpin stability, security and liberal democracy and human rights in Latin America. For the Americans, however, it also had the merit of meshing with broader US foreign policy interests and provided a new forum or framework within which 'to pursue its long-standing quest for stability in its own backyard and to deal with problems such as the Colombian drugs trade'.[28] There are, then, both economic and political motives for the FTAA. But if it is true that a successful FTAA will strengthen Latin American economies by unleashing a wave of export-led growth and capital inflows into countries desperate for foreign investment, technology and management skills, the real significance of this contemporaneous event, above and beyond the national interests of the USA, remains highly questionable.

Certainly the approval of the free trade accord and the idea of extending and intensifying hemispheric integration and cooperation in the Americas signify an interesting new dimension to the regrouping of established regional organisations such as NAFTA and MERCOSUR, but it does not have the socio-economic and political-constitutional significance that inheres in the EU model as a new federal model. Enlargement of the EU in 2004, like the recent consolidation of the FTAA, will serve to widen an already diverse array of interests with an even wider range of viewpoints, but the level of institutionalisation in the former is much more developed and sophisticated than the latter is ever likely to be. Moreover, the recent trade agreement between the region's two customs unions, MERCOSUR and the Andean Community, adds a new twist to this formative relationship. The economic *rapprochement* signalled the future creation of the South American Community of Nations (SACN) designed to foster political, economic and infrastructural integration, but if it serves to buttress the bloc's bargaining position in trade negotiations with developed countries (including the USA) its prospects for the future must remain unclear. What these two contemporaneous developments on opposite sides of the world have in common is a response to globalisation: in promoting economic prosperity and security by tearing down barriers to trade and competition, both levels of institutionalisation create at least the potential for the national state to adapt and adjust to the new world of global linkages, especially in trade, IT and finance capital.

Whether or not this represents 'deepening integration in the Americas' or just the plain old pursuit of USA superpower interests depends upon the standpoint of the observer and what particular interests are at stake. Currently, in the early years of the new millennium, it is much too early to make serious, detailed assessments of the centennial prospects of either the European or the Americas projects. However, both of them raise questions about precisely how such political organisations as international actors can develop new forms of democratic decision-making processes. Indeed, the democratic problems associated with the emergence of an EU that is 'neo-confederal' – a unique mixture of both federal and confederal elements – are among the most daunting that confront the advocates of wider and deeper European economic and political integration. With these thoughts in mind, it is appropriate for us to examine the relevance of federalism and confederalism in the specific context of globalisation.

Federalism, confederalism and federation

It is precisely at the point where Held considers the need to rethink democracy in the context of globalisation that he makes the following statement:

As fundamental processes of governance escape the categories of the nation state, the traditional national resolutions of the key questions of democratic theory and practice are open to doubt. ... We are compelled to recognise that we live in a complex interconnected world where the extent, intensity, and impact of issues (economic, political or environmental) raise questions about where those issues are most appropriately addressed.[29]

There is a good deal of common sense to this way of thinking which leads Held down the path to what he calls the 'cosmopolitan model of democracy'. This model, first introduced in the early 1990s, is worth more than a moment's reflection here.[30] Held draws attention to the sobering fact that if the reality of global forces, pressures and structures is not acknowledged and integrated into both national and international political processes, 'they will tend to bypass or circumvent the democratic state system'.[31] Consequently a 'democratic public law' needs to be established, incorporating 'a cluster of rights and obligations' that will form the basis of 'a common structure of political action' designed to link 'the ideas of democracy and of the modern state'. For Held 'democratic law' must be internationalised so that what he calls 'a cosmopolitan democratic law' and the establishment of 'a community of all democratic communities' will effectively re-conceptualise sovereignty by articulating and relocating national states within 'an overarching democratic law' that will be just one focus for 'legal development, political reflection and mobilization'. Sovereignty would then be 'stripped away from the idea of fixed borders and territories' and become instead an attribute of 'the democratic law'. Cosmopolitan law therefore would demand 'the subordination of regional, national and local sovereignties to an overarching legal framework, but in this framework these associations would be self-governing at different levels'.[32] Held's vision of the global future, in summary, seems logical:

> A new possibility is anticipated: the recovery of an intensive and more participatory democracy at local levels as a complement to the public assemblies of the wider global order; that is, a political order of democratic associations, cities and nations as well as of regions and global networks. ... It is a legal basis of a global and divided authority system, a system of diverse and overlapping power centres, shaped and delimited by democratic law.[33]

What are we to make of this bold, imaginative proposal? Can Held's ideas be translated into practical action? We cannot present a detailed critique of his 'transformation of political community' here, but it is nonetheless important to underline just how reminiscent it is of both federalism and confederalism.

Federalism and confederalism are terms that we can use here to refer to the variety of forces and pressures that mobilise specific interests, values and beliefs in support of particular forms of association. In some cases these forces and pressures lead to a fundamental transformation of the national state so that a new federation is created as, for example, in the case of Belgium in 1993. Or it may be that these factors combine, as in Spain, to produce a different kind of state reformation, namely, a 'State of the Autonomies' that sustains federal values without resorting to formal federation as conventionally defined in this book. Federalism, we are reminded, is a multidimensional phenomenon that reveres and celebrates the preservation of difference and diversity and seeks in federation the constitutional and institutional practices that protect, promote and preserve the assortment of interests, identities and beliefs that naturally inhere in all societies. But in many national states federal values and practices exist without evidence of a formal written federal constitution. The point is that the federal–confederal formula is extremely versatile and can create the political spaces deemed necessary, indeed vital, to engage the impact of globalisation. It can be adapted and adjusted to suit a variety of different circumstances. And this includes the movement of power resources and decision-making capacities upwards as well as downwards. Accordingly, in the international arena where there may be pressures to create new forms of association between states, without wishing to cross the threshold into a new federal statehood, the confederal possibilities are infinite. Held's analysis of the new global context that all states are now compelled to confront simply underlines the fact that contemporary realities have created novel opportunities for neo-confederal or confederal-type unions that can be shaped and moulded to respond effectively to this challenge. The EU, MERCOSUR, NAFTA, FTAA and the emergent SACN are each illustrative of the different kinds and levels of institutionalisation that have evolved recently in international relations.

It is important, as we have already noted, to emphasise that the EU – as a neo-confederal union – may in some respects have only a patchy relationship to contemporary globalisation. This means that it is inescapably enmeshed in the heterogeneity of global processes, such as trade and investment, finance capital and environmental policy, but not necessarily in all of them nor, indeed, with the same levels of intensity. Consequently, while the SEM and EMU might indicate a firm relationship between European integration and globalisation, the same cannot be said of the EU's embryonic information and telecommunications policy and its media and culture programmes that currently have only a tangential relationship to global forces. The francophone reality in the EU, for example, has so far resisted the dominant anglophone pressures of linguistic uniformity in these policy arenas. As a result, it is easy to oversimplify the EU's relationship to globalisation, which is part cause and part effect of European integration.

This suggests that global pressures, even if they seem both ubiquitous and uniform, have different effects upon different states and, in turn, upon different communities within those states. The reality of globalisation will mean different things to different groups and communities simply because they will experience it in different ways. Some local businesses will face enormous convulsions in their traditional economic activities while others will continue to trade, seemingly unaffected, in their domestic markets. There is no uniform impact nor is there a uniform response. It is precisely in these complex circumstances, where the implications of globalisation are so diffuse and unpredictable, that both federal and confederal responses can furnish connecting links to what has been called 'glocalisation'. If they have any significance in this putative new world it will lie in their capacity creatively to combine both the local and the global spheres of human agency.

If we return to Held's projected world of cosmopolitan governance and law, we will recall that it is a distinctively new polity that 'in form and substance' would reflect and embrace 'the diverse forms of power and authority that operate within and across borders'. In essence, it would be 'a transnational, common structure of political action'.[34] But when he refers to 'diverse self-regulating realms, from regions and states to cities and local associations' and the self-governing capacity of associations 'at different levels', this is a language and discourse that comes very close to the European tradition of federalism that we surveyed in Chapter 6. The strong Althusian overtones of self-governing regions, cities and local associations smack very much of a federal imprint. Indeed, Held himself acknowledged his own references to 'the federal model' in his earlier work but confessed in almost furtive manner in a footnote that he substituted the term 'cosmopolitan' for the 'federal' concept because the latter word was too controversial in the specific context of the debate about European integration. In hindsight, he seems to have found the terminology of federalism distinctly 'unhelpful in conveying his intentions', but he seems, nonetheless, to have located his cosmopolitan democratic order as somewhere between federalism and confederalism.[35] Could Held's 'political order of democratic associations, cities and nations as well as of regions and global networks', then, be something that might resemble a new form of federal order or confederal governance? It is at least theoretically conceivable. If we are compelled to rethink our basic conceptual categories to try to engage and encapsulate the new global realities identified earlier in this chapter, it is eminently reasonable to contemplate new unions of states and citizens as unique forms of global association.

In the event that sceptics might regard some of these remarks as either too fanciful or far-fetched, it is instructive to note that the EU remains a repository of innovative ideas and experiments. In December 1999, in the wake of the calamity in Seattle, Pascal Lamy, the EU's Commissioner for Trade, urged the international community to give priority to WTO reform that would improve its efficiency, transparency and accountability. But he also renewed his call for the serious consideration of a WTO parliament – originally proposed by some elected representatives of the EU's European Parliament (EP) – together with better coordination between the WTO and the global financial institutions. One option was to create a global 'economic security council', an idea originally floated by Jacques Delors, a former President of the European Commission (1985–95) and Lamy's former boss.[36] This is a good example of how the global backlash in Seattle has sparked a new bout of imaginative thinking about the international response to the global disorder. We should also mention in this context the simmering debate about the eponymous Tobin tax, a proposal to introduce the first-ever global tax on currency transactions in order to reduce the instability and volatility of international financial markets.[37] This idea, which has been taken very seriously by the governments of Finland and Canada and by the EP in the EU, could involve either the IMF or the World Bank, as well as a reformed UN, to manage the revenues and subsequent expenditures, but it has also been linked to a new supranational organisation independent of the existing organisational structure of international relations. Heikki Patomaki's recent work, *Democratising Globalisation: The Leverage of the Tobin Tax*, is another shining example of the innovative possibilities of global governance that compel us to return to some deep-rooted assumptions about traditional democratic theory.[38] His challenge to democratic theorists is to ask precisely how democratic ideals in the world of globalised power and dependency relations could be worked out. He is right: in raising questions about the nature of consent and legitimacy, the nature of a constituency, the meaning of representation, and the proper form and scope of political participation, we go to the very heart of democratic theory.[39] These sorts of practical proposals, then, serve to vindicate the main thrust of Held's proposal for a new political order and they also reinforce the argument advanced in this chapter for the utilisation of federal and confederal elements in a future global (liberal) democracy.

Conclusion: confederal governance

This chapter has provided a sketch outline of some of the main issues and relationships that continue to characterise the era of globalisation. Its principal focus has been conceptual clarity, the nature of linkages and relationships and the analysis of explanation. We have seen that globalisation is a multidimensional phenomenon that incorporates a huge heterogeneity of processes rather than a singular set of homogenous processes. It is also a portmanteau term that has two seemingly contradictory implications, namely, integration and fragmentation. But these two processes are in reality two sides of the same coin and are best understood as indissolubly connected parts of a broadly uneven impact that affects some states, some communities and some businesses more than others.

The political implications of globalisation are correspondingly uneven and unpredictable. Nonetheless, it is clear that there is sufficient empirical evidence to justify referring to an era of 'globalisation' in the sense that finance capital, information technology, trade and investment, and environmental issues have combined to produce a level, scope and intensity of global market pressures upon daily life that is unprecedented. It is not enough to claim that this era reflects the circumstances of previous historical epochs when time, distance and space have been so radically transformed. There is probably a case to be made for historical relativism, as some commentators mentioned above do, but the capacity of some contemporary global forces to extend well beyond the reach of the national state and to be able simply to bypass or circumvent liberal democratic governments at will is surely without precedent. Lessons can certainly be learned from earlier economic transitions, but our survey hints at something more akin to qualitative rather than just quantitative change. It is a question of kind as well as degree.

Leaving this intellectual debate aside, it nonetheless remains the case that the constitutional and political implications of globalisation demand imagination, innovation and international leadership if we are to secure a firm grip on these elusive contemporary developments. It is no accident that the underlying theme of much of the outpouring of political science literature on globalisation seems to embrace a strong normative tendency in favour of a 'cosmopolitan democracy' (what is in reality a disguised confederal governance) that has the potential to emancipate states and citizens from the power of increasingly global financial markets. New institutions and new forms of representation are implicit in the reappraisal of contemporary relationships and linkages between states, governments, citizens and the invasive, penetrating forces that characterise the new global order. It is a golden opportunity to look again at what inventive ideas and practices federal and confederal elements could bring to the debate about the new political order. And they would be practical proposals. It would, indeed, be ironic if human invention could achieve so much in the realms of science, information technology, medicine and knowledge yet fail lamentably to match these achievements with sufficient political sophistication. These thoughts are appropriately paraphrased by Quentin Peel:

> Never before have we known so much about the world around us, about the laws of physics and of nature, about the most obscure peoples in forgotten corners of the globe, what they believe in and how they eke out their existence. Never before have we been able to communicate so easily with each other, regardless of distance, and travel around the world in hours, not days or weeks or even years. Never before have borders meant so little, and never has one language been so universally understood. The nation state is ever less relevant, and supranational entities, bureaucracies, broadcasters, businesses, banks set the international agenda. Never before have secrets been so difficult to keep, as satellites scour the airwaves and the fields, listening and watching, quite capable of monitoring the minutiae of human life.[40]

In the year 2005 we still stand on the threshold of the new millennium that promises much and will probably deliver less. Globalisation has the possibility to be put to the service of all mankind: to eradicate disease and poverty, to expunge the North–South divide; to combat tribal strife, to eliminate some environmental disasters, to promote education, to regulate material consumption, to help to control population increases, and ultimately, to manage human diversity itself. It has the possibility to do all of these things, but it must also be 'democratised' if it is to become a stepping stone rather than a stumbling block to greater human welfare. It is hard to imagine a more important challenge and a more important role that warrants the prescription of federalism and confederalism.

11 The success and failure of federation

Introduction

This study has examined federalism and federation from a number of different comparative perspectives. It has broadly shown that there are many ways in which we can seek to explain and understand these two discrete concepts and their complex interrelationship. We have explored this relationship in the origins and formation of federations, the motives for union, the various types of socio-economic and cultural-ideological diversity that sustain this kind of state structure, the institutional strengths and weaknesses of federation and, ultimately its constitutional foundation in the fundamental concept of liberal democracy that is itself rooted in the moral imperatives of justice, respect, toleration, reciprocity and mutual recognition – themselves linked, in turn, to legitimacy, welfare and political stability.

So what does this study tell us about the question of success and failure? How do we judge whether or not a particular federation is either successful or unsuccessful? If the overall integrity of the state is preserved, can we presume that, short of the complete disintegration of the federation, secession is the strongest indicator of failure while political stability is the hallmark of success? If so, is mere endurance and longevity sufficient to warrant the label 'success'? It would seem that the answer to the question of success and failure is much more complex than might initially be expected. The case of Malaysia, for example, would suggest that it has combined both failure and success: the secession-expulsion of Singapore in 1965 and the subsequent long-term political stability evident in the one-party hegemony of the United Malays National Organisation (UMNO). In this area of enquiry, then, we might do well to remember Preston King's assertion that failed federations – for example, Czechoslovakia, Yugoslavia and the Soviet Union (admittedly not genuine liberal democracies) – signify the failure of particular experiments rather than the demonstrable failure of federation itself. We might therefore conclude that it is indeed crass to see in these examples of 'failed' unions of states an automatic deficiency in federation *qua* federation. The point is that it is impossible to establish a firm set of criteria by which to judge success and failure. All we can do is to construct a framework of analysis that can enable us to identify certain features common to the federations placed under the microscope so that we can isolate and distil sets of factors present in the case studies that might allow us to discern regular patterns of activity capable of sustaining some broad generalisations. The first problem, however, lies in the terms 'success' and 'failure' themselves. They are blanket terms that admit of neither gradations of judgment nor nuances of informed opinion. The student of federalism and federation is presented with a stark choice at the outset: federations are either a success or a failure.

Almost forty years ago Thomas M. Franck looked at the pathology of federations in a study entitled 'Why Federations Fail', first published in 1968.[1] He, too, began his survey with a preliminary caution about the use of terminology – what he called 'semantic hazards' – and the danger of facile generalisations. 'What', he asked, 'is meant by the term "failure"? If "failure" is generally the non-achievement of certain goals', then it could be defined as 'specifically a non-achievement of the necessary conditions for survival of a federation as initially conceived'.[2] However, he was at pains to point out that failure was a relative not an absolute term. No federal experiment was ever a complete failure: failed federations frequently accomplished some very important objectives during their lifetimes, however brief. Indeed, he claimed that these objectives could 'arguably be said to be more important than the continuation of federation itself'.[3] This was evidently the case in the three failed federations that were the subject of his brief comparative analysis, namely, the West Indies (1962), the Central African Federation (1963) and Malaysia (1965), while East Africa (Kenya, Uganda and Tanganyika) was an example of a federation that simply failed to emerge. Accordingly these three federations together with the East African association were successful in reaching at least some of the socio-economic and cultural objectives that they were originally designed to achieve.[4] Franck's essay remains of enduring significance to us today because it continues to raise important questions about both the success and failure of federation as a particular form of state structure that is a tangible institutional reality designed to accommodate different kinds of socio-economic and cultural-ideological diversities. In hindsight, his use of the term 'failure' was actually quite modest and mundane. He referred to it as mere historical fact: 'the discontinuation of a constitutional association between certain units of the union, or the end of the negotiations designed to produce such a constitutional arrangement'.[5]

Following Franck, Ursula Hicks also looked at the particular question of success and failure in considerable detail in 1978 but did not resolve it. She did, however, acknowledge the complexity of the question by distinguishing between those federations that simply fell apart and whose constituent units subsequently struggled to survive as separate entities (as occurred in the Federation of the British West Indies), and those that did as well, or even better, than if the original federation had continued (as occurred after the expulsion of Singapore from Malaysia).[6] She was therefore astute in seeking to assess the impact of a perceived failure by asking what had subsequently become of its members. It was necessary to look at what happened to the former constituent units in cases of complete disintegration and (in the case of secession) the remaining members of the federation. Moreover, it was also important to examine the consequences of failure from the standpoint of their impact upon the former federation's neighbours and upon the rest of the world. Nonetheless, this study did seem to assume that failure in federation was largely self-evident.

It is at least clear that when we seek to explain the causes of failure in particular federal experiments we are engaged in the pathology of federation, and it is important for us to look for both general and particular factors in each case. But this must also apply to the causes of success. Hicks was particularly perceptive about this matter, observing that 'it is seldom a matter of identifying a unique factor; it is rather a question of judging which elements in a complex situation were most responsible for the result'. After all, 'many of the general or environmental factors which have influenced failures or success' were not 'peculiar to federal systems', but were actually 'shared by unitary countries of many complexions'.[7] Here, once again, we confront some of the basic problems inherent in the very nature of comparative political science. Secession is just such a case in point. Leaving aside the examples of federations that either collapsed in their entirety, as with the West Indies and the Central African Federation, or those that simply failed to materialise, as in the case of East Africa, the particular question of secession in federations is illustrative of the sort of perceived failure of the federal state that could be and often is just as pertinent to so-called unitary states. This is an interesting area of further research in comparative federalism and federation and, as we shall see, one that impels us to look again at the contemporary significance of studying the origins and formation of federations. Let us therefore turn our attention briefly to the question of secession in federation.

Secession in federation

In this section I do not wish to address the broad question of secession. There are already plenty of detailed studies that do so.[8] There is also a burgeoning literature on theories of secession that is certainly important for the particular study of comparative federalism and federation but which, for our very limited purposes here, has only a tangential relevance to the present survey.[9] Instead my purpose is to focus our attention upon secession and federation.

Given the principal focus of this book, it is certainly worth pointing out that a conventional wisdom has evolved in the mainstream literature which asserts that secession on the part of the constituent units of a federation is candidly incompatible with the notion of federation *qua* federation. Edward Freeman remarked over a century ago that a federation was 'essentially a perpetual union' and that a federal constitution could not 'any more than any other constitution, contain provisions for its own dissolution'. The federal power, he claimed, was 'entitled to full obedience within its own sphere, and the refusal of that obedience, whether by states or by individuals, was unequivocally an act of rebellion'.[10] Yet Freeman did not deny that circumstances could arise when certain parts of a federation might 'have ceased to have that community of feeling and interest with certain other parts' deemed so essential to the integrity of the union.[11] In such cases he judged that the weakness of the federal tie might actually bring with it 'some incidental advantages':

> At any rate a plausible case may be made out in favour of this facility of secession. Rebellion is sometimes necessary, and secession is certainly the mildest form that rebellion can take. For, beyond all doubt, secession is legally and formally, rebellion. ... It does not at all follow that such rebellion is necessarily either wrong or inexpedient; but it does follow that secession is not an everyday right to be exercised at pleasure.[12]

He concluded, then, that a seceding state might be fully justified in its secession. There were circumstances that could conceivably justify such a rupture. Indeed, separation between members of a federation might sometimes be expedient, and if the federal system was undoubtedly an 'ingenious and nicely-balanced system' it also supplied 'the means of a peaceable divorce'.[13] His conclusion was based largely upon a brief comparative survey of the American Civil War (1861–65) and the earlier Swiss *Sonderbund* Civil War (1847) and the contrast between these two case studies, less than two decades apart, prompted him to regard the American episode (whose outcome was still unknown when he wrote) as somewhat untypical of federal experiments. Indeed, in his eulogy of Switzerland he was at pains to emphasise that 'if anyone is tempted to draw shallow inferences against federalism in general from mistaken views of one single example, he may at once correct his error by looking at that nearer federation which has weathered so many internal and external storms'.[14] A century later, Kenneth Wheare's summary of Freeman's position that secession was 'theoretically inconsistent' with federation but 'probably desirable in practice' was an accurate assessment.[15]

Freeman's conclusions about secession were originally written in 1863 and they seemed to have survived largely intact a century later when Wheare wrote his own short commentary on the subject. Referring principally to the USA, Switzerland, Canada and Australia, he noted that the constituent units *acting alone* had no more right to leave the federation than the federal government *acting alone* had any right to expel a member state. This was because both secession and expulsion were tantamount to the end of federation.[16] His general position on secession in federations was therefore fundamentally in tune with Freeman's conclusions:

> Yet I doubt whether it can be maintained that a right to secede unilaterally is inconsistent with the federal principle *as a matter of logic*. ... The right to secede does not make the general government the agent of the states ... on the contrary, it recognizes that the general government is to be either co-ordinate with a state government *within the area of the state*, or is to have no connection with it. ... But while the existence of a right to secede unilaterally or a right to expel unilaterally may be quite consistent with federal government, it is not, I believe, consistent, as a rule, with good federal

government …. It will usually be true that a unilateral power to secede or to expel makes for bad federal government.[17]

The nub of Wheare's dilemma with secession in federations appears to have hinged on the idea of *acting alone* – the notion of the federal government and the constituent state governments in a federation behaving unilaterally in constitutional law. Yet, as a matter of logic, there seemed to be no reason why unilateral secession was inconsistent with the federal principle. Presumably Wheare followed Freeman in the view that secession in federations was 'far more easy to carry out into practice than similar schemes of secession could be under any other form of government'. Moreover, Freeman might already have resolved Wheare's dilemma when he observed that 'a federation, though legally perpetual, is something which is in its own nature essentially voluntary: there is a sort of inconsistency in retaining members against their will'.[18] Clearly, in this light, there was a moral basis for secession. The law and the constitution might understandably be silent about it, but in terms of the nature of federation itself as essentially a voluntary union of states and citizens secession was always at least a logical possibility as well as a moral imperative.

When Ronald Watts addressed the question of secession in federations in his classic survey of new federations in the Commonwealth, first published in 1966, he, too, followed in the path of Freeman and Wheare.[19] British imperial experience in seeking to promote federal experiments in India, Pakistan, Malaysia, Nigeria, the West Indies and the Central African Federation revealed, as a general proposition, that none of these new independent federations formally permitted unilateral regional secession. Obviously the specific context of Watts' comparative analysis was crucial. Such a constitutional concession would have seriously impeded the early stages of nation-building in these countries where the bonds of unity had not yet had time to strengthen and develop. The main conclusion of this study regarding secession was therefore hardly surprising: 'the independent federations have not been unwise in their denial of any right for regions to secede unilaterally'.[20] This foreshadowed the later study by Franck, who claimed that the historic successes of the USA, Canada, Australia and Switzerland had very little to teach the newly independent nations of Africa and Asia. Certainly, some lessons of experience were relevant to them and could be learned, but to suggest that the classic analogies could be used as a solution to their own problems was chimerical:

> Much of the superficial analogy drawn between the successful applications of federalisms of the past and the present needs of the developing nations is apt to be misleading, and reliance upon it has already led to disappointment both among well-wishers in the old states and among the intellectual leaders of the new nations. It has led to the creation of false-analogy federalism.[21]

Ivo Duchacek also addressed the question of secession in his detailed survey of comparative federalism published in 1970.[22] He set his comparative analysis

in the context of the observation that the late 1960s were the years when secession seemed to have become a veritable fashion: 'the temptation to secede and
form an independent territorial unit had assumed epidemic proportions'.[23] But
even when these words alluding to the previous decade were first published,
Duchacek noted that 'national self-determination and the concomitant territorial
disintegration are high and certainly will remain so for some time on the agenda
of the last third of the twentieth century'.[24] His study seemed to suggest that
federations were no more prone to secessionist pressures than unitary states,
adding that 'the separatist ferment in all corners of the world has different inten-
sities, and very different chances of eventual success, either in the form of
independence or broader territorial autonomy'.[25]

Later, in 1977, Watts returned to the subject of secession but this time with
particular regard to Canada.[26] As we have seen, the decade of the 1960s seemed
to have been a period of great uncertainty in respect of the perceived failure of
federations, especially in Africa and Asia, with either the attenuation or the
outright collapse of particular experiments in Nigeria, Malaysia, the West Indies
and the Central African Federation. However, the election in 1976 of the Parti
Quebecois – an avowedly separatist provincial political party – as the provincial
government in Quebec seemed to usher in a new era of self-doubt. Suddenly
and dramatically the prospect of secession in Canada – one of the classic federations – sparked a serious public debate about the future of the federation, a
debate that has subsequently waxed and waned as a constitutional issue up until
the present day.

Watts' essay focused upon the sources of stress in federations and suggested
that no single condition or institutional arrangement could be held responsible
for crises in federations that were actually the result of a cumulative combination
of factors. Obviously, socio-economic and cultural-ideological cleavages
combined with institutional and procedural deficiencies served to polarise
Canadians into predominantly francophone Quebecois and the overwhelmingly
anglophone population of the Rest of Canada (known today as ROC), and
Watts noted exactly this as federal institutions failed to moderate cleavages so
that a decline in support for political compromise occurred and the controversy
became a zero-sum contest between two opposing forces with very high stakes.[27]
But as Franck had already stated in his comparative survey of federal failures,
the principal cause of failure could not be found in 'an analysis of economic
statistics or in an inventory of social, cultural or institutional diversity'.[28] In the
light of Canadian circumstances in the late 1970s and the subsequent provincial
referendum in 1980 on 'sovereignty-association' in Quebec, it would presumably
have meant explaining precisely why Quebecois no longer believed that federation was in their long-term national interest. In the event, secession was rejected
in the referendum.

In his classic *Federalism and Federation*, first published in 1982, Preston King
followed in the footsteps of previous contributors when he observed that the
important point to note about secession in federations was 'less that federal
constitutions say that they allow secession, or say that they disallow it, but that

the structure of these governments is heavily weighted against it' principally because the central government in a federation was 'significantly distinguished from its constitutive member governments by virtue of ... its exercise of national functions which engage and affect the system as a whole'.[29] Clearly the very structure of all federations impelled them towards 'the retention of some form of unity' so that a formal provision conceding a retreat from this basic objective would be 'inconsistent with it'.[30] Accordingly, the basic assumption upon which all federations are ultimately founded is that the constituent territorial units are structurally incorporated in such a manner that they constitute a 'single, coherent decision-procedure' and do not expect to 'enjoy an independent power to negate that procedure'.[31] This is why King concluded that secession in federations cannot be conceded 'in any clear-cut or coherent way, legally speaking, within a federal union':

> For the central government is not only dealing with interest-bearing territorial units, but also with interest-bearing individuals. Constitutionally, in law, the federal centre owes a duty to both. ... The important point is that, legally, whatever tacit or express undertakings may have been made to localities about secession, the actual granting of this remains at the discretion of the centre in all federations.[32]

For King, this constitutional duty of the federal government simultaneously to its constituent units as *collective* territorial interests and to its citizens as *individuals* in the larger federal polity was the nub of the dilemma regarding secession. And even if some region or province did manage to break away from the federation, this would be tantamount to a *political* not a *legal* act. There was, after all, no legal provision preventing constituent territorial units from holding local referenda on citizens' preferences regarding secession. But the bottom line, according to King, was that any 'formal move towards secession' would conflict with the formal duty of the federal government towards those of its citizenry in the particular seceding locality who opposed 'the forcible transfer of their allegiance'. He warned that in any federal constitution 'there would always be grounds for regarding any acquiescence in local secession by the federal centre as illegal – as an abrogation of its duty'.[33] However, King's important distinction between the political and the legal dimensions of secession, while certainly fundamental in its theoretical implications for federation *qua* federation, was not quite the insurmountable obstacle to this separatist goal, even in terms of legal practicalities, that he seemed to suggest. The recent case of the Supreme Court decision in the Quebec secession issue in 1998 demonstrated that, according to the Canadian Constitution, Quebec did not have a unilateral right to secede from Canada. The ruling clearly specified that secession was tantamount to a profound constitutional change that was not a matter to be decided by a simple majority vote in the seceding province, but must be achieved by formal constitutional amendment through a process of negotiation. And while it was silent about the specific mode of constitutional amendment, it did concede that if and when there was a 'clear majority' in Quebec in favour of secession in answer to a 'clear question' concerning secession, the Canadian government and other 'participants in Confederation' would have a duty to negotiate the possible secession of Quebec in accordance with the four basic principles assumed by the written text of the Canadian Constitution, namely, constitutionalism and the rule of law, democracy, federalism and the protection of minority rights.

The upshot of this remarkable episode in the history of Canadian constitutional law and politics is twofold: first, the confirmation that unilateral secession by Quebec is forbidden; and, second, the acknowledgement that Quebec does have the right to initiate the political process that might lead to secession via a process negotiation. Secession would therefore be justified only by deliberative democracy, consent and in accordance with the four fundamental principles identified above. Allen Buchanan endorsed the unprecedented nature of the Supreme Court judgment in this particularly controversial area of Canadian constitutional reform:

> It attempts to do something of great importance that has not been done before: to subject the potentially destructive issue of secession to the rule of law by constitutionalizing the secession process, but in the absence of an existing explicit constitutional provision for secession.[34]

Not only did this break new ground in the nebulous area of the law and politics of secession but it also formally addressed the critical distinction identified by King above, namely, that between the constituent units as *collective* territorial interests and citizens as *individuals* in the larger federal polity. This judicial decision, as Buchanan has emphasised, was based upon a subtle understanding of the crucial relationship between *legality* and *legitimacy*.[35] The legality of a future secession based upon this understanding, then, would seem to resolve the problem identified above by King about secession as a political not a legal act. Provided that the act of secession via negotiation and public debate satisfied the stringent test(s) of democracy implicit in the judicial ruling, it could no longer be construed as illegal. In other words, if the act of secession was founded upon the recognition that all citizens, not just those in Quebec, should have a say in the decision on secession 'on the premise that proper respect for the equality of persons requires that each should have a say on important political decisions', especially those that would alter the boundaries of the federation and the character of a person's citizenship, then the legitimacy inherent in the democratic process – along with respect for the attendant principles of federalism, the protection of minorities, and constitutionalism and the rule of law – would effectively guarantee the legality of secession.[36]

The Quebec secession issue therefore serves to confirm the received wisdom established at least as far back as Freeman in the 1860s in regarding 'the facility of secession' as theoretically inconsistent with federation but probably desirable in practice. We might also add that there could very well be circumstances in some federal experiments in which it would also be morally justifiable. But there is yet another aspect to this subject that is worth more than a moment's reflection before we turn away from secession in federation. This is the neglected relationship between secession and the origins and formation of federations that we surveyed in Chapter 3. As we shall see, this relationship has an important bearing upon the question of success and failure in federations.

If we recall Franck's important essay entitled 'Why Federations Fail', we are reminded that his comparative analysis of federal failures in East Africa, Malaysia, the West Indies and Central Africa did not enable him to identify a list of prerequisites that, if not possessed more or less equally by all the parts of a proposed federation, would assure its failure. Indeed, he denied that such a list could be made. The analytical and interpretive difficulties defied neat causal classification. The best that one could do was much more modest: it was to concede that the sharing of such things as culture, language and other socio-economic factors, while helpful to the cause of federation, could not assure its success. They could never be an ultimate guarantee against failure.[37]

In pursuit of the sources of failure and success, then, Franck developed what he called 'the factor–goal components in federation motivation' and began by dividing the factors making for federation and the goals sought to be achieved by federation-building into three categories: namely, primary, secondary and tertiary. We shall paraphrase Franck's framework of analysis in the following way.[38] *Tertiary* goal-factors gave rise to a federal condition that could be described as bargain-striking, in which a federation was formed not so much to harness a genuine mutuality of interest as to prevent a clash of disparate racial or economic interests, or to take advantage of some temporary coincidence of interests to secure an immediately achievable objective. *Secondary* goal-factors gave rise to a federal condition that could best be described as a genuine coalition in which a profound coincidence of parallel interests could be advanced through cooperation and merger. *Primary* goal-factors gave rise to a federal condition that elevated the federal value above all other political values and in which the ideal of the federal nation represented the most important political fact in the lives of the people and leaders of each part of the federation.

In drawing upon his four case studies mentioned above, Franck then identified the following four tentative hypotheses:

1   The presence of certain secondary factors, such as common colonial heritage, a common language and the prospect of complementary economic advantages might be either *useful* or even *necessary*, but are not *sufficient* to ensure success.

2   The absence of a positive political or ideological commitment to the *primary* goal of federation *as an end in itself* among the leaders and people of each of the federating units made success improbable, if not impossible. This was the one consistent factor found in the four federal failures. There must be an ideological commitment not to federation only as a means but also as an *end*, as good *for its own sake*. In a developed community, the impetus for successful federation can come either from the ideological commitment of charismatic

leaders transmitted to the people or from the broadly shared values of the people, culminating in a *federal* value, originating in charismatic *events* and transmitted to the leaders, or built gradually out of common secondary factors.

3   If the political commitment to federation is only a commitment to short-term goals based upon *tertiary* factors, federal institutions survive as long as the tertiary goals continue to be important or new goals are substituted, but once the tertiary goals are attained, this very achievement becomes in a sense a factor making for disintegration.

4   Where there is no paramount ideological commitment to the federal ideal, the mere creation of federal institutions will not resolve the conflicts that will arise within the federation, nor will it of itself transform *secondary* or *tertiary* into the requisite *primary* goal-factor motivation.

Although these hypotheses derived from four case studies of federations in developing countries that were deemed to have failed, there is some basis for the view that 'each experiment with federalism shares something with all other federal experiences' even if 'our Western-centred experience relevant to the causation of federalism does not tell us all about newly-independent Asia and Africa'.[39] Besides it was perfectly possible for these new federations to seek to redefine the federal form that was characteristic of the classic federations in their own unique Third World contexts. This might not lead to 'neat packages of classical federalism' but it did not prevent new forms of association based upon loose confederal or federal-type arrangements being invented.[40]

Almost forty years later, what does this short summary of Franck's 'factor–goal components in federation motivation' tell us about success and failure in federations? Can we make any further advances in our current reappraisal of both the principal causes of failure and the necessary preconditions of success in federations? One area of research that suggests itself to us in the light of our brief reassessment of Franck's framework of analysis is a closer look at the origins and formation of federations. It seems clear that one potentially fruitful line of enquiry would be to return to the intellectual debate about how and why federations are formed. In many cases this would help us to better understand not only the motives for union but also particular problems that confronted elites during the critical period of federation-building. These might conceivably furnish important clues to contemporary cultural-ideological challenges and to the perceived deficiencies in institutional design that often become apparent only much later in federal evolution. In short, we need to re-examine the unique combination of general factors and historical specificities that originally drove political elites to champion the federal cause in different case studies and subsequently to sustain it in the age of emergent mass democracy during the late nineteenth and twentieth centuries.

Recent research on the accommodation of territorial cleavages in federal and non-federal states has pointed up the renewed interest among scholars in the origins of federations.[41] Given the essentially contractual basis of federation as a union of states and citizens, the forensic re-examination of the origins and formation of federations has an obvious logic of its own. It makes perfect sense to explore the relationship between the origins and formation of federations and their effects. Sometimes the sources of contemporary stresses and strains can be directly located in more sophisticated versions of Riker's so-called 'federal bargain' and sometimes they are the result of later unresolved conflicts and challenges. The point is that we need to return to the historical analyses of the formation and evolution of federations if we want to explain the desire on the part of a constituent unit or units to leave the federation. Both the historical context and the point of departure of each federation matter in the search for understanding. In explaining the peculiarities of federal experiments in the former Soviet Union and Eastern Europe, Nancy Bermeo has arrived at the same destination:

> The contrast between the effects of federalism in Eastern Europe and elsewhere highlights the importance of considering the origins of federal systems when making projections about their effects. Federal systems that are imposed by outside forces are always troubled and usually short-lived. … Every federalist system that either split apart or turned toward unitarism was one that was forced upon regions by an outside, usually colonial power. This pattern is not the fruit of coincidence, but, rather, a strong signal that *origins matter.*[42]

This recent comparative study informs us that while it remains important to examine the relationship between the institutional configuration of federations and their socio-economic and cultural profiles – the interaction between federalism and federation – it is nonetheless the case that detailed contemporary analyses of constitutions, political institutions and decision-making procedures alone do not tell the whole story.

Secession and federation are therefore related in a complex fashion that can be properly explained and understood only by paying attention to historical context and the point of departure. The origins and formation of federations provides the key to a contextual understanding of contemporary stresses and strains.

This is the case, for example, with separatist ideas and movements in Western Australia in 1933 and in Quebec in the years since 1976. In the former case, we can already detect a major problem in Western Australia's desire to enter the projected federation in 1900 as an 'original state' but on terms slightly different from those provided in the new constitution. When introducing the Commonwealth of Australia Bill in Parliament in May 1900, Joseph Chamberlain, the British Secretary of State for the Colonies, acknowledged the existence of 'a difference of opinion arising between the Australian colonies' over the question of tariffs, and this is why the colony was recognised in only oblique fashion in the Act of Parliament Establishing the Constitution of the Commonwealth of Australia in July 1900.[43] Western Australia entered the federation on generous terms that allowed it to retain tariff barriers against the other

states for a transitional period but it was 'an unwilling partner', delaying its referendum of federation for three years while its colonial government sought
concessions from its potential partners and from the imperial government.[44] As
early as 1906, only five years after federation, both houses of the state parliament
adopted a separatist resolution while discontent with the constituent state's position in the national political economy became endemic after the First World War.
Support for secession continued to gain ground with the onset of the Great
Depression in the early 1930s that culminated in April 1933 in a referendum on
the issue organised by the state government. Despite a clear majority voting in
favour of secession in Western Australia, the movement petered out once it
became clear that separation from Australia was inconsistent with the Statute of
Westminster (1931), and in the same year voters elected a new government
opposed to this option.[45] Nonetheless, we can detect the earliest signs of this
whole secessionist episode in Australian constitutional and political history simply
by a reinvestigation of the circumstances that surrounded the formation of the
federation.

The case of Quebec is similar to that of Western Australia in respect of
historical context and the point of departure. The literature on Quebec separatism is vast and we will engage it only briefly in this short summary of
secession and federation, but the fundamental point remains the same: political scientists have to go back to the 1860s in Canadian constitutional and
political history in order to understand and appreciate the sources, complexities and subtleties of Quebec separatism.[46] The origins of Quebec secession
must be seen in terms of competing conceptions of the nature and purpose of
Canada itself. Charles Taylor explained it from the standpoint of the politics
of recognition. Confederation was 'a marriage of reason' for Quebec and it
has been the continued denial of its own conception and understanding of
Canada that has led to disillusion with it. The fact that 'Canada never gelled
as a nation for them', combined with the growth of specifically 'French
power' inside Canada, resulted in the demand for Quebec to be recognised as
'a crucial component of the country, as an entity whose survival and flourishing was one of the main purposes of Canada as a political society'. What
has been missing is 'the clear recognition that this was part of our purpose as
a federation'.[47]

The case has been made, then, that part of the explanation for secession from
any state, whether federal or non-federal, can be found in the historical specificities that characterise the processes of state-building and national integration
evident in each case study. But the specific relationship between secession and
federation is complex because of the nature of federation itself. The literature on
federations is predicated on the assumption that this kind of state is essentially a
contract between recognised partners that binds them together on a moral basis
of equality, mutual respect, trust, tolerance and reciprocity so that the idea of
secession must be construed in this light. Secession, it follows, can be justified on
the moral basis that the federal bargain or contract has been either abandoned
or undermined to such an extent that it neither satisfies the goals nor meets the

basic needs of one or several parts of the federation. Indeed, continued membership might even be damaging to a particular constituent identity or interest. The most common justification of secession in federations therefore is that the federation has somehow become less federal in its nature and operation. This is precisely why it is necessary to return to the historical sources and debates that surround the origins and formation of each federation. And this brings us back full circle to the question of success and failure in federations. Let us conclude the chapter by returning to the problems associated with this question.

Conclusion

The words 'failure' and 'success' are relative not absolute terms when seeking to assess federations from a comparative perspective. As Franck noted in his pioneering essay on the pathology of federations, putative 'failures' must be seen 'in shades of grey, rather than as altogether black'.[48] Nevertheless, he believed that the principal cause of failure could be found only in 'the absence of a suffi-cient political-ideological commitment to the *primary* concept or value of federation itself'.[49] The absence of this ideological commitment to the *primary* goal of federation *as an end in itself* among the leaders and people of each of the federating units made success 'improbable, if not impossible'. This meant that conceptions of a single, common self-interest had to emerge that would override previous interests so that the leaders and their followers had to *feel federal*, making their identities and loyalties compatible with the federation as a whole. In short, they had to commit to federation as an *end*, as good *for its own sake*.[50]

This opened the door for political scientists to examine each case study of failed federation in its own right in order to establish a hierarchy of causes that might furnish the basis for a set of generalisations about the disintegration of federations. There was, then, still much for political scientists to investigate, and this approach also paved the way for future comparative surveys, including those that chose to focus upon secession and federation. As we have seen, Franck's comparative analysis was devoted to four principal case studies of newly inde-pendent federations that were deemed to have failed and he concluded that ultimately they did not succeed in the way that the old federations did because they 'did not call forth a commitment to the primary ideal of federalism compa-rable to that of their classical antecedents'. They failed because the attendant *secondary* factors 'did not alone add up to the primary factor of a sense of nation-hood'.[51]

There is, however, another way to look at this question of success and failure. Secession, expulsion or the complete disintegration of a federation are tanta-mount, as Franck suggested, to the discontinuation of a constitutional association. It is nothing less than the truncation or dissolution of the state. They are therefore a somewhat crude measure of failure with a strong element of finality about them. However, it is also important to construe failure and success in federations in terms of the endurance of federal values. Federations endure; they survive and prosper by adaptation and adjustment to change, even by adding new bargains to the original binding contract that brought them together in the first place. But sometimes the resilience and survival of a federation tells us nothing about what we might call its *federality*, that is, its success or failure in sustaining federal values.

There is, then, another important question that needs to be considered when assessing failure and success in federations: 'how *federal* is the federation?' Has a particular federation been successful in preserving, protecting and promoting federal values that can be briefly summarised as mutual respect, recognition, toleration, dignity, consent, trust and reciprocity? This is admittedly an extremely difficult question to answer, but it remains an important one nonetheless because it raises the possibility that federations which have survived might have done so at the price of undermining federal values. Probably the most common threat to federal values during the past century has been the insidious centralisation of federal government in virtually all public policy sectors in the federation. It is certainly the main source of complaints from constituent units that perceive an almost relentless encroachment upon their own particular policy preferences. We have already witnessed this with the *lander* in Germany and Austria, the province and nation of Quebec in Canada, Western Australia, Kashmir in India and Kelantan in Malaysia. If this is the case, then we must consider the possibility of federations being successful in respect of their longevity, governmental stability and territorial integrity but a failure in the sense of their preservation of local autonomy and political accommodation. Thus if one constituent unit of a federation perceives that its own interests or identity are imperilled by membership of the union and that its very survival might be endangered, this would constitute a legitimate grievance that could conceivably furnish a strong moral basis for separation.

Mindful of the moral basis to federalism and federation, it is time to turn to the final chapter of the book. We have traversed a huge area of scholarly enquiry and we have examined the many faces of success and failure in federation. Our survey indicates that while federations, like any other states, are prone to different kinds of threats and challenges (both territorial and non-territorial) from different parts of the state, they are often although not always fractures or fault lines that can be traced back to old cleavages. This does not mean that new challenges, such as multicultural communities, language minorities and gender-based issues, are less significant. Nor does it mean that we should forget to factor these into the equation when we consider success and failure in federations. Indeed, they often have more political salience than traditional conflict alignments, but they are generally less threatening in terms of secession because they are not largely territorially based. In any case these issues usually have more to do with the quality of federal democracy than with the state of the federation itself.

12 Conclusion

Comparative federalism in theory and practice

We began our comparative study of federalism and federation by concentrating on the problem of studying federalism construed in its broadest sense in the mainstream literature. One of the main problems that we identified at the outset was that while there is such a thing as federal theory, there is no fully fledged theory of federalism. Several of the leading contributors to the intellectual debate about federalism acknowledged this conspicuous lacuna and some suggested reasons for it. Daniel Elazar claimed that the source of the problem lay, ironically, in one of federalism's main strengths, namely, its flexibility. Its very flexibility and adaptability made it 'difficult to discuss satisfactorily on a theoretical level'. He believed that while the federal principle of self-rule and shared rule had been successfully applied in a great many different ways, under a wide variety of circumstances, it seemed to 'complicate theory-building' because flexibility 'leads to ambiguity, which has great operational advantages even as it creates severe theoretical problems'.[1]

Part of the price of flexibility inherent in the federal idea, then, would seem to be theoretical disarray. Since, according to Elazar, there are several varieties of political arrangements to which the term 'federal' can be appropriately applied, it is hardly surprising that the conceptual basis for theory-building furnishes only shaky foundations. Ambiguity certainly has practical advantages in the tangible institutional world of federation but it is a real handicap for those who search for a theory of federalism. There would seem therefore to be something of a dilemma in the relationship between flexibility, adaptability and ambiguity and the pursuit of theory. This predicament is also reminiscent of what Murray Forsyth had earlier referred to as 'the natural and inevitable' use of the term 'federalism' 'in a very wide and overarching sense'. He suggested that it could conceivably be used not only to span the spectrum of federal union and that of the federal state but that it could also be used 'in a hundred other contexts as well'. This meant that its 'all-pervasive character' made it 'a dangerous object of study' because 'with sufficient effort it can be detected almost everywhere, and endless pursuit can take the place of hard analysis'.[2]

Both Elazar and Forsyth seemed to have arrived at the same conclusion: federalism's practical strengths were at the expense of its theoretical deficiencies. Ronald Watts also seemed to come close to this destination when he too acknowledged in 1994 that federalism was both 'flexible and varied' and re-emphasised in 1999 that its increasing popularity in the world was characterised by 'an enormous variety of forms' and 'new and innovative variants'. It is fair to say that Watts' intellectual position on the comparative study of federal political systems has always been one of consistent pragmatism that refused to be 'constrained to traditional arrangements or theories about federalism'.[3] But this observation brings us back to what we mean by theory itself. Moreover, is federalism something about which it is possible to theorise? Here it is appropriate to recall Maurice Vile's explanation in 1977 for the absence of a theory of federalism. He lamented that this was because 'much of the theoretical effort of the past thirty years has been devoted to the discussion of the definition of federalism in such a way as to leave little or no basis upon which to build any sustained theoretical structure'.[4] The implication once again was that the obsession with finding a precise definition of federalism, together with the very variety and widespread application of the federal idea, made it very difficult to develop a theory of the subject. Indeed, this strong strand of pessimism in thinking about federalism can be detected as recently as 1995 when S. Rufus Davis declared that 'we are at the crossroads of federal theory because we have been borne along ... on the tide of a vast literature that has evolved over long stretches of time'. To continue on the same path, he believed, would be both 'barren and futile' because it would only 'encourage new fictions'.[5]

Is this any longer the case? Can we not use the conceptual progress that has been made so far to attempt to take at least a few modest steps in the direction of building a theory of federalism? Theory in its simplest sense is about explaining and understanding the world that we inhabit and political theory is ultimately about explaining human behaviour – identifying relationships, exploring inter-relationships and examining motivations, intentions, actions and outcomes. Since federalism, broadly conceived, is complex precisely because it is multi-dimensional, we have to develop concepts that can successfully accommodate this complexity. Consequently a theory of federalism, to be of any practical utility, would have to accommodate both empirical and normative aspects and embrace a whole host of dimensions that together constitute the federal totality, historical, philosophical, constitutional, legal, political, economic, social, ideological and cultural.

It is here that our conceptual distinction between federalism and federation can be put to effective use. There is no doubt that federation *qua* federation is something that has firm conceptual boundaries. This was something acknowledged by Carl Friedrich at least as far back as the early 1950s in his essay 'Federal Constitutional Theory and Emergent Proposals', which stated quite categorically that federalism was 'one of the most important aspects of modern constitutionalism'.[6] Leaving aside his predilections for Althusian perspectives, Friedrich clearly tied his understanding of federalism to notions of contract, autonomy, reciprocity, consent, consultation and participation. This is why the idea of the written constitution was so important, indeed pivotal, to his interpretation of federalism. 'True federalism', he claimed, was 'the federalizing process under constitutionalism' and it was characterised by the permanent interplay between the inclusive community and the component communities so that this interrelationship, cooperation and exchange was a 'universal principle of political organization'.[7] This implied that 'every federal community, to be truly federal', would organize its amending process in such a way that it involved 'the effective cooperation of the inclusive and the component communities' in amending the federal constitution. For Friedrich, the constitutional amending process was vital because it regulated the relationship between 'two competing autonomies' that determined 'from time to time whether and how ... powers should be altered'.[8] But the crucial feature for Friedrich was the nature of the relationship between what he regarded as the two fundamental federal concepts of autonomy and participation. He put it thus:

> Autonomy is here taken in its original meaning as signifying the power and authority, the legitimate right, to govern oneself, but not excluding the participation in a group of similar entities which form in turn an autonomous community. In other words, the autonomy of a community is not considered as impaired by participation in a wider community *if* the sphere of authority of the wider community is instituted, maintained and altered only with effective participation of the component community. It is evident that this intertwining of participating communities can only be accomplished within the context of a constitution, and ... that it necessarily and significantly divides governmental power and authority over the citizens of such federal (or federated) communities.[9]

The influence of Althusius in this understanding of federalism is crystal clear and the implicit assumptions – the basic federal values – of mutual respect, recognition, dignity, reciprocity, toleration and consent are self-evident. It is precisely these values, beliefs and interests that combine to produce the tangible institutional reality that we know as federation – with 'union' and 'autonomy' as its characteristic hallmark.

The notion of federation as a particular species of the larger genus 'fully constitutional government' has been part and parcel of established federal scholarship that dates back several centuries and includes, in this study, John Stuart Mill, Edward Freeman, Albert Venn Dicey, James Bryce, Henry Sidgwick, Kenneth Wheare, Christopher Hughes, Carl Friedrich, Ronald L. Watts, William Riker, Maurice Vile, S. Rufus Davis, Daniel Elazar, Ivo Duchacek and Preston King. Probably the most significant development in this accumulated intellectual wisdom has been the theoretical shift away from the state and sovereignty. Friedrich noted this trend half a century ago: 'the attempts of jurists to narrow the focus of federalism and to restrict it to thinking in terms of the "federal state" have not succeeded'. New federal systems, such as India and the post-war European project, were 'in the making' while 'older federal communities', such as the United States and (West) Germany were 'evolving novel solutions to the difficult problems of associated territories, like Puerto Rico and

Berlin'.[10] Since then Daniel Elazar has been the most vociferous advocate of widening both the scope and meaning of federalism: 'using the federal principle does not necessarily mean establishing a federal system in the conventional sense of a modern federal state'. This understanding was too narrow and restrictive. Instead Elazar emphasised that 'the essence of federalism is not to be found in a particular set of institutions but in the institutionalization of particular relationships among the participants in political life', but he also acknowledged that it is 'based on a particular kind of constitutional framework'.[11]

Consequently Preston King was on solid ground when he too referred to 'the federal variety of constitutionalism' and insisted that 'the key to federation is its universal constitutional attribution of entrenched powers at the centre to constitutive and non-sovereign territorial units'.[12] The gist of recent scholarly analyses of federation regarding its constitutionality, then, is that it is constitutional autonomy which matters rather than the particular division of powers between central and regional governments. Friedrich also anticipated this shift of emphasis when he noted that there may be 'different powers for different federal systems'.[13] And as Elazar observed, because federalism was a value concept, it was a term that carried with it 'an essence' which could be interpreted in a variety of ways under different circumstances as long as people adhered *to the essentials of the concept*.[14] We can see therefore that in terms of the conceptual distinction between federalism and federation used in this book, federal values are construed in terms of social diversity having political salience – the variety of different identities and interests that we take to be *federalism* – and are expressed in *federation* as a form of constitutionalism which rests upon both autonomy and representation. This brings us inescapably to the question of federal democracy that has been implicit in our concluding survey.

The debate about federal democracy is usually couched in terms of Madisonian principles that date back to *The Federalist Papers*. We are reminded from Chapter 2 that in *Federalist* 10 James Madison went to the very heart of the subject by distinguishing between a democracy and a republic. The former he called a 'pure democracy', by which he meant 'a society consisting of a small number of citizens, who assemble and administer the government in person', and in terms of late eighteenth-century intellectual thought in the New World this was something that was palpably incompatible with minority interests, individual security and property rights.[15] 'Theoretic politicians', he declared, 'have erroneously supposed that by reducing mankind to a perfect equality in their political rights, they would at the same time be perfectly equalized and assimilated in their possessions, their opinions and their passions'.[16] The republican remedy, as we will recall from Chapter 2, was to introduce the principle of representation and the notion of the extended republic. Today the intellectual debate about federal governance, broadly conceived, is still preoccupied with the implications that divided and shared political authority among its citizens has for the quality of federal democracy.

The creation of fragmented, constrained political institutions, designed to augment minority influence in federal government, acts as a safeguard against

arbitrariness and furnishes the basis for overall political stability and such institutions remain at the heart of the current debate about just how 'democratic'
federal democracy can be. In hindsight it is quite remarkable how far the federal
idea of dividing and sharing political authority among citizens so that they
occupy, so to speak, different policy spaces in separate but overlapping areas of
political authority has continued to challenge, and sometimes even confound,
modern democratic theory and practice. A constitutional and political arrangement that seems, at least on the surface, to be fairly simple and straightforward –
in Madison's language 'a happy combination' of 'the great and aggregate interests' to be referred to the national, the local and the particular state legislatures –
has continued to fuel what Elazar dubbed a 'continuing seminar in
governance'.[17] But this is not something that we should consider to be problematic. On the contrary, it is in the nature of the thing itself. Inherent in the notion
of federal government (and increasingly of federal governance) is the recognition
that citizens in both their individual and collective communitarian capacities will
have separate but overlapping identities, loyalties and interests. This is, after all,
the very *raison d'être* of the federal idea. Consequently, the theoretical and practical problems that inhere in federal democracy – such as the agenda problem,
the majority principle and the nature of the democratic unit itself – should really
be construed as part of the larger debate about the nature and meaning of
modern liberal democracy in the twenty-first century. On this reckoning, the
problems identified in federation by theorists of democracy, such as Robert
Dahl, can be partly rationalised as the price to be paid for seeking to constitu-
tionalise and institutionalise federal values or federalism.[18] Every form of
democracy has theoretical problems and practical pitfalls and federal democracy
is no exception. Elazar shared a similar view: 'federalism is analogous to other
great concepts such as democracy, which offer a similar spread of ambiguities
and variety of applications'.[19]

What, then, does the future hold for federalism and federation in the new
millennium? How can the discrete set of values, beliefs and interests that we
have defined as federalism be effectively enshrined and formally integrated in
federation or (to use Elazar's terminology) in some other flexible form of federal
arrangement? In this book we have tried to demonstrate how far the federal idea
is relevant to our understanding of both the EU and the complex relationship
between democracy and globalisation. Certainly the regularity with which the
term 'federal' recurs as a potential solution to difficult conflicts in different parts
of the world – currently in Cyprus, Sri Lanka, Iraq, Sudan and even Indonesia –
reinforces its contemporary significance as a subject that merits serious study. But
in theoretical terms each of these case studies involving complicated ethnic
conflicts suggests that it might now be appropriate to develop and sustain a
normative theory of the federal state or, at least, of federal governance. Let us
look a little closer at this intellectual development that will serve as the final part
of the concluding chapter.

In recent years the notion of a moral basis to contemporary federal thought
has been increasingly explicit in much of the mainstream literature on modern

federalism. It has been particularly notable in the theoretical, philosophical and empirical analyses of Canadian scholars who have addressed the contemporary problems of Canada. This outpouring of scholarly literature is a particular response to a range of difficult problems: the role of Quebec in the federation, the constitutional position of the Aboriginal peoples, the significance of bilingualism, multiculturalism and multinationalism, minority rights and federal–provincial relations.[20] In political theory the federal idea has loomed large in the major debates about nationalism, liberalism, cultural diversity, identity politics, citizenship, justice, legitimacy and stability.[21] These broad areas of research have spawned a huge literature on federalism and nationalism, federalism and secession, federalism and citizenship, asymmetrical federalism and the nature of federal democracy. And the consistent theme that has underpinned this literature has been the moral basis to federalism.

In their recent edited collection of essays entitled *Theories of Federalism: A Reader*, Dimitrios Karmis and Wayne Norman sketch out the evidence of a revival of interest in the theory of federalism from a primarily normative perspective.[22] Their main purpose is to investigate and explore theories of federalism that consistently emphasise the normative arguments in favour of federal and confederal arrangements compared to those of unitary states, that is, 'from the perspective of evaluating and recommending institutions and not merely explaining and comparing them'.[23] There is strong evidence to suggest that this theoretical approach to the study of federalism and federation is consonant with contemporaneous change. Normative empirical theory *prescribes* federal arrangements as an appropriate tangible institutional response to a variety of contemporary problems of the new millennium. It does not necessarily *recommend* federation *qua* federation, nor does it suggest that the federal idea will be sufficiently flexible and adaptable to address *every* socio-economic and cultural-ideological problem of the age, but it does recommend the federal ideals and norms of constitutionalism, republicanism and power-sharing – 'self-rule and shared rule' – in some combination as the best form of compound governance in the pursuit of justice.[24]

This 'normative turn' in the theoretical debate about federalism is essentially a moral debate because it is based upon underlying notions of justice. Where this applies to sub-state national identities, cultural minorities, linguistic communities and indigenous peoples, the pursuit of justice requires the following three things: first, that citizens in their collective capacities must have channels of expression in order to access their culture; second, the capacity to use their language to achieve things in public life, in the worlds of economic management, of technology and of learning in general; and, third, the formal recognition of their worth that serves as the indispensable basis of dignity, self-confidence and self-respect.[25] Together these goals reflect the normative values of 'community, culture, identity and heritage' that breathe life into social relations in general. In short, they represent different conceptions of what are public goods.[26]

This brief focus upon the contemporary intellectual trend in the direction of normative empirical theory in the comparative study of federalism and federation enables us to bring our study to a convenient close. It is clear that there is no longer any need to despair about the study of federalism and federation.[27] The concepts have been lucidly defined and their interrelationship has been thoroughly examined and explored from several comparative perspectives. The inherent ambiguities that remain in the subject are no more and no less than what we might expect to find in comparable studies in political science that examine, for example, democracy, pluralism and political integration. Moreover, the variety of theoretical constructs and structural arrangements that result from these ambiguities demonstrates, as Elazar observed, 'the richness of the concept and its continued importance in political life and thought'.[28] It is time to be bold and imaginative in the area of federal studies and to look with a great deal more confidence than has been displayed in the past to the increasing significance of federalism and federation in the world of the twenty-first century. The moral value of federalism will be judged ultimately by the shortcomings of the few alternatives that exist to varieties of the federal form.

Notes and references

Introduction: the problem with studying federalism

1 Preston King, *Federalism and Federation* (London: Croom Helm, 1982).
2 King, *Federalism and Federation*, 14.
3 A.H. Birch, 'Approaches to the Study of Federalism', *Political Studies*, XIV(1) (1966), 15.
4 S. Rufus Davis, *The Federal Principle: A Journey Through Time in Quest of a Meaning* (London: University of California Press, 1978).
5 Davis, *The Federal Principle*, 2–3.
6 Davis, *The Federal Principle*, 216.
7 H.R.G. Greaves, *Federal Union in Practice* (London: George Allen & Unwin, 1940), 120.
8 Greaves, *Federal Union in Practice*, 11.

1 Federalism and federation: the quest for meaning

1 C. Rossiter (Ed.), *The Federalist Papers* (New York: The New American Library, 1961), xii.
2 A. de Tocqueville, *Democracy in America*, ed. and abridg. R.D. Heffner (London: The New English Library, 1956), 36.
3 Tocqueville, *Democracy in America*, 46.
4 Tocqueville, *Democracy in America*, 61 and 80.
5 J.S. Mill, *Utilitarianism, On Liberty and Considerations on Representative Government*, ed. H.B. Acton (London: J.M. Dent & Sons, 1972). It should be noted that the father of 'utilitarianism', Jeremy Bentham, also contributed to the intellectual debate in relation to British imperial considerations. See *The Works of Jeremy Bentham*, ed. J. Bowring (New York: Russell & Russell, 1962).
6 Mill, *Representative Government*, 367.
7 Mill, *Representative Government*, 367–68.
8 Freeman's *History of Federal Government* was republished posthumously in a new form in 1893 edited by J.E. Bury and entitled *The History of Federal Government in Greece and Italy*, ed. J.E. Bury (Freeport, NY: Books for Libraries Press, 1972). The latter work was a reprint of the original volume but with the addition of a new chapter on Italy and a new fragment on Germany which were discovered among Freeman's papers and intended for his second volume.
9 For a detailed analysis of Freeman's federal ideas, see M. Burgess, *The British Tradition of Federalism* (London: Cassell, 1995).
10 S. Mogi, *The Problem of Federalism: A Study in the History of Political Theory*, 2 vols (London: George Allen & Unwin, 1931), Vol. I, 290.
11 Freeman, *History of Federal Government*, Preface, xiii.

12 S. Collini, D. Winch and J. Burrow, *That Noble Science of Politics: A Study in Nineteenth Century Intellectual History* (Cambridge: Cambridge University Press, 1983), 220.

13 Collini *et al.*, *That Noble Science of Politics*, 222.

14 Freeman, *History of Federal Government*, 13.

15 Freeman, *History of Federal Government*, 3.

16 J. Bryce, *The American Commonwealth*, 2 vols (London: Macmillan & Co. 1919).

17 Bryce, *The American Commonwealth*, Vol. I, Introduction, 4.

18 Bryce, *The American Commonwealth*, Vol. I, 341.

19 Bryce, *The American Commonwealth*, Vol. I, 342.

20 Bryce, *The American Commonwealth*, Vol. I, 342.

21 Bryce, *The American Commonwealth*, Vol. I, 348.

22 Bryce, *The American Commonwealth*, Vol. I, 350–53.

23 Bryce, *The American Commonwealth*, Vol. I, 350.

24 Bryce, *The American Commonwealth*, Vol. I, 350–51.

25 Bryce, *The American Commonwealth*, Vol. I, 356.

26 Bryce, *The American Commonwealth*, Vol. I, 356.

27 Bryce, *The American Commonwealth*, Vol. I, 357.

28 Bryce, *The American Commonwealth*, Vol. I, 357.

29 Bryce, *The American Commonwealth*, Vol. I, 357.

30 Bryce, *The American Commonwealth*, Vol. I, 359.

31 J. Bryce, *Studies in History and Jurisprudence*, 2 vols (Oxford: Clarendon Press, 1901).

32 Bryce, *Studies in History*, Vol. I, 256.

33 Bryce, *Studies in History*, Vol. I, 262–63.

34 Bryce, *Studies in History*, Vol. I, 265–67.

35 Bryce, *Studies in History*, Vol. I, 268–69.

36 Bryce, *Studies in History*, Vol. II, 56.

37 A.V. Dicey, *Introduction to the Study of the Law of the Constitution* (London: Macmillan & Co. 1950), 9th edn.

38 Dicey, *Law of the Constitution*, 141.

39 Dicey, *Law of the Constitution*, 143.

40 Dicey, *Law of the Constitution*, 144.

41 Dicey, *Law of the Constitution*, 172–73.

42 Dicey, *Law of the Constitution*, 171–79.

43 For this interpretation of Dicey's impact upon British political thought, see Burgess, *The British Tradition of Federalism*, 17–18.

44 H. Sidgwick, *The Elements of Politics* (London: Macmillan & Co. 1891) and *The Development of European Polity* (London: Macmillan & Co. 1903).

45 Sidgwick, *European Polity*, 433.

46 Sidgwick, *Elements of Politics*, 507.

47 Sidgwick, *Elements of Politics*, 508.

48 Sidgwick, *Elements of Politics*, 508.

49 Sidgwick, *Elements of Politics*, 509.i

50 Sidgwick, *Elements of Politics*, 509–10.

51 Sidgwick, *Elements of Politics*, 511.

52 Sidgwick, *Elements of Politics*, 511–12.

53 Sidgwick, *Elements of Politics*, 516.

54 Sidgwick, *Elements of Politics*, 513–14.

55 Sidgwick, *Elements of Politics*, 518.

56 Collini *et al.*, *That Noble Science of Politics*, 281–82. See also S. Collini, 'The Ordinary Experience of Civilized Life: Sidgwick's Politics and the Method of Reflective Analysis' in B. Schultz (Ed.), *Essays on Henry Sidgwick* (Cambridge: Cambridge University Press, 1992), Chap. 12, 333–67.

57 Sidgwick, *Elements of Politics*, 519.

58 Collini *et al.*, *That Noble Science of Politics*, 281–82 and 290–307.

59 Sidgwick, *Elements of Politics*, 507.
60 S. Mogi, *The Problem of Federalism: A Study in the History of Political Theory*, 2 vols (London: George Allen & Unwin, 1931).
61 H. Laski, 'Preface' in Mogi (Ed.), *The Problem of Federalism*, 7.
62 S. Mogi, 'Note' in Mogi (Ed.), *The Problem of Federalism*, 9.
63 H. Laski, 'The Obsolescence of Federalism', *The New Republic*, 3 May 1939, 367–69.
64 See in particular J.D. Wilkinson, *The Intellectual Resistance in Europe* (Cambridge, MA: Harvard University Press, 1981) and R. Mayne and J. Pinder, *Federal Union: The Pioneers* (London: Macmillan, 1990).
65 H.R.G. Greaves, *Federal Union in Practice* (London: George Allen & Unwin 1940).
66 Greaves, *Federal Union*, 11.
67 K.C. Wheare, *Federal Government* (Oxford: Oxford University Press, 1963), 4th edn, 10.
68 Wheare, *Federal Government*, 1.
69 Wheare, *Federal Government*, 11.
70 Greaves, *Federal Union*, 16.
71 W.S. Livingston, 'A Note on the Nature of Federalism', *Political Science Quarterly*, 67 (March 1952), 81–95.
72 Livingston, 'A Note on the Nature of Federalism', 83–84.
73 Livingston, 'A Note on the Nature of Federalism', 88.
74 Livingston, 'A Note on the Nature of Federalism', 88.
75 Livingston, 'A Note on the Nature of Federalism', 91–92.
76 Livingston, 'A Note on the Nature of Federalism', 93–94.
77 Livingston, 'A Note on the Nature of Federalism', 95.
78 Livingston, 'A Note on the Nature of Federalism', 95.
79 Livingston, 'A Note on the Nature of Federalism', 85–86.
80 S. Rufus Davis, 'The "Federal Principle" Reconsidered', Part I, *Australian Journal of Politics and History*, 1(1) (November 1955), 59–85 and 'The "Federal Principle" Reconsidered', Part II, *Australian Journal of Politics and History*, 1(2) (May 1956), 223–44.
81 Davis, 'The "Federal Principle" Reconsidered', Part II, 243–49.
82 Davis, 'The "Federal Principle" Reconsidered', Part II, 243.
83 Davis, 'The "Federal Principle" Reconsidered', Part II, 243.
84 Davis, 'The "Federal Principle" Reconsidered', Part II, 242.
85 A.H. Birch, *Federalism, Finance and Social Legislation in Canada, Australia and the United States* (Oxford: Clarendon Press, 1955).
86 Birch, *Federalism, Finance and Social Legislation*, 290.
87 Birch, *Federalism, Finance and Social Legislation*, 291.
88 Birch, *Federalism, Finance and Social Legislation*, 305.
89 Birch, *Federalism, Finance and Social Legislation*, 306.
90 Birch, *Federalism, Finance and Social Legislation*, 306.
91 A.H. Birch, 'Approaches to the Study of Federalism', *Political Studies*, XIV(1) (1966), 15–33.
92 Birch, 'Approaches', 17–18.
93 Birch, 'Approaches', 32–33.
94 M.J.C. Vile, *The Structure of American Federalism* (Oxford: Oxford University Press, 1961).
95 C.J. Friedrich, 'New Tendencies in Federal Theory and Practice', Sixth World Congress of IPSA (September 1964), Geneva, Switzerland, 1–14.
96 Friedrich, 'New Tendencies', 2.
97 C.J. Friedrich, 'Federal Constitutional Theory and Emergent Proposals' in A.W. Macmahon (Ed.), *Federalism: Mature and Emergent* (New York: Russell & Russell, 1962).
98 Friedrich, 'Federal Constitutional Theory', 528–29.
99 Friedrich, 'Federal Constitutional Theory', 518.
100 Friedrich, 'Federal Constitutional Theory', 514 and 517.

101 K.W. Deutsch *et al.*, *Political Community and the North Atlantic Area* (Princeton, NJ: Princeton University Press, 1957).

102 Birch, 'Approaches', 19.

103 C.J. Hughes, *Confederacies* (Leicester: Leicester University Press, 1963). 50.

104 Hughes, *Confederacies*, 11.

105 W.H. Riker, *Federalism: Origin, Operation, Significance* (Boston: Little, Brown & Company, 1964), 2.

106 Riker, *Federalism*, 11.

107 Riker, *Federalism*, 11.

108 Riker, *Federalism*, 11–12.

109 Riker, *Federalism*, 37 and 157.

110 Riker, *Federalism*, 12–15, 91–101 and 136.

111 Riker, *Federalism*, 155.

112 W.H. Riker, 'Six Books in Search of a Subject or Does Federalism Exist and Does it Matter?', *Comparative Politics*, 2(1) (October 1969), 135–46.

113 Riker, 'Six Books', 146.

114 Riker, 'Six Books', 145.

115 Riker, 'Six Books', 142.

116 W.H. Riker, 'Federalism' in F.I. Greenstein and N.W. Polsby (Eds), *The Handbook of Political Science*, Vol. V (Reading, MA: Addison-Wesley, 1975), 93–172.

117 S. Rufus Davis, *The Federal Principle: A Journey Through Time in Quest of a Meaning* (London: University of California Press, 1978), Chap. 6, 155–203.

118 M. Grodzins, *The American System: A New View of Government in the United States*, ed. D. Elazar (Chicago, IL: Rand McNally, 1966).

119 D.J. Elazar, *The American Partnership: Intergovernmental Cooperation in the Nineteenth-Century United States* (Chicago and London: University of Chicago Press, 1962) and his *American Federalism: A View from the States* (New York: Harper & Row, 1984), 4th edn.

120 'Publius' was the pen name used by Alexander Hamilton, John Jay and James Madison during 1787–88 when they published 85 articles entitled 'The Federalist' in defence of the new American Constitution which was ratified in 1789.

121 R.L. Watts, *New Federations: Experiments in the Commonwealth* (Oxford: Clarendon Press, 1966).

122 Watts, *New Federations*, Chap. 1, 3–16.

123 Watts, *New Federations*, Chap. 3, 41–66.

124 T.M. Franck, 'Why Federations Fail' in T.M. Franck (Ed.), *Why Federations Fail* (London: London University Press, 1968), Chap. 5, 167–99.

125 F.N. Trager, '"Introduction": On Federalism' in Franck (Ed.), *Why Federations Fail*, xv.

126 Franck, 'Why Federations Fail', 169.

127 M.B. Stein, 'Federal Political Systems and Federal Societies', *World Politics*, 20 (1968), 721–47.

128 Stein, 'Federal Political Systems', 729.

129 Stein, 'Federal Political Systems', 729.

130 Stein, 'Federal Political Systems', 731.

131 Stein, 'Federal Political Systems', 733.

132 G. Sawer, *Modern Federalism* (London: Pitman 1969).

133 Sawer, *Modern Federalism*, 98.

134 Sawer, *Modern Federalism*, 2.

135 Sawer, *Modern Federalism*, 147.

136 Sawer, *Modern Federalism*, 153.

137 I.D, Duchacek, *Comparative Federalism: The Territorial Dimension of Politics* (London: Holt, Reinhart & Winston 1970), 189–91.

138 This quotation is taken from S. Rufus Davis, 'The Federal Principle Revisited' in D.P. Crook (Ed.), *Questioning the Past* (Brisbane: University of Queensland Press, 1972). See Davis, *The Federal Principle*, fn. 1, 205.

139 Davis, *The Federal Principle*, 205–13. Davis was still claiming in 1995 that 'the state of the federal art is uncertain' and that there was 'undoubtedly a crisis'. See S. Rufus Davis, *Theory and Reality: Federal Ideas in Australia, England and Europe* (Queensland: University of Queensland Press, 1995), 34–35.

140 Preston King, 'Against Federalism' in R. Benewick, R.N. Berki and B. Parekh (Eds), *Knowledge and Belief in Politics* (London: Allen & Unwin, 1973), 151–76.

141 King, 'Against Federalism', 174.

142 M.J.C. Vile, 'The Definition of Federalism', Appendix A in 'Federalism in the United States, Canada and Australia', Research Papers 2, *Commission on the Constitution* (London: HMSO, 1973), 35.

143 M.J.C. Vile, 'Federal Theory and the "New Federalism" in D. Jaensch (Ed.), *The Politics of New Federalism* (Adelaide: Australian Political Studies Association, 1977), 1.

144 Vile, 'Federal Theory', 2.

145 Vile, 'Federal Theory', 2.

146 Vile, 'Federal Theory', 2.

147 Vile, 'Federal Theory', 2–3.

148 Vile, 'Federal Theory', 3.

149 King, 'Against Federalism', 161.

150 Birch, 'Approaches', 15.

151 Vile, 'Federal Theory', 4 and 11.

152 King, *Federalism and Federation* (London: Croom Helm, 1982).

153 M. Forsyth, 'Book Review' of *Comparative Federalism and Federation: Competing Traditions and Future Directions* by M. Burgess and A.-G. Gagnon, *West European Politics*, 19(1) (January 1996), 200–1 and J. Robinson, 'Federalism and the Transformation of the South African State' in G. Smith (Ed.), *Federalism: The Multiethnic Challenge* (London: Longman, 1995), 274.

154 Wheare, *Federal Government*, 11.

155 King, *Federalism and Federation*, 76.

156 See R.L. Watts, 'Contemporary Views on Federalism' in B. De Villiers (Ed.), *Evaluating Federal Systems* (London: Juta & Co. 1994), Chap. 1, 1–29 and 'Federalism, Federal Political Systems and Federations', *Annual Review of Political Science*, I (1998), 117–37. See also D.V. Verney, 'Federalism, Federative Systems, and Federations: The United States, Canada and India', *Publius: The Journal of Federalism*, 25(2) (Spring 1995), 81–97 for a modest revision of Watts' three-fold distinction.

157 D.J. Elazar, *Exploring Federalism* (Tuscaloosa, AL: University of Alabama Press, 1987).

158 Elazar, *Exploring Federalism*, 38 and Watts, 'Contemporary Views on Federalism', 8.

159 M. Forsyth, *Unions of States: The Theory and Practice of Confederation* (Leicester: Leicester University Press, 1981), 7.

160 C.S. McCoy and J. Wayne Baker, *Fountainhead of Federalism: Heinrich Bullinger and the Covenantal Tradition* (Louisville, KE: Westminster/John Knox Press, 1991).

161 D.J. Elazar, *Exploring Federalism*, 138–45.

162 D.S. Lutz, 'From Covenant to Constitution in American Political Thought', *Publius: The Journal of Federalism*, 10 (Fall 1980), 101–33.

2   The American federal experience

1 See G. Martin, 'Empire Federalism and Imperial Parliamentary Union, 1820–1870', *The Historical Journal*, XVI(I) (1973), 65–92 and G. Martin, 'The Idea of "Imperial Federation"' in R. Hyam and G. Martin (Eds), *Reappraisals in British Imperial History* (London: Macmillan, 1975), Chap. 6 and M. Burgess, *The British Tradition of Federalism* (London: Cassell, 1995).

2 Martin, 'Empire Federalism', 71–72.
3 D. Lutz, 'The Articles of Confederation as the Background to the Federal Republic', *Publius: The Journal of Federalism*, 20 (Winter 1990), 57.
4 Lutz, 'Articles of Confederation', 57.
5 Lutz, 'Articles of Confederation', 57.
6 Lutz, 'From Covenant to Constitution in American Political Thought', *Publius: The Journal of Federalism*, 10 (Fall 1980), 102.
7 Lutz, 'Articles of Confederation', 58–61. For a detailed survey of Whig political theory in colonial America, see D.S. Lutz, *Popular Consent and Popular Control: Whig Political Theory in the Early State Constitutions* (Baton Rouge, LO: Louisiana State University Press, 1980) and C.S. Hyneman and D.S. Lutz (Eds), *American Political Writing during the Founding Era, 1760–1805*, 2 vols (Indianapolis, IN: Liberty Press, 1983).
8 For a list of proposals and plans for federating or uniting the colonies or states, see Lutz, 'From Covenant to Constitution', 132–33. Mention should also be made of the significance of the Iroquois confederation to early American colonial thought about continent-wide federal union. On this subject, see D. Lutz, 'The Iroquois Confederation Constitution: An Analysis', *Publius: The Journal of Federalism*, 28(2) (Spring 1998), 99–127.
9 Lutz, 'Articles of Confederation', 58.
10 C.S. McCoy and J. Wayne Baker, *Fountainhead of Federalism: Heinrich Bullinger and the Covenantal Tradition* (Louisville, KE: Westminster/John Knox Press, 1991), 88.
11 McCoy and Baker, *Fountainhead of Federalism*, 93–94.
12 See Madison, *Federalist* 10 and Hamilton, *Federalist* 85 in C. Rossiter (Ed.), *The Federalist Papers* (New York: The New American Library, 1961), 77–84 and 520–27 respectively.
13 Lutz, 'From Covenant to Constitution', 102.
14 McCoy and Baker, *Fountainhead of Federalism*, 89.
15 Alexis de Tocqueveille, *Democracy in America*, trans. G. Lawrence, ed. J.P. Mayer (London: Fontana Press, 1994), 157.
16 Madison, *Federalist* 37 in Rossiter (Ed.), *The Federalist Papers*, 230.
17 Madison, *Federalist* 37 in Rossiter (Ed.), *The Federalist Papers*, 229.
18 Madison, *Federalist* 40 in Rossiter (Ed.), *The Federalist Papers*, 247–48.
19 Madison, *Federalist* 39 in Rossiter (Ed.), *The Federalist Papers*, 246.
20 M. Diamond, 'The Federalist's View of Federalism' in G.C.S. Benson (Ed.), *Essays on Federalism* (Claremont: Institute for Studies in Federalism, 1961), 23–24.
21 For a contending view of the status of the new American union in 1789 as 'a federal union of states rather than … a federal state', see M. Forsyth, *Unions of States: The Theory and Practice of Confederation* (Leicester: Leicester University Press, 1981), 60–72.
22 Diamond, 'The Federalist's View of Federalism', 38–40.
23 Hamilton, *Federalist* 22 and 23 in Rossiter (Ed.), *The Federalist Papers*, 151 and 154.
24 Diamond, 'The Federalist's View of Federalism', 41.
25 Tocqueville, *Democracy in America*, 157.
26 M. Farrand (Ed.), *The Records of the Federal Convention of 1787*, Vol. I (New Haven, CT: Yale University Press, 1937), rev. edn, 18.
27 Forsyth, *Unions of States*, 4.
28 E.C. Burnett, *The Continental Congress* (New York: The Macmillan Co. 1941), 257. Lutz, 'Articles of Confederation', also provides further important information about the misrepresentation of the anti-federalists.
29 Forsyth, *Unions of States*, 4.
30 Hamilton, *Federalist* 15 in Rossiter (Ed.), *The Federalist Papers*, 108 (italics in original).
31 Hamilton, *Federalist* 9 in Rossiter (Ed.), *The Federalist Papers*, 76.
32 Madison (with Hamilton), *Federalist* 20 in Rossiter (Ed.), *The Federalist Papers*, 138.
33 'Brutus', Antifederalist, No. 17, 'Federalist Power Will Ultimately Subvert State Authority' in M. Borden (Ed.), *The Antifederalist Papers* (Michigan: Michigan State University Press, 1965), 42–43.

34 'A Farmer', Antifederalist, No. 39, 'Appearance and Reality – The Form is Federal; The Effect is National' in Borden (Ed.), *The Antifederalist Papers*, 106–7.

35 Patrick Henry, Antifederalist, No. 40, 'On The Motivations and Authority of the Founding Fathers' in Borden (Ed.), *The Antifederalist Papers*, 109–110.

36 'Centinel', Antifederalist, No. 21, 'Why The Articles Failed' in Borden (Ed.), *The Antifederalist Papers*, 51.

37 M. Borden (Ed.), Intro., 'The Antifederalist Mind' in Borden (Ed.), *The Antifederalist Papers*, viii.

38 'A Farmer', Antifederalist, No. 3, 'New Constitution Creates a National Government; Will Not Abate Foreign Influence; Dangers of Civil War and Despotism' in Borden (Ed.), *The Antifederalist Papers*, 6 (italics added).

39 Farrand (Ed.), *Federal Convention*, Vol. I, 37.

40 Hamilton, *Federalist* 9 in Rossiter (Ed.), *The Federalist Papers*, 75–76.

41 Hamilton, *Federalist* 9 in Rossiter (Ed.), *The Federalist Papers*, 76.

42 See F.K. Lister, *The European Union, The United Nations and the Revival of Confederal Governance* (London: Greenwood Press, 1996).

43 M. Diamond, 'What the Framers Meant by Federalism' in R.A. Goldwin (Ed.), *A Nation of States: Essays on the American Federal System* (Chicago: Rand McNally, 1964), 24–41.

44 Diamond, 'What the Framers Meant', 26.

45 Diamond, 'What the Framers Meant', 27.

46 Diamond, 'What the Framers Meant', 32.

47 Lutz, 'The Articles of Confederation', 70.

48 See D. Lutz, 'The Relative Influence of European Writers on Late-Eighteenth Century American Political Thought', *American Political Science Review*, 78 (1984), 189–97.

49 Lutz, 'The Relative Influence', 196.

50 See Table 2, 'Most Cited Thinkers by Decade' in Lutz, 'The Relative Influence', 193.

51 This point is made by I. Hampsher-Monk in '"Publius": The Federalist' in I. Hampsher-Monk (Ed.), *A History of Modern Political Thought: Major Thinkers from Hobbes to Marx* (Oxford: Blackwell, 1992), 204.

52 B. Bailyn, *The Ideological Origins of the American Revolution* (London: The Belknap Press of Harvard University Press, 1967), 285.

53 M. Kammen (Ed.), *The Origins of the American Constitution: A Documentary History* (London: Penguin Books 1986), Intro., viii.

54 Madison, *Federalist* 39. He also surveyed the difference between a republic and a democracy in *Federalist* 10. See Rossiter (Ed.), *The Federalist Papers*, 240–41 and 82–84 respectively.

55 Hampsher-Monk, '"Publius": The Federalist', 206.

56 He uses the term to describe the word 'government' but it applies equally to the word 'democracy'. See S.E. Finer, *Comparative Government* (Harmondsworth: Penguin Books 1982), 3.

57 Bailyn, *The Ideological Origins*, 282.

58 For a discussion of constitutionalism and federalism as essentially restraints on the exercise of governmental power for the protection of individual rights, see C.J. Friedrich, 'Federal Constitutional Theory and Emergent Proposals' in A.W. MacMahon (Ed.), *Federalism: Mature and Emergent*: (New York: Russell & Russell Inc., 1962), Chap. 26, 510–33 and C.J. Friedrich, *Constitutional Government and Democracy: Theory and Practice in Europe and America* (Waltham, MA: Blaisdell Publishing Co., 1968), 4th edn.

59 Hampsher-Monk, '"Publius": The Federalist', 217.

60 Madison, *Federalist* 10 in Rossiter (Ed.), *The Federalist Papers*, 78.

61 Madison, *Federalist* 10 in Rossiter (Ed.), *The Federalist Papers*, 80 and 82.

62 Madison, *Federalist* 10 in Rossiter (Ed.), *The Federalist Papers*, 82.

63 Madison, *Federalist* 10 in Rossiter (Ed.), *The Federalist Papers*, 84.
64 Madison, *Federalist* 51 in Rossiter (Ed.), *The Federalist Papers*, 324.
65 S.H. Beer, *To Make a Nation: The Rediscovery of American Federalism* (London: The Belknap Press of Harvard University Press, 1994), 196–206.
66 Diamond, 'What the Framers Meant', 39.
67 M. Jensen, *The Articles of Confederation: An Interpretation of the Socio-Constitutional History of the American Revolution, 1774–1781* (Madison, WI: The University of Wisconsin Press, 1962), 245.
68 C.J. Hughes, *Confederacies* (Leicester: Leicester University Press, 1963), 5.

3 Federalism and federation: the origins and formation of federal states

1 M. Forsyth, *Unions of States: The Theory and Practice of Confederation* (Leicester: Leicester University Press, 1981), 160.
2 See especially Hamilton, *Federalist* 1 and 6–9 and Jay *Federalist* 2–5 in C. Rossiter (Ed.), *The Federalist Papers* (New York: The New American Library, 1961), 33–76.
3 W.H. Riker, *Federalism: Origin, Operation, Significance* (Boston: Little, Brown & Company, 1964), 19.
4 Riker, *Federalism*, 20 and Hamilton, *Federalist* 11–13 in Rossiter (Ed.), *The Federalist Papers*, 84–99.
5 Forsyth, *Unions of States*, 160.
6 Riker, *Federalism*, 12.
7 Riker, *Federalism*, 20 and 25.
8 Riker, *Federalism*, 12–13.
9 Riker, *Federalism*, 48.
10 A.H. Birch, 'Approaches to the Study of Federalism', *Political Studies*, XIV(I) (1966), 32.
11 W.H. Riker, 'Federalism' in F.I. Greenstein and N.W. Polsby (Eds), *The Handbook of Political Science: Governmental Institutions and Processes*, Vol. 5 (Reading, MA: Addison Wesley, 1975), Chap. 2, 93–172.
12 Riker, 'Federalism', *Handbook of Political Science*, 114.
13 Riker, 'Federalism', *Handbook of Political Science*, 114–16 and 127–28.
14 M.J.C. Vile, 'Federal Theory and the "New Federalism"' in D. Jaensch (Ed.), *The Politics of New Federalism* (Adelaide: Australian Political Studies Association, 1977), 1.
15 Riker, 'Federalism', *Handbook of Political Science*, 129.
16 S. Rufus Davis, *The Federal Principle: A Journey Through Time in Quest of a Meaning* (London: University of California Press, 1978), 126 and 132.
17 Davis, *The Federal Principle*, 132–33.
18 Preston King, *Federalism and Federation* (London: Croom Helm, 1982), 34.
19 King, *Federalism and Federation*, 34.
20 King, *Federalism and Federation*, 36.
21 King, *Federalism and Federation*, 82–87.
22 Riker, 'Federalism', *Handbook of Political Science*, 113.
23 Riker, *Federalism*, 11.
24 Riker, *Federalism*, 12.
25 I am indebted to Kurt R. Luther for these interesting and important observations that can be found in K.R. Luther, 'Federalism and Federation in Europe: A Comparative Study of the Germanic Tradition', Ph.D. thesis., University of Plymouth (August 1989), 15–16.
26 Davis, *The Federal Principle*, 136.
27 I have used the excellent historical summaries in Forsyth, *Unions of States*, 18–30 and W. Linder, *Swiss Democracy: Possible Solutions to Conflict in Multicultural Societies* (London: Macmillan, 1994), 5–18 .

28 B. de Villiers (Ed.), *Bundestreue: The Soul of an Intergovernmental Partnership*, Occasional Papers (Johannesburg, RSA: Konrad Adenauer Stiftung, March 1995), 1–36.
29 Linder, *Swiss Democracy*, 15–18.
30 Forsyth, *Unions of States*, 29.
31 Linder, *Swiss Democracy*, 15.
32 J. Bryce, *Modern Democracies*, Vol. I (London: Macmillan and Co., 1929), Chap. XXVIII, 371–75.
33 Linder, *Swiss Democracy*, 16–18.
34 R. Gibbins, *Conflict and Unity: An Introduction to Canadian Political Life* (Scarborough, Ont.: Nelson Canada, 1994), 10–21.
35 G. Martin, *Britain and the Origins of the Canadian Confederation, 1837–67* (London: Macmillan, 1995), 15 and 6–7.
36 Martin, *Britain and the Origins of the Canadian Confederation*, 292.
37 Martin, *Britain and the Origins of the Canadian Confederation*, 294 and 296.
38 For further information about the anti-confederationists in the Maritimes, see G. Martin, 'The Case Against Canadian Confederation, 1864–1867', in G. Martin (Ed.), *The Causes of Canadian Confederation* (Fredericton, NB: Acadiensis Press, 1990), 19–49.
39 Riker, 'Federalism', *Handbook of Political Science*, 120.
40 Martin, *Britain and the Origins of the Canadian Confederation*, 6.
41 Riker, 'Federalism', *Handbook of Political Science*, 120.
42 J. Bryce, *Modern Democracies*, Vol. II (London: Macmillan & Co., 1929), 182.
43 G. Blainey, *The Tyranny of Distance: How Distance Shaped Australia's History* (Melbourne: Sun Books, 1966) and J.D.B. Miller, *Australian Government and Politics: An Introductory Survey* (London: Gerald Duckworth & Co., 1954), 43.
44 J. Holmes and C. Sharman, *The Australian Federal System* (London: George Allen & Unwin, 1977), 13–14.
45 Holmes and Sharman, *The Australian Federal System*, 12.
46 G. Sawer, *Modern Federalism* (London: Pitman, 1976), 31.
47 Riker, *Federalism*, 28.
48 Riker, 'Federalism', *Handbook of Political Science*, 120.
49 Miller, *Australian Government and Politics*, 42 and Sawer, *Modern Federalism*, 31.
50 W.H. Riker, 'Federalism' in R.E. Goodin and P. Pettit (Eds), *A Companion to Contemporary Political Philosophy* (Oxford: Basil Blackwell, 1993), 508–14.
51 B. Galligan, *A Federal Republic: Australia's Constitutional System of Government* (Cambridge: Cambridge University Press, 1995), 56.
52 Holmes and Sharman, *The Australian Federal System*, 14.
53 G. Austin, *The Indian Constitution: Cornerstone of a Nation* (Oxford: Clarendon Press, 1966), xii.
54 R. Dikshit, *The Political Geography of Federalism: An Inquiry into Origins and Stability* (London: Macmillan, 1976), 115.
55 B. Chakrabarty, 'India's Federalism: An Infantile Disorder' in B. Chakrabarty (Ed.), *Centre–State Relations in India* (New Delhi: Segment Book Distributors, 1990), 191.
56 These factors are taken from the following two sources: R.L. Watts, *New Federations: Experiment in the Commonwealth* (Oxford: Clarendon Press, 1966), 17–18 and R.L. Hardgrave, Jr and S.A. Kochanek, *India: Government and Politics in a Developing Nation* (London: Harcourt Brace Jovanovich, 1986), 4th edn, 114–15.
57 Hardgrave and Kochanek, *India: Government and Politics in a Developing Nation*, 115. See also Austin, *The Indian Constitution*, 188–94.
58 Austin, *The Indian Constitution*, 186.
59 See Riker, *Federalism*, 29–30.
60 R.H. Hickling, *An Introduction to the Federal Constitution* (Kuala Lumpur: Federation of Malaya Information Services, 1960), 4.
61 There is a useful summary of these developments in Watts, *New Federations*, 23–27.

62 This is well documented in R.S. Milne, *Government and Politics in Malaysia* (Boston: Houghton Mifflin Company, 1957) and in F.G. Carnell, 'Political Implications of Federalism in New States' in U.K. Hicks *et al.*, *Federalism and Economic Growth in Underdeveloped Countries* (London: Allen & Unwin, 1961), 16–59.

63 Dikshit, *The Political Geography of Federalism*, 128–29.

64 Watts, *New Federations*, 25–26.

65 See H.E. Groves and L.A. Sheridan, *The Constitution of Malaysia* (New York: Oceana Publications, 1967).

66 Watts, *New Federations*, 27.

67 Riker, *Federalism*, 30–31 and Riker, 'Federalism', *Handbook of Political Science*, 124.

68 See B. Simandjuntak, *Malayan Federalism, 1945–1963: A Study of Federal Problems in a Plural Society* (London: Oxford University Press, 1969) and a good summary of these constitutional developments can be found in H.P. Lee, *Constitutional Conflicts in Contemporary Malaysia* (Oxford: Oxford University Press, 1995).

69 Dikshit, *The Political Geography of Federalism*, 136.

70 Dikshit, *The Political Geography of Federalism*, 136.

71 A.H. Birch, 'Approaches to the Study of Federalism', *Political Studies*, XIV(1) (1966), 29–32.

72 Riker, 'Federalism', *Handbook of Political Science*, 114.

73 M. Macdonald, *The Republic of Austria, 1918–1934* (London: Oxford University Press, 1946), 2.

74 K.R. Luther and W.C. Muller (Eds), *Politics in Austria: Still a Case of Consociationalism?* (London: Frank Cass & Co., 1992), 4.

75 Luther and Muller (Eds), *Politics in Austria*, 8–9.

76 Riker, *Federalism*, 38.

77 Dikshit, *The Political Geography of Federalism*, 162.

78 Luther and Muller (Eds), *Politics in Austria*, 4–5.

79 Dikshit, *The Political Geography of Federalism*, 162.

80 R.D. Dikshit, 'Military Interpretation of Federal Constitutions: A Critique', *Journal of Politics*, 33 (1971), 180–89.

81 Dikshit, *The Political Geography of Federalism*, 141.

82 Riker, *Federalism*, 37.

83 Riker, *Federalism*, 37.

84 N. Johnson, 'Territory and Power: Some Historical Determinants of the Constitutional Structure of the Federal Republic of Germany' in C. Jeffery (Ed.), *Recasting German Federalism: The Legacies of Unification* (London: Pinter, 1999), Chap. 2, 29.

85 Dikshit, *The Political Geography of Federalism*, 144.

86 Dikshit, *The Political Geography of Federalism*, 144–45.

87 Riker, *Federalism*, 37.

88 Dikshit, *The Political Geography of Federalism*, 154.

89 Dikshit, *The Political Geography of Federalism*, 154–56.

90 Riker, 'Federalism', *Handbook of Political Science*, 121.

91 Riker, *Federalism*, 13.

92 D. McKay, 'On the Origins of Political Unions: The European Case', *Journal of Theoretical Politics*, 9(3) (1997), 287.

93 A. Stepan, *Arguing Comparative Politics* (Oxford: Oxford University Press, 2001), 318–20.

94 Watts, *New Federations*, 65.

95 D. McKay, 'On the Origins of Political Unions: The European Case', *Journal of Theoretical Politics*, 9(3) (1997), 287.

4 Federalism, nationalism and the national state: legitimacy and the problem of national identity

1 The only references I could find that approximate to this category are M. Forsyth (Ed.), *Federalism and Nationalism* (Leicester: Leicester University Press, 1989), R.A. Goldwin, A. Kaufman and W.A. Schambra (Eds), *Forging Unity Out Of Diversity: The Approaches of Eight Nations* (Washington, DC: American Enterprise Institute for Public Policy Research, 1989) and G. Smith (Ed.), *Federalism: The Multiethnic Challenge* (London: Longman, 1995). A recent edited collection of essays is very useful but is not solely concerned with comparative federalism and federation: A.-G. Gagnon and J. Tully (Eds), *Multinational Democracies* (Cambridge: Cambridge University Press, 2001).

2 See A.D. Smith, *Theories of Nationalism* (London: Duckworth, 1971) and his *National Identity* (London: Penguin, 1991).

3 W.L. Morton quoted in D.V. Smiley, *The Canadian Political Nationality* (Toronto and London: Methuen, 1967), 130.

4 E.A. Freeman, *History of Federal Government in Greece and Italy*, ed. J.E. Bury (Freeport, NY: Books for Libraries Press, 1972), 13.

5 J. Bryce, *Studies in History and Jurisprudence*, 2 vols, Vol. II (Oxford: Clarendon Press, 1901), 268.

6 S. Collini, D. Winch and J. Burrow, *That Noble Science of Politics: A Study in Nineteenth Century Intellectual History* (Cambridge: Cambridge University Press, 1983), 222.

7 J. Bryce, *The American Commonwealth*, Vol. I (New York: The Macmillan Company, 1928), 357.

8 See, for example, the following sources: W. Kymlicka, *Liberalism, Community and Culture* (Oxford: Clarendon Press, 1989), his *Multicultural Citizenship: A Liberal Theory of Minority Rights* (Oxford: Oxford University Press, 1995) and his *Politics in the Vernacular: Nationalism, Multiculturalism and Citizenship* (Oxford: Oxford University Press, 2001), M. Canovan, *Nationhood and Political Theory* (Cheltenham: Edward Elgar, 1996), Y. Tamir, *Liberal Nationalism* (Princeton, NJ: Princeton University Press, 1993), D. Miller, *On Nationality* (Oxford: Clarendon Press, 1995) and his *Citizenship and National Identity* (Cambridge: Polity Press, 2000), and Gagnon and Tully (Eds), *Multinational Democracies*.

9 G. Varouxakis, *Mill on Nationality* (London: Routledge, 2002), 3.

10 Varouxakis, *Mill on Nationality*, 3.

11 Varouxakis, *Mill on Nationality*, 4.

12 J.S. Mill, *Utilitarianism, On Liberty and Considerations on Representative Government*, ed. H.B. Acton (London: J.M. Dent & Sons, 1972), 367.

13 Mill, *Representative Government*, 374–76.

14 Varouxakis, *Mill on Nationalism*, is a vigorous defence of Mill's liberal political thought on nationalism and takes to task his contemporary liberal critics.

15 See Y. Tamir, *Liberal Nationalism* and D. Miller, *On Nationality*. I do not wish to suggest that their theoretical positions are the same. For a detailed analysis of their different views on nations and nationality, see M. Canovan, *Nationhood and Political Theory*, Chap. 10, 115–24.

16 Sir John (later Lord) Acton, 'Nationality' in his *History of Freedom and Other Essays* (London: Macmillan & Co., 1907), 289.

17 Acton, 'Nationality', 289.

18 Acton, 'Nationality', 289.

19 Acton, 'Nationality', 290.

20 Acton, 'Nationality', 298.

21 Varouxakis, *Mill on Nationalism*, 7.

22 Tamir, *Liberal Nationalism*, 143–44.

23 Tamir, *Liberal Nationalism*, 144.

24 Tamir, *Liberal Nationalism*, 150.
25 D.J. Elazar, *Exploring Federalism* (Tuscaloosa, AL: University of Alabama Press, 1987), 85.
26 For further information about the creation of the Jura, see W. Linder, *Swiss Democracy: Possible Solutions to Conflict in Multicultural Societies* (London: Macmillan, 1994), 25–27 and 65–68; for the new Indian states, see H. Bhattacharyya, 'India Creates Three New States', *Federations: What's New in The Practice of Federalism?*, 1(3) (2001); and for Nunavut, see A. Cairns, *Citizens Plus: Aboriginal Peoples and the Canadian State* (Vancouver: University of British Columbia Press, 2000).
27 Kymlicka, *Politics in the Vernacular*, 92–96.
28 Kymlicka, *Politics in the Vernacular*, 96.
29 Studies of the theoretical concerns inherent in liberal multinationalism can be found in Tamir, *Liberal Nationalism*, Gagnon and Tully (Eds), *Multinational Democracies* and Kymlicka, *Politics in the Vernacular*.
30 W.S. Livingston, 'A Note on the Nature of Federalism', *Political Science Quarterly*, 67 (March 1952), 81–95. The debate about the meaning and empirical implications of the phrase 'federal society' was explored in M.B. Stein, 'Federal Political Systems and Federal Societies', *World Politics*, 20 (1968), 721–47.
31 B. Galligan, *A Federal Republic: Australia's Constitutional System of Government* (Cambridge: Cambridge University Press, 1995), 55.
32 Galligan, *A Federal Republic*, 61–62.
33 Galligan, *A Federal Republic*, 62.
34 Galligan, *A Federal Republic*, 55. He referred his readers to a list of 'federal failures' in M. Frenkel, *Federal Theory* (Canberra: Centre for Research on Federal Financial Relations, The Australia National University, 1986), 102–3.
35 K.C. Wheare, *Federal Government* (London: Oxford University Press, 1963), 4th edn, 38–41.
36 Wheare, *Federal Government* (italics added).
37 Elazar, *Exploring Federations*, 38–64.
38 Tamir, *Liberal Nationalism*, 144.
39 C. Taylor, 'Why do Nations have to become States?' in C. Taylor, *Reconciling the Solitudes: Essays on Canadian Federalism and Nationalism*, ed. G. Laforest (London: McGill-Queens University Press, 1993), Chap. 3, 40–58.
40 Taylor, 'Why do Nations have to Become States?', 45.
41 Tamir, *Liberal Nationalism*, 145.
42 Tamir, *Liberal Nationalism*, 163.
43 R. Maiz, 'Democracy, Federalism and Nationalism in Multinational States' in W. Safran and R. Maiz (Eds), *Identity and Territorial Autonomy in Plural Societies* (London: Frank Cass, 2000), 35–60.
44 Maiz, 'Democracy, Federalism and Nationalism', 36 (italics in original).
45 A.-G. Gagnon, 'The Moral Foundations of Asymmetrical Federalism: A Normative Exploration of the Case of Quebec and Canada' in Gagnon and Tully (Eds), *Multinational Democracies*, Chap. 13, 319–37.
46 Gagnon, 'The Moral Foundations', 321.
47 Maiz, 'Democracy, Federalism and Nationalism', 36.
48 Maiz, 'Democracy, Federalism and Nationalism', 36.
49 See R. Agranoff (Ed.), *Accommodating Diversity: Asymmetry in Federal States* (Baden-Baden: Nomos Verlag., 1999).
50 See B. de Villiers, *Bundestreue: The Soul of an Intergovernmental Partnership*, Occasional Papers (Johannesburg, RSA: Konrad Adenauer Stiftung, March 1995), 3–36, S. LaSelva, *The Moral Foundations of Canadian Federalism: Paradoxes, Achievements and Tragedies of Nationhood* (London: McGill-Queen's University Press, 1996) and M. Burgess, 'The Federal Spirit as a Moral Basis to Canadian Federalism', *International Journal of Canadian Studies*, 22 (Fall 2000), 13–35.

51 Wheare, *Federal Government*, 50.
52 C. Taylor, 'Shared and Divergent Values' in R.L. Watts and D.M. Brown (Eds), *Options for a New Canada* (Toronto: University of Toronto Press, 1991), Chap. 4, 64–65.
53 Tamir, *Liberal Nationalism*, 145.
54 Kymlicka, *Politics in the Vernacular*, 92.
55 Taylor, 'Why do Nations have to become States?', 57.
56 See J. Tully, *Strange Multiplicity: Constitutionalism in an Age of Diversity*, Chap. 6 (Cambridge: Cambridge University Press, 1995) and his 'Introduction' in Gagnon and Tully (Eds), *Multinational Democracies*, 1–33.
57 Tully, 'Introduction', 5.
58 Tully, 'Introduction', 32.
59 Tully, 'Introduction', 33. This observation is reminiscent of Elazar's emphasis upon the need to have 'a continuing stream of constitutional questions that require public attention … a continuing referendum on first principles' in *Exploring Federalism*, 85.
60 Quoted in F. Delmartino, 'Belgium: A Regional State or a Federal State in the Making?' in M. Burgess (Ed.), *Federalism and Federation in Western Europe* (London: Croom Helm, 1986), Chap. 3, 38.
61 J. Fitzmaurice, *The Politics of Belgium: A Unique Federalism* (London: Hurst & Company, 1996), 49.
62 On the 'personality' principle and the special status of the Brussels Capital Region, see W. Swenden, 'Asymmetric Federalism and Coalition-Making in Belgium', *Publius: The Journal of Federalism*, 32(3) (2002), 67–87 and D. Jacobs and M. Swyngedouw, 'Territorial and Non-Territorial Federalism: Reform of the Brussels Capital Region, 2001', *Regional and Federal Studies*: 13(2) (Summer 2003), 127–39.
63 J. Poirier, 'Formal Mechanisms of Intergovernmental Relations in Belgium', *Regional and Federal Studies*, 12(3) (Autumn 2002), 24–54.
64 Poirier, 'Formal Mechanisms', 26. On the issue of ambiguity, see C. Erk and A.-G. Gagnon, 'Constitutional Ambiguity and Federal Trust: Codification of Federalism in Canada, Spain and Belgium', *Regional and Federal Studies*, 10(1) (Spring 2000), 92–111.
65 De Villiers, *Bundestreue*, 1–36.
66 See Linder, *Swiss Democracy*, 18–25.
67 V. Bogdanor, 'Federalism in Switzerland', *Government and Opposition*, 23(1) (Winter 1988), 71.
68 See T. Fleiner, 'Commentary' that follows the chapter by O.K. Kaufmann, 'Swiss Federalism' in Goldwin, Kaufman and Schambra (Eds), *Forging Unity Out Of Diversity*, 240.
69 K. McRae (Ed.), *Conflict and Compromise in Multilingual Societies: Switzerland* (Waterloo, Ont.: Wilfrid Laurier University Press, 1983), 232.
70 Linder, *Swiss Democracy*, 130.
71 Hughes claimed that 'each canton has become almost an ethnicity in its own right'. See C. Hughes, 'Cantonalism: Federation and Confederacy in the Golden Epoch of Switzerland' in M. Burgess and A.-G. Gagnon (Eds) *Comparative Federalism and Federation: Competing Traditions and Future Directions* (Hemel Hempstead: Harvester Wheatsheaf, 1993), Chap. 9, 156.
72 Linder describes it as 'an 'artificial multicultural nation' that is 'an independent political nation', having renounced 'a "nation-state" of one culture, one religion and one language'. See Linder, *Swiss Democracy*, xvi–xviii.
73 Kymlicka, *Politics in the Vernacular*, 92 and A. Stepan, *Arguing Comparative Politics* (Oxford: Oxford University Press, 2001), 327.
74 See the preamble to the new Federal Constitution of Switzerland formally adopted in 1999.
75 See Taylor, 'Shared and Divergent Values', Chap. 4, 53–76.
76 See D.J. Horton, *Andre Laurendeau: French-Canadian Nationalist, 1912–1968* (Oxford: Oxford University Press, 1993), 225. The debate about protecting and promoting Quebec's

distinct identity in Canada is examined in M. Burgess, 'Ethnicity, Nationalism and Identity in Canada–Quebec Relations: The Case of Quebec's "Distinct Society"', *Journal of Commonwealth and Comparative Politics*, XXXIV(2) (July 1996), 46–64.

77 Rene Levesque, quoted in N. Bissoondath, *Selling Illusions: The Cult of Multiculturalism in Canada* (Toronto: Penguin Books, 1994), 40.

78 On the idea of English Canada, see J.L. Granatstein and K. McNaught (Eds), *English Canada Speaks Out* (Toronto: Doubleday Canada, 1991) and P. Resnick, *Thinking English Canada* (Toronto: Stoddart, 1994); and on the anglophone Quebecois, see R. Rudin, 'English-Speaking Quebec: The Emergence of a Disillusioned Minority' in A.-G. Gagnon (Ed.), *Quebec: State and Society* (Scarborough, Ont.: Nelson Canada, 1993), 2nd edn, Chap. 19, 338–48.

79 Wheare, *Federal Government*, 27.

80 These trends and developments have been researched in B. Chakrabarty (Ed.), *Centre–State Relations in India* (New Delhi: Segment Book Distributors, 1990).

81 See B. Arora, 'Adapting Federalism to India: Multilevel and Asymmetrical Innovations' in B. Arora and D.V. Verney (Eds), *Multiple Identities in a Single State: Indian Federalism in a Comparative Perspective* (New Delhi: Konark Publishers, 1995), Chap. 3, 72.

82 Arora, 'Adapting Federalism to India', 78.

83 There is a useful survey of constitutional and institutional responses to the challenge of social diversity in India in H. Bhattacharyya, *India as a Multicultural Federation: Asian Values, Democracy and Decentralisation (in comparison with Swiss Federalism)* (Basel: Helbing & Lichtenhahn, 2001), Chaps 2 and 6.

84 Arora, 'Adapting Federalism to India', 78.

85 H.P. Lee, *Constitutional Conflicts in Contemporary Malaysia* (Oxford: Oxford University Press, 1995), 120.

86 R.L. Watts, *New Federations: Experiments in the Commonwealth* (Oxford: Clarendon Press, 1966), 24.

87 See *Federal Constitution [Laws of Malaysia]*, Article 153(1–10), 15 January 2003 (Kuala Lumpur: International Law Book Series, 2003), 188–91.

88 For the details see V. Sinnadurai, 'Unity and Diversity: The Constitution of Malaysia' in Goldwin, Kaufman and Schambra (Eds), *Forging Unity Out Of Diversity*, Chap. 7, 334–41.

89 Paragraph 165 of the Reid Commission Report, quoted in Sinnadurai, 'Unity and Diversity', 337 (italics in original).

90 Sinnadurai's account points out that the interpretation of the federal court in 1982 'arrived at an interpretation so obviously not intended by the drafters of the constitution', 'Unity and Diversity', 340.

91 See Articles 161 and 161A of the Federal Constitution.

92 The Boon Eng, 'Commentary' in Sinnadurai, 'Unity and Diversity', 350.

93 See J.M. Fernando, *The Making of the Malayan Constitution*, MBRAS monograph, No. 31 (Kuala Lumpur: The Malaysian Branch of the Royal Asiatic Society, 2002).

94 C. Taylor, 'Foreword' in Gagnon and Tully (Eds), *Multinational Democracies*, xiv.

95 J. Tully, 'Introduction', 1–33.

96 See, for example, D. Miller, 'Nationality in Divided Societies' in Gagnon and Tully, *Multinational Democracies*, Chap. 12, 306–7 and M. Keating, *Plurinational Democracy: Stateless Nations in a Post-Sovereignty Era* (Oxford: Oxford University Press, 2001), 26–27.

97 K. McRoberts, 'Canada and the Multinational State', *Canadian Journal of Political Science*, XXXIV(4) (December 2001), 683–713.

98 McRoberts, 'Canada and the Multinational State', 686–88.

99 Apart from those mentioned whose work has already been cited in the text, we can also include two additional Canadian scholars, namely, Philip Resnick, 'Toward a Multinational Federalism: Asymmetrical Confederal Alternatives' in F.L. Seidle (Ed.),

Seeking a New Canadian Partnership: Asymmetrical and Confederal Options (Montreal: Institute for Research on Public Policy, 1994), 71–90 and Wayne Norman, 'Justice and Stability in Multinational Societies' in Gagnon and Tully (Eds), *Multinational Democracies*, Chap. 3, 90–109.

100 M. Canovan, *Nationhood and Political Theory*, 3.
101 McRoberts, 'Canada and the Multinational State', 694–97. It must be pointed out that this article was published before Gagnon and Tully's *Multinational Democracies* appeared.
102 McRoberts, 'Canada and the Multinational State', 710.
103 Canovan, *Nationhood and Political Theory*, 2–3.
104 R. Simeon and D.-P. Conway, 'Federalism and the Management of Conflict in Multinational Societies' in Gagnon and Tully (Eds), *Multinational Democracies*, Chap. 14, 361 and 364.

5   The comparative study of federal political systems

1   W. Riker, *Federalism: Origin, Operation, Significance* (Boston: Little, Brown & Company, 1964), see 'Suggestions for further reading', 157 and 'Preface', xi–xiii. Riker was using the term 'federalism' to apply to both federations and federal political systems.
2   Riker, *Federalism*, xii.
3   K.C. Wheare, *Federal Government* (Oxford: Oxford University Press, 1963), 4th edn.
4   Riker, *Federalism*, 157.
5   R.L. Watts, *Comparing Federal Systems* (London, Montreal and Kingston, Ont.: McGill-Queen's University Press, 1999), 2nd edn, 35–41.
6   D.J. Elazar, *Exploring Federalism* (Tuscaloosa, AL: University of Alabama Press, 1987), 12.
7   Watts, *Comparing Federal Systems*, 35.
8   G. Austin, *The Indian Constitution: Cornerstone of a Nation* (Oxford: Clarendon Press, 1966), 207.
9   Austin, *The Indian Constitution*, xii.
10 For a detailed examination of the history of constitutional rule in Malaysia, see H.P. Lee, *Constitutional Conflicts in Contemporary Malaysia* (Oxford: Oxford University Press, 1995), Chap. 5, 100–25.
11 Lee, *Constitutional Conflicts*, 119–20.
12 For further details about 'executive federalism', see D.V. Smiley, *The Federal Condition in Canada* (Toronto: McGraw-Hill Ryerson, 1987), R.L. Watts, *Executive Federalism: A Comparative Analysis* (Kingston, Ont.: Queen's University, Institute of Intergovernmental Relations, 1989), J. Stefan Dupre, 'Reflections on The Workability of Executive Federalism' in R.S. Blair and J.T. McLeod (Eds), *The Canadian Political Tradition: Basic Readings* (Scarborough, Ont.: Nelson, 1993), 472–500 and R.L. Watts, 'German Federalism in Comparative Perspective' in C. Jeffery (Ed.), *Recasting German Federalism: The Legacies of Unification* (London: Pinter, 1999), Chap. 12, 265–84.
13 R. Gibbins, 'Federal Societies, Institutions and Politics' in H. Bakvis and W.M. Chandler (Eds), *Federalism and the Role of the State* (Toronto: University of Toronto Press, 1987), Chap. 2, 18.
14 Preston King, 'Against Federalism' in R. Benewick, R.N. Berki and B. Parekh (Eds), *Knowledge and Belief in Politics* (London: Allen & Unwin, 1973), 153.
15 In Canada the work of Alan C. Cairns on the relationship between federal state, government and society is worth more than a passing glance. See his 'The Governments and Societies of Canadian Federalism', *Canadian Journal of Political Science*, 10 (1977), 695–726.
16 M.J.C. Vile, 'Federal Theory and the "New Federalism"' in D. Jaensch (Ed.), *The Politics of New Federalism* (Adelaide: Australian Political Studies Association, 1977), 3.

17 R. Simeon and D.-P. Conway, 'Federalism and the Management of Conflict in Multinational Societies' in A.-G. Gagnon and J. Tully (Eds), *Multinational Democracies* (Cambridge: Cambridge University Press, 2001), Chap. 14, 361.

18 B. Galligan, *A Federal Republic: Australia's Constitutional System of Government* (Cambridge: Cambridge University Press, 1995), 55 and W.S. Livingston, 'A Note on the Nature of Federalism', *Political Science Quarterly*, 67 (March 1952), 81–95.

19 The contemporary debate was sparked by Livingston's article identified in fn. 18 above, but it developed to include I.D. Duchacek, *Comparative Federalism: The Territorial Dimension of Politics* (New York: Holt, Reinhart & Winston Inc., 1970), R.D. Dikshit, *The Political Geography of Federalism: An Inquiry into Origins and Stability* (New Delhi: The Macmillan Company of India Limited, 1975) and Vile, 'Federal Theory and the "New Federalism"', 1–14.

20 F.N. Trager, '"Introduction": On Federalism' in T.M. Franck (Ed.), *Why Federations Fail* (London: London University Press, 1968), x.

21 J.G. Ruggie, 'Territoriality and Beyond: Problematizing Modernity in International Relations', *International Organization*, 47(1) (Winter 1993), 149–50.

22 See F. Prinz, 'A Model of a Multinational Society as Developed in Austria-Hungary before 1918' in N. Rhoodie (Ed.), *Intergroup Accommodation in Plural Societies* (London: Macmillan, 1978), Chap. 3, 44–52.

23 For further information about the religious cleavage in Swiss federalism see W. Linder, *Swiss Democracy: Possible Solutions to Conflict in Multicultural Societies* (London: Macmillan, 1994), 18–21.

24 Figures taken from K.M. Mathew (Ed.), *Manorama Yearbook 1997*, Part IV, 'India and the States' (Kottayam, Kerala: 1998), 460.

25 See the chapter by Ismail Bakar entitled 'Multinational Federation: The Case of Malaysia' in the collection of essays currently being edited by M. Burgess and J. Pinder as *Multinational Federations*.

26 See, for example, P.L. Chartrand, 'The Aboriginal Peoples in Canada and Renewal of the Federation' in K. Knop (Ed.), *Rethinking Federalism: Citizens, Markets and Governments in a Changing World* (Vancouver: University of British Columbia Press, 1995), Chap. 8, 119–31, F. Abele and M.J. Prince, 'Alternative Futures: Aboriginal Peoples and Canadian Federalism' in H. Bakvis and G. Skogstad (Eds), *Canadian Federalism: Performance, Effectiveness and Legitimacy* (Oxford: Oxford University Press, 2002), Chap. 12, 220–37, F. Abele and M.J. Prince, 'Aboriginal Governance and Canadian Federalism: A To-Do List for Canada' in F. Rocher and M. Smith (Eds), *New Trends in Canadian Federalism* (Peterborough, Ont.: Broadview Press, 2003), Chap. 6, 135–65 and K.L. Ladner, 'Treaty Federalism: An Indigenous Vision of Canadian Federalisms' in Rocher and Smith (Eds), *New Trends in Canadian Federalism*, Chap. 7, 167–94.

27 Elazar, *Exploring Federalism*, 85.

28 Preston King, *Federalism and Federation* (London: Croom Helm, 1982), 76.

29 See W. Clement and G. Williams, 'Introduction' in W. Clement and G. Williams (Eds), *The New Canadian Political Economy* (London: McGill-Queen's University Press, 1989), 7.

30 Clement and Williams (Eds), *The New Canadian Political Economy*, 10.

31 See M. Burgess, 'From Trudeau to Mulroney: The Political Economy of Constitutional Reform in Canada, 1980–1990' in C.H.W. Remie and J.-M. Lacroix (Eds), *Canada on the Threshold of the 21st Century: European Reflections upon the Future of Canada* (Amsterdam: John Benjamins Publishing Company, 1991).

32 R. Simeon, 'National Reconciliation: The Mulroney Government and Federalism' in A.B. Gollner and D. Salee (Eds), *Canada Under Mulroney: An End of Term Report* (Montreal: Vehicle Press, 1988), 45–46.

33 G. Stevenson, 'Federalism and the Political Economy of the Canadian State' in L. Panitch (Ed.), *The Canadian State: Political Economy and Political Power* (Toronto: University of Toronto Press, 1977), Chap. 3, 71–100.

34 Stevenson, 'Federalism and the Political Economy of the Canadian State', 78.

35 See, for example, R. Hudon, 'Quebec, the Economy and the Constitution' in K. Banting and R. Simeon (Eds), *And No One Cheered: Democracy and the Constitution Act* (Toronto: Methuen, 1983), Chap. 7, 133–53 and A.-G. Gagnon and M.B. Montcalm, *Quebec: Beyond The Quiet Revolution* (Scarborough, Ont.: Nelson Canada, 1990).

36 See R. Voigt, 'Financing the German Federal System in the 1980s', *Publius: The Journal of Federalism*, 19(4) (fall 1989), 99–113.

37 There is an excellent survey by H. Mackenstein and C. Jeffery, 'Financial Equalisation in the 1990s: On the Road Back to Karlsruhe?' in C. Jeffery (Ed.) *Recasting German Federalism: The Legacies of Unification* (London: Pinter, 1999), Chap. 7, 155–76. See also A. Gunlicks, *The Lander and German Federalism* (Manchester: Manchester University Press, 2003), Chap. 5, 163–211.

38 The Constitution Act (1982).

39 Three recent comparative surveys can be found in R.M. Bird and F. Vaillancourt, *Fiscal Decentralisation in Developing Countries* (Cambridge: Cambridge University Press, 1998) and C. Jeffery and D. Heald (Eds), 'Money Matters: Territorial Finance in Decentralised States', *Regional and Federal Studies*, Special Issue, 13(4) (Winter 2003).

40 See M.G. Rao, 'Indian Fiscal Federalism from a Comparative Perspective' in B. Arora and D.V. Verney (Eds), *Multiple Identities in a Single State: Indian Federalism in Comparative Perspective* (New Delhi: Konark Publishers, 1995), Chap. 9, 272–316.

41 See A. Mozoomdar, 'The Political Economy of Modern Federalism' in Arora and Verney (Eds), *Multiple Identities in a Single State*, Chap. 7, 197–233 and S. Guhan, 'Federalism and the New Political Economy in India' in the same volume of essays, Chap. 8, 237–71.

42 See R.L. Watts, *The Spending Power in Federal Systems: A Comparative Study* (Kingston, Ont.: Queen's University, Institute of Intergovernmental Relations, 1999) and his *Comparing Federal Systems* (London, Montreal and Kingston, Ont.: McGill-Queen's University Press, 1999), 2nd edn, Chap. 4, 43–55.

43 The classic texts are J.M. Buchanan, 'Federalism and Fiscal Equity', *American Economic Review*, 40(4) (1950), 421–32, R.N. Bhargava, 'The Theory of Federal Finance', *The Economic Journal*, 63(249) (1953), 84–97, R. Musgrave, *Essays in Fiscal Federalism* (Washington, DC: The Brookings Institute, 1965) and W.E. Oates, *Fiscal Federalism* (New York: Harcourt Brace Jovanovich, 1972).

44 R.L. Watts, 'Introduction: Comparative Research and Fiscal Federalism', *Regional and Federal Studies*, 13(4) (Winter 2003), 1–6 (italics in original).

45 For the view that fiscal federalism and the federal spirit are intimately interrelated see I. Bakar, 'Fiscal Federalism: The Study of Federal–State Fiscal Relations in Malaysia', Ph.D. thesis, University of Hull (2004).

46 See K.C. Wheare, *Federal Government* (Oxford: Oxford University Press, 1963), 4th edn, 82–85, D.B. Truman, 'Federalism and the Party System' in A.W. Macmahon (Ed.), *Federalism: Mature and Emergent* (New York: Russell & Russell, 1962), Chap. 8, 115–36, W.H. Riker, *Federalism: Origin, Operation, Significance* (Boston: Little, Brown & Company, 1964), 91–101 and 136 and A. Wildavsky (Ed.), *American Federalism in Perspective* (Boston: Little, Brown & Company, 1967), Section III. It is worth pointing out that Truman's seminal paper was first published in 1955 under the copyright of Columbia University and that Wildavsky's interest in political parties and federal systems dates back at least to his 'Party Discipline under Federalism', *Social Research*, 28 (1961), 437–58. See also S. Rufus Davis, 'The "Federal Principle" Reconsidered', Part II, *Australian Journal of Politics and History*, 1(2) (May 1956), 223–44.

47 Riker, *Federalism: Origin, Operation, Significance*, 136.

48 Riker, *Federalism: Origin, Operation, Significance*, 125–36 and 'Federalism' in F.I. Greenstein and N.W. Polsby (Eds), *The Handbook of Political Science: Governmental Institutions and Processes*, Vol. 5 (Reading, MA: Addison Wesley, 1975), 131–41.

49 Riker, *Federalism: Origins, Operation, Significance*, 129–30.

50 Riker, *Federalism: Origin, Operation, Significance*, 130. His empirical evidence for this claim was derived from W.H. Riker and R. Schaps, 'Disharmony in Federal Government', *Behavioral Science*, 2 (1957), 276–90.

51 Riker, 'Federalism', 134.

52 Riker, 'Federalism', 137.

53 Riker, 'Federalism', 140.

54 The notions of 'symmetry' and 'asymmetry' were first introduced to the debate about federalism by Charles D. Tarlton in 'Symmetry and Asymmetry as Elements of Federalism: A Theoretical Speculation', *Journal of Politics*, 27 (1965), 861–74.

55 G. Sawer, *Modern Federalism* (London: Pitman Publishing, 1976), 121.

56 D.J. Elazar, *Exploring Federalism*, 178–79.

57 See R. Gibbins, *Regionalism: Territorial Politics in Canada and the United States* (Toronto: Butterworths, 1982), 130–40.

58 Elazar, *Exploring Federalism*, 180.

59 See J.D.B. Miller, *Australian Government and Politics: An Introductory Survey* (London: Gerald Duckworth & Co. Ltd, 1954), 53 (my italics) and J. Rydon, 'The Australian Tradition of Federalism and Federation' in M. Burgess and A.-G. Gagnon (Eds), *Comparative Federalism and Federation: Competing Traditions and Future Directions* (Hemel Hempstead: Harvester Wheatsheaf, 1993), 231.

60 Miller, *Australian Government and Politics*, 53.

61 See J. Chin, 'Politics of Federal Intervention in Malaysia, with Reference to Sarawak, Sabah and Kelantan', *Journal of Commonwealth and Comparative Politics*, 19(2) (April 1997), 159–72.

62 See B.H. Shafruddin, *The Federal Factor in the Government and Politics of Peninsular Malaysia* (Singapore: Oxford University Press, 1987).

63 See A. Zakaria (Ed.), *The Government and Politics of Malaysia* (Singapore: Oxford University Press, 1987).

64 See M.A. Yusoff, 'Federalism in Malaysia: A Study of the Politics of Centre–State Relations', Ph.D. thesis, University of Manchester (1998), 26.

65 S. Barraclough, 'Barisan Nasional Dominance and Opposition Fragmentation: The Failure of Attempts to Create Opposition Cooperation in the Malaysian Party System', *Asian Profile*, 13(1) (1985), 33–43.

66 See T.B. Eng, 'Commentary' in V. Sinnadurai, 'Unity and Diversity: The Constitution of Malaysia' in R.A. Goldwin, A. Kaufman and W.A. Schambra (Eds) *Forging Unity Out of Diversity: The Approach of Eight Nations* (Washington, DC: American Enterprise Institute for Public Policy Research, 1989), Chap. 7, 351.

67 Riker, *Federalism: Origin, Operation, Significance*, Preface, xi–xiii. For a summary of Riker's intellectual contribution to the study of federalism in particular and to the discipline of political science in general, see A. Stepan, *Arguing Comparative Politics* (Oxford: Oxford University Press, 2001), 316–18.

68 S. Rufus Davis, 'The "Federal Principle" Reconsidered', Part II, 242.

69 I.D. Duchacek, *Comparative Federalism*, 193 (italics in original).

70 Duchacek, *Comparative Federalism*, 192. For a detailed exposition of the 'federal spirit', see M. Burgess, 'The Federal Spirit as a Moral Basis to Canadian Federalism', *International Journal of Canadian Studies*, 22 (Fall 2000), 13–35.

71 King, *Federalism and Federation*, 14 and 75.

72 A.C. Cairns, 'The Living Canadian Constitution', *Queen's Quarterly*, LXXVII (Winter 1970), 1–16. Reprinted in J.P. Meekison (Ed.), *Canadian Federalism: Myth or Reality* (London: Methuen, 1977), 3rd edn, Chap. 6, 86–99.

73 See Watts, *Comparing Federal Systems*, 101–4.

74 R. Simeon, 'Political Pragmatism Takes Precedence Over Democratic Process' in M.D. Behiels (Ed.), *The Meech Lake Primer: Conflicting Views of the 1987 Constitutional Accord* (Ottawa: University of Ottawa Press, 1989), Chap. 3, 131–35.

75 Watts, *Comparing Federal Systems*, 99.

76 Watts, *Comparing Federal Systems*, 100.
77 Elazar, *Exploring Federal Systems*, 216.
78 See the following sources: J. Smith, 'The Origins of Judicial Review in Canada', *Canadian Journal of Political Science*, 16 (March 1983), J. Smith, 'Judicial Review and Modern Federalism: Canada and the United States' in Bakvis and Chandler (Eds), *Federalism and the Role of the State*, Chap. 7, 113–26, G. Baier, 'Judicial Review and Canadian Federalism' in H. Bakvis and G. Skogstad (Eds), *Canadian Federalism: Performance, Effectiveness and Legitimacy* (Oxford: Oxford University Press, 2002), Chap. 2, 24–39, G. Baier, 'The Law of Federalism: Judicial Review and the Division of Powers' in Rocher and Smith (Eds), *New Trends in Canadian Federalism*, Chap. 5, 111–33.
79 Quebec has its own bill of rights, the Quebec Charter of Human Rights and Freedoms, adopted by the provincial National Assembly in June 1975. For the argument that this might form the basis of a series of multiple charters throughout Canada, see D. Schneiderman, 'Human Rights, Fundamental Differences? Multiple Charters in a Partnership Frame' in R. Gibbins and G. Laforest (Eds), *Beyond the Impasse: Toward Reconciliation* (Montreal: Institute for Research on Public Policy, 1998), Part Three, 147–85. For the view that the centralisation thesis is questionable, see J.B. Kelly, 'Reconciling Rights and Federalism during Review of the Charter of Rights and Freedoms: the Supreme Court of Canada and the Centralization Thesis, 1982 to 1999', *Canadian Journal of Political Science*, XXXIV(2) (June 2001), 321–55.
80 For a detailed examination of judicial review in West Germany, see P. Blair, *Federalism and Judicial Review in West Germany* (Oxford: Clarendon Press, 1981) but see also the insightful article by G. Kisker, 'The West German Federal Constitutional Court as Guardian of the Federal System', *Publius: The Journal of Federalism*, 19(4) (Fall 1989), 35–52. For the recent revival of federal comity in law, see P. Blair and P. Cullen, 'Federalism, Legalism and Political Reality: The Record of the Federal Constitutional Court' in C. Jeffery (Ed.), *Recasting German Federalism: The Legacies of Unification* (London: Pinter, 1999), Chap. 6, 119–54.
81 B. Galligan, *A Federal Republic*, 171.
82 See Articles 188–91, The Federal Constitution of Switzerland, Title 5, Federal Authorities, Chap. 4, Federal Supreme Court, 45.
83 See C. Rothmayr, '"Towards the Judicialisation of Swiss Politics?" in J.-E. Lane (Ed.), The Swiss Labyrinth: Institutions, Outcomes and Redesign', *West European Politics*, 24(2) (April 2001), 77–94.
84 Rothmayr, 'Towards the Judicialisation of Swiss Politics?', 78–79.
85 Kisker, 'The West German Federal Constitutional Court', 43.
86 Elazar, *Exploring Federal Systems*, 215.
87 S. Rufus Davis, 'The "Federal Principle" Reconsidered', Part II, 242.

6   The Anglo-American and Continental European federal political traditions

1 F.H. Hinsley, *Power and the Pursuit of Peace* (Cambridge: Cambridge University Press, 1980), 13.
2 G. Sartori, 'Concept Misformation in Comparative Politics', *American Political Science Review*, 64 (1970), 1033–53.
3 F.H. Hinsley, *Sovereignty* (London: C.A. Watts, 1966).
4 See M.J. Tooley (Ed.), *Six Books of the Commonwealth* (Oxford: Basil Blackwell, 1955).
5 S. Rufus Davis, *The Federal Principle: A Journey Through Time in Quest of a Meaning* (London: University of California Press, 1978), 46–47. Davis' view is confirmed by S. Mogi who also noted that Bodin was curiously 'the first advocate of the federal idea

on a theoretical basis' in his classic *The Problem of Federalism: A Study in the History of Political Theory*, Vol. I (London: George Allen & Unwin, 1931), 26.

6 See P. Riley, 'The Origins of Federal Theory in International Relations Ideas', *Polity*, VI(1) (1973), 87–121.

7 S. Lakoff, 'Between Either/Or and More or Less: Sovereignty Versus Autonomy Under Federalism', *Publius: The Journal of Federalism*, 24 (Winter 1994), 68.

8 On the ambiguity evident in Rousseau's political thought about federalism, see P. Riley, 'Rousseau as a Theorist of National and International Federalism', *Publius: The Journal of Federalism*, 3(1) (1973), 5–17.

9 Riley, 'The Origins of Federal Theory', 87–121.

10 Riley, 'The Origins of Federal Theory' and 'Three 17th Century German Theorists of Federalism: Althusius, Hugo and Leibniz', *Publius: The Journal of Federalism*, 6(3), 1976, 7–41.

11 Riley, 'The Origins of Federal Theory', 92.

12 Riley, 'The Origins of Federal Theory', 94.

13 M. Stein, 'Changing Concepts of Federalism since World War II: Anglo-American and Continental European Traditions', paper presented to the Workshop on Genealogy and Concept Formation, International Committee for the Study of the Development of Political Science, Mexico City, 24–27 May 1994, 1–31. Daniel Elazar had already alluded to the political-theological ideas of Heinrich Bullinger that had influenced Johannes Althusius in his *Exploring Federalism* (Tuscaloosa, AL: University of Alabama Press, 1987), 138–39.

14 C. Pentland, *International Theory and European Integration* (London: Faber & Faber, 1973), 159–60.

15 Stein, 'Changing Concepts of Federalism since World War II', 15.

16 See M. Fogarty, *Christian Democracy in Western Europe, 1820–1953* (London: Routledge & Kegan Paul, 1957), Ilan Greilsammer, 'Some Observations on European Federalism' in D. Elazar (Ed.), *Federalism and Political Integration* (Israel: Turtledove, 1979), T.O. Hueglin, 'Johannes Althusius: Medieval Constitutionalist or Modern Federalist?', *Publius: The Journal of Federalism*, 9(4) (Fall 1979), 9–41, M. Burgess, 'Federalism and Federation in Western Europe' in M. Burgess (Ed.), *Federalism and Federation in Western Europe* (London: Croom Helm, 1986), Chap. 2, 15–33 and M. Burgess, 'The European Tradition of Federalism: Christian Democracy and Federalism' in M. Burgess and A.-G. Gagnon (Eds), *Comparative Federalism and Federation: Competing Traditions and Future Directions* (Hemel Hempstead: Harvester Wheatsheaf, 1993), Chap. 8, 138–53.

17 A. Osiander, 'Sovereignty, International Relations, and the Westphalian Myth', *International Organization*, 55(2) (Spring 2001), 270.

18 Osiander, 'Sovereignty', 279.

19 The classic work on this remains E.A. Freeman, *History of Federal Government in Greece and Italy*, ed. J.E. Bury (Freeport, NY: Books For Libraries Press, 1972). It was first published in 1893.

20 J.G. Ruggie, 'Territoriality and Beyond: Problematizing Modernity in International Relations', *International Organization*, 47(1) (Winter 1993), 149–50.

21 In the IR literature, see for example J.G. Ruggie, 'Continuity and Transformation in the World Polity: Towards a Neorealist Synthesis', *World Politics*, 35 (January 1983), 261–85, M. Fischer, 'Feudal Europe, 800–1300: Communal Discourse and Conflictual Practices', *International Organization*, 46 (Spring 1992), 427–66, and M.W. Zacher, 'The Territorial Integrity Norm: International Boundaries and the Use of Force', *International Organization*, 55(2) (Spring 2001), 215–50. In the EI literature, see for example J.A. Caporaso, 'The European Union and Forms of State: Westphalian, Regulatory or Post-Modern?', *Journal of Common Market Studies*, 34(1) (March 1996), 29–52, M. Smith, 'The European Union and a Changing Europe: Establishing the Boundaries of Order', *Journal of Common Market Studies*, 34(1), 5–28 and J. Zielonka,

'How New Enlarged Borders will Reshape the European Union', *Journal of Common Market Studies*, 39(3) (September 2001), 507–36.

22   See D. Nicholls, *The Pluralist State* (London: Macmillan Press, 1975), 32.

23   Elazar, *Exploring Federalism*, 87 and 90–91.

24   For those interested in this intellectual debate, see the following studies: Nicholls, *The Pluralist State*, S. Ehrlich, *Pluralism on and off Course* (London: Pergamon Press, 1982), P. Hirst, *The Pluralist Theory of the State: Selected Writings of G.D.H. Cole, J.N. Figgis and H.J. Laski* (London: Routledge 1989) and P. Hirst, *Associative Democracy: New Forms of Economic and Social Governance* (Cambridge: Polity Press, 1994).

25   Johannes Althusius, *Politica* (1614), an abridged translation of *Politics Methodically Set Forth and Illustrated with Sacred a nd Profane Examples* by F.S. Carney (Ed.), *Politica* (Indianapolis, IN: Liberty Fund, 1995).

26   D.J. Elazar, 'Federal-Type Solutions and European Integration' in C.L. Brown-John (Ed.), *Federal-Type Solutions and European Integration* (Lanham, MD: University Press of America, 1995), Chap. 20, 443.

27   S. Mogi, *The Problem of Federalism*, Vol. I, 27–29 (italics added).

28   The standard work on Althusius is F.S. Carney, *The Politics of Johannes Althusius* (London: Eyre & Spottiswoode, 1964), but the most recent detailed, comprehensive survey of his life and work is T.O. Hueglin, *Early Modern Concepts for a Late Modern World: Althusius on Community and Federalism* (Waterloo, Ont.: Wilfrid Laurier University Press, 1999).

29   Carney (Ed.), 'The General Elements of Politics', in *Politica*, 17.

30   Carney (Ed.), 'Political Sovereignty and Ecclesiastical Communication', in *Politica*, 73.

31   See A. Lijphart, 'Consociational Democracy', *World Politics*, 21 (1969), 207–25, K. McRae (Ed.), *Consociational Democracy* (Toronto: McClelland & Stewart, 1974) and A. Lijphart, *Democracy in Plural Societies: A Comparative Exploration* (London: Yale University Press, 1977).

32   Ehrlich, *Pluralism on and off Course*, 71–75. There is also a useful summary of Gierke's importance in 69–80 and an excellent survey in Hueglin, *Early Modern Concepts for a Late Modern World*, 17–20.

33   See P.-J. Proudhon, *Du Principe fédératif*, trans. and intro. R. Vernon (Ed.), *The Principle of Federalism by P.-J. Proudhon* (Toronto: University of Toronto Press, 1979). See also A. Ritter, *The Political Thought of Pierre-Joseph Proudhon* (Princeton: Princeton University Press, 1969) and R. Nelson, 'The Federal Idea in French Political Thought', *Publius: The Journal of Federalism*, 5(3), 1976, 9–62.

34   Stein, 'Changing Concepts of Federalism since World War II', 17–18 and Hueglin, *Early Modern Concepts for a Late Modern World*, 222.

35   Vernon, 'Introduction', in *The Principle of Federalism*, xii–xiii.

36   Vernon, 'Introduction', in *The Principle of Federalism*, xviii.

37   Elazar referred to 'the necessarily utopian character of his thought' in his *Exploring Federalism*, 147.

38   Proudhon's appeal was doubtless attractive to the millions of industrial workers and landless peasants in Spain more for his anarchist-socialist ideas than for his advocacy of federalism.

39   I have discussed these ideas at greater length in M. Burgess, *Federalism and European Union: The Building of Europe, 1950–2000* (London: Routledge, 2000), 10–11 and 39–41 and in 'Federalism' in A. Wiener and T. Diez (Eds), *European Integration Theory* (Oxford: Oxford University Press, 2004), Chap. 2, 25–43.

40   A. Fremantle (Ed.), *The Papal Encyclicals in their Historical Context* (London: Mentor-Omega, 1963).

41   Some readers might detect a certain irony in the notion that the Roman Catholic Church, with its centralised, authoritarian tradition of papal decision-making might be associated with a constitutional and political idea based upon ideas of power-sharing, divided sovereignty and republican democracy.

42 Burgess, 'The European Tradition of Federalism: Christian Democracy and Federalism' in Burgess and Gagnon (Eds), *Comparative Federalism and Federation*, 138–53.
43 Fremantle (Ed.), *The Papal Encyclicals*, 342.
44 See M. Burgess, 'Political Catholicism, European Unity and the Rise of Christian Democracy' in M.L. Smith and P.M.R. Stirk (Eds), *Making the New Europe: European Unity and the Second World War* (London, Pinter Publishers, 1990), 142–55.
45 Fremantle (Ed.), *The Papal Encyclicals*, 420.
46 I have drawn heavily on pages 51–54 of Chapter 2 in order more firmly to integrate this information and interpretation into a different, specifically comparative context for the purposes of this chapter.
47 The source of one of the most famous intellectual debates about this issue is L. Hartz, *The Liberal Tradition in America* (New York: Harcourt, Brace & World, 1955) and the same author's, *The Founding of New Societies* (New York: Harcourt, Brace & World, 1964). For an excellent critique of the Hartz thesis as applied to Canada, see G. Horowitz, *Canadian Labour in Politics* (Toronto: University of Toronto Press, 1968).
48 Stein, 'Changing Concepts of Federalism Since World War II', 9–10.
49 See J. Kincaid and D.J. Elazar (Eds), *The Covenant Connection: Federal Theology and the Origins of Modern Politics* (Durham, NC: Carolina Academic Press, 1985) and D.J. Elazar, *Exploring Federalism*, esp. Chap. 1, 214.
50 V. Ostrom, *The Political Theory of a Compound Republic: Designing the American Experiment* (Lincoln, NE and London: University of Nebraska Press, 1987).
51 C.S. McCoy and J. Wayne Baker, *Fountainhead of Federalism: Heinrich Bullinger and the Covenantal Tradition* (Louisville, KE: Westminster/John Knox Press, 1991).
52 McCoy and Baker, *Fountainhead of Federalism*, 11.
53 S.Rufus Davis, *The Federal Principle: Journey Through Time in Quest of a Meaning* (London: University of California Press, 1978), 3.
54 McCoy and Baker, *Fountainhead of Federalism*, 11–12.
55 McCoy and Baker, *Fountainhead of Federalism*, 12.
56 Mc Coy and Baker, *Fountainhead of Federalism*, 12–14.
57 McCoy and Baker, *Fountainhead of Federalism*, 21.
58 McCoy and Baker, *Fountainhead of Federalism*, 53.
59 McCoy and Baker, *Fountainhead of Federalism*, 27–28.
60 D.S. Lutz, 'From Covenant to Constitution in American Political Thought', *Publius: The Journal of Federalism*, 10 (Fall, 1980), 128. On the fascination of early colonial Americans with the idea of the Jewish people and the Jewish biblical experience, see Lutz above, 102–3 and D.J. Elazar, 'Covenant as the Basis of the Jewish Political Tradition', *Jewish Journal of Sociology*, 20 (June 1978), 5–37.
61 Lutz, 'From Covenant to Constitution', 101 and 106.
62 McCoy and Baker, *Fountainhead of Federalism*, 28.
63 See G. Martin, 'Empire Federalism and Imperial Parliamentary Union, 1820–1870', *The Historical Journal*, XVI(I) (1973), 65–92 and G. Martin, 'The Idea of "Imperial Federation"' in R. Hyam and G. Martin (Eds), *Reappraisals in British Imperial History* (London: Macmillan, 1975), Chap. 6. See also M. Burgess, *The British Tradition of Federalism* (London: Cassell, 1995), Chaps 2 and 3.
64 Martin, 'Empire Federalism', 71–72.
65 D. Lutz, 'The Articles of Confederation as the Background to the Federal Republic', *Publius: The Journal of Federalism*, 20 (Winter 1990), 57. See also A. de Tocqueville, *Democracy in America*, trans. G. Lawrence, ed. J.P. Mayer (London: Fontana Press, 1994), Chap. 5, 61–98.
66 Tocqueville, *Democracy in America*, 61 (italics added).
67 Lutz, 'Articles of Confederation', 57.
68 Lutz, 'Articles of Confederation', 57.
69 Lutz, 'From Covenant to Constitution', 102.

70 Lutz, 'Articles of Confederation', 58–61. For a detailed survey of Whig political theory in colonial America, see D.S. Lutz, *Popular Consent and Popular Control: Whig Political Theory in the Early State Constitutions* (Baton Rouge, LO: Louisiana State University Press, 1980), and C.S. Hyneman and D.S. Lutz (Eds), *American Political Writing during the Founding Era, 1760–1805*, 2 vols (Indianapolis, IN: Liberty Press, 1983).

71 For a list of proposals and plans for federating or uniting the colonies or states, see Lutz, 'From Covenant to Constitution', 132–33. Mention should also be made of the importance of the Iroquois confederation to early American colonial thinking about continent-wide confederation. On this subject, see Lutz, 'Articles of Confederation', 59.

72 Lutz, 'Articles of Confederation', 58.

73 McCoy and Baker, *Fountainhead of Federalism*, 88.

74 McCoy and Baker, *Fountainhead of Federalism*, 93–94.

75 See Madison, *Federalist* 10, and Hamilton, *Federalist* 85 in C. Rossiter (Ed.), *The Federalist Papers* (New York: The New American Library, 1961), 77–84 and 520–27.

76 Rossiter, *The Federalist Papers*, Introduction, vii and xii.

77 K.C. Wheare, *Federal Government* (Oxford: Oxford University Press, 1963), 4th edn, 1.

78 D. Kwavnick (Ed.), *The Tremblay Report* (The Carleton Library, Toronto, no. 64: McClelland & Stewart, 1973), Introduction, viii.

79 Kwavnick (Ed.), *The Tremblay Report*, Vol. II, Chap. 7, 87–104.

80 Kwavnick (Ed.), *The Tremblay Report*, Introduction, vii.

81 A. Brady, 'Quebec and Canadian Federalism', *Canadian Journal of Economic and Political Science*, 25(3) (1959), 259.

82 W.D. Coleman, *The Independence Movement in Quebec, 1945–1980* (Toronto: University of Toronto Press, 1984), 17–18.

83 F.-P. Gingras and N. Nevitte, 'The Evolution of Quebec Nationalism' in A.-G. Gagnon (Ed.), *Quebec: State and Society* (Toronto: Methuen, 1984), Chap. 1, 3.

84 G. Stevenson, *Unfulfilled Union: Canadian Federalism and National Unity* (Toronto: Gage, 1982), 162.

85 McCoy and Baker, *Fountainhead of Federalism*, 89.

86 McCoy and Baker, *Fountainhead of Federalism*, 8.

87 S. Mogi, *The Problem of Federalism*, Vol. I, 323.

7 The concept of representation in federalism and federation

1 H.F. Pitkin, *The Concept of Representation* (Berkeley and Los Angeles, CA: University of California Press, 1967), 2.

2 Pitkin, *Concept of Representation*, 3.

3 H.F. Pitkin, 'The Concept of Representation' in Pitkin, *Representation* (New York: Atherton Press, 1969), 16.

4 Pitkin, 'The Concept of Representation' in Pitkin, *Representation*, 16.

5 See Madison, *Federalist* 10 in C. Rossiter (Ed.), *The Federalist Papers* (New York: The New American Library, 1961), 82–83.

6 Madison, *Federalist* 54 in Rossiter (Ed.), *The Federalist Papers*, 339.

7 Madison, *Federalist* 54 in Rossiter (Ed.), *The Federalist Papers*, 340.

8 Madison, *Federalist* 10 in Rossiter (Ed.), *The Federalist Papers*, 78.

9 Madison, *Federalist* 10 in Rossiter (Ed.), *The Federalist Papers*, 82.

10 Madison, *Federalist* 10 in Rossiter (Ed.), *The Federalist Papers*, 83.

11 Madison, *Federalist* 10 in Rossiter (Ed.), *The Federalist Papers*, 84.

12 Madison, *Federalist* 62 in Rossiter (Ed.), *The Federalist Papers*, 377.

13 Madison, *Federalist* 62 in Rossiter (Ed.), *The Federalist Papers*, 378.

14 Madison, *Federalist* 62 in Rossiter (Ed.), *The Federalist Papers*, 377.

15 Madison, *Federalist* 55 in Rossiter (Ed.), *The Federalist Papers*, 342.

16 Vincent Ostrom, *The Meaning of American Federalism: Constituting a Self-Governing Society* (San Francisco, CA: Institute for Contemporary Studies, 1991), 45.

17 Ostrom, *The Meaning of American Federalism*, 17.

18 S.M. Lipset, *American Exceptionalism: A Double-Edged Sword* (New York: W.W. Norton & Co., 1996), 46.

19 D.J. Elazar, *Exploring Federalism* (Tuscaloosa, AL: University of Alabama Press, 1987), 34.

20 Ostrom, The *Meaning of American Federalism*, 51 See also S. Lakoff, 'Between Either/Or and More or Less: Sovereignty Versus Autonomy Under Federalism', *Publius: The Journal of Federalism*, 24 (Winter 1994), 63–78.

21 S.H. Beer, 'Federalism, Nationalism and Democracy in America', *American Political Science Review*, 72(1) (1978), 319. For an interesting comparative survey of the evolution of American and Canadian federalism which summarises the various factors that led to the gradual centralisation of American federalism, see R.L. Watts, 'The American Constitution in Comparative Perspective: A Comparison of Federalism in the United States and Canada', *The Journal of American History*, 74(3) (December 1987), 769–91.

22 H. Maier, 'Der Föderalismus – Ursprunge und Wandlegen', *Archiv des Öffentlichen Rechts*, 115(2) (1990), 223. The view of Madison on this aspect of German history can be found in *Federalist 19*, where he sees it as a 'history of wars among the princes and states themselves; of the licentiousness of the strong and the oppression of the weak; ... of general imbecility, confusion and misery'; see Rossiter (Ed.), *The Federalist Papers*, 130.

23 H. Plessner, *Die verspätete Nation* (Stuttgart: Kohlhammer Press, 1959).

24 U. Munch, 'Entwicklungen und Perspektiven des deutschen Föderalismus', *Aus Politik und Zeitgeschehen (13)* (1999), 3.

25 J. Bodin, *Les six Livres de la republique avec l'apologie de R. Herpin* quoted in U. Bermbach, 'Widerstandsrecht, Souveränität, Kirche und Staat' in I. Fetscher and H. Munkler (Eds), Vol. 3, *Pipers Handbuch der politischen Ideen* (Munich/Zurich: Piper, Verlag., 1985), 137.

26 E. Schmitt, 'Abbe Sieyès' in H. Rauch, *Politische Denker*, Vol. II (Munich: Bayerische Landeszentrale für politische Bildungsarbeit, 1977), 91; H. Dippel, 'Die politischen Ideen der Franzosischen Revolution' in I. Fetscher and H. Munkler (Eds), *Piper's Handbuch der politischen Ideen*, Vol. IV (Munich/Zurich: Piper, Verlag., 1986), 21–69.

27 Emmanuel Joseph Sieyès, *Politische Schriften, 1788–1790*, ed. E. Schmitt and R. Reichardt (Darmstadt/Neuwied: Luchterhand, 1975), 217.

28 R.H. Foerster (Ed.), *Emmanuel Sieyès: Was ist der dritte Stand?* (Frankfurtam Main: Insel Verlag, 1968), 60.

29 See C.J. Hughes, 'Cantonalism: Federation and Confederacy in the Golden Epoch of Switzerland' in M. Burgess and A.-G. Gagnon (Eds), *Comparative Federalism and Federation: Competing Traditions and Future Directions* (Hemel Hempstead: Harvester Wheatsheaf, 1993), Chap. 9, 154–67.

30 D. Freiburghaus, *Die Schweiz: Eidgenossischer Föderalismus oder die Ungleichheit der Lebensverhaltnisse'* in Europäisches Zentrum für Föderalismus-Forschung (Ed.), *Jährbuch des Föderalismus*, Vol. I (Baden-Baden: Nomos Verlag., 2000), 296.

31 See R.L. Watts, *Comparing Federal Systems in the 1990s* (Kingston, Ont.: Queen's University, Institute of Intergovernmental Relations, 1996).

32 For a cursory glance at what cries out for a detailed up-to-date research survey, see Watts, *Comparing Federal Systems*, Chap. 3.

33 For a radical view that Canada needs to federalise the federation, see M. Burgess, 'Obstinate or Obsolete? The State of the Canadian Federation', *Regional and Federal Studies*, 9(2) (Summer, 1999), 1–15.

34 Hamilton, *Federalist 15*, in Rossiter (Ed.), *The Federalist Papers*, 108 (capitals in original).

35 Madison, *Federalist 51*, in Rossiter (Ed.), *The Federalist Papers*, 323.

36 President Andrew Jackson's Proclamation to the People of South Carolina, 1832 in K.L. Hall (Ed.), *Major Problems in American Constitutional History*, Vol. I (Lexington, MA: Heath & Co., 1992), 383.

37 J.C. Calhoun, 'A Discourse on the Constitution and Government of the United States, 1849–1850' in R.M. Lence (Ed.), *Union and Liberty: The Political Philosophy of John C. Calhoun* (Indianapolis, IN: Liberty Fund, 1992), 82.

38 On 'secession potential' in the United States, see C.D. Tarlton, 'Symmetry and Asymmetry as Elements of Federalism: A Theoretical Speculation', *Journal of Politics*, 27 (1965), 861–74 and M. Burgess and F. Gress, 'Symmetry and Asymmetry Revisited', in R. Agranoff (Ed.), *Accommodating Diversity: Asymmetry in Federal States* (Baden-Baden: Nomos Verlag, 1999).

39 I have provided a detailed conceptual comparison of these two projects, two centuries apart, in M. Burgess, *Federalism and European Union: The Building of Europe, 1950–2000* (London: Routledge, 2000).

40 J. Fischer, 'Das Ziel ist die Europäische Föderation', *Frankfurter Allgemeine Zeitung (FAZ)* (112) (15 May 2000), 12. The original text is: 'den Unbergang vom Staatenverbund der Union hin zur vollen Parlamentarisierung in einer Europäische Föderation'.

41 H. Vedrine, 'Klassischer Föderalismus oder Föderation von Nationalstaaten?', *FAZ* (115) (13 June 2000), 4.

42 A. Sbragia, 'Thinking about the European Future: The Uses of Comparison' in A.M. Sbragia (Ed.), *Euro Politics: Institutions and Policymaking in the 'New' European Community* (Washington, DC: The Brookings Institute, 1992), 258 and M. Burgess, *Federalism and European Union*.

43 See I.D. Duchacek, *Comparative Federalism: The Territorial Dimension of Politics* (New York: Holt, Reinhart, & Winston, Inc., 1970), especially 7–15 and 192. For Preston King, the claim that a bicameral legislature is a 'distinct and essential characteristic of federations' is 'inappropriate' because it is 'the entrenchment of regional representation' that makes them 'distinctive'. See his *Federalism and Federation* (London: Croom Helm, 1982), Chap. 7, 94–95.

44 Watts, *Comparing Federal Systems in the 1990s*, 87.

45 B. Kohler-Koch (Ed.), 'Regieren in entgrenzten Raumen', *Politische Viertel – jahresschrift*, 39 (1998), Special Edition, No. 29 and Sbragia (Ed.), 'Thinking about the European Future', 278.

46 King used a similar example in *Federalism and Federation*, 91.

47 King, *Federalism and Federation*, 91.

48 See P.G. Kielmansegg, 'Integration and Demokratie' in M. Jachtenfuchs and B. Kohler-Koch (Eds), *Europäische Integration* (Opladen: Leske and Budrich, 1996), 64 and F.W. Scharpf, 'The Joint-Decision Trap: Lessons from German Federalism and European Integration', *Public Administration*, 66 (Autumn 1988), 239–78. This does not, however, imply that the German *lander* governments in the Bundesrat no longer vote according to perceived territorial state interests. See C. Jeffery, 'Party Politics and Territorial Representation in the Federal Republic of Germany', *West European Politics*, 22(2) (1999), 130–66.

49 F. Gress, 'Interstate Cooperation and Territorial Representation in Intermestic Politics', *Publius: The Journal of Federalism*, 26(1) (Winter 1996), 68.

50 For a contemporary comparison of the Australian and German second chambers, see W. Swenden, *Federalism and Second Chambers. Regional Representation in Parliamentary Federations: The Australian Senate and German Bundesrat Compared* (Oxford: P.I.E. – Peter Lang, 2004) See also L. Thorlakson, 'Comparing Federal Institutions: Power and Representation in Six Federations', *West European Politics*, 26(2) (April 2003), 1–22.

51 King noted in 1993 that 'When we are speaking of representation, it is never self-evident in the abstract as to what it is that is to be represented'. See Preston King, 'Federation and Representation' in Burgess and Gagnon (Eds), *Comparative Federalism and Federation*, Chap. 5, 95.

52 Pitkin, *The Concept of Representation*, 244.
53 C. Tuschoff, 'The Compounding Effect: The Impact of Federalism on the Concept of Representation', *West European Politics*, Special Issue, 22(2) (1999), 16.
54 J.B. Brzinski, T.D. Lancaster and C. Tuschoff, 'Introduction', *West European Politics*, Special Issue (1999), 4–5.

8 Asymmetrical federalism and federation

 1 See R. Agranoff, 'Power Shifts, Diversity and Asymmetry' in R. Agranoff (Ed.), *Accommodating Diversity: Asymmetry in Federal States* (Baden-Baden: Nomos Verlag., 1999), Chap. 1, 21–22.
 2 W.S. Livingston, 'A Note on the Nature of Federalism', *Political Science Quarterly*, 67 (March 1952), 81–95. Livingston referred to 'Differences of economic interest, religion, race, nationality, language, variations in size, separation by great distances, differences in historical background, previous existence as separate colonies or states, dissimilarity of social and political institutions' (89).
 3 I.D. Duchacek, *Comparative Federalism: The Territorial Dimension of Politics* (New York: Holt, Reinhart & Winston, 1970).
 4 Duchacek, *Comparative Federalism*, 288.
 5 See R.L. Watts, 'Multicultural Societies and Federalism', *Studies of the Royal Commission on Bilingualism and Biculturalism*, No. 8 (Ottawa: Ministry of Supply and Services, 1970), 47–50 and R.L. Watts, *New Federations: Experiments in the Commonwealth* (Oxford: Clarendon Press, 1966), 149–55, 176–77 and 248–51.
 6 R.M. Stevens, 'Asymmetrical Federalism: The Federal Principle and the Survival of the Small Republic', *Publius: The Journal of Federalism*, 5 (1977), 177–203.
 7 See M. Frenkel, *Federal Theory* (Canberra: Centre for Research on Federal Financial Relations, The Australian National University, 1986), 79 and D.J. Elazar, *Exploring Federalism* (Tuscaloosa, AL: University of Alabama Press, 1987), 54–58.
 8 See, in particular, the chapters by A. Mullins and C. Saunders, 'Different Strokes for Different Folks?: Some Thoughts on Symmetry and Difference in Federal Systems', Chap. 3, 41–60, R. Agranoff, 'Asymmetrical and Symmetrical Federalism in Spain: An Examination of Intergovernmental Policy', Chap. 4, 61–89, J.P. Boase, 'Faces of Asymmetry: German and Canadian Federalism', Chap. 5, 90–110 and C.L. Brown-John, 'Asymmetrical Federalism: Keeping Canada Together?', Chap. 6, 111–24, in B. De Villiers (Ed.), *Evaluating Federal Systems* (London: Juta and Co. Ltd, 1994). The term has even entered the political vocabulary in respect of unitary states. See M. Keating, 'What's Wrong With Asymmetrical Government?', *Regional and Federal Studies: An International Journal*, Special Issue, 'Remaking the Union: Devolution and British Politics in the 1990s, 8(1) (Spring 1998), 195–218.
 9 Agranoff (Ed.), *Accommodating Diversity*.
10 C.D. Tarlton, 'Symmetry and Asymmetry as Elements of Federalism: A Theoretical Speculation', *Journal of Politics*, 27 (1965), 861–74.
11 Tarlton, 'Symmetry and Asymmetry', 861.
12 Tarlton, 'Symmetry and Asymmetry', 867.
13 Tarlton, 'Symmetry and Asymmetry', 865–67 and Livingston, 'A Note on the Nature of Federalism, 81–95.
14 Tarlton, 'Symmetry and Asymmetry', 867.
15 Tarlton, 'Symmetry and Asymmetry', 867.
16 Tarlton, 'Symmetry and Asymmetry', 867.
17 Tarlton, 'Symmetry and Asymmetry', 867–68.
18 Tarlton, 'Symmetry and Asymmetry', 868.
19 Tarlton, 'Symmetry and Asymmetry', 868.
20 Tarlton, 'Symmetry and Asymmetry', 869.

21 Tarlton, 'Symmetry and Asymmetry', 869.
22 Tarlton, 'Symmetry and Asymmetry', 869.
23 See W.H. Riker, *Federalism: Origin, Operation, Significance* (Boston: Little, Brown & Company, 1964) and S.H. Beer, *To Make a Nation: The Rediscovery of American Federalism* (Cambridge, MA: The Belknap Press of Harvard University Press, 1993).
24 Tarlton, 'Symmetry and Asymmetry', 871.
25 Tarlton, 'Symmetry and Asymmetry', 874.
26 Tarlton, 'Symmetry and Asymmetry', 873.
27 See M. Burgess, 'Federalism and Federation: A Reappraisal' in M. Burgess and A.-G. Gagnon (Eds), *Comparative Federalism and Federation: Competing Traditions and Future Directions* (Hemel Hempstead: Harvester Wheatsheaf, 1993), Chap. 1, 3–14.
28 Article 72(3), *Basic Law*, for the Federal Republic of Germany (Bonn: Press and Information Office of the Federal Government, 1994), 44 and Article 36, 'Canada Act (1982)' in R. Cheffins and P.A. Johnson, *The Revised Canadian Constitution: Politics as Law* (Toronto: McGraw-Hill Ryerson Ltd, 1986), 226.
29 See F. Gress, 'Interstate Cooperation and Territorial Representation in Intermestic Politics', *Publius: The Journal of Federalism*, 26(1) (Winter 1996), 53–71.
30 Duchacek, *Comparative Federalism*, 280.
31 Duchacek, *Comparative Federalism*, 282.
32 Duchacek, *Comparative Federalism*, 282.
33 D. Milne, 'Challenging Constitutional Dependency: A Revisionist View of Atlantic Canada' in J.N. McCrorie and M.L. MacDonald (Eds), *The Constitutional Future of the Prairie and Atlantic Regions of Canada* (Regina, Sas.: University of Regina, 1992), Chap. 17, 308–17.
34 Tarlton, 'Symmetry and Asymmetry', 869.
35 For further detailed information about asymmetrical federalism concerning Quebec in Canada, see D. Milne, 'Equality or Asymmetry: Why Choose?' in R.L. Watts and D.M. Brown (Eds), *Options for a New Canada* (Toronto: University of Toronto Press, 1991), Chap. 15, 285–307 and R.L. Watts, 'The Canadian Experience with Asymmetrical Federalism' in Agranoff (Ed.), *Accommodating Diversity*, Chap. 7, 118–36.
36 See R. Hrbek (Ed.), *Regional Parties and Party Systems in Federal States* (Baden-Baden: Nomos Verlag., 2004).
37 Tarlton, 'Symmetry and Asymmetry', 872.
38 See R. Agranoff, 'Intergovernmental Relations and the Management of Asymmetry in Spain' and L. Moreno, 'Asymmetry in Spain: Federalism in the Making?' in Agranoff (Ed.), *Accommodating Diversity*, respectively, Chap. 6, 94–117 and Chap. 9, 149–68.
39 See D. Jacobs and M. Swyngedouw, 'Territorial and Non-territorial Federalism: Reform of the Brussels Capital Region, 2001', *Regional and Federal Studies*, 13(2) (Summer 2003), 127–39.
40 On asymmetry in Germany, see R. Sturm, 'The Constitution under Pressure: Emerging Asymmetrical Federalism in Germany' in Agranoff (Ed.), *Accommodating Diversity*, Chap. 8, 137–48.
41 See T. Diez (Ed.), *The European Union and the Cyprus Conflict: Modern Conflict, Postmodern Union* (Manchester: Manchester University Press, 2002), T. Bahcheli, 'Searching for a Cyprus Settlement: Considering Options for Creating a Federation, a Confederation, or Two Independent States', *Publius: The Journal of Federalism*, 30(1–2) (Winter/Spring, 2000), 203–16 and A. Theophanous, 'Prospects for Solving the Cyprus Problem and the Role of The European Union, *Publius: The Journal of Federalism*, 30(1–2) (Winter/Spring, 2000), 217–41.
42 Tarlton, 'Symmetry and Asymmetry', 861.
43 Duchacek, *Comparative Federalism*, 283.
44 Tarlton, 'Symmetry and Asymmetry', 870 and 872.

45 B. Galligan, *A Federal Republic: Australia's Constitutional System of Government* (Cambridge: Cambridge University Press, 1995), 55.

46 For a detailed discussion of asymmetrical federalism as normative political theory, see A.-G. Gagnon and C. Gibbs, 'The Normative Basis of Asymmetrical Federalism' in Agranoff (Ed.), *Accommodating Diversity*, Chap. 5, 73–93 and A.-G. Gagnon, 'The Moral Foundations of Asymmetrical Federalism: A Normative Exploration of the Case of Quebec and Canada' in A.-G. Gagnon and J. Tully (Eds), *Multinational Democracies* (Cambridge: Cambridge University Press, 2001), Chap. 13, 319–37.

47 See D. Karmis and W. Norman, 'The Revival of Federalism in Normative Political Theory' in D. Karmis and W. Norman (Eds), *Theories of Federalism: A Reader* (London: Palgrave, 2005), Chap. 1, 1–30.

9 The European Union as a federal model

1 D.J. Elazar, 'From Statism to Federalism: A Paradigm Shift', *Publius: The Journal of Federalism*, 25(2) (1995), 5.

2 Elazar, 'From Statism to Federalism', 6.

3 See D.J. Elazar, *Exploring Federalism* (Tuscaloosa, AL: University of Alabama Press, 1987), 12.

4 D.J. Elazar, 'Federal-Type Solutions and European Integration' in C.L. Brown-John (Ed.), *Federal-Type Solutions and European Integration* (Lanham, MD: University Press of America, 1993), Chap. 20, 441.

5 G. Sartori, 'Concept Misformation in Comparative Politics', *American Political Science Review*, 64 (1970), 1033–53.

6 'The Schuman Declaration' in B.F. Nelsen and A. C.-G. Stubb (Eds), *The European Union: Readings on the Theory and Practice of European Integration* (Boulder, CO: Lynne Riener Publishers, 1994), 11–12 (italics in original).

7 See J. Monnet, *Memoirs* (New York: Doubleday, 1978) and the most recent biography of Monnet by F. Duchene, *Jean Monnet: The First Statesman of Interdependence* (London: W.W. Norton & Co., 1994).

8 Monnet, *Memoirs*, 367.

9 For a more detailed examination of this complex relationship, see M. Burgess, *Federalism and European Union: The Building of Europe, 1950–2000* (London: Routledge, 2000), Chap. 2, 23–53.

10 Duchene, *Jean Monnet*, 405.

11 For further details about Spinelli, see J. Pinder (Ed.), *Altiero Spinelli and the British Federalists* (London: Federal Trust, 1998) and Burgess, *Federalism and European Union*.

12 Monnet, *Memoirs*, 394–95.

13 Burgess, *Federalism and European Union*, 58.

14 If the Constitutional Treaty is ratified, co-decision will be extended to 95% of EU legislation.

15 A.L. Milward, *The Reconstruction of Western Europe, 1945–51* (London: Methuen & Co., 1984).

16 Milward, *The Reconstruction of Western Europe*, Preface, xvi.

17 Milward, *The Reconstruction of Western Europe*, 492.

18 Milward, *The Reconstruction of Western Europe*, 493–94.

19 A.L. Milward, *The European Rescue of the Nation-State* (London: Routledge, 1992).

20 Milward, *The European Rescue of the Nation-State*, 2–4.

21 A.L. Milward *et al.* (Eds), *The Frontier of National Sovereignty: History and Theory, 1945–1992* (London: Routledge, 1993).

22 Milward *et al.* (Eds), *The Frontier of National Sovereignty*, 31.

23 Fischer's famous speech presaged a sudden flurry of statements about the future of Europe by the EU's leading statesmen, including Jacques Chirac, the French

President (June 2000), Tony Blair, the British Prime Minister (October 2000), Guy Verhofstadt, the Belgian Prime Minister (October 2000), Gerhard Schröder, the German Chancellor (April 2001), Lionel Jospin, the French Prime Minister (May 2001) and Romano Prodi, the President of the European Commission (May 2001). For Fischer's speech, 'From Confederacy to Federation – Thoughts on the Finality of European Integration', see http://www.dgap.org/englishtip/tip-4/fischer120500.html.

24 A. Moravcsik, 'Negotiating the Single European Act: National Interest and Traditional Statecraft in the European Community', *International Organization*, 45(1) (1991), 651–88.

25 See A. Moravcsik, 'Preferences and Power in the European Community: A Liberal Intergovernmentalist Approach', *Journal of Common Market Studies*, 31(4) (1993), 473–524.

26 B. Rosamond, *Theories of European Integration* (Basingstoke: Palgrave, 2000), 142.

27 Rosamond, *Theories of European Integration*, 139.

28 See A. Moravcsik, 'Taking Preferences Seriously: A Liberal Theory of International Politics', *International Organization*, 51(4) (1997) 513–53, his 'Federal Ideals and Constitutional Realities in the Treaty of Amsterdam', *Journal of Common Market Studies* (Annual Review), 36 (1998), 13–38, his *The Choice For Europe: Social Purpose and State Power* (London: UCL Press, 1999) and his 'A New Statecraft? Supranational Entrepreneurs and International Cooperation', *International Organization*, 53(2) (1999), 267–306.

29 See the sources for Moravcsik's writings identified above for 1998–99.

30 This is the title of a well-known article by T. Risse-Kappen, 'Explaining the Nature of the Beast: International Relations Theory and Comparative Public Policy Analysis Meet the EU', *Journal of Common Market Studies*, 34(1) (1996), 53–80.

31 A. Moravcsik, 'Federalism in the European Union: Rhetoric and Reality' in K. Nicolaidis and R. Howse (Eds), *The Federal Vision: Legitimacy and Levels of Governance in the United States and the European Union* (Oxford: Oxford University Press, 2001), 186.

32 Moravcsik, 'Federalism in the European Union', 186–87.

33 Moravcsik, 'Federalism in the European Union', 163–64.

34 N. Nugent, *The Government and Politics of the European Union* (London: Macmillan, 1999), 469.

35 I.D. Duchacek, *Comparative Federalism: The Territorial Dimension of Politics* (New York: Holt, Reinhart & Winston, 1970), 202.

36 Moravcsik, 'Federalism in the European Union', 163.

37 See Burgess, *Federalism and European Union*, Chap. 8, 253–72.

38 See J. Fischer, <http://www.dgap.org/englishtip/tip-4/fischer120500.html>.

39 For this viewpoint, see J. Pinder, *The Building of the European Union* (Oxford: Oxford University Press, 1998), D. McKay, *Federalism and European Union* (Oxford: Oxford University Press, 1999), Burgess, *Federalism and European Union*, D. McKay, *Designing Europe: Comparative Lessons from the Federal Experience* (Oxford: Oxford University Press, 2001), M. Burgess, 'Federalism and Federation' in M. Cini (Ed.), *European Union Politics* (Oxford: Oxford University Press, 2003), Chap. 5, 65–79 and M. Burgess, 'Federalism' in A. Wiener and T. Diez (Eds), *European Integration Theory* (Oxford: Oxford University Press, 2004), Chap. 2, 25–43.

40 Monnet, *Memoirs*, 394–95.

41 See the website address: http://europa.eu.int/futurumforum_convention.

42 For the full text of the Constitutional Treaty, see <http://europa.eu.int/constitution/constitution_en.htm> and for the European Commission 'non-paper' entitled 'Summary of the agreement on the Constitutional Treaty', see the Futurum web site: <http://europa.eu.int/futurum>.

43 I have relied upon the Commission 'non-paper' for the short summary on which my brief analysis is based.

44 *Financial Times*, 30 October 2004, 12.

45 P. Riley, 'The Origins of Federal Theory in International Relations Ideas', *Polity*, VI(I) (1973), 89 (italics added).
46 Monnet, *Memoirs*, 367.
47 For a more detailed historical and conceptual analysis of this argument, see Burgess, *Federalism and European Union*, Chap. 8, 253–72.

10 Federalism, democracy and the state in the era of globalisation

1 Podium: 'Globalisation – America's Final Frontier', from the State of the Union Address by the President of the United States, given in the Capitol Building in Washington, DC, *The Independent*, 31 January 2000, 4.
2 I.D. Duchacek, *Comparative Federalism: The Territorial Dimension of Politics* (New York: Holt, Reinhart & Winston, 1970), 191.
3 H.M. Schwartz, *States Versus Markets: The Emergence of a Global Economy* (London: Macmillan Press, 2000), 317 and Preface, xii.
4 Schwartz, *States and Markets*, 2.
5 Schwartz, *States and Markets*, Preface, xii.
6 C.N. Murphy, 'Globalization and Governance: A Historical Perspective' in R. Axtmann (Ed.), *Globalization and Europe: Theoretical and Empirical Investigations* (London: Pinter, 1998), Chap. 9, 144.
7 Murphy, 'Globalization and Governance', 147.
8 D. Held, 'The Transformation of Political Community: Rethinking Democracy in the Context of Globalization' in I. Shapiro and C. Hacker-Corson (Eds), *Democracy's Edges* (Cambridge: Cambridge University Press, 1999), Chap. 6, 92.
9 A. Giddens, *Consequences of Modernity* (Cambridge: Polity Press, 1990), 64 quoted in Held, 'The Transformation of Political Community', 92.
10 D. Kellner, 'Globalization and the Post-Modern Turn', in Axtmann (Ed.), *Globalization and Europe*, Chap. 2, 23.
11 Held, 'The Transformation of Political Community', 93.
12 Kellner, 'Globalization and the Post-Modern Turn', 24–25.
13 See S. Strange, *States and Markets* (London: Pinter Publishers, 1989) and her later work, *The Retreat of the State: The Diffusion of Power in the World Economy* (Cambridge: Cambridge University Press, 1996).
14 Commission on Global Governance, *Our Global Neighbourhood. The Report* (Oxford: Oxford University Press, 1995).
15 A. Pagden, 'The Genesis of "Governance" and Enlightenment Conceptions of the Cosmopolitan World Order', *International Social Science Journal (ISSJ)*, 50(155) (1998), 7–15.
16 C. Hewitt de Alcantara, 'Uses and Abuses of the Concept of Governance', *ISSJ*, 155 (1998), 105–13.
17 Hewitt de Alcantara, 'Uses and Abuses of the Concept of Governance', 105–6.
18 Pagden, 'The Genesis of Governance', 7.
19 Hewitt de Alcantara, 'Uses and Abuses of the Concept of Governance', 106.
20 Pagden, 'The Genesis of Governance', 8 and 14.
21 A. Smith, 'National Identity and the Idea of European Unity', *International Affairs*, 68(1) (1992), 55–76.
22 Held, 'The Transformation of Political Community', 90.
23 Held, 'The Transformation of Political Community', 90–91.
24 See M. Castells, *The Informational City: Information Technology, Economic Restructuring and the Urban–Regional Process* (Oxford: Basil Blackwell, 1989).
25 G. Ross, 'European Integration and Globalization' in Axtmann (Ed.), *Globalization and Europe*, Chap. 10, 164.

26 A. Giddens, *The Third Way and its Critics* (Cambridge: Polity Press, 2000), 160.
27 M. Rhodes, P. Heywood and V. Wright, 'Towards a New Europe?' in M. Rhodes, P. Heywood and V. Wright (Eds), *Developments in West European Politics* (London: Macmillan Press Ltd, 1997), 8.
28 Guy de Jonquieres and Edward Alden, 'American Ties', *Financial Times*, 20 April 2001, 8.
29 Held, 'The Transformation of Political Community', 105–6.
30 See D. Held, 'Democracy: From City States to a Cosmopolitan Order?' in D. Held (Ed.), *Prospects for Democracy, Political Studies*, Special Issue, , XL (1992), 10–39, his *Democracy and the Global Order: From Modern State to Cosmopolitan Governance* (Cambridge: Polity Press, 1995) and his *Models of Democracy* (Cambridge: Polity Press, 1996).
31 Held, 'The Transformation of Political Community', 103.
32 Held, 'The Transformation of Political Community', 105–7.
33 Held, 'The Transformation of Political Community', 107.
34 Held, 'The Transformation of Political Community', 106–7.
35 See Held, 'Democracy: From City States to a Cosmopolitan Order?', 33, fn. 77 and his *Democracy and the Global Order*, 229–31.
36 See 'Collapse of Seattle Talks Blamed on US', *Financial Times*, 6 December 1999, 16.
37 James Tobin's seminal article entitled 'A Proposal for International Monetary Reform' seems to have been first published in the *Eastern Economic Journal*, 4(3–4) (1978), 153–59, but the origins of the idea can be traced back to 1972.
38 H. Patomaki, *Democratising Globalisation: The Leverage of the Tobin Tax* (London: Zed Books, 2001).
39 Patomaki, *Democratising Globalisation*, 200–1.
40 See 'Walls of the World Come Tumbling Down', *Financial Times*, 6 December 1999 (Supplement).

11 The success and failure of federation

1 T.M. Franck, 'Why Federations Fail' in T.M. Franck (Ed.), *Why Federations Fail* (London: London University Press, 1968), Chap. 5, 167–99.
2 Franck, 'Why Federations Fail', 169.
3 Franck, 'Why Federations Fail', 169.
4 Franck, 'Why Federations Fail', 169.
5 Franck, 'Why Federations Fail', 170.
6 U.K. Hicks, *Federalism, Failure and Success: A Comparative Study* (London: The Macmillan Press Ltd, 1978), Chap. 8, 171. Strictly speaking, Singapore's separation from Malaysia was a case of expulsion rather than secession.
7 Hicks, *Federalism, Failure and Success*, 171.
8 See, for example, A. Buchanan, *Secession: The Morality of Political Divorce from Fort Sumter to Lithuania and Quebec* (Oxford: Westview Press, 1991), M. Moore (Ed.), *National Self-Determination and Secession* (Oxford: Oxford University Press, 1998) and S. Macedo and A. Buchanan (Eds), *Secession And Self-Determination*, Nomos, XLV, *Yearbook of the American Society for Political and Legal Philosophy* (New York: New York University Press, 2003).
9 These are usually construed as liberal and communitarian theories. See, for example, H. Berran, 'A Liberal Theory of Secession', *Political Studies*, 32 (1984), 20–31, D. Miller, *Citizenship and National Identity* (Cambridge: Polity Press, 2000) and P.B. Lehning (Ed.), *Theories of Secession* (New York: Routledge, 1998). The work of W. Norman in this regard is also of great interest. See his 'The Ethics of Secession as the Regulation of Secessionist Politics' in Moore (Ed.), *National Self-Determination and Secession*, Chap. 3, 34–61, 'Justice and Stability in Multinational Societies' in A.-G. Gagnon and J. Tully (Eds), *Multinational Democracies* (Cambridge: Cambridge University Press, 2001), Chap.

3, 90–109 and 'Domesticating Secession' in Macedo and Buchanan (Eds), *Secession and Self-Determination*, Chap. 8, 193–237.

10 E.A. Freeman, *History of Federal Government in Greece and Italy*, ed. J.E. Bury (Freeport, NY: Books For Libraries Press, 1972), 90.

11 Freeman, *History of Federal Government*, 89.

12 Freeman, *History of Federal Government*, 90.

13 Freeman, *History of Federal Government*, 90 and 94.

14 Freeman, *History of Federal Government*, 93.

15 K.C. Wheare, *Federal Government* (Oxford: Oxford University Press, 1963), 4th edn, fn. 1, 86 .

16 Wheare devoted only two pages to the question of secession. See his *Federal Government*, 85–87 (italics in original).

17 See Wheare, *Federal Government*, 86–87 (italics in original).

18 Freeman, *History of Federal Government*, 89 and 91.

19 R.L. Watts, *New Federations: Experiments in the Commonwealth* (Oxford: Clarendon Press, 1966).

20 Watts, *New Federations*, 312.

21 Franck, 'Why Federations Fail', 184.

22 I.D. Duchacek, *Comparative Federalism: The Territorial Dimension of Politics* (New York: Holt, Rinehart & Winston, 1970).

23 Duchacek, *Comparative Federalism*, 69.

24 Duchacek, *Comparative Federalism*, 79.

25 Duchacek, *Comparative Federalism*, 77.

26 R.L. Watts, 'Survival or Disintegration' in R. Simeon (Ed.), *Must Canada Fail?* (London: McGill-Queen's University Press, 1977), Chap. 3, 42–60.

27 Watts, 'Survival or Disintegration', 53–54.

28 Franck, 'Why Federations Fail', 177.

29 Preston King, *Federalism and Federation* (London: Croom Helm, 1982), 109.

30 King, *Federalism and Federation*, 112.

31 King, *Federalism and Federation*, 112.

32 King, *Federalism and Federation*, 118.

33 King, *Federalism and Federation*, 118.

34 A. Buchanan, 'The Quebec Secession Issue: Democracy, Minority Rights and the Rule of Law' in Macedo and Buchanan (Eds), *Secession and Self-Determination*, Chap. 9, 239.

35 Buchanan, 'The Quebec Secession Issue', 240.

36 Buchanan, 'The Quebec Secession Issue', 246–47.

37 Franck, 'Why Federations Fail', 171.

38 I have drawn heavily on 'Why Federations Fail', 171–74.

39 Entitled 'On Federalism', this was the view of Frank N. Trager in his brief introduction to Franck's edited collection of essays, xiv.

40 Franck, 'Why Federations Fail', 192. In this context it is worth calling attention here to the short commentaries on secession in D.J. Elazar, *Exploring Federalism* (Tuscaloosa, AL: University of Alabama Press, 1987), 240–44 and R.L. Watts, *Comparing Federal Systems* (London, Montreal and Kingston, Ont.: McGill-Queen's University Press, 1999), 2nd edn, 107–8 and 114–15.

41 U.M. Amoretti and N. Bermeo (Eds), *Federalism and Territorial Cleavages* (London: The Johns Hopkins University Press, 2004).

42 N. Bermeo, 'Conclusion: The Merits of Federalism' in Amoretti and Bermeo (Eds), *Federalism and Territorial Cleavages*, 472 (italics added).

43 See the 'Speech of the Secretary of State for the Colonies', 14 May 1900 in A.P. Newton, *Federal and Unified Constitutions: A Collection of Constitutional Documents for the Use of Students* (London: Longmans, Green & Co., 1923), 311–23, followed by the proposed Constitution of Australia, 324–58.

44 See G. Stevenson, 'Western Alienation in Australia and Canada' in L. Pratt and G. Stevenson (Eds), *Western Separatism: The Myths, Realities and Dangers* (Edmonton: Hurtig Publishers, 1981), 121.

45 The whole episode is sketched out in Stevenson, 'Western Alienation in Australia and Canada', 119–34.

46 The literature on Quebec separatism is vast, but a start can be made by consulting J. Jacobs, *The Question of Separatism: Quebec and the Struggle over Sovereignty* (New York: Random House, 1980), W.D. Coleman, *The Independence Movement in Quebec, 1945–1980* (Toronto: University of Toronto Press, 1984), J. Lemco, *Turmoil in the Peaceable Kingdom: The Quebec Sovereignty Movement and its Implications for Canada and the United States* (Toronto: University of Toronto Press, 1994), J. Webber, *Reimagining Canada: Language, Culture, Community and the Canadian Constitution* (London: McGill-Queen's University Press, 1994) and S. LaSelva, *The Moral Foundations of Canadian Federalism: Paradoxes, Achievements and Tragedies of Nationhood* (London: McGill-Queen's University Press, 1996).

47 C. Taylor, 'Shared and Divergent Values' in R.L. Watts and D.M. Brown (Eds), *Options For a New Canada* (Toronto: University of Toronto Press, 1991), 64–65. See also M. Burgess, 'Ethnicity, Nationalism and Identity in Canada–Quebec Relations: The Case of Quebec's "Distinct Society"', *Journal of Commonwealth and Comparative Politics*, XXXIV(2) (July 1996), 46–64.

48 Franck, 'Why Federations Fail', 171.

49 Franck, 'Why Federations Fail', 177 (italics in original).

50 Franck, 'Why Federations Fail', 173–74.

51 Franck, 'Why Federations Fail', 183 and 190.

12 Conclusion: comparative federalism in theory and practice

1 D.J. Elazar, *Exploring Federalism* (Tuscaloosa, AL: University of Alabama Press, 1987), 38.

2 M. Forsyth, *Unions of States: The Theory and Practice of Confederation* (Leicester: Leicester University Press, 1981), 6–7.

3 R.L. Watts, 'Contemporary Views on Federalism' in B. De Villiers (Ed.), *Evaluating Federal Systems* (London: Juta and Co. Ltd, 1994), Chaps 1 and 7 and *Comparing Federal Systems* (London, Montreal and Kingston, Ont.: McGill-Queen's University Press, 1999), 2nd edn, xi and 121.

4 M.J.C. Vile, 'Federal Theory and the "New Federalism"' in D. Jaensch (Ed.), *The Politics of New Federalism* (Adelaide: Australian Political Studies Association, 1977), 1.

5 S. Rufus Davis, *Theory and Reality: Federal Ideas in Australia, England and Europe* (Queensland: University of Queensland Press, 1995), 37.

6 C.J. Friedrich, 'Federal Constitutional Theory and Emergent Proposals' in A.W. Macmahon (Ed.), *Federalism: Mature and Emergent* (New York: Russell & Russell Inc., 1962), Chap. 26, 510.

7 Friedrich, 'Federal Constitutional Theory', 513–14.

8 Friedrich, 'Federal Constitutional Theory', 514.

9 Friedrich, 'Federal Constitutional Theory', 515 (italics in original).

10 Friedrich, 'Federal Constitutional Theory', 514.

11 Elazar, *Exploring Federalism*, 12 and 34.

12 Preston King, *Federalism and Federation* (London: Croom Helm, 1982), 146–48.

13 Friedrich, 'Federal Constitutional Theory', 512.

14 Elazar, *Exploring Federalism*, 15–16 (italics in original).

15 Madison, *Federalist 10* in C. Rossiter (Ed.), *The Federalist Papers* (New York: The New American Library, 1961), 77–84.

16 Madison, *Federalist* 10 in Rossiter (Ed.), *The Federalist Papers*, 81.
17 Madison, *Federalist* 10 in Rossiter (Ed.), *The Federalist Papers*, 83 and Elazar, *Exploring Federalism*, 85.
18 R.A. Dahl, 'Federalism and the Democratic Process' in J.R. Pennock and J.W. Chapman (Eds), *Liberal Democracy*, Nomos XXV (New York: New York University Press, 1983), Chap. 3, 95–108. See also in this volume of essays, D. Braybrooke, 'Can Democracy be Combined with Liberalism or with Federalism?', Chap. 4, 109–18.
19 Elazar, *Exploring Federalism*, 83.
20 The list would include the following sources: W. Kymlicka, *Liberalism, Community and Culture* (Oxford: Clarendon Press, 1989), R.L. Watts and D.M. Brown (Eds), *Options for a New Canada* (Toronto: University of Toronto Press, 1991), C. Taylor, *Multiculturalism and the Politics of Recognition* (Princeton, NJ: Princeton University Press, 1992), C. Taylor (with an introduction by G. Laforest), *Reconciling the Solitudes: Essays on Canadian Federalism and Nationalism* (London: McGill-Queen's University Press, 1993), J. Webber, *Reimagining Canada: Language, Culture and Community and the Canadian Constitution* (London: McGill-Queen's University Press, 1994), J. Tully, *Strange Multiplicity: Constitutionalism in an Age of Diversity* (Cambridge: Cambridge University Press, 1995), W. Kymlicka, *Multicultural Citizenship: A Liberal Theory of Minority Rights* (Oxford: Clarendon Press, 1995), S. LaSelva, *The Moral Foundations of Canadian Federalism: Paradoxes, Achievements and Tragedies of Nationhood* (London: McGill-Queen's University Press, 1996), K. McRoberts, *Misconceiving Canada: The Struggle for National Unity* (Oxford: Oxford University Press, 1997) and R. Gibbins and G. Laforest (Eds), *Beyond the Impasse: Toward Reconciliation* (Montreal: Institute for Research on Public Policy, 1998). See also M. Burgess, 'The Federal Spirit as a Moral Basis to Canadian Federalism', *International Journal of Canadian Studies*, 22 (Fall 2000), 13–35.
21 See for example the collection of essays in A.-G. Gagnon and J. Tully (Eds), *Multinational Democracies* (Cambridge: Cambridge University Press, 2001).
22 D. Karmis and W. Norman (Eds), *Theories of Federalism: A Reader* (New York: Palgrave Macmillan, 2005).
23 Karmis and Norman, 'The Revival of Federalism in Normative Political Theory' in Karmis and Norman (Eds), *Theories of Federalism*, Chap. 1, 1–30.
24 Elazar, *Exploring Federalism*, 12 and 192.
25 These are the three conceptions that form the basis of Charles Taylor's famous essay entitled 'Why do Nations have to become States?' in C. Taylor, *Reconciling The Solitudes: Essays on Canadian Federalism and Nationalism*, ed. G. Laforest (London: McGill-Queen's University Press, 1993), Chap. 3, 40–58.
26 See A.-G. Gagnon, 'The Moral Foundation of Asymmetrical Federalism: A Normative Exploration of the Case of Quebec and Canada' in Gagnon and Tully (Eds), *Multinational Democracies*, Chap. 13, 321 and 325.
27 Davis' dark despair must not be confused with his positive plea for a different approach to the study of federalism that he believes must embrace 'the paramountcy of history and culture' as the proper basis for understanding the subject. He may, however, be tilting at windmills because the former obsession with competing definitions of federalism seems today to have finally petered out and left us to concentrate upon history and context, which has been the principal focus of this book. See Davis, *Theory and Reality*, 38.
28 Elazar, *Exploring Federalism*, 83.

Bibliography

Abele, F. and Prince, M.J., 'Alternative Futures: Aboriginal Peoples and Canadian Federalism' in H. Bakvis and G. Skogstad (Eds), *Canadian Federalism: Performance, Effectiveness and Legitimacy* (Oxford: Oxford University Press, 2002), Chap. 12, 220–37.

Abele, F. and Prince, M.J., 'Aboriginal Governance and Canadian Federalism: A To-Do List for Canada' in F. Rocher and M. Smith (Eds), *New Trends in Canadian Federalism* (Peterborough, Ont.: Broadview Press, 2003), Chap. 6, 135–65.

Acton, Sir John (later Lord), 'Nationality' in *History of Freedom and Other Essays* (London: Macmillan & Co. Ltd, 1907), 289.

Agranoff, R., 'Asymmetrical and Symmetrical Federalism in Spain: An Examination of Intergovernmental Policy' in B. de Villiers (Ed.), Evaluating Federal Systems, (London: Juta & Co. Ltd., 1994), Chap. 4, 61–89.

Agranoff, R. (Ed.), *Accommodating Diversity: Asymmetry in Federal States* (Baden-Baden: Nomos Verlag., 1999).

Agranoff, R. (Ed.), 'Intergovernmental Relations and the Management of Asymmetry in Spain' in *Accommodating Diversity: Asymmetry in Federal States* (Baden-Baden: Nomos Verlag., 1999), Chap. 6, 94–117.

Agranoff, R. (Ed.), 'Power Shifts, Diversity and Asymmetry' in *Accommodating Diversity: Asymmetry in Federal States* (Baden-Baden: Nomos Verlag., 1999), Chap. 1, 21–22.

Althusius, J., *Politica* (1614), an abridged translation of *Politics Methodically Set Forth and Illustrated with Sacred and Profane Examples* by F.S. Carney (Ed.), *Politica* (Indianapolis, IN: Liberty Fund, 1995).

Amoretti, U.M. and Bermeo, N. (Eds), *Federalism and Territorial Cleavages* (London: The Johns Hopkins University Press, 2004).

Arora, B., 'Adapting Federalism to India: Multilevel and Asymmetrical Innovations' in B. Arora and D.V. Verney (Eds), *Multiple Identities in a Single State: Indian Federalism in a Comparative Perspective* (New Delhi: Konark Publishers, 1995), Chap. 3, 72.

Austin, G., *The Indian Constitution: Cornerstone of a Nation* (Oxford: Clarendon Press, 1966).

Bahcheli, T., 'Searching for a Cyprus Settlement: Considering Options for Creating a Federation, a Confederation, or Two Independent States', *Publius: The Journal of Federalism*, 30(1–2) (Winter/Spring 2000), 203–16.

Baier, G., 'Judicial Review and Canadian Federalism' in H. Bakvis and G. Skogstad (Eds), *Canadian Federalism: Performance, Effectiveness and Legitimacy* (Oxford: Oxford University Press, 2002), Chap. 2, 24–39.

Baier, G., 'The Law of Federalism: Judicial Review and the Division of Powers' in F. Rocher and M. Smith (Eds), *New Trends in Canadian Federalism* (Peterborough, Ont.: Broadview Press, 2003), Chap. 5, 111–33.

Bailyn, B., *The Ideological Origins of the American Revolution* (London: The Belknap Press of Harvard University Press, 1967), 285.

Bakar, I., 'Fiscal Federalism: The Study of Federal–State Fiscal Relations in Malaysia', Ph.D. thesis, University of Hull (2004).

Bakar, I., 'Multinational Federation: The Case of Malaysia' in M. Burgess and J. Pinder (Eds), *Multinational Federations* (forthcoming).

Barraclough, S., 'Barisan Nasional Dominance and Opposition Fragmentation: The Failure of Attempts to Create Opposition Cooperation in the Malaysian Party System', *Asian Profile*, 13(1) (1985), 33–43.

Basic Law, for the Federal Republic of Germany, Article 72(3) (Bonn: Press and Information Office of the Federal Government, 1994), 44.

Beer, S.H., 'Federalism, Nationalism and Democracy in America', *American Political Science Review*, 72(1) (1978), 319.

Beer, S.H., *To Make a Nation: The Rediscovery of American Federalism* (Cambridge, MA: The Belknap Press of Harvard University Press, 1993); repr. (London: The Belknap Press of Harvard University Press, 1994).

Bentham, J, *The Works of Jeremy Bentham*, ed. J. Bowring (New York: Russell & Russell Inc., 1962).

Bermeo, N., 'Conclusion: The Merits of Federalism' in U.M. Amoretti and N. Bermeo (Eds), *Federalism and Territorial Cleavages* (London: The Johns Hopkins University Press, 2004).

Berran, H., 'A Liberal Theory of Secession', *Political Studies*, 32 (1984), 20–31.

Bhargava, R.N., 'The Theory of Federal Finance', *The Economic Journal*, 63(249) (1953), 84–97.

Bhattacharyya, H., 'India Creates Three New States', *Forum of Federations: What's New in The Practice of Federalism?*, 1(3) (2001).

Bhattacharyya, H., *India as a Multicultural Federation: Asian Values, Democracy and Decentralisation, in Comparison with Swiss Federalism* (Basel: Helbing & Lichtenhahn, 2001), Chaps 2 and 6.

Birch, A.H., *Federalism, Finance and Social Legislation in Canada, Australia and the United States* (Oxford: Clarendon Press, 1955).

Birch, A.H., 'Approaches to the Study of Federalism', *Political Studies*, XIV(1) (1966), 15–33.

Bird, R.M. and Vaillancourt, F., *Fiscal Decentralisation in Developing Countries* (Cambridge: Cambridge University Press, 1998).

Bissoondath, N., *Selling Illusions: The Cult of Multiculturalism in Canada* (Toronto: Penguin Books, 1994), 40.

Blainey, G., *The Tyranny of Distance: How Distance Shaped Australia's History* (Melbourne: Sun Books, 1966).

Blair, P., *Federalism and Judicial Review in West Germany* (Oxford: Clarendon Press, 1981).

Blair, P. and Cullen, P., 'Federalism, Legalism and Political Reality: The Record of the Federal Constitutional Court' in C. Jeffery (Ed.), *Recasting German Federalism: The Legacies of Unification* (London: Pinter, 1999), Chap. 6, 119–54.

Boase, J.P., 'Faces Of Asymmetry: German and Canadian Federalism' in B. de Villiers (Ed.), Evaluating Federal Systems, (London: Juta & Co. Ltd, 1994), Chap. 5, 90–110.

Bodin, J., *Les Six Livres de la republique avec l'apologie de R. Herpin* quoted in U. Bermbach, 'Widerstandsrecht, Souveränität, Kirche und Staat' in I. Fetscher and H. Munkler (Eds), *Pipers Handbuch der politischen Ideen*, Munich/Zurich: Piper, Verlag., Bd.3, 1985), 137.

Bogdanor, V., 'Federalism in Switzerland', *Government and Opposition*, 23(1) (Winter 1988), 71.

Borden, M. (Ed.), Intro., 'The Antifederalist Mind' in *The Antifederalist Papers* (Michigan, MI: Michigan State University Press, 1965), viii.

Brady, A., 'Quebec and Canadian Federalism', *Canadian Journal of Economic and Political Science*, 25(3) (1959), 259.

Braybrooke, D., 'Can Democracy be Combined with Liberalism or with Federalism?' in J.R. Pennock and J.W. Chapman (Eds), *Liberal Democracy*, Nomos XXV (New York: New York University Press, 1983), Chap. 4, 109–18.

Brown-John, C.L., 'Asymmetrical Federalism: Keeping Canada Together?' in B. De Villiers (Ed.), *Evaluating Federal Systems* (London: Juta & Co. Ltd, 1994), Chap. 6, 111–24.

'Brutus', Antifederalist, No. 17, 'Federalist Power Will Ultimately Subvert State Authority' in M. Borden (Ed.), *The Antifederalist Papers* (Michigan, MI: Michigan State University Press, 1965), 42–43.

Bryce, J., *Studies in History and Jurisprudence*, 2 vols (Oxford: Clarendon Press, 1901).

Bryce, J., *The American Commonwealth*, 2 vols (London: Macmillan & Co. Ltd, 1919); repr. (New York: The Macmillan Company, 1928).

Bryce, J., *Modern Democracies* (London: Macmillan and Co. Ltd, 1929), 2 vols.

Brzinski, J.B., Lancaster, T.D. and Tuschoff, C., 'Introduction', *West European Politics*, Special Issue (1999), 4–5.

Buchanan, A., *Secession: The Morality of Political Divorce from Fort Sumter to Lithuania and Quebec* (Oxford: Westview Press, 1991).

Buchanan, A., 'The Quebec Secession Issue: Democracy, Minority Rights and the Rule of Law' in S. Macedo and A. Buchanan (Eds), *Secession And Self-Determination*, Nomos, XLV, *Yearbook of the American Society for Political and Legal Philosophy* (New York: New York University Press, 2003), Chap. 9, 239.

Buchanan, J.M., 'Federalism and Fiscal Equity', *American Economic Review*, 40(4) (1950), 421–32.

Burgess, M. (Ed.), 'Federalism and Federation in Western Europe' in *Federalism and Federation in Western Europe* (London: Croom Helm, 1986), Chap. 2, 15–33.

Burgess, M., 'Political Catholicism, European Unity and the Rise of Christian Democracy' in M.L. Smith and P.M.R. Stirk (Eds), *Making the New Europe: European Unity and the Second World War* (London: Pinter Publishers, 1990), 142–55.

Burgess, M., 'From Trudeau to Mulroney: The Political Economy of Constitutional Reform in Canada, 1980–1990' in C.H.W. Remie and J.-M. Lacroix (Eds), *Canada on the Threshold of the 21st Century: European Reflections upon the Future of Canada* (Amsterdam: John Benjamins Publishing Company, 1991).

Burgess, M., 'The European Tradition of Federalism: Christian Democracy and Federalism' in M. Burgess and A.-G. Gagnon (Eds), *Comparative Federalism and Federation: Competing Traditions and Future Directions* (Hemel Hempstead: Harvester Wheatsheaf, 1993), Chap. 8, 138–53.

Burgess, M., 'Federalism and Federation: A Reappraisal' in M. Burgess and A.-G. Gagnon (Eds), *Comparative Federalism and Federation: Competing Traditions and Future Directions* (Hemel Hempstead: Harvester Wheatsheaf, 1993), Chap. 1, 3–14.

Burgess, M., *The British Tradition of Federalism* (London: Cassell, 1995).

Burgess, M., 'Ethnicity, Nationalism and Identity in Canada–Quebec Relations: The Case of Quebec's "Distinct Society"', *Journal of Commonwealth and Comparative Politics*, XXXIV(2) (July 1996), 46–64.

Burgess, M., 'Obstinate or Obsolete? The State of the Canadian Federation', *Regional and Federal Studies*, 9(2) (Summer 1999), 1–15.

Burgess, M., *Federalism and European Union: The Building of Europe, 1950–2000* (London: Routledge, 2000).

Burgess, M., 'The Federal Spirit as a Moral Basis to Canadian Federalism', *International Journal of Canadian Studies*, 22 (Fall 2000), 13–35.

Burgess, M., 'Federalism and Federation' in M. Cini (Ed.), *European Union Politics* (Oxford: Oxford University Press, 2003), Chap. 5, 65–79.

Burgess, M., 'Federalism' in A. Wiener and T. Diez (Eds), *European Integration Theory* (Oxford: Oxford University Press, 2004), Chap. 2, 25–43.

Burgess, M. and Gress, F., 'Symmetry and Asymmetry Revisited' in R. Agranoff (Ed.), *Accommodating Diversity: Asymmetry in Federal States* (Baden-Baden: Nomos Verlag., 1999).

Burnett, E.C., *The Continental Congress* (New York: The Macmillan Co. Ltd, 1941), 257.

Cairns, A.C., *Citizens Plus: Aboriginal Peoples and the Canadian State* (Vancouver: University of British Columbia Press, 2000).

Cairns, A.C., 'The Living Canadian Constitution', *Queen's Quarterly*, LXXVII (Winter 1970), 1–16; repr. in J.P. Meekison (Ed.), *Canadian Federalism: Myth or Reality* (London: Methuen, 1977), 3rd edn, Chap. 6, 86–99.

Cairns, A.C., 'The Governments and Societies of Canadian Federalism', *Canadian Journal of Political Science*, 10 (1977), 695–726.

Calhoun, J.C., 'A Discourse on the Constitution and Government of the United States, 1849–1850' in R.M. Lence (Ed.), *Union and Liberty: The Political Philosophy of John C. Calhoun* (Indianapolis, IN: Liberty Fund, 1992), 82.

'Canada Act (1982)', Article 36, in R. Cheffins and P.A. Johnson, *The Revised Canadian Constitution: Politics as Law* (Toronto: McGraw-Hill Ryerson Ltd, 1986), 226.

Canovan, M., *Nationhood and Political Theory*, Cheltenham: Edward Elgar, 1996).

Caporaso, J.A., 'The European Union and Forms of State: Westphalian, Regulatory or Post-Modern?', *Journal of Common Market Studies*, 34(1) (March 1996), 29–52.

Carnell, F.G., 'Political Implications of Federalism in New States' in U.K. Hicks *et al.*, *Federalism and Economic Growth in Underdeveloped Countries* (London: Allen & Unwin, 1961), 16–59.

Carney, F.S., *The Politics of Johannes Althusius* (London: Eyre & Spottiswoode, 1964).

Carney, F.S. (Ed.), 'The General Elements of Politics' in Althusius's *Politica*, ed. and abridg. F.S. Carney (Indianapolis, IN: Liberty Fund, 1995).

Carney, F.S. (Ed.), 'Political Sovereignty and Ecclesiastical Communication' in Althusius's *Politica*, ed. and abridg. F.S. Carney (Indianapolis, IN: Liberty Fund, 1995).

Castells, M., *The Informational City: Information Technology, Economic Restructuring and the Urban–Regional Process* (Oxford: Basil Blackwell, 1989).

'Centinel', Antifederalist, No. 21, 'Why The Articles Failed' in M. Borden (Ed.), *The Antifederalist Papers* (Michigan, MI: Michigan State University Press, 1965), 51.

Chakrabarty, B. (Ed.), *Centre–State Relations in India* (New Delhi: Segment Book Distributors, 1990).

Chartrand, P.L., 'The Aboriginal Peoples in Canada and Renewal of the Federation' in K. Knop (Ed.), *Rethinking Federalism: Citizens, Markets and Governments in a Changing World*, Vancouver: University of British Columbia Press, 1995), Chap. 8, 119–31.

Chin, J., 'Politics of Federal Intervention in Malaysia, with Reference to Sarawak, Sabah and Kelantan', *Journal of Commonwealth and Comparative Politics*, 19(2) (April 1997), 159–72.

Clement, W. and Williams, G. (Eds), 'Introduction' in *The New Canadian Political Economy* (London: McGill-Queen's University Press, 1989), 7.

Coleman, W.D., *The Independence Movement in Quebec, 1945–1980* (Toronto: University of Toronto Press, 1984).

Collini, S., 'The Ordinary Experience of Civilized Life: Sidgwick's Politics and the Method of Reflective Analysis' in B. Schultz (Ed.), *Essays on Henry Sidgwick* (Cambridge: Cambridge University Press, 1992), Chap. 12, 333–67.

Collini, S., Winch, D. and Burrow, J., *That Noble Science of Politics: A Study in Nineteenth Century Intellectual History* (Cambridge: Cambridge University Press, 1983).

Commission on Global Governance, *Our Global Neighbourhood. The Report* (Oxford: Oxford University Press, 1995).

Constitutional Treaty, available at: http://europa.eu.int/constitution/constitution_en. htm.

Dahl, R.A., 'Federalism and the Democratic Process' in J.R. Pennock and J.W. Chapman (Eds), *Liberal Democracy*, Nomos XXV (New York: New York University Press, 1983), Chap. 3, 95–108.

Davis, S. Rufus, 'The "Federal Principle" Reconsidered', Part I, *Australian Journal of Politics and History*, 1(1) (November 1955).

Davis, S. Rufus, 'The "Federal Principle" Reconsidered', Part II, *Australian Journal of Politics and History*, 1(2) (May 1956).

Davis, S. Rufus, 'The Federal Principle Revisited' in D.P. Crook (Ed.), *Questioning the Past*, Brisbane: University of Queensland Press, 1972).

Davis, S. Rufus, *The Federal Principle: A Journey Through Time in Quest of a Meaning* (London: University of California Press, 1978).

Davis, S. Rufus, *Theory and Reality: Federal Ideas in Australia, England and Europe* (Queensland: University of Queensland Press, 1995).

Delmartino, F., 'Belgium: A Regional State or a Federal State in the Making?' in M. Burgess (Ed.), *Federalism and Federation in Western Europe* (London: Croom Helm, 1986), Chap. 3, 38.

Deutsch, K.W., *et al.*, *Political Community and the North Atlantic Area* (Princeton, NJ: Princeton University Press, 1957).

Diamond, M., 'The Federalist's View of Federalism' in G.C.S. Benson (Ed.), *Essays on Federalism* (Claremont: Institute for Studies in Federalism, 1961), 23–24.

Diamond, M., 'What the Framers Meant by Federalism' in R.A. Goldwin (Ed.), *A Nation of States: Essays on the American Federal System* (Chicago, IL: Rand McNally, 1964), 24–41.

Dicey, A.V., *Introduction to the Study of the Law of the Constitution* (London: Macmillan & Co., 1950), 9th edn.

Diez, T. (Ed.), *The European Union and the Cyprus Conflict: Modern Conflict, Postmodern Union* (Manchester University Press, 2002).

Dikshit, R., *The Political Geography of Federalism: An Inquiry into Origins and Stability* (London: Macmillan, 1976), 115.

Dikshit, R.D., 'Military Interpretation of Federal Constitutions: A Critique', *Journal of Politics*, 33 (1971), 180–89.

Dikshit, R.D., *The Political Geography of Federalism: An Inquiry into Origins and Stability* (New Delhi: The Macmillan Company of India, 1975).

Dippel, H., 'Die politischen Ideen der Französischen Revolution' in I. Fetscher and H. Munkler (Eds), *Piper's Handbuch der politischen Ideen*, Vol. IV (Munich/Zurich: Piper, Verlag., 1986), 21–69.

Duchacek, I.D., *Comparative Federalism: The Territorial Dimension of Politics* (New York: Holt, Rinehart, & Winston, 1970).

Duchene, F., *Jean Monnet: The First Statesman of Interdependence* (London: W.W. Norton & Co., 1994).

Dupre, J. Stephan, 'Reflections on The Workability of Executive Federalism' in R.S. Blair and J.T. McLeod (Eds), *The Canadian Political Tradition: Basic Readings* (Scarborough, Ont.: Nelson, 1993), 472–500.

Ehrlich, S., *Pluralism on and off Course* (London: Pergamon Press, 1982).

Elazar, D.J., *The American Partnership. Intergovernmental Cooperation in the Nineteenth-Century United States* (Chicago, IL and London: University of Chicago Press, 1962).

Elazar, D.J., 'Covenant as the Basis of the Jewish Political Tradition', *Jewish Journal of Sociology*, 20 (June 1978), 5–37.

Elazar, D.J., *American Federalism: A View from the States* (New York: Harper & Row, 1984), 4th edn.

Elazar, D.J., *Exploring Federalism* (Tuscaloosa, AL: University of Alabama Press, 1987).

Elazar, D.J., 'Federal-Type Solutions and European Integration' in C.L. Brown-John (Ed.), *Federal-Type Solutions and European Integration* (Lanham, MD: University Press of America, 1993), Chap. 20.

Elazar, D.J., 'From Statism to Federalism: A Paradigm Shift', *Publius: The Journal of Federalism*, 25(2) (1995), 5.

Eng, T.B., 'Commentary' in V. Sinnadurai, 'Unity and Diversity: The Constitution of Malaysia' in R.A. Goldwin, A. Kaufman and W.A. Schambra (Eds), *Forging Unity Out of Diversity: The Approach of Eight Nations* (Washington, DC: American Enterprise Institute for Public Policy Research, 1989), Chap. 7, 351.

Erk, C. and Gagnon, A.-G., 'Constitutional Ambiguity and Federal Trust: Codification of Federalism in Canada, Spain and Belgium', *Regional and Federal Studies*, 10(1) (Spring 2000), 92–111.

European Commission 'non-paper' entitled 'Summary of the agreement on the Constitutional Treaty', available at: http://europa.eu.int/futurum.

'A Farmer', Antifederalist, No. 3, 'New Constitution Creates a National Government; Will Not Abate Foreign Influence; Dangers of Civil War and Despotism' in M. Borden (Ed.), *The Antifederalist Papers* (Michigan, MI: Michigan State University Press, 1965), 6.

'A Farmer', Antifederalist, No. 39, 'Appearance and Reality – The Form is Federal; The Effect is National' in M. Borden (Ed.), *The Antifederalist Papers* (Michigan, MI: Michigan State University Press, 1965), 106–7.

Farrand, M. (Ed.), *The Records of the Federal Convention of 1787*, Vol. 1 (New Haven, CT: Yale University Press, 1937), rev. edn, 18.

Federal Constitution [Laws of Malaysia], Article 153(1–10), 15 January 2003 (Kuala Lumpur: International Law Book Series, 2003), 188–91.

Fernando, J.M., *The Making of the Malayan Constitution*, MBRAS monograph, No. 31 (Kuala Lumpur: The Malaysian Branch of the Royal Asiatic Society, 2002).

Financial Times, 'Collapse of Seattle Talks Blamed on US', 6 December 1999, 16.

Financial Times, 'Walls of the World Come Tumbling Down', 6 December 1999 (Supplement).

Financial Times, 30 October 2004, 12.

Finer, S.E., *Comparative Government* (Harmondsworth: Penguin Books Ltd, 1982), 3.

Fischer, J., 'Das Ziel ist die Europäische Föderation', *Frankfurter Allgemeine Zeitung (FAZ)*, (112) (15 May 2000), 12.

Fischer, J., 'From Confederacy to Federation – Thoughts on the Finality of European Integration', available at: http://www.dgap.org/englishtip/tip-4/fischer120500.html.

Fischer, M., 'Feudal Europe, 800–1300: Communal Discourse and Conflictual Practices', *International Organization*, 46 (Spring 1992), 427–66.

Fitzmaurice, J., *The Politics of Belgium: A Unique Federalism* (London: Hurst & Company, 1996), 49.

Fleiner, T., 'Commentary' on 'Swiss Federalism' in R.A. Goldwin, A. Kaufman and W.A. Schambra (Eds), *Forging Unity Out Of Diversity: The Approaches of Eight Nations* (Washington, DC: American Enterprise Institute for Public Policy Research, 1989), 240.

Foerster, R.H. (Ed.), *Emmanuel Sieyès: Was ist der dritte Stand?* (Frankfurt, 1968), 60.

Fogarty, M., *Christian Democracy in Western Europe, 1820–1953* (London: Routledge & Kegan Paul, 1957).

Forsyth, M., *Unions of States: The Theory and Practice of Confederation* (Leicester: Leicester University Press, 1981).

Forsyth, M. (Ed.), *Federalism and Nationalism* (Leicester: Leicester University Press, 1989).

Forsyth, M., 'Book Review' of *Comparative Federalism and Federation: Competing Traditions and Future Directions* by M. Burgess and A.-G. Gagnon, *West European Politics*, 19(1) (January 1996), 200–1.

Franck, T.M. (Ed.), 'Why Federations Fail' in *Why Federations Fail* (London: London University Press, 1968), Chap. 5, 167–99.

Franck, T.M. (Ed.), *Why Federations Fail* (London: London University Press, 1968).

Freeman, E.A., *History of Federal Government in Greece and Italy*, ed. J.E. Bury (Freeport, NY: Books For Libraries Press, 1972).

Freiburghaus, D., *Die Schweiz: Eidgenossischer Föderalismus oder die Ungleichheit der Lebensverhaltnisse'* in Europäisches Zentrum für Föderalismus-Forschung (Ed.), *Jährbuch des Föderalismus*, Vol. I (Baden-Baden: Nomos Verlag., 2000), 296.

Fremantle, A. (Ed.), *The Papal Encyclicals in their Historical Context* (London: Mentor-Omega, 1963).

Frenkel, M., *Federal Theory* (Canberra: Centre for Research on Federal Financial Relations, The Australia National University, 1986).

Friedrich, C.J., 'Federal Constitutional Theory and Emergent Proposals' in A.W. Macmahon (Ed.), *Federalism: Mature and Emergent* (New York: Russell & Russell, 1962), Chap. 26, 510–33.

Friedrich, C.J., 'New Tendencies in Federal Theory and Practice', Sixth World Congress of IPSA (September 1964), Geneva, Switzerland, 1–14.

Friedrich, C.J., *Constitutional Government and Democracy: Theory and Practice in Europe and America* (Waltham, MA: Blaisdell Publishing, 1968), 4th edn.

Gagnon, A.-G., 'The Moral Foundation of Asymmetrical Federalism: A Normative Exploration of the Case of Quebec and Canada' in A.-G. Gagnon and J. Tully (Eds), *Multinational Democracies* (Cambridge: Cambridge University Press, 2001), Chap. 13.

Gagnon, A.-G. and Gibbs, C., 'The Normative Basis of Asymmetrical Federalism' in R. Agranoff (Ed.), *Accommodating Diversity: Asymmetry in Federal States* (Baden-Baden: Nomos Verlag., 1999), Chap. 5, 73–93.

Gagnon, A.-G. and Montcalm, M.B., *Quebec: Beyond The Quiet Revolution* (Scarborough, Ont.: Nelson Canada, 1990).

Gagnon, A.-G. and Tully, J. (Eds), *Multinational Democracies* (Cambridge: Cambridge University Press, 2001).

Galligan, B., *A Federal Republic: Australia's Constitutional System of Government* (Cambridge: Cambridge University Press, 1995).

Gibbins, R., *Regionalism: Territorial Politics in Canada and the United States* (Toronto: Butterworths, 1982), 130–40.

Gibbins, R., 'Federal Societies, Institutions and Politics' in H. Bakvis and W.M. Chandler (Eds), *Federalism and the Role of the State* (Toronto: University of Toronto Press, 1987), Chap. 2, 18.

Gibbins, R., *Conflict and Unity: An Introduction to Canadian Political Life* (Scarborough, Ont.: Nelson Canada, 1994), 10–21.

Gibbins, R. and Laforest, G. (Eds), *Beyond the Impasse: Toward Reconciliation* (Montreal: Institute for Research on Public Policy, 1998).

Giddens, A., *Consequences of Modernity* (Cambridge: Polity Press, 1990), 64.

Giddens, A., *The Third Way and its Critics* (Cambridge: Polity Press, 2000), 160.

Gingras, F.-P. and Nevitte, N., 'The Evolution of Quebec Nationalism' in A.-G. Gagnon (Ed.), *Quebec: State and Society* (Toronto: Methuen, 1984), Chap. 1, 3.

Goldwin, R.A., Kaufman, A. and Schambra, W.A. (Eds), *Forging Unity Out Of Diversity: The Approaches of Eight Nations* (Washington, DC: American Enterprise Institute for Public Policy Research, 1989).

Granatstein, J.L. and McNaught, K. (Eds), *English Canada Speaks Out* (Toronto: Doubleday Canada, 1991).

Greaves, H.R.G., *Federal Union in Practice* (London: George Allen & Unwin, 1940).

Greilsammer, I., 'Some Observations on European Federalism' in D. Elazar (Ed.), *Federalism and Political Integration* (Israel: Turtledove, 1979).

Gress, F., 'Interstate Cooperation and Territorial Representation in Intermestic Politics', *Publius: The Journal of Federalism*, 26(1) (Winter 1996), 53–71.

Grodzins, M., *The American System: A New View of Government in the United States*, ed. D. Elazar (Chicago, IL: Rand McNally, 1966).

Groves, H.E. and Sheridan, L.A., *The Constitution of Malaysia* (New York: Oceana Publications, 1967).

Guhan, S., 'Federalism and the New Political Economy in India' in B. Arora and D.V. Verney (Eds), *Multiple Identities in a Single State: Indian Federalism in a Comparative Perspective* (New Delhi: Konark Publishers, 1995), Chap. 8, 237–71.

Gunlicks, A., *The Lander and German Federalism* (Manchester: Manchester University Press, 2003), Chap. 5, 163–211.

Hall, K.L. (Ed.), *Major Problems in American Constitutional History*, Vol. I (Lexington, MA: Heath & Co., 1992), 383.

Hampsher-Monk, I., '"Publius": The Federalist' in *A History of Modern Political Thought: Major Thinkers from Hobbes to Marx* (Oxford: Blackwell, 1992), 204.

Hardgrave, R.L., Jr and Kochanek, S.A., *India: Government and Politics in a Developing Nation* (London: Harcourt Brace Jovanovich, 1986), 4th edn, 114–15.

Hartz, L., *The Liberal Tradition in America* (New York: Harcourt, Brace & World, 1955).

Hartz, L., *The Founding of New Societies* (New York: Harcourt, Brace & World, 1964).

Held, D., 'Democracy: From City States to a Cosmopolitan Order?' in D. Held (Ed.), *Prospects for Democracy, Political Studies*, Special Issue, XL (1992), 10–39,.

Held, D., *Democracy and the Global Order: From Modern State to Cosmopolitan Governance* (Cambridge: Polity Press, 1995).

Held, D., *Models of Democracy* (Cambridge: Polity Press, 1996).

Held, D., 'The Transformation of Political Community: Rethinking Democracy in the Context of Globalization' in I. Shapiro and C. Hacker-Corson (Eds), *Democracy's Edges* (Cambridge: Cambridge University Press, 1999), Chap. 6, 92.

Henry, Patrick, Antifederalist, No. 40, 'On The Motivations and Authority of the Founding Fathers' in M. Borden (Ed.), *The Antifederalist Papers* (Michigan, MI: Michigan State University Press, 1965), 109–10.

Hewitt de Alcantara, C., 'Uses and Abuses of the Concept of Governance', *ISSJ*, 155 (1998), 105–13.

Hickling, R.H., *An Introduction to the Federal Constitution*, Kuala Lumpur: Federation of Malaya Information Services, 1960), 4.

Hicks, U.K., *Federalism, Failure and Success: A Comparative Study* (London: The Macmillan Press, 1978), Chap. 8, 171.

Hinsley, F.H., *Sovereignty* (London: C.A. Watts, 1966).

Hinsley, F.H., *Power and the Pursuit of Peace* (Cambridge: Cambridge University Press, 1980), 13.

Hirst, P., *The Pluralist Theory of the State: Selected Writings of G.D.H. Cole, J.N. Figgis and H.J. Laski* (London: Routledge 1989).

Hirst, P., *Associative Democracy: New Forms of Economic and Social Governance* (Cambridge: Polity Press, 1994).

Holmes, J. and Sharman, C., *The Australian Federal System* (London: George Allen & Unwin, 1977), 13–14.

Horowitz, G., *Canadian Labour in Politics* (Toronto: University of Toronto Press, 1968).

Horton, D.J., *Andre Laurendeau: French-Canadian Nationalist, 1912–1968* (Oxford: Oxford University Press, 1993), 225.

Hrbek, R. (Ed.), *Regional Parties and Party Systems in Federal States* (Baden-Baden: Nomos Verlag., 2004).

Hudon, R., 'Quebec, the Economy and the Constitution' in K. Banting and R. Simeon (Eds), *And No One Cheered: Democracy and the Constitution Act* (Toronto: Methuen, 1983), Chap. 7, 133–53.

Hueglin, T.O., 'Johannes Althusius: Medieval Constitutionalist or Modern Federalist?', *Publius: The Journal of Federalism*, 9(4) (Fall 1979), 9–41.

Hueglin, T.O., *Early Modern Concepts for a Late Modern World: Althusius on Community and Federalism* (Waterloo, Ont.: Wilfrid Laurier University Press, 1999).

Hughes, C.J., *Confederacies* (Leicester: Leicester University Press, 1963).

Hughes, C.J., 'Cantonalism: Federation and Confederacy in the Golden Epoch of Switzerland' in M. Burgess and A.-G. Gagnon (Eds), *Comparative Federalism and Federation: Competing Traditions and Future Directions* (Hemel Hempstead: Harvester Wheatsheaf, 1993), Chap. 9, 154–67.

Hyneman, C.S. and Lutz, D.S. (Eds), *American Political Writing during the Founding Era, 1760–1805*, 2 vols (Indianapolis, IN: Liberty Press, 1983).

Jacobs, D. and Swyngedouw, M., 'Territorial and Non-Territorial Federalism: Reform of the Brussels Capital Region, 2001', *Regional and Federal Studies*, 13(2) (Summer 2003), 127–39.

Jacobs, J., *The Question of Separatism: Quebec and the Struggle over Sovereignty* (New York: Random House, 1980).

Jeffery, C., 'Party Politics and Territorial Representation in the Federal Republic of Germany', *West European Politics*, 22(2) (1999), 130–66.

Jeffery, C. and Heald, D. (Eds), 'Money Matters: Territorial Finance in Decentralised States', *Regional and Federal Studies*, Special Issue, 13(4) (Winter 2003).

Jensen, M., *The Articles of Confederation: An Interpretation of the Socio-Constitutional History of the American Revolution, 1774–1781* (Madison, WI: The University of Wisconsin Press, 1962), 245.

Johnson, N., 'Territory and Power: Some Historical Determinants of the Constitutional Structure of the Federal Republic of Germany' in C. Jeffery (Ed.), *Recasting German Federalism: The Legacies of Unification* (London: Pinter, 1999), Chap. 2, 29.

Jonquieres, G. de and Alden, E., 'American Ties', *Financial Times*, 20 April 2001, 8.

Kammen. M. (Ed.), *The Origins of the American Constitution: A Documentary History* (London: Penguin Books, 1986), Intro., viii.

Karmis, D. and Norman, W. (Eds), *Theories of Federalism: A Reader* (New York: Palgrave Macmillan, 2005).

Karmis, D. and Norman, W. (Eds), 'The Revival of Federalism in Normative Political Theory' in *Theories of Federalism: A Reader* (New York: Palgrave Macmillan, 2005), Chap. 1, 1–30.

Keating, M., 'What's Wrong With Asymmetrical Government?' *Regional and Federal Studies: An International Journal*, Special Issue, 'Remaking the Union: Devolution and British Politics in the 1990s, 8(1) (Spring 1998), 195–218.

Keating, M., *Plurinational Democracy: Stateless Nations in a Post-Sovereignty Era* (Oxford: Oxford University Press, 2001), 26–27.

Kellner, D., 'Globalization and the Post-Modern Turn' in R. Axtmann (Ed.), *Globalization and Europe: Theoretical and Empirical Investigations* (London: Pinter, 1998), Chap. 2, 23.

Kelly, J.B., 'Reconciling Rights and Federalism during Review of the Charter of Rights and Freedoms: the Supreme Court of Canada and the Centralization Thesis, 1982 to 1999', *Canadian Journal of Political Science*, XXXIV(2) (June 2001), 321–55.

Kielmansegg, P.G., 'Integration and Demokratie' in M. Jachtenfuchs and B. Kohler-Koch (Eds), *Europäische Integration* (Opladen: Leske and Budrich, 1996), 64.

Kincaid, J. and Elazar, D.J. (Eds), *The Covenant Connection: Federal Theology and the Origins of Modern Politics* (Durham, NC: Carolina Academic Press, 1985).

King, P., 'Against Federalism' in R. Benewick, R.N. Berki and B. Parekh (Eds), *Knowledge and Belief in Politics* (London: Allen & Unwin, 1973), 151–76.

King, P., *Federalism and Federation* (London: Croom Helm, 1982).

King, P., 'Federation and Representation' in M. Burgess and A.-G. Gagnon (Eds), *Comparative Federalism and Federation: Competing Traditions and Future Directions* (Hemel Hempstead: Harvester Wheatsheaf, 1993), Chap. 5, 95.

Kisker, G., 'The West German Federal Constitutional Court as Guardian of the Federal System', *Publius: The Journal of Federalism*, 19(4) (Fall 1989), 35–52.

Kohler-Koch, B. (Ed.), 'Regieren in entgrenzten Raumen', *Politische Viertel – jahresschrift*, 39 (1998), Special Edition, No. 29.

Kwavnick, D. (Ed.), *The Tremblay Report* (The Carleton Library, Toronto, no. 64: McClelland & Stewart, 1973).

Kymlicka, W., *Liberalism, Community and Culture* (Oxford: Clarendon Press, 1989).

Kymlicka, W., *Multicultural Citizenship: A Liberal Theory of Minority Rights* (Oxford: Clarendon Press, 1995).

Kymlicka, W., *Politics in the Vernacular: Nationalism, Multiculturalism and Citizenship* (Oxford: Oxford University Press, 2001).

Ladner, K.L., 'Treaty Federalism: An Indigenous Vision of Canadian Federalisms' in F. Rocher and M. Smith (Eds), *New Trends in Canadian Federalism* (Peterborough, Ont.: Broadview Press, 2003), Chap. 7, 167–94.

Lakoff, S., 'Between Either/Or and More or Less: Sovereignty Versus Autonomy Under Federalism', *Publius: The Journal of Federalism*, 24 (Winter 1994), 63–78.

LaSelva, S., *The Moral Foundations of Canadian Federalism: Paradoxes, Achievements and Tragedies of Nationhood* (London: McGill-Queen's University Press, 1996).

Laski, H., 'The Obsolescence of Federalism', *The New Republic*, 3 May 1939, 367–69.

Lee, H.P., *Constitutional Conflicts in Contemporary Malaysia* (Oxford: Oxford University Press, 1995).

Lehning, P.B. (Ed.), *Theories of Secession* (New York: Routledge, 1998).

Lemco, J., *Turmoil in the Peaceable Kingdom: The Quebec Sovereignty Movement and its Implications for Canada and the United States* (Toronto: University of Toronto Press, 1994).

Lijphart, A., 'Consociational Democracy', *World Politics*, 21 (1969), 207–25.

Lijphart, A., *Democracy in Plural Societies: A Comparative Exploration* (London: Yale University Press, 1977).

Linder, W., *Swiss Democracy: Possible Solutions to Conflict in Multicultural Societies* (London: Macmillan, 1994).

Lipset, S.M., *American Exceptionalism: A Double-Edged Sword* (New York: W.W. Norton & Co., 1996), 46.

Lister, F.K., *The European Union, The United Nations and the Revival of Confederal Governance* (London: Greenwood Press, 1996).

Livingston, W.S., 'A Note on the Nature of Federalism', *Political Science Quarterly*, 67 (March 1952), 81–95.

Luther, K.R., 'Federalism and Federation in Europe: A Comparative Study of the Germanic Tradition', Ph.D. thesis., University of Plymouth (August 1989), 15–16.

Luther, K.R. and Muller, W.C. (Eds), (1992) *Politics in Austria: Still a Case of Consociationalism?* (London: Frank Cass & Co., 1992), 4.

Lutz, D., 'The Relative Influence of European Writers on Late Eighteenth Century American Political Thought', *American Political Science Review*, 78 (1984), 189–97.

Lutz, D., 'The Articles of Confederation as the Background to the Federal Republic', *Publius: The Journal of Federalism*, 20 (Winter 1990), 57.

Lutz, D., 'The Iroquois Confederation Constitution: An Analysis', *Publius: The Journal of Federalism*, 28(2) (Spring 1998), 99–127.

Lutz, D.S., 'From Covenant to Constitution in American Political Thought', *Publius: The Journal of Federalism*, 10 (Fall 1980), 101–33.

Lutz, D.S., *Popular Consent and Popular Control: Whig Political Theory in the Early State Constitutions* (Baton Rouge, LO: Louisiana State University Press, 1980).

Macedo, S. and Buchanan, A. (Eds), *Secession And Self-Determination*, Nomos, XLV, *Yearbook of the American Society for Political and Legal Philosophy* (New York: New York University Press, 2003).

Mackenstein, H. and Jeffery, C., 'Financial Equalisation in the 1990s: On the Road Back to Karlsruhe?' in C. Jeffery (Ed.), *Recasting German Federalism: The Legacies of Unification* (London: Pinter, 1999), Chap. 7, 155–76.

Maier, H., 'Der Föderalismus – Ursprunge und Wandlegen', *Archiv des Öffentlichen Rechts*, 115(2) (1990), 223.

Martin, G., 'Empire Federalism and Imperial Parliamentary Union, 1820–1870', *The Historical Journal*, XVI(I) (1973), 65–92.

Martin, G., 'The Idea of "Imperial Federation"' in R. Hyam and G. Martin (Eds), *Reappraisals in British Imperial History* (London: Macmillan, 1975), Chap. 6.

Martin, G. (Ed.), 'The Case Against Canadian Confederation, 1864–1867' in *The Causes of Canadian Confederation* (Fredericton, NB: Acadiensis Press, 1990), 19–49.

Martin, G., *Britain and the Origins of the Canadian Confederation, 1837–67* (London: Macmillan, 1995), 15 and 6–7.

Maiz, R., 'Democracy, Federalism and Nationalism in Multinational States' in W. Safran and R. Maiz (Eds), *Identity and Territorial Autonomy in Plural Societies* (London: Frank Cass, 2000), 35–60.

Mathew, K.M. (Ed.), *Manorama Yearbook 1997*, Part IV, 'India and the States' (Kottayam, Kerala: 1998), 460.

Mayne, R. and Pinder, J., *Federal Union: The Pioneers* (London: Macmillan, 1990).

McCoy, C.S. and Baker, J.W., *Fountainhead of Federalism: Heinrich Bullinger and the Covenantal Tradition* (Louisville, KE: Westminster/John Knox Press, 1991).

Macdonald, M., *The Republic of Austria, 1918–1934* (London: Oxford University Press, 1946), 2.

McKay, D., 'On the Origins of Political Unions: The European Case', *Journal of Theoretical Politics*, 9(3) (1997), 287.

McKay, D., *Federalism and European Union* (Oxford: Oxford University Press, 1999).

McKay, D., *Designing Europe: Comparative Lessons from the Federal Experience* (Oxford: Oxford University Press, 2001).

McRae, K. (Ed.), *Consociational Democracy* (Toronto: McClelland & Stewart, 1974).

McRae, K. (Ed.), *Conflict and Compromise in Multilingual Societies: Switzerland* (Waterloo, Ont.: Wilfrid Laurier University Press, 1983), 232.

McRoberts, K., *Misconceiving Canada: The Struggle for National Unity* (Oxford: Oxford University Press, 1997).

McRoberts, K., 'Canada and the Multinational State', *Canadian Journal of Political Science*, XXXIV(4) (December 2001), 683–713.

Mill, J.S., *Utilitarianism, On Liberty and Considerations on Representative Government*, ed. H.B. Acton (London: J.M. Dent & Sons, 1972).

Miller, D., *On Nationality* (Oxford: Clarendon Press, 1995).

Miller, D., *Citizenship and National Identity* (Cambridge: Polity Press, 2000).

Miller, D., 'Nationality in Divided Societies' in A.-G. Gagnon and J. Tully (Eds), *Multinational Democracies* (Cambridge: Cambridge University Press, 2001), Chap. 12, 306–7.

Miller, J.D.B., *Australian Government and Politics: An Introductory Survey* (London: Gerald Duckworth & Co., 1954).

Milne, D., 'Equality or Asymmetry: Why Choose?' in R.L. Watts and D.M. Brown (Eds), *Options for a New Canada* (Toronto: University of Toronto Press, 1991), Chap. 15, 285–307.

Milne, D., 'Challenging Constitutional Dependency: A Revisionist View of Atlantic Canada' in J.N. McCrorie and M.L. MacDonald (Eds), *The Constitutional Future of the Prairie and Atlantic Regions of Canada* (Regina, Sas.: University of Regina, 1992), Chap. 17, 308–17.

Milne, R.S., *Government and Politics in Malaysia* (Boston: Houghton Mifflin Company, 1957).

Milward, A.L., *The Reconstruction of Europe, 1945–51* (London: Methuen & Co., 1984).

Milward, A.L., *The European Rescue of the Nation-State* (London: Routledge, 1992).

Milward, A.L., F.M.B. Lynch, F. Romero, R. Ranieri and V. Sorensen . (Eds), *The Frontier of National Sovereignty: History and Theory, 1945–1992* (London: Routledge, 1993).

Mogi, S., *The Problem of Federalism: A Study in the History of Political Theory*, 2 vols (London: George Allen & Unwin, 1931).

Monnet, J., *Memoirs* (New York: Doubleday, 1978).

Moore, M. (Ed.), *National Self-Determination and Secession* (Oxford: Oxford University Press, 1998).

Moravcsik, A., 'Negotiating the Single European Act: National Interest and Traditional Statecraft in the European Community', *International Organization*, 45(1) (1991), 651–88.

Moravcsik, A., 'Preferences and Power in the European Community: A Liberal Intergovernmentalist Approach', *Journal of Common Market Studies*, 31(4) (1993), 473–524.

Moravcsik, A., 'Taking Preferences Seriously: A Liberal Theory of International Politics', *International Organization*, 51(4) (1997) 513–53.

Moravcsik, A., 'Federal Ideals and Constitutional Realities in the Treaty of Amsterdam', *Journal of Common Market Studies* (Annual Review), 36 (1998), 13–38.

Moravcsik, A., *The Choice For Europe: Social Purpose and State Power* (London: UCL Press, 1999).

Moravcsik, A., 'A New Statecraft? Supranational Entrepreneurs and International Cooperation', *International Organization*, 53(2) (1999), 267–306.

Moravcsik, A., 'Federalism in the European Union: Rhetoric and Reality' in K. Nicolaidis and R. Howse (Eds), *The Federal Vision: Legitimacy and Levels of Governance in the United States and the European Union* (Oxford: Oxford University Press, 2001), 186.

Moreno, L., 'Asymmetry in Spain: Federalism in the Making?' in R. Agranoff (Ed.), *Accommodating Diversity: Asymmetry in Federal States* (Baden-Baden: Nomos Verlag., 1999), Chap. 9, 149–68.

Mozoomdar, A., 'The Political Economy of Modern Federalism' in B. Arora and D.V. Verney (Eds), *Multiple Identities in a Single State: Indian Federalism in a Comparative Perspective* (New Delhi: Konark Publishers, 1995), Chap. 7, 197–233.

Mullins, A. and Saunders, C., 'Different Strokes for Different Folks?: Some Thoughts on Symmetry and Difference in Federal Systems' in B. de Villiers, (Ed.), Evaluating Federal Systems (London: Juta & Co. Ltd, 1994), Chap. 3, 41–60.

Munch, U., 'Entwicklungen und Perspektiven des deutschen Föderalismus', *Aus Politik und Zeitgeschehen*, (13) (1999), 3.

Murphy, C.N., 'Globalization and Governance: A Historical Perspective' in R. Axtmann (Ed.), *Globalization and Europe: Theoretical and Empirical Investigations* (London: Pinter, 1998), Chap. 9.

Musgrave, R., *Essays in Fiscal Federalism* (Washington, DC: The Brookings Institute, 1965).

Nelsen, B.F. and Stubb, A.C.-G. (Eds), 'The Schuman Declaration' in *The European Union: Readings on the Theory and Practice of European Integration* (Boulder, CO: Lynne Riener Publishers, 1994), 11–12.

Nelson, R., 'The Federal Idea in French Political Thought', *Publius: The Journal of Federalism*, 5(3), 1976, 9–62.

Nicholls, D., *The Pluralist State* (London: Macmillan Press, 1975), 32.

Norman, W., 'The Ethics of Secession as the Regulation of Secessionist Politics' in M. Moore (Ed.), *National Self-Determination and Secession* (Oxford: Oxford University Press, 1998), Chap. 3, 34–61.

Norman, W., 'Justice and Stability in Multinational Societies' in A.-G. Gagnon and J. Tully (Eds), *Multinational Democracies* (Cambridge: Cambridge University Press, 2001), Chap. 3, 90–109.

Norman, W., 'Domesticating Secession' in S. Macedo and A. Buchanan (Eds), *Secession And Self-Determination*, Nomos, XLV, *Yearbook of the American Society for Political and Legal Philosophy* (New York: New York University Press, 2003), Chap. 8, 193–237.

Nugent, N., *The Government and Politics of the European Union* (London: Macmillan, 1999), 469.

Oates, W.E., *Fiscal Federalism* (New York: Harcourt Brace Jovanovich, 1972).

Osiander, A., 'Sovereignty, International Relations, and the Westphalian Myth', *International Organization*, 55(2) (Spring 2001), 270.

Ostrom, V., *The Political Theory of a Compound Republic: Designing the American Experiment* (Lincoln, NE and London: University of Nebraska Press, 1987).

Ostrom, V., *The Meaning of American Federalism: Constituting a Self-Governing Society* (San Francisco, CA: Institute for Contemporary Studies, 1991), 45.

Pagden, A., 'The Genesis of "Governance" and Enlightenment Conceptions of the Cosmopolitan World Order', *International Social Science Journal (ISSJ)*, 50(155) (1998), 7–15.

Patomaki, H., *Democratising Globalisation: The Leverage of the Tobin Tax* (London: Zed Books, 2001).

Pentland, C., *International Theory and European Integration* (London: Faber & Faber, 1973), 159–60.

Pinder, J. (Ed.), *Altiero Spinelli and the British Federalists* (London: Federal Trust, 1998).

Pinder, J., *The Building of the European Union* (Oxford: Oxford University Press, 1998).

Pitkin, H.F., *The Concept of Representation* (Berkeley and Los Angeles, CA: University of California Press, 1967), 2.

Pitkin, H.F., 'The Concept of Representation' in *Representation* (New York: Atherton Press, 1969), 16.

Plessner, H., *Die verspätete Nation* (Stuttgart: Kohlhammer Press, 1959).

Podium: 'Globalisation – America's Final Frontier', from the State of the Union Address by the President of the United States, given in the Capitol Building in Washington, DC, *The Independent*, 31 January 2000, 4.

Poirier, J., 'Formal Mechanisms of Intergovernmental Relations in Belgium', *Regional and Federal Studies*, 12(3) (Autumn 2002), 24–54.

Prinz, F., 'A Model of a Multinational Society as Developed in Austria-Hungary before 1918' in N. Rhoodie (Ed.), *Intergroup Accommodation in Plural Societies* (London: Macmillan, 1978), Chap. 3, 44–52.

Proudhon, P.-J., *Du Principe federatif*, trans. and intro by R. Vernon (Ed.), *The Principle of Federalism by P.-J. Proudhon* (Toronto: University of Toronto Press, 1979).

Rao, M.G., 'Indian Fiscal Federalism from a Comparative Perspective' in B. Arora and D.V. Verney (Eds), *Multiple Identities in a Single State: Indian Federalism in Comparative Perspective* (New Delhi: Konark Publishers PVT Ltd, 1995), Chap. 9, 272–316.

Resnick, P., *Thinking English Canada* (Toronto: Stoddart, 1994).

Resnick, P., 'Toward a Multinational Federalism: Asymmetrical Confederal Alternatives' in F.L. Seidle (Ed.), *Seeking a New Canadian Partnership: Asymmetrical and Confederal Options* (Montreal: Institute for Research on Public Policy, 1994), 71–90.

Rhodes, M. Heywood, P. and Wright, V. (Eds), 'Towards a New Europe?' in *Developments in West European Politics* (London: Macmillan Press Ltd, 1997), 8.

Riker, W.H., 'Six Books in Search of a Subject or Does Federalism Exist and Does it Matter?', *Comparative Politics*, 2(1) (October 1969), 135–46.

Riker, W.H., 'Federalism' in F.I. Greenstein and N.W. Polsby (Eds), *The Handbook of Political Science*, Vol. 5 (Reading, MA: Addison-Wesley, 1975), 93–172.

Riker, W.H., 'Federalism' in R.E. Goodin and P. Pettit (Eds), *A Companion to Contemporary Political Philosophy* (Oxford: Basil Blackwell, 1993), 508–14.

Riker, W.H. and Schaps, R., 'Disharmony in Federal Government', *Behavioral Science*, 2 (1957), 276–90.

Riley, P., 'Rousseau as a Theorist of National and International Federalism', *Publius: The Journal of Federalism*, 3(1) (1973), 5–17.

Riley, P., 'The Origins of Federal Theory in International Relations Ideas', *Polity*, VI(1) (1973), 87–121.

Riley, P., 'Three 17th Century German Theorists of Federalism: Althusius, Hugo and Leibniz', *Publius: The Journal of Federalism*, 6(3), 1976, 7–41.

Risse-Kappen, T., 'Explaining the Nature of the Beast: International Relations Theory and Comparative Public Policy Analysis Meet the EU', *Journal of Common Market Studies*, 34(1) (1996), 53–80.

Ritter, A., *The Political Thought of Pierre-Joseph Proudhon*, Princeton, NJ: Princeton University Press, 1969).

Robinson, J., 'Federalism and the Transformation of the South African State' in G. Smith (Ed.), *Federalism: The Multiethnic Challenge* (London: Longman, 1995), 274.

Rosamond, B., *Theories of European Integration* (Basingstoke: Palgrave, 2000), 142.

Ross, G., 'European Integration and Globalization' in R. Axtmann (Ed.), *Globalization and Europe: Theoretical and Empirical Investigations* (London: Pinter, 1998), Chap. 10, 164.

Rossiter, C. (Ed.), *The Federalist Papers* (New York: The New American Library and London: The New English Library Limited, 1961).

Rothmayr, C., 'Towards the Judicialisation of Swiss Politics?' in J.-E. Lane (Ed.), The Swiss Labyrinth: Institutions, Outcomes and Redesign', *West European Politics*, 24(2) (April 2001), 77–94.

Rudin, R., 'English-Speaking Quebec: The Emergence of a Disillusioned Minority' in A.-G. Gagnon (Ed.), *Quebec: State and Society*, Scarborough, Ont.: Nelson Canada, 1993), 2nd edn, Chap. 19, 338–48.

Ruggie, J.G., 'Continuity and Transformation in the World Polity: Towards a Neorealist Synthesis', *World Politics*, 35 (January 1983), 261–85.

Ruggie, J.G., 'Territoriality and Beyond: Problematizing Modernity in International Relations', *International Organization*, 47(1) (Winter 1993), 149–50.

Rydon, J., 'The Australian Tradition of Federalism and Federation' in M. Burgess and A.-G. Gagnon (Eds), *Comparative Federalism and Federation: Competing Traditions and Future Directions* (Hemel Hempstead: Harvester Wheatsheaf, 1993), 231.

Sartori, G., 'Concept Misformation in Comparative Politics', *American Political Science Review*, 64 (1970), 1033–53.

Sawer, G., *Modern Federalism* (London: Pitman Publishing, 1969); repr. (London: Pitman Publishing Ltd, 1976).

Sbragia, A.M. (Ed.), 'Thinking about the European Future: The Uses of Comparison' in *Euro Politics: Institutions and Policymaking in the 'New' European Community* (Washington, DC: The Brookings Institute, 1992), 258.

Scharpf, F.W., 'The Joint-Decision Trap: Lessons from German Federalism and European Integration', *Public Administration*, 66 (Autumn 1988), 239–78.

Schmitt, E., 'Abbe Sieyès' in H. Rauch, *Politische Denker*, Vol. II (Munich: Bayerische Landeszentrale für politische Bildungsarbeit, 1977), 91.

Schneiderman, D., 'Human Rights, Fundamental Differences? Multiple Charters in a Partnership Frame' in R. Gibbins and G. Laforest (Eds), *Beyond the Impasse: Toward Reconciliation* (Montreal: Institute for Research on Public Policy, 1998), Part III, 147–85.

Schwartz, H.M., *States Versus Markets: The Emergence of a Global Economy* (London: Macmillan Press Ltd, 2000).

Shafruddin, B.H., *The Federal Factor in the Government and Politics of Peninsular Malaysia*, Singapore: Oxford University Press, 1987).

Simandjuntak, B., *Malayan Federalism, 1945–1963: A Study of Federal Problems in a Plural Society* (London: Oxford University Press, 1969).

Sidgwick, H., *The Elements of Politics* (London: Macmillan & Co., 1891).

Sidgwick, H., *The Development of European Polity* (London: Macmillan & Co., 1903).

Sieyès, E.J. *Politische Schriften, 1788–1790*, ed. E. Schmitt and R. Reichardt, (Darmstadt/Neuwied: Luchterhand, 1975), 217.

Simeon, R., 'National Reconciliation: The Mulroney Government and Federalism' in A.B. Gollner and D. Salee (Eds), *Canada Under Mulroney: An End of Term Report*, (Montreal: Vehicle Press, 1988), 45–46.

Simeon, R., 'Political Pragmatism Takes Precedence Over Democratic Process' in M.D. Behiels (Ed.), *The Meech Lake Primer: Conflicting Views of the 1987 Constitutional Accord* (Ottawa: University of Ottawa Press, 1989), Chap. 3, 131–35.

Simeon, R. and Conway, D.-P., 'Federalism and the Management of Conflict in Multinational Societies' in A.-G. Gagnon and J. Tully (Eds), *Multinational Democracies* (Cambridge: Cambridge University Press, 2001), Chap. 14, 361 and 364.

Sinnadurai, V., 'Unity and Diversity: The Constitution of Malaysia' in R.A. Goldwin, A. Kaufman and W.A. Schambra (Eds), *Forging Unity Out Of Diversity: The Approaches of Eight Nations* (Washington, DC: American Enterprise Institute for Public Policy Research, 1989), Chap. 7, 334–41.

Smiley, D.V., *The Canadian Political Nationality* (Toronto and London: Methuen, 1967), 130.

Smiley, D.V., *The Federal Condition in Canada* (Toronto: McGraw-Hill Ryerson, 1987).

Smith, A., 'National Identity and the Idea of European Unity', *International Affairs*, 68(1) (1992), 55–76.

Smith, A.D., *Theories of Nationalism* (London: Duckworth, 1971).

Smith, A.D., *National Identity* (London: Penguin, 1991).

Smith, G. (Ed.), *Federalism: The Multiethnic Challenge* (London: Longman, 1995).

Smith, J., 'The Origins of Judicial Review in Canada', *Canadian Journal of Political Science*, 16 (March 1983).

Smith, J., 'Judicial Review and Modern Federalism: Canada and the United States' in H. Bakvis and W.M. Chandler (Eds), *Federalism and the Role of the State* (Toronto: University of Toronto Press, 1987), Chap. 7, 113–26.

Smith, M., 'The European Union and a Changing Europe: Establishing the Boundaries of Order', *Journal of Common Market Studies*, 34(1), 5–28.

'Speech of the Secretary of State for the Colonies', 14 May 1900 in A.P. Newton, *Federal and Unified Constitutions: A Collection of Constitutional Documents for the Use of Students* (London: Longmans, Green & Co., 1923), 311–23,.

Stein, M., 'Changing Concepts of Federalism since World War II: Anglo-American and Continental European Traditions', paper presented to the Workshop on Genealogy and Concept Formation, International Committee for the Study of the Development of Political Science, Mexico City, 24–27 May 1994, 1–31.

Stein, M.B., 'Federal Political Systems and Federal Societies', *World Politics*, 20 (1968), 721–47.

Stepan, A., *Arguing Comparative Politics* (Oxford: Oxford University Press, 2001).

Stevens, R.M., 'Asymmetrical Federalism: The Federal Principle and the Survival of the Small Republic', *Publius: The Journal of Federalism*, 5 (1977), 177–203.

Stevenson, G., 'Federalism and the Political Economy of the Canadian State' in L. Panitch (Ed.), *The Canadian State: Political Economy and Political Power* (Toronto: University of Toronto Press, 1977), Chap. 3, 71–100.

Stevenson, G., 'Western Alienation in Australia and Canada' in L. Pratt and G. Stevenson (Eds), *Western Separatism: The Myths, Realities and Dangers* (Edmonton: Hurtig Publishers, 1981), 121.

Stevenson, G., *Unfulfilled Union: Canadian Federalism and National Unity* (Toronto: Gage, 1982), 162.

Strange, S., *States and Markets* (London: Pinter Publishers, 1989).

Strange, S., *The Retreat of the State: The Diffusion of Power in the World Economy* (Cambridge: Cambridge University Press, 1996).

Sturm, R., 'The Constitution under Pressure: Emerging Asymmetrical Federalism in Germany' in R. Agranoff (Ed.), *Accommodating Diversity: Asymmetry in Federal States* (Baden-Baden: Nomos Verlag., 1999), Chap. 8, 137–48.

Swenden, W., 'Asymmetric Federalism and Coalition-Making in Belgium', *Publius: The Journal of Federalism*, 32(3) (2002), 67–87.

Swenden, W., *Federalism and Second Chambers. Regional Representation in Parliamentary Federations: The Australian Senate and German Bundesrat Compared* (Oxford: P.I.E. – Peter Lang, 2004).

Tamir, Y., *Liberal Nationalism* (Princeton, NJ: Princeton University Press, 1993).

Tarlton, C.D., 'Symmetry and Asymmetry as Elements of Federalism: A Theoretical Speculation', *Journal of Politics*, 27 (1965), 861–74.

Taylor, C., 'Shared and Divergent Values' in R.L. Watts and D.M. Brown (Eds), *Options for a New Canada* (Toronto: University of Toronto Press, 1991), Chap. 4, 64–65.

Taylor, C., *Multiculturalism and the Politics of Recognition* (Princeton, NJ: Princeton University Press, 1992).

Taylor, C. (with an introduction by G. Laforest), *Reconciling the Solitudes: Essays on Canadian Federalism and Nationalism* (London: McGill-Queen's University Press, 1993).

Taylor, C., 'Why do Nations have to become States?' in *Reconciling the Solitudes: Essays on Canadian Federalism and Nationalism*, ed. G.. Laforest (London: McGill-Queens University Press, 1993), Chap. 3, 40–58.

Taylor, C., 'Foreword' in A.-G. Gagnon and J. Tully (Eds), *Multinational Democracies* (Cambridge: Cambridge University Press, 2001), xiv.

Theophanous, A., 'Prospects for Solving the Cyprus Problem and the Role of The European Union', *Publius: The Journal of Federalism*, 30(1–2) (Winter/Spring 2000), 217–41.

Thorlakson, L., 'Comparing Federal Institutions: Power and Representation in Six Federations', *West European Politics*, 26(2) (April 2003), 1–22.

Tobin, J., 'A Proposal for International Monetary Reform', *Eastern Economic Journal*, 4(3–4) (1978), 153–59.

Tocqueville, A. de *Democracy in America*, ed. and abridg. R.D. Heffner (London: The New English Library Ltd, 1956); repr. as *Democracy in America*, trans. G. Lawrence, ed. J.P. Mayer (London: Fontana Press, 1994).

Tooley, M.J. (Ed.), *Six Books of the Commonwealth* (Oxford: Basil Blackwell, 1955).

Trager, F.N., '"Introduction": On Federalism' in T.M. Franck (Ed.), *Why Federations Fail* (London: London University Press, 1968), xv.

Truman, D.B., 'Federalism and the Party System' in A.W. Macmahon (Ed.), *Federalism: Mature and Emergent* (New York: Russell & Russell, 1962), Chap. 8, 115–36.

Tully, J., *Strange Multiplicity: Constitutionalism in an Age of Diversity* (Cambridge: Cambridge University Press, 1995).

Tully, J., 'Introduction' in A.-G. Gagnon and J. Tully (Eds), *Multinational Democracies* (Cambridge: Cambridge University Press, 2001), 1–33.

Tuschoff, C., 'The Compounding Effect: The Impact of Federalism on the Concept of Representation', *West European Politics*, Special Issue, 22(2) (1999), 16.

Varouxakis, G., *Mill on Nationality* (London: Routledge, 2002), 3.

Vedrine, H., 'Klassischer Föderalismus oder Föderation von Nationalstaaten?', *FAZ*, (115) (13 June 2000), 4.

Verney, D.V., 'Federalism, Federative Systems, and Federations: The United States, Canada and India', *Publius: The Journal of Federalism*, 25(2) (Spring 1995), 81–97.

Vile, M.J.C., *The Structure of American Federalism* (Oxford: Oxford University Press, 1961).

Vile, M.J.C., 'The Definition of Federalism', Appendix A in 'Federalism in the United States, Canada and Australia', Research Papers 2, *Commission on the Constitution* (London: HMSO, 1973), 35.

Vile, M.J.C., 'Federal Theory and the "New Federalism"' in D. Jaensch (Ed.), *The Politics of New Federalism* (Adelaide: Australian Political Studies Association, 1977).

Villiers, B. de (Ed.), *Bundestreue: The Soul of an Intergovernmental Partnership*, Occasional Papers (Johannesburg, RSA: Konrad Adenauer Stiftung, March 1995), 1–36.

Villiers, B. de (Ed.), Evaluating Federal Systems (South Africa: Juta & Co. Ltd, 1994).

Voigt, R., 'Financing the German Federal System in the 1980s', *Publius: The Journal of Federalism*, 19(4) (Fall 1989), 99–113.

Watts, R.L., *New Federations: Experiments in the Commonwealth* (Oxford: Clarendon Press, 1966).

Watts, R.L., 'Multicultural Societies and Federalism', *Studies of the Royal Commission on Bilingualism and Biculturalism*, No. 8 (Ottawa: Ministry of Supply and Services, 1970), 47–50.

Watts, R.L., 'Survival or Disintegration' in R. Simeon (Ed.), *Must Canada Fail?* (London: McGill-Queen's University Press, 1977), Chap. 3, 42–60.

Watts, R.L., 'The American Constitution in Comparative Perspective: A Comparison of Federalism in the United States and Canada', *The Journal of American History*, 74(3) (December 1987), 769–91.

Watts, R.L., *Executive Federalism: A Comparative Analysis* (Kingston, Ont.: Queen's University, Institute of Intergovernmental Relations, 1989).

Watts, R.L., 'Contemporary Views on Federalism' in B. De Villiers (Ed.), *Evaluating Federal Systems* (London: Juta & Co. Ltd, 1994).

Watts, R.L., *Comparing Federal Systems in the 1990s* (Kingston, Ont.: Queen's University, Institute of Intergovernmental Relations, 1996).

Watts, R.L., 'The Canadian Experience with Asymmetrical Federalism' in R. Agranoff (Ed.), *Accommodating Diversity: Asymmetry in Federal States* (Baden-Baden: Nomos Verlag., 1999), Chap. 7, 118–36.

Watts, R.L., 'Federalism, Federal Political Systems and Federations', *Annual Review of Political Science*, I (1998), 117–37.

Watts, R.L., *Comparing Federal Systems*, London, Montreal and Kingston, Ont.: McGill-Queen's University Press, 1999), 2nd edn.

Watts, R.L., 'German Federalism in Comparative Perspective' in C. Jeffery (Ed.), *Recasting German Federalism: The Legacies of Unification* (London: Pinter, 1999), Chap. 12, 265–84.

Watts, R.L., *The Spending Power in Federal Systems: A Comparative Study* (Kingston, Ont.: Queen's University, Institute of Intergovernmental Relations, 1999).

Watts, R.L., 'Introduction: Comparative Research and Fiscal Federalism', *Regional and Federal Studies*, 13(4) (Winter 2003), 1–6.

Watts, R.L. and Brown, D.M. (Eds), *Options for a New Canada* (Toronto: University of Toronto Press, 1981).

Webber, J., *Reimagining Canada: Language, Culture and Community and the Canadian Constitution* (London: McGill-Queen's University Press, 1994).

Wheare, K.C., *Federal Government* (Oxford: Oxford University Press, 1963), 4th edn.

Wildavsky, A., 'Party Discipline under Federalism', *Social Research*, 28 (1961), 437–58.

Wildavsky, A. (Ed.), *American Federalism in Perspective* (Boston, MA: Little, Brown & Company, 1967), Section III.

Wilkinson, J.D., *The Intellectual Resistance in Europe* (Cambridge, MA: Harvard University Press, 1981).

Yusoff, M.A., 'Federalism in Malaysia: A Study of the Politics of Centre–State Relations', Ph.D. thesis, University of Manchester (1998), 26.

Zacher, M.W., 'The Territorial Integrity Norm: International Boundaries and the Use of Force', *International Organization*, 55(2) (Spring 2001), 215–50.

Zakaria, A. (Ed.), *The Government and Politics of Malaysia* (Singapore: Oxford University Press, 1987).

Zielonka, J., 'How New Enlarged Borders will Reshape the European Union', *Journal of Common Market Studies*, 39(3) (September 2001), 507–36.

Index

eBooks

eBooks – at www.eBookstore.tandf.co.uk

A library at your fingertips!

eBooks are electronic versions of printed books. You can store them on your PC/laptop or browse them online.

They have advantages for anyone needing rapid access to a wide variety of published, copyright information.

eBooks can help your research by enabling you to bookmark chapters, annotate text and use instant searches to find specific words or phrases. Several eBook files would fit on even a small laptop or PDA.

NEW: Save money by eSubscribing: cheap, online access to any eBook for as long as you need it.

Annual subscription packages

We now offer special low-cost bulk subscriptions to packages of eBooks in certain subject areas. These are available to libraries or to individuals.

For more information please contact webmaster.ebooks@tandf.co.uk

We're continually developing the eBook concept, so keep up to date by visiting the website.

www.eBookstore.tandf.co.uk

DATE DUE

Demco, Inc. 38-293